THE STRUCTURE OF LEARNING
From Sign Stimuli to Sign Language

◆ ❖ ◆

THE STRUCTURE OF LEARNING
From Sign Stimuli to Sign Language

◆❖◆

R. Allen Gardner
Beatrix T. Gardner
University of Nevada, Reno

LEA LAWRENCE ERLBAUM ASSOCIATES, PUBLISHERS
1998   Mahwah, New Jersey   London

Lawrence Erlbaum Associates, Inc., Publishers
10 Industrial Avenue
Mahwah, NJ 07430

Cover design by Kathryn Houghtaling Lacey

Library of Congress Cataloging-in-Publication Data

    Gardner, R. Allen, 1930-
The structure of learning : from sign stimuli to sign language / R. Allen Gardner and Beatrix
T. Gardner.
      p.   cm.
    Included bibliographical references and index.
    ISBN 0-8058-2603-3 (cloth : alk. paper)
    1. Learning, Psychology of. 2. Psychology, Comparative.
    3. Conditioned response. 4. Learning strategies. 5. Psychology, Experimental. I. Title.
    BF318.G38 1998
    153.1'5--dc21
                                 97-44357
                                 CIP

Books published by Lawrence Erlbaum Associates are printed on acid-free paper, and their
bindings are chosen for strength and durability.

Printed in the United States of America
10 9 8 7 6 5 4 3 2 1

Contents

Preface

Throughout history, people have believed in mumbo jumbo: in ghosts, voodoo dolls, and witches who could make rivers run backward and pull the moon down from the sky. People have believed that pouring vinegar on door hinges cured headaches, that pentagrams neutralized demons, and that applying a toad to a woman's breast speeded up alchemical reactions. Even today, people believe in spoon-bending, channeling, astrology, the healing power of pyramids, clairvoyance, communication with the dead, and abduction by extraterrestrials. Polls in the 1980s showed that 23% of Americans believed in reincarnation. Polls regularly show that less than half of Americans who graduate from U.S. colleges and universities accept the theory of evolution.

How to tell science from mumbo jumbo? Honest scientists admit that there is a certain amount of mumbo jumbo in most science and a certain amount of science in most mumbo jumbo. Separating the two is a matter of evaluating evidence. This book emphasizes the rules of evidence in a field of intersection between psychology and animal behavior. Scientific rules of evidence only lead to relative answers. All scientific evidence may be flawed but some evidence is more flawed than other evidence. This book aims to show how the difference between poor evidence and better evidence, though always relative, is well worth the effort.

Books that offer an encyclopedia-style compendium of current theory and research are often truly valuable introductions to a field.

A compendium can also be a valuable addition to a reference shelf, providing that the definition of "current" is wide enough to keep the contents from falling rapidly out of date. The trouble with a compendium is that it must sacrifice depth of detail for breadth of coverage. It must omit basic details of evidence. Within the covers of a compendium, readers must accept predigested assertions on faith as received wisdom. This common practice dulls rather than sharpens any taste for inquiry.

The primary subject of this book is the tools of inquiry in this field. Consequently, descriptions of experiments and series of experiments that build on each other appear in some depth, more depth than in the usual compendium. Experimental methods usually have an instructive history. Early questions and early techniques lead to more advanced questions and advanced techniques. Later experiments build on the successes and failures of earlier work. This book shows how experimental operations develop from experiment to experiment by describing experiments in historical series and in enough detail to show continuity.

This book offers enough detail and background information to make it accessible to nonspecialists. The same rules of evidence are useful in many related fields. Skill in relating theoretical interpretation to experimental operations should transfer beyond the limited number of topics in this book to other topics in this field as well as to topics in related fields. Mastering this skill is at least as valuable as mastering a compendium of predigested facts and theories, and many students and colleagues find it more exciting.

The strategy of this book is to provoke interest in experimental operations by questioning traditional views. Many readers are surprised to find that it is possible to question folk wisdom about reward, punishment, and cognition. Attempting, and sometimes failing, to defend the traditional view, is a way to find out how advances depend on operational definition.

In contrast with the top-down, feed backward viewpoint of tradition, this book offers a bottom-up, feed forward alternative, which has the advantage of freshness and novelty for many beginners. Contrasting traditional views with reasonable alternatives is a way to get readers to attend to crucial problems of experimental operations. This book presents the major traditional positions in detail, but it demands that readers examine evidence, recognize weaknesses, and consider alternatives.

Inexpensive videotape technology has brought a steadily increasing amount of ethological observation into modern conditioning laboratories. The results of these ethological observations have profound implications for basic theories of learning. This book emphasizes these implications and relates them to classical questions in the ethology and experimental psychology of learning.

Recent developments in computer science have produced a new breed of autonomous robots and autonomous system controllers. Modern robots and system controllers are truly autonomous. Like living systems they operate spontaneously under unexpected conditions. The new breed of autonomous robots and controllers operate on bottom-up principles that are refreshingly ethological. These advances in computer science have profound implications for basic theories of learning. This book emphasizes these implications and relates them to basic problems in the ethology and experimental psychology of learning.

Beatrix Gardner and I collaborated on earlier versions of this book until her recent death, which left me to bring it to its present form. When we met, she had just returned to American experimental psychology fresh from taking her D.Phil. in Zoology at Oxford with the nobelist Niko Tinbergen, a towering figure in experimental ethology. My mentor had been Benton J. Underwood of Northwestern, known throughout his career for experimental methods in the study of learning. Our sign language studies of cross-fostered chimpanzees express a life-long interest in ethology, learning, and experimental operations. Those studies grew out of the same principles that led to this book and appear appropriately in the concluding chapters. They extend the principles of the earlier chapters with unusual conditions and tasks, and with free-living, well-fed, nearly human, experimental subjects as opposed to rats and pigeons in boxes. They also show how rigorous laboratory studies can apply to broadly interesting scientific questions.

Although we planned from the beginning to write a book like this one, our sign language studies of chimpanzees absorbed most of our efforts for many years. Meanwhile, a wave of new experiments appeared that challenged the folk wisdom in traditional theories and traditional books. By now these findings have been well documented and thoroughly replicated. The new findings point to the same ethological pattern, in the nursery school and the Skinner box, in rats and pigeons, in children and chimpanzees. At the same time, fresh developments in computer science offer fresh insights into the behavior of autonomous living systems. It seems like a good time to incorporate the new developments into this new book.

Allen Gardner
November 1997

CHAPTER I

Introduction

DISCOVERY VERSUS UNDERSTANDING

Science promises discovery. Great industries and great nations spend huge sums of money hoping that further discoveries will make them richer and more powerful. Publishers and broadcasters retail news to audiences eager to share in the adventure and the profits of scientific discovery. Philosophy promises understanding. But, what makes us say that we understand this or that idea? What makes us say that students understand? Is it that they can repeat back what they have heard or read, that they can pass examinations, that they say they understand? Those who promise adventure, profit, power, must have something concrete to offer: mushroom-shaped clouds, moon rocks, chess-playing machines. Where philosophy can be lofty and noble, science must be crass and materialistic.

Scientists must work with practical possibilities rather than ideals. All experiments are flawed, but they are not all equally flawed. Some are much better than others. There are significant degrees of difference between disciplined, publicly verifiable observation and ordinary, subjective experience. Several hundred years of scientific history have demonstrated that each level of improvement is well worth the effort. The whole structure rests on operational definitions.

1

BELIEF VERSUS EVIDENCE

Early in the 20th century, Robert H. Goddard patented the basic rocket design that remains in use to this day. In a 1919 report, Goddard described the principles of rocket travel in outer space, and in 1920 the Smithsonian Institution, which had financed some of Goddard's work, summarized the gist of this article in a press release. Journalists were skeptical. An editorial in *The New York Times* reminded the public that it would be impossible for a rocket to function in a vacuum, and dismissed Goddard with, "Of course, he only seems to lack the knowledge ladled out daily in high schools." To its credit the *Times* eventually printed a retraction, but not until 1969 as U.S. astronauts prepared for the first moon landing (Wohleber, 1996).

Before he wrote this article, Goddard first proved that rocket engines could operate in a vacuum by testing an actual engine in a vacuum chamber. This early model not only worked in a vacuum, but it worked 20% better in the vacuum than in air. Goddard was well aware of the traditional belief that engines cannot work in a vacuum, but he settled the question with experimental evidence rather than plausible arguments. The chief objective of this book is to offer tools for distinguishing between belief and evidence.

OPERATIONAL DEFINITION

Goddard did much more than assert that his rocket engine could work in a vacuum. He described his experiments in detail: how he created a vacuum in his experimental chamber, how he measured the vacuum, how he measured the output of his engine, and so on. He described his experimental operations in such detail that other scientists could evaluate his evidence and repeat his experiments. They could reach their own conclusions. Operational definitions tie theories and explanations to observation and experiment.

Facial Vision

Can blind human beings locate objects at a distance? For hundreds, perhaps thousands, of years natural philosophers debated this question. Many cultures believe that losses such as blindness stimulate compensation. To skeptics, compensation seems like a sentimental denial of the harshness of nature and the principle of survival through fitness. Believers retold dramatic stories about the remarkable abilities of blind people. Skeptics found it easy to discount such informal, unverified anecdotes. Without direct experimental tests, the debate could have continued for hundreds of years more.

The dispute ended in 1944 when Dallenbach and his associates placed a 4-ft wide by 7-ft high Masonite screen at random places across the path of blind subjects. The path ran lengthwise through a 60×20 foot corridor. The blind subjects were asked to signal by raising one arm when they first detected the screen, and to stop walking and raise the other arm when they were about to collide with it. There were also catch trials without any obstacle. Blind subjects were quite good at detecting and locating the screen. Next, normal-sighted student volunteers attempted the same task while blindfolded. They failed at first, but within about 20 trials they, also, could detect and locate the obstacle and their performance approached the accuracy of the blind subjects after a few hours of practice (Supa, Cotzin, & Dallenbach, 1944).

The experimenters asked both the blind and the sighted subjects to explain how they detected the screen. About half of the blind and the sighted subjects were convinced that they felt it on the skin of their faces—their foreheads or their cheeks. This agreed with the consensus of blind people in centuries of introspective inquiry into this phenomenon. In fact, the phenomenon had come to be known as "facial vision."

Further experiments showed that blind and blindfolded people could do just as well when their heads were covered with hoods, so long as their ears were exposed. When their faces were bare, but their ears were stopped, they failed. Both blind and blindfolded subjects also failed when the corridor was covered with a thick carpet and they had to walk without shoes. Eventually, the experimenters devised an apparatus that emitted artificial tones and picked up echoes with a microphone. They suspended this contraption from an overhead track so that it could be moved through the corridor by remote control. Under these conditions, subjects could control the movements of the apparatus and locate the obstacles from another room by listening with headphones to the sounds received by the microphone (Cotzin & Dallenbach, 1950).

Dependent Variable

Notice the difference between armchair argument about whether or not a blind person can locate objects at a distance, and an operational test. Dallenbach and his associates devised a way of observing— and better still, measuring—the alleged abilities of blind human beings. It is always the most critical, and often the most difficult, step in any experiment.

Clearly, the responses of the subjects—raising one arm when they first detected the screen, stopping and raising the other arm when they were about to collide with it—*depended* on their ability to locate an object at a distance without sight. In general, the dependent variable in a behavioral experiment is some form of observable response.

Independent Variable

An independent variable is a variable that the dependent variable depends on. The terms mean just what they seem to mean. About half of the blind and blindfolded subjects claimed that they felt the screen on the skin of their cheeks or foreheads. When the experimenters eliminated that source of information with thick hoods, subjects could still locate the screen as long as their ears remained outside of the hoods. This eliminated skin sensation as an independent variable. When the experimenters eliminated hearing with ear stoppers, the subjects failed to detect the obstacles, even when their faces were completely exposed. This identifies hearing as the sense that the ability depends on, and further eliminates facial sensations. The subjects also failed when they had to remove their shoes and walk over a carpeted floor. This identifies the sound of footsteps as the sound that the ability depends on.

Experimental Control

To isolate the effect of an independent variable, everything else must be held constant. In the case of hearing, the experimenters deafened the subjects with ear stoppers while keeping all other aspects of the task constant. By *controlling* for all other independent variables the experimenters isolated hearing as an independent variable.

Experimental control defines the independent variable. Control conditions ask the questions that advertising slogans want you to forget. When the ad says that a brand of soap flakes "washes clothes whiter," you are not supposed to ask, "Whiter than what?" Suppose the ad only means whiter than no soap at all, or whiter than coal dust. The control group defines the "what" in whiter than what, faster than what, and so on.

Introspection

Both the blind and the sighted university students learned to locate obstacles in the dark by listening to the echoes of their own footsteps. It is hard to believe that they accomplished this demanding task without any awareness of which sense organ they were using. Blind people down through the ages solved the same problem for themselves outside of the laboratory, most of them also unaware of which sense organ they were using. They could do it even when their mental imagery of facial vision was quite vivid. One of the blind subjects, for example, described faint shadows on his face that became clear and sharp as he approached an obstacle. That so many agreed in their reports of facial images, and that they were so firmly convinced that they used facial images, is a very interesting phenomenon. And yet, neither the numbers of those who agreed nor the strength of their convictions are evidence for the validity or even the relevance of their subjective reports.

Intervening Variable

Usually, the independent variable in expermental psychology is some sort of stimulus input arranged by the experimenter, and the dependent variable is some sort of response output of the subject. In an experiment in learning, the independent variable is often a series of trials that can be read on the horizontal axis of a graph as in Fig. 1.1, and the dependent variable, which rises or falls as a function of the independent variable, usually appears on the vertical axis of a graph as also shown in Fig. 1.1.

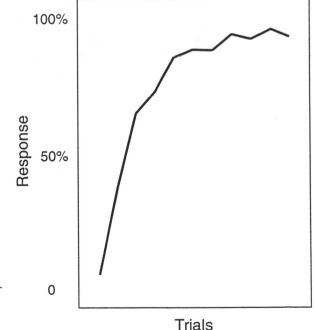

FIG. 1.1.   A curve of percent response plotted against trials in a typical graph of a learning experiment. Copyright © 1997 by R. Allen Gardner.

Intervening variables are relationships between independent and dependent variables. Suppose that Fig. 1.1 plotted the results of an experiment in classical conditioning (chap. 2). On each trial the experimenter lighted a light and then gave the dog some food. The experimenter measured the number of drops of saliva collected in a test tube on each trial, after lighting the light, but before presenting the food. Figure 1.1 would then show how the number of drops of saliva increased from trial to trial. This is called a *learning curve*.

Where is the learning in this curve? Obviously, there is no learning in the saliva in the test tube. Equally obviously, there is no learning in the light or in the food. A single trial cannot show any evidence of learning. The only evidence of learning is in the relationship between trials. We can see and measure the saliva, and we can see and measure the light and the food and the time between them, but we can only infer the relationship from trial to trial by looking at the record and making inferences.

Unseen and unseeable relationships are commonplace in all sciences. Suppose you hold a pencil out at arm's reach and then release it. The pencil usually drops in this experiment. Why does it drop instead of drifting gently up to the sky, or just floating there in the air? The phenomenon is called gravity, of course. Where is the gravity in this experiment? You cannot see gravity any more than you can see learning. The gravity is not in the pencil, and it is not in the floor. There is gravity in the relationship between the pencil and the earth, and all that anyone can see or measure is the rate of fall of the pencil. Once again, a single observation of the position of the pencil at any point in time or space cannot show evidence of gravity.

All sciences must deal with phenomena that can only be inferred from a series of observations. Intervening variables involve additional problems of operational definition over and above the definitions of directly observable dependent and independent variables. These problems of operational definition are straightforward, but the rules of operational definition must be obeyed.

Figure 1.1 is a typical learning curve. The vertical axis represents some measure of response, usually related to probability. The horizontal axis represents some time series, usually trials. Notice that the level of response is greater than zero at the start of learning, even before the first food on the first trial. Anybody who is at all familiar with dogs knows that they are practically always salivating. Pavlov never had to teach any dog to salivate. All he could do was to increase the rate of salivation at certain times. This is typical of all learning situations. The to-be-learned response is always something that the subject does in the learning situation before the start of learning. Otherwise, it could never be affected by experience.

Notice that the curve approaches 100% but never quite reaches it. This is also typical of learning curves. As well as a habit may be learned, behavior is never perfectly stereotyped. Some variation always remains. Without this variability, nothing new could ever be learned and all habits would be permanent.

The curve in Fig. 1.1 is also typical in that it rises rapidly at first and then rises more and more slowly as it approaches 100%. This is called *negative acceleration*.

Experiment Versus Correlation

Since the 19th century, experts have advised parents against picking up a crying baby. They argue that picking up babies and cuddling them only rewards crying. The baby will learn to get affection and attention by crying and become a whimpering, cranky child. This is very difficult advice to take. Most parents cannot resist picking up a crying baby, even when they believe the traditional advice. A baby's cry seems to evoke cuddling and comforting.

Ainsworth and her associates (Ainsworth & Bell, 1977) produced the first actual evidence on this subject by observing parents in their homes and recording how quickly they picked up newborn infants. These investigators found that the babies who were picked up sooner actually cried less at the end of their first year than the children who were picked up later. Not only did the babies who were picked up sooner cry less, but they started to speak earlier. Many parents who picked up their crying infants in spite of the conventional advice have felt vindicated by this result. But, does this study really prove that it is better to pick up a crying baby?

Is it likely that the kind of mother or father who can let their baby cry piteously without responding is the same sort of person as the mother or father that rushes in with comfort at the first sign of distress? It seems very likely that we have two different human types here, one that is more nurturing than the other. If that is true, then it is also likely that nurturance is a genetic trait passed on from parent to child. Nurturing parents might very well have nurturing children who calm down sooner and are more sensitive, responsive, and communicative than the offspring of nonnurturing parents. Perhaps, if nurturing parents could only control themselves and refrain from picking up their squalling infants for a few years, their offspring would be even calmer and more communicative.

This argument can only be settled with an experiment. Correlational studies can never answer questions of this kind. To eliminate (*control for*) genetic factors, experimenters have to manipulate conditions. One possibility is to switch half of the babies at birth and have half the nurturing parents raise the children of nonnurturing parents, while half of the nonnurturing parents raise the children of nurturing parents. The other half of each group would raise their own children. In that way we could see if picking up the crying infants made them calmer and more communicative whether or not they had nurturing genes—and vice versa, if letting them lie crying in their cribs made them more cranky and less communicative whether or not they had nonnurturing genes. This experimental design is called *cross-fostering*. The object of cross-fostering is to distinguish between two independent variables—in this case inheritable nurturing traits of the parents as distinct from the nurturing behavior of the parents.

Alas, it seems very unlikely that we could get a significant sample of parents to cooperate in this fascinating experiment in child rearing. The experiment is also flawed with respect to the central question of whether or not to pick up a crying baby. Very likely nurturing parents have a whole pattern of nurturing behaviors, and picking up the crying infant is only a part of their nurturing parental style. The cross-fostering experiment is too general to answer a question as specific as the one we have here. To test the specific question, the experimenter should let nurturing parents treat their babies as they wish in every way except that half must pick them up as soon as they start crying and half must let them cry for some specified interval, say 15 minutes, before picking them up. The nonnurturing parents would be divided in half in the same way.

Despite its logical advantages as an operational definition of the independent variable, the more specific experiment may be quite as impractical as the cross-fostering experiment. Often in a natural science, particularly a biological science, the necessary experimental conditions are so impractical that critical questions remain unanswered. Practical difficulties have a way of resolving themselves with time, however. Questions about what is on the other side of the moon, for example, were once thought to be unanswerable. Also, bright young minds often discover practical solutions to problems that baffled their elders for generations.

Adaptive Versus Maladaptive

The staggering variety of life forms on our planet is plainly related to specialized adaptations for different ecological niches. The hovering flight of the hummingbird and the treetop feeding of the giraffe are familiar examples. Increasingly specialized wings, hooves, necks, and so on, appear clearly in the fossil record. The geological record also tells a tale of flux and change. Inevitably, the environment changes, and those creatures that are most finely tuned to the environment of their ancestors perish when conditions change. The paths of specialization are also paths to extinction. The ancestors of the giant panda lived in a time when bamboo shoots were plentiful. In that place, and in those times it was highly adaptive to specialize in that one kind of food. Now that bamboo is scarce, the panda is rapidly approaching extinction.

Human beings are remarkably unspecialized. We live in the Arctic and at the Equator, in the mountains and by the sea, in deserts and in marshlands, and we eat just about everything. We are the least specialized of species and that is probably why we are overrunning the earth. Our ability to learn to alter our habits with changing conditions is a vitally adaptive asset. Nevertheless, anyone old enough to read this book probably has already acquired a long list of bad habits. This baggage of maladaptive habits that most adult human beings carry with them is quite as well learned as their adaptive habits—often, maddeningly better learned. Clearly, the mechanisms of learning fail to protect us from acquiring maladaptive habits. Any general theory of learning must account for maladaptive habits as well as for adaptive habits.

ETHOLOGICAL EXPERIMENTS

Color Vision

The experience of color is plainly subjective. Isaac Newton, who discovered the relationship between the physics of light and the experience of color, said it best: "the Rays to speak properly are not coloured" (1730/1952, p. 124). Color vision must be somewhere in the beholder. Although about 2 in 25 European men have deficient color vision, color blindness was unknown to the scientific world until 1798 when John Dalton described his own anomalous experiences. Moreover, that brilliant scientist was in his mid-20s before he realized that his visual world was severely abnormal.

How about other animals? Do they also have color vision? Early naturalists attempted to answer this question by looking at the habits and neurology of other species to see whether they were similar enough to the human case to suppose that this or that nonhuman being might see the world in color, as humans see it. The habits of honeybees, for example, seem to indicate that they distinguish flowers on the basis of color, but the anatomy and neurology of their eyes and brains are far from human. Some argued that honeybees only seem to be distinguishing the color of the flowers and that simpler explanations could account for their behavior. Others argued that the apparent color vision of the honeybee is only another case of anthropomorphism, of projecting human traits into other animals. Still others argued for the simplicity of color vision itself, that it might not require organs as complex as the human eye and brain. There the matter stood, perennial fuel for debate, until the rigorous and precise experiments of von Frisch early in this century.

Von Frisch showed that bees not only discriminate colors, but that they sort them into groups of primary colors the way human beings do, although they may group them more crudely than humans. He also showed that the spectrum of colors visible to the honeybee is shifted away from the red and into the ultraviolet; they confuse red with black and see ultraviolet as a distinct color. Plainly, the cleverest philosophers could never have achieved these discoveries by deep thought on the subject. Von Frisch had to devise measures of color vision for bees, by *operational definition* (Lindauer, 1961; von Frisch, 1950).

Before von Frisch, experimenters had found that bees without previous experience find some colors much more attractive than others. If colored patches are laid out in a field in a random array, many more bees investigate patches with colors near the middle of their visible spectrum and hardly any investigate colors near the ends of their visible spectrum. This only proves that the honeybees have species-specific color preferences. Scientists of the early 20th century concluded that true color vision was obviously beyond the capacity of such a tiny brain. Of course, human beings also have species-specific color preferences and this hardly proves that they are color-blind.

Von Frisch made history by laying out squares of colored paper on a table in a meadow. He placed a small dish on each square. All of the dishes were empty except for one dish that he baited with a small amount of syrup. Honeybees soon found the syrup and returned to the same dish time after time. When von Frisch randomly rearranged the squares on the table, the bees returned to the same colored square, even if he washed out all of the dishes so that the only remaining cue was the color of the square (von Frisch, 1950). Von Frisch had devised an operational definition of color vision in honeybees.

Von Frisch demonstrated that he could manipulate the color preferences of bees arbitrarily. That is, he could teach them to approach any visible color that he chose. A stimulus that is arbitrarily interchangeable with other stimuli in this sense is an *arbitrary stimulus*, a useful term that plays a central role in the descriptions of this book.

Honeybees can remember more than the color of flowers; they can also remember some flower shapes (Gould, 1985; Plowright, 1997). Thus, operational definitions derived from careful experiments permit us to speak with some confidence about the perception of a creature as alien to human beings a honeybee.

Further experiments show that when they return to the hive, these simple creatures with their tiny brains routinely communicate to other bees about distant sources of food. Rather than pinpointing precise targets, scouts only indicate a promising area to forage. Followers are free to take advantage of other targets that may present themselves, as when a change of wind across the flight path carries the scent of richer or closer forage (Gould, 1975; Gould, Henerey, & MacLeod, 1970).

When bees swarm, they form a mass clinging to a convenient branch while scouts search out a favorable site for the new hive. Returning scouts dance on the surface of the mass to communicate their findings. Sometimes their reports disagree. "Prime location, 100 meters due south," dances one scout. "Spectacular site 75 meters north by northwest," dances another. Each scout recruits followers who reconnoiter the proposed sites for themselves and return to join the debate. The swarm remains until there is consensus, with disastrous results if the debate goes on too long (Lindauer, 1961, pp. 34–58).

Arbitrary and Obligatory

Honeybees investigate patches of color. It is a prominent response that generations of human beings observed long before von Frisch arrived on the scene. Bees are more likely to investigate some colors than others and most bees have approximately the same color preferences. No one had to teach them that. The arbitrary effects of experience, however dramatic, are always superimposed on obligatory species-specific patterns of response.

Human beings in widely separated communities all over the world have the same repertoire of facial expressions. The same expressions of anger, disgust, happiness, and sadness are associated with the same types of affective stimuli, but the particular stimuli that evoke these responses, the stimulus events as well as the language in which the events are described, depend on cultural experience. Ekman (1973) demonstrated this by trekking to a remote village in New Guinea where all of the inhabitants had formerly been so isolated that they had never met any foreigner nor had they met anyone else who had ever met a foreigner. Ekman asked these people to make the facial expressions for four basic emotions and photographed their responses. He also showed them photographs of American college students who had been asked to make the same facial expressions. The New Guinea villagers named the facial expressions in the American photographs easily and accurately and, later, American college students named the facial expressions in the New Guinea photographs, also easily and accurately. Ekman's most difficult technical problem (apart from finding a sufficiently isolated village and getting there) was translating the descriptions of basic emotional experience from one language to another.

Not only the pairing of events and emotions, but also the social conditions in which some responses are suppressed and others counterfeited, depend on social learning. Facial expressions of anger and disgust seemed to be absent in native Japanese and, indeed, these expressions fail to appear in ordinary social situations. They appeared quite readily, however, when Ekman (1973) secretly photographed the same Japanese while they were alone in the dark watching films of emotionally charged material, such as surgery.

Along the same lines, young chimpanzees, born in American laboratories and cross-fostered by human beings, have the same repertoire of emotional vocalization observed in young chimpanzees reared by their own mothers under wild conditions in Africa. Positive events and situations evoke positive vocalizations such as pants and grunts, while negative events evoke negative vocalizations, such as whimpers, whether the infant chimpanzees are reared by human psychologists in a U.S. suburb or by wild chimpanzee mothers in an African forest. But, for the cross-fostered infants, the cookies or ice cream that evoked pleasure grunts and the bath preparations that evoked whimpers can only have acquired their affective values through experience (R. A. Gardner, B. T. Gardner, & Drumm, 1989).

Whether we are interested in species identity or gender identity, eating habits or mating habits, survival skills or drug addictions, we must study the *obligatory* consequences of species membership as well as the *arbitrary* effects of individual experience.

Obligatory Patterns

The traditional view acknowledges the existence of obligatory species-specific responses while claiming that there is also a contrasting class of arbitrary behaviors that are "malleable" or "plastic" so that they can be "modified" or "shaped" by consequences, in Skinner's words "as the sculptor shapes his figure from a lump of clay" (1953, p. 93). Pressing a lever, riding a bicycle, playing a violin all look quite arbitrary, but only if we treat them as acts defined by their effects on particular human artifacts and ignore the patterns of behavior that go into the acts.

Popular animal shows amaze audiences with bears riding bicycles and porpoises walking backward on their tails, but knowledgeable ethologists point out how skillful trainers systematically capitalize on the species-specific patterns of behavior that go into the amazing acts (cf. Hediger, 1955). Male bears fight by striking with their forepaws while standing erect on their hind legs. They must balance on two legs to engage in this species-specific pattern. Circus trainers claim that bears transfer this two-legged pattern to "dancing" to music or riding a bycicle. Backward tail walking appears spontaneously in untrained porpoises (Pryor, Haag, & O'Reilly, 1969). The dancing of the famous Lipizaner stallions is their species-specific mating display set to music. The arbitrary effect of experience lies in the connection of obligatory patterns of response to arbitrary patterns of stimulation.

Observation and Experiment

By the end of the 19th century, *field naturalists* formed a prominent group within biology. In the 20th century, behavioral biologists led by Tinbergen, Lorenz, and von Frisch and their followers carried on this tradition as *ethology*. They studied the stream of ongoing behavior under natural conditions in great detail.

> When a bird is sitting on its eggs you know that it is incubating. When it delivers heavy wing-blows at another bird you know that it is fighting. But when two gulls, standing opposite each other, are pecking into the soil, or are tearing at grass tufts, or are walking around each other with the neck drawn in and the bill pointing upward, you have not the slightest idea what they are doing, at least at first. (Tinbergen, 1953a, p. 51)

Tinbergen and his students found that male gulls attack and retreat at the borders of disputed territory but, at the same time, they engage in apparently irrelevant behavior such as pulling up clumps of grass and preening their feathers. A prospective female mate approaches the borders to be met with a mixture of courtship and defense. These are all patterns that ethologists must observe directly and describe in detail.

Field studies continue to enrich science and culture. Goodall's (1986) monumental study of the chimpanzees of East Africa is an inspiring recent example. Field studies emphasize obligatory behavior unfolding under natural conditions.

Species-specific behavior, the domain of field naturalists, used to be called *instinctive* or inborn as opposed to learned by experience. For example, the mating songs of many birds are so species-specific that an ornithologist can identify a bird from its song without ever seeing a feather or a beak. English chaffinches are a typical example. Normally, chaffinches hatch in the spring and migrate south for the winter. During that first spring the immature males never sing, but they hear the normal songs of adult males. Adult males sing in the spring and summer. The young males begin to sing the chaffinch mating song the following spring when they return to the breeding grounds and become sexually mature. Thorpe (1961) gathered chaffinch eggs in the field before they hatched and raised the young birds in his laboratory in isolated cages. Deprived of experience with adult male songs, the isolated males failed to sing normal chaffinch songs the next spring when they became sexually mature. A whole field of research grew out of Thorpe's discoveries (King & West, 1989; Slater & Williams, 1994; West, King, & Freeberg, 1997). Many birds have to learn vital elements of their species-specific songs. Rather than asking whether species-specific behavior is instinctive or learned, modern experimenters ask how much is learned, and when and how is it learned.

Ethologists led by Tinbergen and von Frisch introduced elegant and rigorous experiments in the field and in the laboratory under natural conditions. In order to demonstrate that bees have color vision, von Frisch had to introduce experience with particular colors under experimental conditions. At the time that von Frisch reported these experiments, of course, it was as revolutionary to claim that a tiny bee's brain could learn anything particular about a flower as to claim that a bee's brain could tell one color from another.

Many animals mark their territories with distinctive scents, but many others have to remember the arbitrary landscape of trees, bushes, and rocks in their territories. In many species, bonding with one mate and caring for one's own young depends on learning to recognize the sights and sounds of individual mates and young. Obligatory and species-specific behavior such as homing, foraging, mating, and caring for young often depends on arbitrary learning. Ethologists must study the arbitrary effects of learning on obligatory, species-specific behavior.

Experimental Psychology

Experimental psychology also has roots in the late 19th century. From its beginning the experimental psychology of learning concentrated on arbitrary learning. In early experiments humans learned arbitrary lists of words and meaningless strings of letters, and both humans and other animals learned arbitrary paths through artificial mazes. Skinner invented the operant conditioning chamber or Skinner box in the 1930s to serve as an artificial learning environment. In the traditional view, learning to press a lever or peck a key is completely arbitrary and independent of the evolutionary history of rats and pigeons.

There are two, closely related, reasons why experimental psychologists looked for arbitrary forms of learning. First, the advance of modern science depends heavily on the discovery of general, widely applicable principles. Physicists look for general laws that apply to all forms of matter and all forms of energy. Physiologists look for general laws that apply, for example, to the blood and circulation of all animals. If mazes and Skinner boxes represent arbitrary forms of learning in artificial situations, then the principles of learning in these situations should be general rather than species-specific. In the traditional view, learning in mazes and Skinner boxes should reveal the basic principles of all animal learning, including human learning.

The second reason for studying arbitrary forms of learning in artificial environments has to do with the traditional and popular view that human behavior transcends human biology and evolution. In this view, human beings live in totally artificial environments of their own recent creation. Most of their learning about speaking and writing, driving cars and flying airplanes, building cities and paying taxes is arbitrary and independent of their evolutionary history. If this is true, then the principles of learning discovered in artificial environments like mazes and Skinner boxes should be the principles that are most relevant to human learning.

Ethology of the Skinner Box

Moving away from the detailed descriptions of the ethologists, the founders of the experimental psychology of learning, such as Pavlov, Hull, and Skinner, insisted on single, arbitrary indexes of learning. They counted drops of saliva or number of lever-presses to the exclusion of all other observations. Chapter 2 discusses a sample of Zener's full description in 1937 of the rich and varied behavior of a dog during a typical trial of salivary conditioning in Pavlov's laboratory in Russia. But, Zener was exceptional. He parted with Pavlov and his colleagues both in methods and conclusions. To the end of his career, Skinner urged readers to study the marks of the pen on the recorder rather than the animal in the box (1988, p. 466). In his view, watching the animals inside the box only diverted the experimenter from the arbitrary principles of learning revealed by the pen writing on the recorder.

Fortunately, in recent decades more and more experimenters have been curious enough to look for themselves to see just what else the animals do in the conditioning chambers besides pressing levers and pecking keys. Relatively inexpensive videotape recording has encouraged this trend. With videotape, observers can describe varied ethological patterns of behavior at leisure and without disturbing the experimental subjects. At the same time, experimenters can compare the descriptions of independent pairs of observers to see whether they agree with each other. Independent agreement between observers is called *reliability*. Descriptions of what the animals are doing besides pressing levers and pecking keys reveal a rich ethological flux of behavior in the conditioning chamber (Timberlake & Silva, 1994).

Despite the fears of traditional experimental psychologists, ethological descriptions of species-specific behavior lead to general laws. By discovering general principles relevant to human welfare, the founders of ethology, Tinbergen, Lorenz, and von Frisch, earned the Nobel Prize for Medicine in 1973. Meanwhile, the International Society of Human Ethology, founded in 1972 to recognize the ethology of human behavior, has flourished and grown. In the traditional view, obligatory, species-specific behaviors were troublesome artifacts to be eliminated from experiments and forgotten in theories. Recent discoveries show that, on the contrary, ethological patterns are at the heart of all animal learning.

As artificial and arbitrary as the conditioning chamber may appear, rats and pigeons bring their species-specific ethology with them into the chamber. Human beings also bring their species-specific ethology into the artificial and arbitrary environments of the modern world. Careful experiments have given us a large body of evidence about the way animals learn in artificial environments. This book looks for fresh insights into the general laws of learning by examining this body of evidence from an ethological and ecological point of view.

This book also looks for fresh insights by examining laboratory evidence from the point of view of experimental operations. Readers who can master the principles of operational definition can test propositions for themseleves and come to their own conclusions about each topic in this book. They can apply the same principles to evaluate theories and evidence that fall outside the limited scope of this book as well as theories and evidence that appear in the future. They should find that the same rules of evidence apply to other fields of animal behavior and psychology.

PLAN OF THIS BOOK

This chapter introduces the main themes of this book: operational definition and an ethological, ecological, and evolutionary perspective. The next two chapters introduce the descriptive terms of most experiments since the 1930s that divide experiments into two procedures: classical conditioning and instrumental conditioning. Later chapters raise questions about this distinction, but the terms in chapters 2 and 3 remain useful for describing experiments.

Chapter 4 introduces a framework for describing basic mechanisms that have emerged as candidates for the fundamental unit of classical conditioning: S-S, S-S*, S-R, and S-R-S*. Chapter 4 also introduces the method of testing the operational implications of theories against experimental findings.

The remaining chapters apply the method of chapter 4 to a selection of central problems in human and nonhuman animal learning. They trace basic themes from their roots early in the 20th century to recent developments in animal behavior and robotics. Concrete operational definitions and modern developments in computer science challenge traditional views. The object of each discussion is to raise questions that remain unanswered or only partially answered at this writing.

The last two chapters discuss research on infant chimpanzees that were cross-fostered by human adults. These chapters apply the ethological principles of learning to a situation in which a free-living, well-fed, infant chimpanzee has to learn something much more advanced than lever-pressing or key-pecking. The results open fundamental questions about learning, intelligence, and language. Here we included some of the texture and detail of a personal adventure in ethology and experimental psychology.

CHAPTER 2

Classical Conditioning

In their attempts to discover the most basic form of learning, early experimenters discovered two procedures, one called *classical* or *Pavlovian conditioning,* the other called *instrumental* or *operant conditioning.* Beginning in the 1930s traditional theorists, such as Skinner (1938), maintained that the two basic procedures represent two distinct forms of learning. This view dominated research and theory throughout the century even though hard evidence frequently contradicts the traditional theoretical distinction. The procedural distinction, however, remains useful as a way to describe experiments in this field. Accordingly, chapter 2 describes the experimental operations that define classical conditioning and chapter 3 describes the experimental operations that define instrumental conditioning. These descriptions should prepare readers to make their own critical analysis of evidence and interpretation that they encounter in this field. Later chapters consider the relation between modern evidence and the traditional distinction.

TYPICAL PROCEDURES

This chapter describes the procedure known as classical or Pavlovian conditioning. Experimental examples that used different species, different responses, and different stimuli illustrate the broad generality of this procedure. Experimental examples from the 1930s to the 1990s illustrate how well the basic findings have survived stringent tests of time and replication.

Salivation

Around 1900 when he started his study of conditioning, Pavlov was already a distinguished scientist who had won a Nobel Prize for his studies of the physiology of digestion. These studies depended on his surgical technique for creating a fistula, or tube, leading from specific regions of the digestive tract to the outside of a living and otherwise healthy animal. In this way, experimenters could observe and measure normal secretions at any stage of digestion. During these experiments, Pavlov noted that experienced dogs often began their secretions on route from their cages to the experimental room. Secretions that appeared without food and before the start of experiments were an inconvenient artifact in his early research. When he began to study "psychic secretions," as he called them, for their own sake he set out on the course of research that made him truly famous.

In a typical experiment on salivary conditioning in Pavlov's laboratory, a hungry dog stood on a table in a special experimental room. The experimenters prepared the dog by surgically diverting a salivary gland so that saliva flowed through the dog's cheek to the outside and collected in a measuring tube. The experimenter first adapted the dog until it would stand quietly on the table in a loose restraining harness. From an adjoining room, the experimenter observed the dog through a small window and presented experimental stimuli with remote controls. A tone sounded and after about 5 seconds a plate containing a small amount of dry food appeared near the dog's mouth. Combinations of tone and food separated by intervals of from 5 to 35 minutes occurred several times during each daily session. From time to time the experimenter presented *probe trials* of tone alone without food for 30 seconds.

Hungry dogs tend to salivate at any sound—a door closing, a tap on the window. The experimental tone is no exception and there was some salivary response the first time an experimenter sounded the tone. But, familiar food always evoked much more salivation than any other stimulus. After 30 to 60 combinations of tone and food, tone alone evoked salivation in *probe trials*. The arbitrary tone evoked salivation without food.

Leg Withdrawal

In a later American example, Liddell (1942, p. 194) attached electrodes to the left foreleg of a sheep. A metronome beat once per second for 5 seconds before the sheep received a mild shock from the electrode. At first, the metronome had little effect, but the shock evoked a sharp

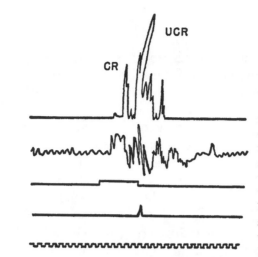

Left forleg

Respiration

Metronome (CS)

Shock (UCS)

Time ($\frac{1}{4}$ sec)

FIG. 2.1. Conditioned responses of sheep. The diagram is from a kymograph record of the 11th pairing of a metronome beat with a shock delivered to the left foreleg. The metronome beat once per second for 5 seconds before the shock. Both conditioned leg movements and respiratory changes began with the beginning of the metronome sound, anticipating the shock that came at the end of the metronome sound. From Liddell (1942).

flexion or withdrawal of the foreleg, accompanied by rapid breathing. After four pairings of the metronome and shock in combination, the metronome evoked clear increases in breathing rate. On the sixth trial the leg flexed, slightly. By the 11th trial, the leg withdrew fully and consistently. Figure 2.1 shows the reactions on the 11th trial.

Eyeblink

Human beings frequently serve as subjects in modern studies of conditioning. Human eyeblinking can be measured with great precision by painting a small silver spot on the subject's eyelid and bouncing a light beam off the spot and onto an electronic recording device. The human eye blinks spontaneously, of course, but it is much more likely to blink when the experimental apparatus blows a slight puff of air against the subject's eye. In a typical experiment, the experimenter pairs a brief flash of light with a puff of air several times during the course of an experimental session. After several pairings the light alone evokes eyeblinks on probe trials (Grant, 1973).

Knee Jerk

In 1902, after Pavlov began his experiments but before news of his findings had reached psychologists in the United States, a student named Edwin Twitmeyer was finishing the experiments for his PhD at the University of Pennsylvania. At the time, many psychologists and neurophysiologists studied the simplest unit of behavior, which they called the reflex arc. The knee jerk, or patellar reflex, is a good example of a simple reflex. Most readers are already familiar with this reflex as tested in thorough medical examinations. A sharp tap on the kneecap, actually the tendon attached to the kneecap, elicits a kicking movement of the lower leg. Repeating this process for many trials increases the extent of the movement. Twitmeyer asked why repetition should enhance this reflex. Why doesn't repetition fatigue and weaken the reflex instead? To find out, he administered many trials over a long series of experimental sessions.

Twitmeyer's experimental apparatus released a hammer that hit the kneecap with a measured amount of force at a precise time. To warn his subjects, the apparatus also struck a bell once just a half-second before the hammer struck the kneecap. One day, the apparatus broke down while a well-practiced subject was in place. When Twitmeyer retested the apparatus, the bell sounded but the hammer failed to operate. To Twitmeyer's surprise, the subject's knee jerked as if struck by the hammer. Twitmeyer thought that the subject, a fellow student, was joking or possibly kicking without waiting for the hammer. The subject reported that he was as surprised as Twitmeyer. The knee seemed to jerk by itself.

Interested, but still skeptical, Twitmeyer repeated the situation, bell without hammer, with a few other subjects. The results were mixed. Some kicked without the hammer, some did not. As he continued, Twitmeyer found that the number of bell-hammer trials was critical. A few subjects responded to the bell without the hammer after only 30 paired trials, but nearly all showed conditioned responses after 130 or more paired trials.

Twitmeyer grasped the significance of his results, writing:

> The movement of the legs following the tap of the bell, without the blows on the tendons, has the characteristics of a simple, immediate reaction to the stimulus. Upon the unanimous testimony of the subjects, it was not produced voluntarily, i.e., there was no idea of the movement in consciousness, antecedent to the movement itself. It may, therefore be held, tentatively at least, that the movement is a reflex action. The afferent excitation must therefore reach the [spinal] cord at the level of the medulla and then pass down to the second or third lumbar segment in which the cell bodies of the efferent conduction path are located. Here then we have a new and unusual reflex arc.
>
> . . . The occurrence of the phenomenon, therefore, depends upon the preliminary simultaneous occurrence of the sound of the bell with the kick produced in the usual way, i.e., a blow on the tendon. After a certain number of such trials, the number varying for different subjects, the association of the sound of the bell and the kick becomes so fixed that the bell itself is capable of serving as a stimulus to the movement. (1974, pp. 1063–1065)

Note how Twitmeyer, like so many others, treats a half-second interval between bell and hammer as equivalent to a zero interval.

Twitmeyer reported and discussed these results in his PhD dissertation together with his main findings that repeated trials increased the reflex. The faculty examining committee approved the dissertation and he received his degree. He also reported his discovery at the annual meeting of the American Psychological Association in a paper called, "Knee-Jerks Without Stimulation of the Patellar Tendon." At that time, the association was so small that there was only one session at any one time, and all members could attend all papers. When he finished, the audience, even the great William James who chaired the session, failed to ask a single question (Dallenbach, 1959). Twitmeyer's experiment first appeared in a regular scientific journal in 1974, long after his death (Twitmeyer, 1974).

Soon after Twitmeyer's paper was so poorly received by the American Psychological Association, Pavlov's work on conditioned reflexes appeared and started a whole new field of research. Pavlov, when he published, was already a Nobel Prize–winning scientist. He published a series of systematic explorations of conditioning and also formulated a new theory of cognitive association to go with his new findings. Twitmeyer had only one experiment to report. He called for further systematic research, but he was only a new PhD without a laboratory of his own. He also titled his dissertation modestly, "A Study of the Knee-Jerk."

It is too bad that others failed to pursue Twitmeyer's procedure even after its belated publication in 1974. His simple method uses a common reflex of human subjects who care for themselves, which avoids the problem of humane animal care. Indeed, Twitmeyer's subjects reported less discomfort than subjects in human eyeblink experiments. The apparatus is also simple and relatively inexpensive. In addition, the neurology of the patellar reflex is well known and its relation to the rest of the nervous system is less elaborate than reflexes that have been popular in laboratories.

BASIC TERMS

Unconditioned Stimulus (UCS)

The UCS is a stimulus that evokes the *unconditioned response* (UCR) with a high probability at the start of the experiment.

Figure 2.2 shows the onset of the UCS, because it is often very difficult to say just when a stimulus such as food comes to an end. In any case, the onset is usually the most significant temporal feature of any stimulus (Albert, Ricker, Bevins, & Ayres, 1993).

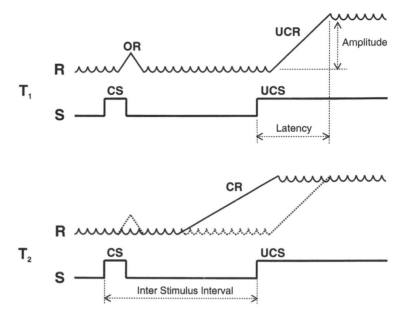

FIG. 2.2.   Classical conditioning. Schematic diagram of two recordings that might have come from a typical experiment. The upper part, T_1, shows the situation on a typical first trial, and the lower part, T_2, shows the situation on a typical late trial. In each part of the diagram, the line labeled R is the response line and the line labeled S is the stimulus line. Copyright © 1997 by R. Allen Gardner.

In the examples in this chapter, the UCS is the food for the hungry dog in the salivary conditioning example, the electric shock for the sheep in the leg withdrawal experiment, the puff of air for the human beings in the eyeblink experiment, and the hammer striking the patellar tendon in Twitmeyer's knee jerk experiment.

The word *unconditioned* can be confusing because it seems to say "never conditioned" or "present at birth" or something of that sort. For an adult dog, the sight of familiar food must have become associated with eating before the start of the experiment. There is weak evidence from Pavlov's laboratory that the sight and smell of milk came to evoke the salivation of milk-fed puppies but not of control puppies. Unfortunately, this experiment was inadequately controlled and never replicated so it gives us only suggestive evidence. Certainly, human beings raised in one culture are attracted by the sight and smell of foods that make members of another culture feel like retching, and vice versa.

In an actual experiment with an adult subject of almost any species, it would be very difficult to prove the absence of any conditioning in a lifetime of experience with a particular UCS. Usually, all we can know about the UCS in any particular experiment is that it evokes the UCR with a high probability at the start of the experiment. The past history of this high probability is a separate question.

Conditioned Stimulus (CS)

The CS is an *arbitrary stimulus* experimentally paired with the UCS. An experiment demonstrates that the CS is arbitrary by using at least two different stimuli, S^a and S^b, and pairing one of these stimuli with the UCS for some subjects and the other with the UCS for the other subjects. The test phase of the experiment presents S^a on some trials and S^b on others for both groups of subjects to test whether there is more response to the stimulus that was paired with the UCS. Since the experimenter flips a coin or uses some other arbitrary device to decide which stimulus to pair with the UCS, the experiment tests whether the response depends on the arbitrary pairing of CS and UCS.

In the examples in this chapter, the CS is the tone for the dog in the salivary example, the metronome for the sheep in the leg withdrawal experiment, the flash of light for the human in the eyeblink experiment, and the bell in Twitmeyer's knee jerk experiment.

The CS usually fails to evoke the full UCR before pairing with the UCS, but often does evoke an orienting response (OR) at the start of the experiment, that Pavlov called an orientation reflex, what-is-it reflex, or investigatory reflex.

Orienting Response (OR)

The OR is a response to the CS at the outset of the experiment. Traditionally, the OR shows that the subject attended to the CS before conditioning. The OR tends to disappear during the course of the experiment as if attention to the CS gradually fades away. A dotted line in T_2 of Fig. 2.2 indicates the place where the OR used to appear.

In most experiments the UCR (or a fractional part of the UCR) is a highly probable response to any stimulus under those conditions. For example, almost any stimulus is likely to evoke some salivation from a hungry dog. Conditioning is impossible if the probability of the conditioned response to the CS is truly zero at the start of the experiment.

Unconditioned Response (UCR)

The UCR is a response that the UCS evokes with a high probability at the start of the experiment.

In many cases, such as salivation to the stimulus of dry food placed in the mouth, the UCR is probably an obligatory, species-specific response to the UCS.

In the examples in this chapter, the UCR is salivation for the dog in the salivary example, leg withdrawal for the sheep in the leg withdrawal experiment, eyeblinking for the human in the eyeblink experiment, knee jerking in Twitmeyer's knee jerk experiment.

Conditioned Response (CR)

The conditioned response (CR) is a response that the CS evokes after paired presentations of the CS and the UCS. In T_2 of Fig. 2.2, the CR appears earlier than the UCS appeared in T_1.

A dotted outline in T_2 of Fig. 2.2 indicates the place where the UCR used to appear. When the CR anticipates the UCS in this way, it leaves a distinct record on every trial. Sometimes, the CR fails to anticipate the UCS. In those cases, experimenters must use *probe trials*. Probe trials present the CS alone to see if a CR appears without any UCS.

In the examples in this chapter, the CR is anticipatory salivation for the dog in the salivary example, anticipatory leg withdrawal for the sheep in the leg withdrawal experiment, anticipatory eyeblinking for the human in the eyeblink experiment, and anticipatory knee jerking in Twitmeyer's knee jerk experiment.

In Fig. 2.2, as in most experiments, the CR is similar to the UCR in form and direction, but the CR can be a decrease in response where the UCR was an increase. D. A. Powell, Gibbs, Maxwell, and Levine-Bryce (1993), for example, used lights, tones, and touch stimuli as CSs and painful shock as the UCS. The UCR that the shock evoked in the rabbit subjects of this experiment was always an increase in heart rate. The CR, however, was a decrease in heart rate for all three types of CS.

Response Measures

The *amplitude* (amount, magnitude) of a response is measured in different units depending on the experiment and the technical resources of the experimenter. Pavlov measured the amount of saliva by reading graduated lines on a measuring tube. Other experimenters have measured leg withdrawal in centimeters of movement, eyeblinks in millimeters of movement, and respiration in millimeters of chest expansion.

The response lines, *R*, in Fig. 2.2 are irregular, wavy lines to indicate the fact that the baselines are not flat zero values under the conditions of any practical experiment. There is always some fluctuation in the level of response. Hungry dogs frequently salivate, human beings frequently blink their eyes, and sheep often flex their legs without any experimental intervention. The amplitude of response to the UCS and CS must always be relative to the average level of background fluctuation.

The *latency* of a response is the time between the onset of a stimulus and the initiation of the response. This is a basic response measure used throughout experimental psychology. The OR, CR, and UCR all have latency as well as amplitude. Figure 2.2 shows the latency of the UCR beginning with the onset of the UCS and ending when the amplitude reaches its maximum level. The level of the amplitude measure that the experimenter uses to define the endpoint of the latency is arbitrary. Individual experimenters can choose some middling value or some value that is just significantly higher than the background fluctuations, whatever seems most useful, just as long as they describe it precisely and stick to the same value throughout the experiment.

The amplitude measure must always refer to the amount of response within some specified time interval. Pavlov and his students would never present a CS and then wait hours or even many minutes before reading the level of saliva collected in the test tube. Because the amplitude measured in any trial is always the amount of response recorded within an arbitrarily defined time interval, and the latency measured in any trial is always the amount of time recorded before an arbitrarily defined amount of response, the two response measures are always interdependent. The experimenter decides which measure to make arbitrarily constant and which to measure as a variable. Usually, the decision depends on the cost and convenience of the technology available to the experimenter.

Pavlov and many other experimenters often report results in terms of the *probability of response,* defined as the number of trials in which there was a recordable response divided by the total number of trials in which the CS appeared. When experimenters report CRs in this way, of course, they are only counting as responses those trials in which there was a response of more than some arbitrarily chosen amount within some arbitrarily chosen interval. They count responses of lower amplitude or longer latency as zero. Responses of higher amplitude or shorter latency are always counted as one. Thus, responses are counted as all-or-none even though they usually vary in amplitude and latency.

Acquisition

Acquisition is a series of trials in which the CS and UCS are paired.

Extinction

Extinction is a series of trials in which the CS appears without the UCS.

Resistance to Extinction

Usually, the CR weakens or ceases entirely during extinction. The rate of decline is called *resistance to extinction.* Responses persist for many trials without the UCS when resistance is high, but die out soon when resistance is low. Experimenters use one of the standard response measures—latency, amplitude, or probability—to measure resistance to extinction. Sometimes experimenters run a fixed number of extinction trials and sometimes they continue running extinction trials until responding drops below some criterion.

Many experiments must use performance during extinction trials as a measure of conditioning during acquisition. Suppose, for example, that after 100 acquisition trials all response measures in a salivation experiment have reached a maximum and stay at the same level for the next 100 trials. How can the experimenter find out whether conditioning is stronger after 200 trials than after 100 trials even though all measures of acquisition have leveled off? The question can be answered by extinguishing one group after 100 trials and a second group after 200 trials to see if the groups differ in resistance to extinction. In cases like this, two groups that performed identically during acquisition may show differences in resistance to extinction.

There are other cases where certain theoretical questions must be investigated by measuring resistance to extinction. These appear in later chapters of this book as these questions become relevant.

Spontaneous Recovery

Pavlov discovered that extinction is only temporary. After a rest, extinguished CRs usually recover substantially, sometimes completely. In one salivary experiment with a dog, Pavlov (1927/1960) reported that, after a series of seven extinction trials, amplitude of the CR decreased from 10 drops of saliva to 3 drops and latency increased from 3 seconds to 13 seconds. The experimenters let the dog rest for

23 minutes. On the first trial after the rest without intervening trials, the CR rose to six drops and the latency dropped to 5 seconds.

Spontaneous recovery after a rest can be tested with or without the UCS. With the UCS, it is called *reacquisition;* without the UCS, it is called *reextinction* (see Fig. 10.1). Spontaneous recovery is a robust phenomenon that appears in virtually all experiments. Plainly, the CR is neither forgotten nor eliminated by extinction. Chapter 10 discusses the theoretical significance of spontaneous recovery.

Habituation

Figure 2.2 illustrates the weakening and eventual loss of the OR over a series of trials. What happens when the experimenter repeats the CS before presenting the UCS? The result is usually the same weakening and eventual loss of the OR. The response *habituates*. What happens if the experimenter now begins pairing the CS and UCS? Conditioning, if it occurs at all, is usually much slower and more difficult after habituation of the OR to the CS. The effect is sometimes called *latent inhibition* (Albert & Ayres, 1989; Lubow, 1989).

Habituation can be stimulus-specific. Whitlow and Wagner (1984) repeatedly presented tones of 530 Hz or 4,000 Hz to rats and found selective weakening of the OR, which they measured by the constriction of surface blood vessels. Habituation was selective in that repetitions of the habituated tone evoked a much weakened OR, while a new, unhabituated tone evoked the full OR. Because habituation can be stimulus-specific, it is a type of conditioning in its own right.

Within an hour of birth human infants begin to fixate objects in their field of view (Prechtl, 1974). Fixation is a kind of orienting response, that appears and then habituates if the object stays the same. The amount of time that newborn babies spend fixating on a particular object, before they habituate and their eyes wander, depends on the amount of structure in the figure. Friedman, Carpenter, and Nagy (1970/1973) studied the habituation of this OR in human neonates when the stimuli consisted of black-and-white checkerboard patterns. Friedman et al. presented either a 2×2 or a 12×12 checkerboard pattern, repeatedly, for 60 seconds at a time. When the amount of fixation fell below the initial average for an infant, the experimenters switched to the other checkerboard pattern. The amount of fixation time recovered to the initial level almost immediately for most of the subjects and the infants scanned the new target with widening eyes as they had initially scanned the first target. Habituation was specific to the first target.

M. H. Bornstein and Benasich (1986) found very similar results with 5-month-old human infants using color slides of human faces and simple red geometric forms as targets. After habituation with one target, fixation and scanning recovered for a fresh target. Reviewing 14 studies of this phenomenon, Bornstein and Sigman (1986) found that the amount of decrement and recovery of attention in habituation tests of this sort correlated with scores on standardized tests of intelligence and language development 2 to 8 years later.

Sensitization

When the UCS is painful or noxious, experimenters often find *sensitization,* which is the opposite of habituation. In an early experiment, Grether (1938) first established that caged monkeys made little response to the sound of a bell. Then he frightened the monkeys several times with loud, noisy powder flashes. After the powder flashes the same bell evoked fright responses. Because the effect of sensitization resembles a conditioned response to a stimulus that was never paired with the UCS, this phenomenon is often called *pseudoconditioning.*

Later, Harlow and Toltzien (1940) demonstrated a similar sensitization effect in cats by presenting a series of 10, 20, or 30 shock trials before the first presentation of a CS. The greater the number of shock trials, the greater the fear response to the CS on its first presentation. Tests were postponed for 5 minutes, 3 hours, or 24 hours after the shock trials. The new CS evoked about the same amount of response in each of these conditions, so an explanation in terms of generalized excitement seems unsatisfactory. Presumably, such excitement (fear, anxiety) would subside in 24 hours. An alternative possibility seems more likely: that responses to shock become conditioned to the experimental room, the apparatus, and the experimental situation in general (Bouton, 1993).

If the CS appears for several trials without the UCS, the CR gradually weakens or ceases completely. This is extinction, of course. Following extinction a few pairings of the CS and UCS can completely restore the conditioned response. This is reacquisition. Presenting the UCS alone, without the CS, for several trials can also restore the CR. In an extensive study comparing several procedures, Harris (1941) measured finger withdrawal of human subjects with painful shock as the UCS. The CS was a loud tone that lasted 4.75 seconds; the UCS was a .25-second shock. All groups received a total of 80 shocks. The measure of the effectiveness of the different procedures was the percentage of conditioned responses on a series of 10 trials without shock. Harris' results actually show more CRs after sensitization (trials with shock alone before the first trial with a CS) than any other procedure that he used. The implication of these and many experiments since (e.g., Servatius & Shors, 1994) is that sensitization may be a part of all conditioning with a painful or noxious UCS.

All good experiments include some control for the effect of sensitization. This is accomplished by exposing one group to the UCS without previous pairing of CS and UCS. Viewed another way, however, if sensitization is specific to the experimental situation and can last as long as 24 hours, it is an elementary form of conditioning, like habituation rather than an annoying artifact.

RELATIONSHIP BETWEEN CONDITIONED AND UNCONDITIONED RESPONSES

The traditional view treats the CR as if it were the same as the UCR that the UCS elicited on the first trial. In this view, the dog that formerly salivated only to food should, after conditioning, salivate in the same way to the metronome. The human that formerly blinked at an air puff should, after conditioning, blink in the same way to the light. This is clearly incorrect. The CR and UCR are rarely, if ever, strictly the same, and the CR is hardly a replica of the UCR (D. A. Powell et al., 1993).

Early experiments tended to use crude measuring instruments and seldom reported more than a single index so that the CR seemed to duplicate the UCR. Thus, Culler, Finch, Girden, and Brogden (1935) and Kellogg (1938) reported that, in the early stages of conditioned leg withdrawal, dogs responded to the CS just as they had to the shock. Similarly Pavlov's records of salivation are seldom precise enough to make exact comparisons between CRs and UCRs. As early as 1948, however, with improved apparatus Konorski could detect clear differences between CRs and UCRs, and this is the usual finding with modern sensitive instruments.

If the CR and UCR are different, what is the relationship between them? The most popular explanation is that the CR is either a fractional component of the UCR or a preparation for the UCS.

Conditioned Response as a Fractional Response

In many experiments, the CR is weaker than the UCR or it is only a component part of the UCR. The amplitude of the conditioned salivary response, for example, is usually significantly lower than the unconditioned salivary response. Moreover, where the UCR to food consists of lapping at the food, salivating, chewing, and then swallowing, the CR usually includes only one or two of these components. A dog that received shock on the leg right after hearing a buzzer may make a conditioned withdrawal response to the buzzer alone without the vocalization that was a part of the reaction to shock.

Conditioned Response as a Preparatory Response

Some theorists claim that the function of the CR is to prepare the organism for the UCS, which would explain the differences between the CR and the UCR. Detailed descriptions certainly support this view. Zener (1937), for example, conditioned salivary responses to a bell that preceded feeding in the usual manner. Zener recorded complete trials on motion picture film.

> Except for the component of salivary secretion the conditioned and unconditioned behavior is not identical. (a) During most of the time in which the bell is reinforced by the presence of food, chewing generally occurs with the head raised out of the food pan but not directed either at the bell or into the food pan, or at any definite environmental object. Yet this posture practically never, even chewing only occasionally, occurs to the conditioned stimulus alone. Despite Pavlov's assertions, the dog does not appear to be eating an imaginary food. (b) Nor is the behavior that does appear an arrested or partial unconditioned reaction consisting of those response elements not conflicting with other actions. It is a different reaction, anthropomorphically describable as a looking for, expecting, the fall of food with a readiness to perform the eating behavior which will occur when the food falls. The effector pattern is not identical with the unconditioned. (c) Movements frequently occur which do not appear as part of the unconditioned response to food: all the restless behavior of stamping, yawning, panting. (p. 393)

When Zener removed the restraining straps, allowing a much greater range of activity, the preparatory character of the behavior became even more evident. At the conditioned signal for food, the dogs approached the food pan; at another signal, which had been associated with the release of acid into the mouth, the dogs either did nothing (since the acid-delivering tube was not attached), or walked away from the neighborhood of the stimulating devices. Furthermore, when satiated with food, their reactions to the CS not only decreased in amount but qualitatively changed.

Zener's (1937) detailed description shows the complexity of behavior in the conditioning situation. Plainly, the common expression, "*the* conditioned response," is misleading.

GENERALITY

Experimental Subjects

Experimenters have conditioned very simple animals with Pavlov's procedure. Planaria, for example, are flat worms, about one centimeter long, three millimeters wide, and one tenth of a millimeter deep. They have two light-sensitive eyespots, bilateral symmetry, and a ganglion at their head end. They are so primitive that, if you cut one in two, the head end grows a new tail and the tail end grows a new head. Thompson and McConnell (1955) conditioned planaria in a light-shock situation. The experimental chamber was a plastic basin filled with water. The CS was the onset of two 100-watt lights. The UCS was a 28-milliampere shock passed through the water. The experimenters observed two different conditioned responses, a turning of the head to one side or the other and a longitudinal contraction of the entire body. In 150 trials the probability of one or the other of these responses increased from just under 30% to just over 40% (see also, Carney & Mitchell, 1978; Krasne & Glanzman, 1995; Levison & Gavurin, 1979).

Conditioning is possible at a very early age, even before birth. Hunt (1949), with chick embryos as subjects, paired a bell with electric shock and obtained conditioning of a gross bodily movement on the 15th day of incubation. In some cases CRs continued to appear after hatching. Spelt (1948) reported conditioning in human fetuses $6\frac{1}{2}$ to $8\frac{1}{2}$ months of age. As the UCS, he used a very loud noise, which produced an unconditioned startlelike response. As the CS he used a tactile vibration of the mother's abdomen. He measured movement of the fetus with tambours attached to the mother's abdomen. Her ears were covered to prevent her from hearing the CS, of course. After pairings of CS and UCS, movement responses occurred to the CS alone. Dorothy Marquis (1931) conditioned the sucking reactions of newborn human infants to the sound of a buzzer. She also altered the feeding schedule of the neonate to a degree by manipulating the amount of time between nursings (Sameroff & Cavanaugh, 1979, reviewed a body of research that grew out of Marquis' pioneering work).

Unconditioned Responses

Pavlov and his students only used food and painful shock as UCSs and consumatory responses such as salivation or defensive responses such as leg withdrawal as UCRs. Since Pavlov's time most experimenters who have used his procedure have also used consumatory responses and defensive responses. Swallowing movements that are a UCR to drinking, pupillary dilation and contraction that are UCRs to sharp changes in illumination, dilation and contraction of surface blood vessels that are UCRs to heating up and cooling down, eye movements that are UCRs to rotation, and even immune reactions to antigens are among the many types of responses that experimenters have successfully used as UCRs in classical conditioning (Turkkan, 1989).

Conditioned Stimuli

From the list of CSs already used in classical conditioning experiments, it looks as though just about any stimulus will serve. Experimenters have used lights of various colors, geometrical forms, and rotating objects; pure tones, horns, buzzers, bubbling water, and metronomes; odors, tastes, and surface pressure on particular spots of the skin. Pavlov tended to prefer continuing stimuli, such as metronomes, electric fans, and rotating disks. Later experimenters tend to prefer stimuli with sharp onset, such as flashes of light, clicks, and touch. An increase or decrease in a stimulus or the termination of a stimulus can also serve as a CS.

Arbitrary Stimuli

If the conditioned result is about the same whether the CS is a tone or a light, a high-pitched tone or a low-pitched tone, a red light or a green light, then we can call it an arbitrary stimulus, S^a. The arbitrariness of stimuli in conditioning experiments is only relative, however.

Chapter 1 described how some colors attract bees more than other colors. It is easier to condition bees to return to those colors. Experiments to see whether noisy flowers are more attractive than silent flowers have not yet appeared. We do know that bees sense noises in the hive because the vibrations made by the dancing scouts are essential to the response of the recruits (Kirchner, Dreller, & Towne, 1991).

An extensive series of experiments with rats that started with Garcia and Koelling (1966) demonstrated that the strength of conditioning can depend critically on the appropriateness of the CS to the UCR. In the typical experiment, innocuous chemicals with novel tastes are added to drinking water. After drinking the novel-tasting water, rats are made ill by injections of poison. After they recover, the rats get a choice between the novel-tasting water and plain tap water. They drink dramatically less of the novel-tasting water. The result is called *taste-aversion conditioning*.

Instead of giving the water a novel taste, the experimenters also sounded buzzers and lighted lights when the rats drank. After illness and recovery, these rats got to choose between a bottle with the noise and lights or a bottle without noise and lights. For rats, illness has markedly less effect on later drinking if the CS is a novel noise or light than if the CS is a taste. Experiments have also conditioned aversion with electric shock. Garcia and Koelling (1966) gave rats painful shocks when they drank novel-tasting water and also when they drank noisy, lighted water. For shocked rats, noise and light depressed drinking more than novel tastes.

Usually, the sensory dimension has a critical effect on conditioning: Different sensory dimensions are more effective for different kinds of conditioning. If the experimenter can arbitrarily choose stimuli within a dimension (colors, tones, tastes) and get much the same effect with a range of stimuli within that dimension, then we call the stimuli arbitrary, with the understanding that this only means relatively arbitrary.

Ethology of Stimulus/Response Compatibility

While it may be true that virtually any animal can be conditioned, that virtually any stimulus can serve as a CS, and that virtually any response can serve as a CR, conditioning is easy with some CS/CR combinations and difficult with others. Differences in the condition-ability of particular stimulus/response combinations are species-specific. Naturally, most experimenters are mostly interested in getting results, so they tend to reuse combinations of stimulus, response, and species that have worked well in the past. In recent times, however, more experimenters have investigated species-specific characteristics that favor certain stimulus/response combinations over others. This leads to a less arbitrary and more ethological and ecological view of conditioning.

Keith-Lucas and Guttman (1975), for example, conditioned aver-sion in rats with painful shock as UCS. They found dramatic condi-tioned effects when they used a toy hedgehog as CS and only weak effects, if any, when they used a flat, striped surface as CS. Ayres,

Haddad, and Albert (1987) and Van Willigen, Emmett, Cote, and Ayres (1987) also conditioned aversive responses in rats using painful shock as the UCS. They found dramatically different amounts of conditioning depending on which CS they used. Conditioning was strong when they used a brief tone as a CS and weak when they used a flash of light.

TIME AND SEQUENCE

In animal behavior, sequence is critical. Suppose I step on your foot and then say, "Excuse me." Your response would be very different if I said, "Excuse me," and then stepped on your foot. The amount of time between events also matters. If "excuse me" and stepping on your foot are separated by an hour, you might fail to associate them at all.

In most experiments in classical conditioning, the CS begins just before the onset of the UCS. It may either overlap with the UCS in time or terminate before the appearance of the UCS. The arrangement illustrated in Fig. 2.2 is by far the most studied and most discussed procedure.

Interstimulus Interval (ISI)

The ISI is measured from the onset of the CS to the onset of the UCS. When the CS starts before the UCS, the ISI is *positive* and the arrangement is called *forward conditioning*. When the CS starts after the UCS, the ISI is *negative* and the arrangement is called *backward conditioning*. When they start at the same time, the ISI is *zero* and the arrangement is called *simultaneous conditioning*.

Length of the Interstimulus Interval

No one would expect much conditioning if we sounded the tone on Monday and gave the dog food on Tuesday. Sounding the tone at noon and giving the food at 1:00 p.m. also seems like a poor arrangement. In general, the shorter the ISI the better the conditioning, as most people would expect. Simultaneous appearance of CS and UCS is the shortest possible interval because in that case the ISI is zero. This extreme value is usually unfavorable for conditioning, however.

The importance of some small amount of offset between CS and UCS suggests that temporal offset plays a significant role in the conditioning process. Many experiments have looked for the shortest or the most favorable ISI in the hope of discovering a critical factor in the process. The shortest possible ISI must depend on the speed of bioelectrical conduction. Conduction in the nervous system is a bit slower than conduction in household wiring, but not much slower and the distances are quite short. Of course, there is a good deal of switching circuitry in the nervous system. There are six synapses between the retina and the optical cortex and a few more at least before an impulse can get to the motor cortex and a few more synapses still before an actual muscle moves. Transmission through all of that neural circuitry must cost some time.

The amount of time it takes for an animal to respond to a stimulus such as a light or a tone with a leg or finger movement is called the *reaction time* and psychologists have studied this interval thoroughly in many animals with many stimuli and many responses. Under favorable experimental conditions simple reaction time (without complex discrimination) takes between one sixth and one eighth of a second from the moment that a light or tone appears to the moment of an overt response such as a leg or finger movement (Wickens, 1984, p. 338). Therefore, the minimum time required for one complete sequence of stimulus in and response out should be between one sixth and one eighth of a second.

Experimenters have studied the ISI in forward classical conditioning (CS then UCS) very thoroughly, and the most favorable interval found in a very large number of forward conditioning studies is roughly one half of a second, depending on experimental particulars, such as subjects, responses, and stimuli (J. F. Hall, 1976, pp. 110–119; Kehoe & Napier, 1991, pp. 195–196). Half a second is at least three to four times as long as the reaction time. And, that is only the most favorable interval; significant amounts of conditioning occur with even longer intervals, under some conditions with intervals of several seconds between CS and UCS. Favorable ISIs that are so much longer than necessary for simple neural circuits to fire indicate strongly that there is more to the process of conditioning than simple association of the CS with the UCS. Chapter 4 discusses the implications of this finding in more detail.

Much of the advance of modern science depends on viewing nature in terms of continuous variables rather than all-or-none categories. Amount of offset between CS and UCS is a variable. The crudeness of Pavlov's early experiments constrained him in his theoretical interpretations. Pavlov had to divide ISIs into crude all-or-none categories of forward, backward, and simultaneous because the early instruments available to him were too crude for precise measurement.

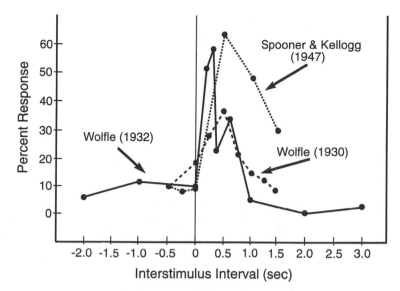

FIG. 2.3.   Results of varying the ISI. From Spooner and Kellogg (1947), from *American Journal of Psychology*. Copyright © 1947 by the Board of Trustees of the University of Illinois. Adapted with permission of the University of Illinois Press.

After Pavlov, however, better apparatus permitted experimenters to explore the ISI as a variable (J. F. Hall, 1976, pp. 110–119). Figure 2.3 illustrates a few typical examples. Modern experiments show a continuous curve rather than any sharp breaks that divide intervals into three types: forward, simultaneous, and backward. Yes, a zero ISI is unfavorable, but relatively long positive intervals can be even more unfavorable than zero. Under the experimental conditions reported in Fig. 2.3, forward intervals of 1.5 seconds or more produced less conditioning than a zero interval.

Experimenters who treat all forward intervals as equivalent members of a single all-or-none category, rather than differing values of a continuous variable, may choose a single value for the positive ISI and compare this with a zero interval. The result, of course, depends entirely on the single interval that the experimenter chooses. Thus, in three of four separate experiments, Rescorla (1980) used a forward offset of 5 or 10 minutes and compared that with zero offset in each case. In the fourth experiment, the forward offset that Rescorla compared with a zero ISI was 30 seconds. It is hardly surprising that such unfavorably long positive intervals would produce less conditioning than a zero interval. This example appears at length here because it illustrates the distortion that results when theorists divide a continuous variable into a few all-or-none categories. Experiments designed to support a particular theoretical interpretation often fall into this trap. Much more can be learned from experiments designed to explore an interesting variable for its own sake.

Chapter 4 discusses the theoretical significance of the ISI as a variable in classical conditioning.

CONDITIONED EMOTIONAL RESPONSE

Human anxiety often interferes with normal, productive behavior. People who suffer from anxiety report physiological reactions such as heart palpitations, shortness of breath, and sweaty palms during attacks of anxiety. Many clinical psychologists interpret these symptoms as conditioned fear. If they are correct, then experiments on classically conditioned defensive behavior should be critically relevant to human anxiety.

Physiological responses to fear, such as heart rate, blood pressure, and breathing rate, are relatively difficult and expensive to measure, but instrumental responses, such as lever-pressing in a Skinner box (chap. 3), are easy and inexpensive to measure. The *conditioned emotional response* (CER) takes advantage of the finding that ongoing instrumental behavior, such as lever-pressing in a Skinner box, is sensitive to the effects of defensive conditioning. Meanwhile, anxiety is debilitating, precisely because it interferes with normal, productive behavior, so conditioned fear that interferes with instrumental responses should be highly relevant to human welfare.

Typically, in a CER procedure, experimenters first train hungry or thirsty rats to press a lever for food or water. Next, they remove the lever from the Skinner box and pair a CS such as a light with a painful UCS such as electric shock. Finally, the experimenters replace the lever in the box and observe the amount of lever-pressing under extinction conditions—that is, no food and no shock. During this test phase of the experiment, however, the experimenters probe by presenting the CS alone to see how much the CS suppresses lever-pressing. If the CS suppresses lever-pressing, this is attributed to an emotional response to the CS that interferes with lever-pressing. The amount of suppression should depend on the amount of emotional response that was conditioned to the CS. It is an indirect way of measuring classical conditioning, but it has the advantage of convenience as well as relevance to the intrusive effects of conditioned fear.

In an important early experiment, Mowrer and Aiken (1954) first trained five groups of rats to press a lever in a Skinner box. Then, after removing the lever from the box, they paired a 3-second flashing light with a 10-second painful electric shock in four different ways as

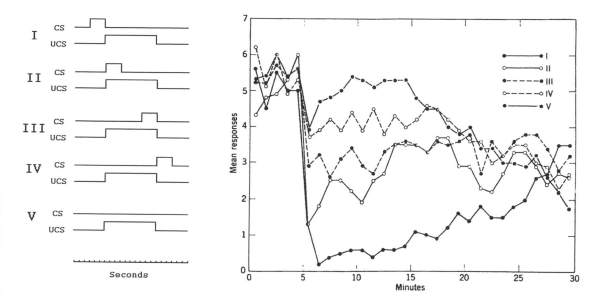

FIG. 2.4. Conditioned emotional response (CER). A flashing light CS was paired with a painful shock UCS for Groups I–IV as shown in the left-hand panel. Group V was a control group with the same number of shocks and lights without pairing. From Mowrer and Aiken (1954), from *American Journal of Psychology*. Copyright © 1954 by the Board of Trustees of the University of Illinois. Used with permission of the University of Illinois Press.

shown in the left-hand panel of Fig. 2.4. Group I received the CS immediately before the onset of the UCS; Group II received the CS immediately after the onset of the UCS; Group III received the CS immediately before the offset of the UCS; and Group IV received the CS immediately after the offset of the UCS. Group V received the same number of shocks and lights as the other four groups, but shocks and lights were separated by at least 2 minutes.

After those differential treatments, Mowrer and Aiken replaced the lever in the box. The results, shown in the right-hand panel of Fig. 2.4, show that the onset of the shock was the most critical point in time for the suppression of food-motivated lever-pressing. The closer the CS to the onset of the shock the greater the suppression. The most effective time was just before the onset of the shock. This is exactly what we would expect if the conditioned emotional response in this experiment was an anticipatory defensive reaction to the flashing light.

SOCIAL CONDITIONING

Following Pavlov, most experiments in classical conditioning have used a rather narrow range of consumatory and defensive responses, such as salivation, leg withdrawal, or eyeblinking. Primitive consumatory and defensive responses are directly involved in emotional conditioning, which is why so many psychologists search for the fundamental laws of classical conditioning. From a broader and more ethological point of view, there is a much wider range of adaptive and maladaptive learning that depends on classical conditioning and that has even more significant implications for human behavior.

Imprinting

A brood of young ducklings following their mother is a common sight in the spring. Ducklings that fail to follow their mother die. How do newly hatched ducklings recognize their own mother? For that matter, how do they recognize an adult duck? How do they tell the difference between adult ducks and other objects anyway? The answer is that newly hatched ducklings follow the first moving object that they see. Following the same object for a while conditions them so that they follow only that object and no others.

Experimenters have exposed ducklings to an arbitrary object such as a red ball or a green shoebox moving back and forth in an enclosure. If the first object is a green shoebox, then after following the shoebox for a while, a duckling always follows that green shoebox, ignoring other objects such as a red ball. Meanwhile, a duckling that has been *imprinted* in this way on a red ball follows the red ball and ignores a green shoebox. Under natural conditions, of course, the mother duck is the first moving object that a duckling sees. Many kinds of social learning in a wide variety of animals show a similar pattern (Suboski, 1990, 1994).

Conditioned Mobbing

Owls, hawks, and other meat-eating birds prey on blackbirds, starlings, and other smaller birds. The smaller birds can often fight off the predator, if they stick together and fly at their enemy from all directions. They usually cannot kill or injure an owl or a hawk, but they can often chase it right out of the area, and possibly condition it to stay away. This pattern of behavior is called *mobbing.*

The sooner they start the mobbing defense the more effective it is, so the defending birds need to recognize potential attackers as soon as possible. The first bird to spot the attacker sounds an alarm call and starts the mobbing. All of the defenders in the area join in when they hear or see the first bird begin the mobbing.

Curio, Ernst, and Vieth (1978) demonstrated that inexperienced blackbirds can learn to mob arbitrary targets by a process that looks very much like classical conditioning. The experimenters housed groups of wild and cage-reared blackbirds in adjacent cages in such a way that they could show a stuffed owl to the wild birds while preventing the cage-reared birds from seeing the owl. Instead of an owl, the cage-reared birds saw an arbitrary object such as a plastic bottle or a stuffed specimen of a harmless honey-eating bird. When the experienced blackbirds sounded their alarm calls and attempted to mob the owl, the inexperienced blackbirds followed them with alarm calls and attempts to mob the plastic bottle or the honey-eating bird.

Soon the inexperienced birds started mobbing the arbitrary object as soon as they saw it, without waiting for the experienced birds to lead the attack. The experimenters then used the now trained, cage-reared blackbirds to train a fresh group of inexperienced blackbirds to mob an arbitrary object. They then let this second generation condition a third generation of inexperienced birds, and so on up to a sixth generation of blackbirds that learned to mob a plastic bottle by following other blackbirds.

Chemical Alarms

When they are injured, many social fish release a chemical that alarms other fish in the school. Experimenters can observe the alarm reactions of a school of fish confined to a laboratory fishtank by stimulating the live fish with the body fluids of a fish killed outside of the tank. The alarm reaction of zebra fish is fairly elaborate and includes swimming toward the source of the alarm chemical, infusion of the substance with tasting movements, followed by rapid darting movements as if trying to disperse and escape from the tank, followed by forming a compact group, dropping to the bottom of the tank, and swimming back and forth as close to the bottom as possible. In their natural habitat, that last maneuver would stir up mud and possibly hide the group from a predator.

Suboski, Bain, Carty, McQuoid, Seelen, and Seifert (1990) first demonstrated that a small school of zebra fish would carry out the full alarm reaction when their only stimulus was the sight of another school of zebra fish in an adjacent tank that was executing the alarm reaction after receiving a dose of the alarm chemical. The experimenters then conditioned a small school of zebra fish to react to an innocuous substance, called morpholine, by pairing morpholine with the alarm chemical. After conditioning, morpholine alone induced the complete alarm reaction.

The experimenters next placed a second group of zebra fish in the same tank as the conditioned group and stimulated both with morpholine alone. When first stimulated with morpholine, the second group continued to swim normally, but they soon followed the conditioned fish in going through the alarm response. In this way the experimenters conditioned the second group to make the alarm response to morpholine. When the second group was responding by themselves without the first group in the tank, Suboski et al. (1990) used these fish (which had never experienced morpholine paired with the alarm chemical) to condition a third group to make the alarm response to the innocuous morpholine.

In both birds and fish, fairly elaborate and sustained patterns of response can be conditioned by classical conditioning. This powerful technique is not restricted to simple responses, such as salivation and leg withdrawal.

Emotional Words

Human language is often described as the highest cognitive achievement of biological evolution. Psychotherapy entirely based on verbal treatment is called cognitive therapy. Human beings have ethological reactions to words. Reading sad stories and sad poetry in a book makes many people weep. Reading horror stories can evoke physiological responses of fear. These are powerful emotional responses to printed words on a page, to totally arbitrary stimuli.

Human beings respond emotionally to printed descriptions of sadness or horror without having any personal experience with the events described, and without personal experience with anything nearly as sad or as horrible. They can only learn these emotional responses to printed words from other human beings by a process very like those used in social learning experiments conducted with other animals.

SUMMARY

This chapter reviews a small, representative sample of the hundreds and hundreds of experiments that have used the procedures of classical conditioning. Throughout the 20th century, thorough replication has established the basic findings with a wide range of different species, different responses, and different stimuli. Chapter 3 is a similar review of instrumental conditioning. Chapter 4 outlines the implications of these findings.

Instrumental Conditioning

Plainly, classical conditioning is both a highly effective laboratory procedure and an essential means of learning for human and nonhuman animals in common situations outside of the laboratory. In the traditional view, classical conditioning may be sufficient for simple, obligatory, physiological responses like salivation, heart rate, and eyeblinks, but a larger class of learning requires a more advanced procedure. In this view, instrumental conditioning seems more appropriate for learning skills, particularly complex skills such as playing a violin, programming a computer, or conducting an experiment.

In *classical conditioning* the experimenter presents, or omits, the UCS according to a predetermined experimental procedure that is independent of anything that the learner does. In *instrumental conditioning* the experimenter presents the UCS if, and only if, the learner makes, or omits, some arbitrary response. From the point of view of the experimenter, the procedural difference is clear. Do these two procedures also represent two different principles of learning? This book takes a hard experimental look at that question.

B. F. Skinner was probably the strongest and most famous advocate of the position that there are two different principles of learning. To emphasize the distinction, Skinner introduced two new terms, *respondent conditioning* for the procedure that others called classical or Pavlovian conditioning, and *operant conditioning* for the procedure that others called instrumental conditioning. The only difference is that the words *respondent* and *operant* (particularly operant) are closely associated with Skinner's view of the learning process.

TYPICAL PROCEDURES

The terms for the principle types of instrumental conditioning refer to different kinds of contingency.

Reward

Thorndike (1898) published the first systematic, scientific accounts of instrumental conditioning. He trained cats to escape from specially designed boxes and rewarded them with food. The cats could see the food through the spaces between the vertical slats that made up the walls of the puzzle boxes. A door opened as soon as the cat pulled on a cord hanging from the top of the box or pressed on a latch. At first, hungry cats engaged in various natural but ineffective activities: reaching between the slats toward the food, scratching at the sides, moving all about the box. Eventually, each cat made the arbitrary response that operated the release mechanism. The door opened immediately, and the cat escaped and got the food. The first successful response appeared to be largely a matter of chance. On successive trials cats concentrated their activity near the release mechanism. Extraneous behavior gradually dropped out until they made the correct response as soon as they found themselves in the box.

The two most common types of apparatus for studying instrumental conditioning are mazes and Skinner boxes. In mazes, a hungry or thirsty learner, usually a laboratory rat and almost always a nonhuman being, typically finds food or water in a goal box at the end of the maze. In Skinner boxes, a hungry or thirsty learner, usually a laboratory rat or pigeon, operates an arbitrary device, typically for food or water reward.

Escape

In escape, the instrumental response turns off a painful or noxious stimulus. In a typical experiment, the floor of the conditioning chamber is an electric grid and a low barrier divides the chamber into two compartments. At intervals the experimenter turns on the current, which delivers painful shocks to the rat's feet. If the rat jumps over the barrier, the experimenter turns off the shock. In this way, the rat *escapes* the shock by making a correct response.

Avoidance

In avoidance, the learner can prevent or postpone a painful or noxious stimulus. In a typical experiment, a human subject places one hand on an electrode that delivers a mildly painful electric shock when the experimenter turns on the current. Three seconds before turning on the shock, the experimenter sounds a tone. If the learner raises his or her index finger within the 3-second warning period, the experimenter omits the shock on that trial. Thus, the subject *avoids* the shock by responding within the warning period.

A standard experiment compares escape and avoidance by testing rats one at a time in a chamber with a grid floor and a signal light mounted in the ceiling. For the escape group, the light comes on followed in 10 seconds by painful shock from the grid floor on every trial. As soon as the rat starts running, the shock stops. Thus, the rat can escape shock by running, but only after the shock begins. For the avoidance group, the light also comes on followed in 10 seconds by painful shock from the grid floor. The avoidance rat, however, can avoid the shock entirely by running before the end of the 10-second warning period.

Punishment

In this procedure, learners receive a painful or noxious stimulus if they make a specified response. Traditionally, *punishment* is the opposite of *reward*. In reward, the learner receives something positive that strengthens a certain response. In punishment, the learner receives something negative that weakens a certain response.

BASIC TERMS

Most of the terms of classical conditioning have parallel meanings in instrumental conditioning. A few terms of classical conditioning are inappropriate for instrumental conditioning and vice versa. The following definitions are mostly parallel to the definitions of the same terms introduced in chapter 2.

Unconditioned Stimulus

Of the four terms used to describe classical conditioning—UCS, CS, UCR, and CR—only UCS (referring to food, water, shock, etc., used in reward training and punishment training) appears in any significant number of descriptions of instrumental conditioning. CR appears occasionally. CS and UCR appear very rarely, if at all.

Response Measures

Experimenters record both the *frequency* of correct and incorrect choices in a maze and the amount of time required to run from the start box to the end of the maze. *Running speed* is a measure of *latency* in one sense, but it is also a measure of *amplitude* in another sense because the harder the animal runs the quicker it gets to the end of the maze. The frequency of correct responses is often expressed as the percentage or *probability* of a correct response.

In a Skinner box, experimenters measure the *frequency* (number of lever-presses in an experimental period), or the *rate* (average number of lever-presses per minute). Lever-presses must activate some device, usually an electric switch, attached to the lever. The animal must press the lever with sufficient force to move it, and for a sufficient distance to activate the switch. If the switch is too sensitive, the apparatus will record minor movements of the animal that happen to jiggle the lever. If the switch requires too much force or travel, the animal may rarely hit the lever hard enough or long enough to activate the recorder. Both force and distance are measures of *amplitude* in a Skinner box.

Experimenters sometimes measure *latency* of lever-pressing by retracting the lever from the box as soon as the animal presses it, then reinserting the lever and measuring the interval between reinsertion and the next response. In a maze-running apparatus, the experimenter usually places the animal in a starting box of some kind and starts the trial by opening the door that allows the animal to enter the maze. Experimenters often measure latency as the interval between the time the door opens and the time the animal leaves the start box.

Response Variability

Variability is a basic dimension of all responses. We have to expect live animals to vary their behavior from moment to moment even under the highly constant conditions of the experimental chamber.

Without some variability animals cannot learn anything new. The following example illustrates the insights that emerge from experiments that report variability.

The switch at the end of the lever in a Skinner box is usually spring-loaded, so that it returns to its resting position after the rat releases the lever. The experimenter can vary the amount of the spring loading, hence the amount of force that the rat must exert in order to operate the switch. A common loading requires the rat to exert about 10 grams of force. Less than 10 grams fails to operate the switch; more than 10 grams earns no additional reward.

Figure 3.1 shows the results of an experiment that raised the force required to operate the reward mechanism first to 21 grams and then to 38 grams and also reported the force exerted on each lever-press. The black bars in Fig. 3.1 show the frequency of different amounts of force under the requirement of at least 21 grams to earn a reward. Under that condition, the rat mostly pressed the lever with 21 grams of force or more, but sometimes it pressed the lever with less than 21 grams and failed to earn a reward. The actual distribution of forces ranged from 13 grams to 44 grams in this condition.

The gray bars in Fig. 3.1 show what happened when the experimenters next raised the requirement to 38 grams. The distribution of forces shifted upward. Now, the rat pressed the lever with more than 38 grams of force most of the time. More often than not the rat still pressed the lever harder than necessary even though this required much more effort than before. Note that the 38-gram requirement

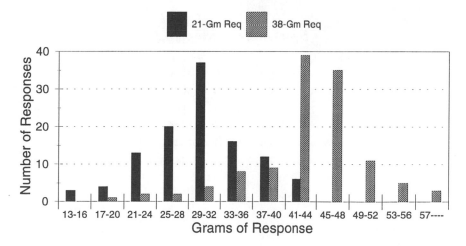

FIG. 3.1. Force exerted by a rat to press a lever in a Skinner box. Black bars show the distribution of frequencies for a 21-gram minimum force requirement. Gray bars show the distribution for a 38-gram minimum requirement. Copyright © 1997 by R. Allen Gardner.

could only affect the rat if 38 grams of force was already within the distribution of response forces under the 21-gram requirement. Response variability is necessary for all new learning.

Acquisition

Acquisition is a series of trials with the UCS.

Extinction

Extinction is a series of trials without the UCS.

Resistance to Extinction

Usually, the response weakens or ceases entirely during extinction. The rate of decline is called *resistance to extinction* and can be measured by one of the standard response measures, such as latency, amplitude, probability, or rate of responding. Some experiments measure resistance to extinction by response during a fixed number of extinction trials and others run extinction trials until the measure of responding drops below some criterion.

There are cases where resistance to extinction is the only measure that can test certain theoretical questions. Later chapters in this book take up these cases as they become relevant.

Spontaneous Recovery

Extinguished responses can recover substantially, sometimes completely, after a rest. Spontaneous recovery can be tested with or without the UCS. With the UCS, it is called *reacquisition*; without the UCS it is called *reextinction* (see Fig. 10.1). Spontaneous recovery is a robust phenomenon that appears in virtually all experiments. Obviously, the CR is neither forgotten nor eliminated by extinction. Chapter 10 discusses the theoretical significance of spontaneous recovery.

GENERALITY

Instrumental conditioning is a much more versatile procedure than classical conditioning and most experiments in instrumental conditioning are less expensive and more convenient to perform. Consequently, instrumental experiments have included a much wider range of subjects, responses, and stimuli.

For example, Gelber conditioned paramecia to approach an arbitrary object. First, she sterilized a platinum wire and then dipped it into a dish of freely swimming paramecia. Then, she counted the number of paramecia that adhered to the sterilized wire. Next, she swabbed the wire with a fluid containing bacteria (the usual food of these animals) and dipped the wire into the dish again. She removed the wire again, and now counted the number of paramecia adhering to the wire. This number increased steadily over a series of 40 trials. In a series of experiments Gelber (1952, 1956, 1957, 1958, 1965) obtained and thoroughly replicated this evidence for instrumental conditioning. D. D. Jensen (1957) and Katz and Deterline (1958) disputed this result, but their experiments omitted safeguards and controls that Gelber included in her experiments. For example, Gelber, unlike her critics, stirred the liquid in the dish to skatter the paramecia between trials and used independent observers who reported that the paramecia swam actively toward the wire.

French (1940) sucked paramecia one at a time up into a capillary tube 0.6 mm in diameter. Paramecia apparently prefer to swim horizontally, which makes a capillary tube into a sort of trap. The lower end of the tube opened into a dish filled with a culture medium. The only way that a paramecium could escape was by swimming down to the open end of the tube. Half of French's paramecia showed a significant improvement in performance in terms of time taken to swim down to the culture medium. Over a series of trials, French observed that his paramecia gradually improved by eliminating ineffective responses such as swimming upward until stopped by the surface and diving downward but stopping before reaching the mouth of the tube. Later, Huber, Rucker, and McDiarmid (1974) replicated French's experiment, extensively.

Much earlier, Fleure and Walton (1907) placed pieces of filter paper on the tentacles of sea anemones at 24-hour intervals. At first the tentacles grasped the filter paper and carried it to the mouth where it was swallowed and, later, rejected. After two to five trials, however, trained animals rejected the paper before carrying it to the mouth and the tentacles failed to grasp the paper at all in later trials.

MAZE LEARNING

Hampton Court Palace just outside of London was an important royal residence from the 16th to the 18th century and remains a fine place to visit. Its most famous attraction is an elaborate maze with tall hedges for walls. Visitors can still try to solve the maze for themselves. An attendant sitting in a wooden tower above the maze used to direct people if they asked for help, but hard times have reduced the palace labor force and this post is usually vacant now. In the early 1900s, experimenters tested rats in mazes that copied the plan of the Hampton Court maze shown in Fig. 3.2. Hungry rats started from the same peripheral point on every trial and found food in the goal box at the center.

Replicas of mazes that wealthy people used to build for human amusement introduce complications that modern experimenters attempt to avoid when searching for general laws of learning. The earliest improvements consisted of a series of uniform T- or Y-shapes with one arm of the T or Y opening into the stem of the next unit and the other arm serving as a cul-de-sac. Gradually, even these were reduced to a single T or Y with only one choice.

Figure 3.3 shows the evolution of maze plans through the first half of the 20th century. The earlier, more elaborate mazes appear at the bottom of Fig. 3.3, the simpler, more modern mazes at the top. The single T or Y became the most popular maze after World War II. In many laboratories, even these simple mazes gave way to the straight alley runway in which learners, usually rats, run from one end to the other of a single alley with no choice except to run or to dawdle.

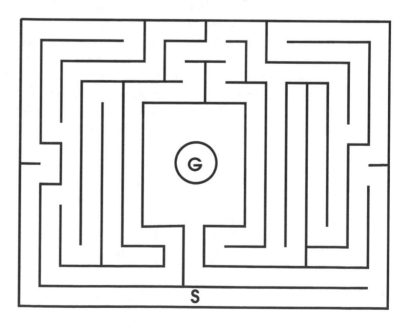

FIG. 3.2.   Plan of the Hampton Court maze used with laboratory rats. The experimenter places the rat at S. The rat can find food by reaching G. From Small (1900).

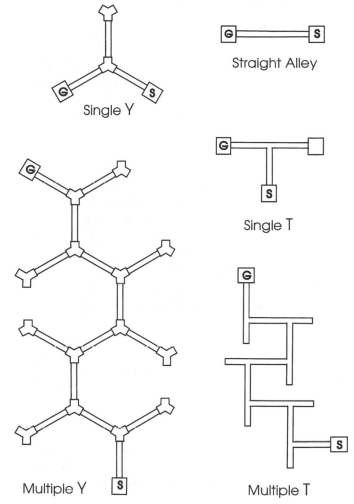

FIG. 3.3. Modern maze plans used with laboratory rats. Copyright © 1997 by R. Allen Gardner.

SKINNER BOX

In the *operant conditioning chamber* or *Skinner box,* the learners, usually rats or pigeons, are deprived to make them hungry or thirsty. The chamber for rats usually has a lever protruding from one wall. The chamber for pigeons usually has a key placed at about the level of a pigeon's beak. When a rat depresses its lever, or a pigeon pecks its key, the apparatus automatically delivers a small portion of a vital commodity, such as food or water. It may take some time before the first lever-press or key-peck, but after a few rewards the rate of responding rises rapidly.

The pattern of responding depends on the pattern of food or water delivery. If the chamber has more than one lever or key, each lever or key can deliver a different amount or rate of food or water. If the chamber has visual and auditory displays, each display can be correlated with a different amount or rate of food or water. With several levers or keys and several displays, experimenters can introduce virtually any level of complexity into the basic procedure.

The only limit on this procedure seems to be the ingenuity of the experimenters. One food-deprived rat learned to go through a doorway, climb a spiral staircase, push down a drawbridge, cross the bridge, climb a ladder, pedal a model railroad car over a track, climb a flight of stairs, play on a toy piano, run through a tunnel, step into an elevator, pull on a chain which lowered the elevator to the starting level, and finally press a lever and receive a small pellet of food (Bachrach & Karen, 1969). In another variant, pigeons learned to push a cube to a point below a suspended lure, climb on the cube, peck the lure, and then receive access to grain. The starting placement of the cube varied randomly from trial to trial and components of the sequence—pushing, climbing, pecking— were learned separately so that the pigeon had to put them together for the first time in test trials. The lure was a miniature yellow plastic banana, perhaps to suggest Köhler's (1925/1959) famous demonstrations of insightful problem-solving by chimpanzees (Epstein, Kirshnit, Lanza, & Rubin, 1984).

Schedules

Variations in the temporal pattern of food or water delivery are called *schedules of reinforcement*. When a Skinner box delivers rewards after every correct response, the schedule is called *continuous reinforcement*. When the apparatus only delivers rewards after some fraction of correct responses, the schedule is called *partial* (or *intermittent*) *reinforcement*.

In modern laboratories, the term schedules of reinforcement almost always refers to the delivery of reward in a Skinner box or some analogous experimental situation. The schedules studied by Skinner and his followers fall into two basic types depending on whether the schedules deliver reward on the basis of time or responses since the last reward. Time-based schedules are called *interval schedules;* response-based schedules are called *ratio schedules*. Regular schedules are called *fixed schedules;* irregular schedules are called *variable schedules*.

Fixed Interval

In a *fixed interval schedule*, rewards follow the first response, which occurs after some specified period of time since the last reward. In a 1-minute fixed-interval schedule, for example, at least 1 minute must elapse between each reward. After each reward a clock measures out

1 minute and at the end of that time sets the apparatus to deliver a reward for the next response. The next response also resets the clock to measure out the next interval. In experimental reports, the abbreviation for a 1-minute fixed interval schedule is "FI 60."

Variable Interval

In a *variable interval schedule,* the time between rewards varies, unpredictably. In a 1-minute variable interval schedule, an average of 1 minute must elapse between rewards. After each reward a clock measures out a particular time interval, say 20, 40, 60, 80, or 100 seconds. An unpredictable program selects one of the intervals before each reward with the restriction that the selected intervals have a mean of 60 seconds. At the end of each interval, the clock sets the apparatus to deliver a reward for the next response. The next response also resets the clock to measure out the next interval. In experimental reports, the abbreviation for a 1-minute variable interval schedule is "VI 60."

Fixed Ratio

A *fixed ratio schedule* delivers a reward immediately after the last of a fixed number of responses, such as 15. The abbreviation for a fixed ratio of 15 responses is "FR 15."

Variable Ratio

A *variable ratio schedule* delivers a reward immediately after the last of a variable number of responses. A "VR 15" schedule could be produced by delivering a reward immediately after the 5th, 10th, 15th, 20th, or 25th response, with the actual number varying unpredictably from reward to reward.

There are many more, mixed types, of schedule that experimenters introduce for special purposes.

Maintenance Versus Conditioning

Each of Skinner's schedules of reinforcement produces a characteristic pattern of responding in the Skinner box. Skinner and his followers have always pointed to the regularity and replicability of these patterns as evidence for the scientific lawfulness of operant conditioning. Closer inspection of these findings, however, leads to serious questions about the relevance of the patterns to laws of conditioning. The major effects look much more like momentary effects of receiving small units of food and water in patterns rather than long-term effects of conditioning. Because the characteristic effects of Skinner's schedules of reinforcement are so closely tied to the procedure of the operant conditioning chamber, they may be irrelevant to behavior outside of the chamber.

Under fixed interval and fixed ratio schedules, each reward signals the beginning of a period without rewards. During these times animals shift to other behavior, such as grooming and exploring the apparatus, and this appears as a pause in lever-pressing or key-pecking. When the passage of time signals the approach of the next reward, the animals shift back to lever-pressing and key-pecking and this appears as a resumption of responding. The animals pause longer when the interval between rewards is greater. Skinner described the records of responding under fixed interval and fixed ratio schedules as "scalloped." That is, they show a pause followed by slow responding followed by more and more rapid responding until the next reward, which is followed by the next pause.

In variable interval and variable ratio schedules, each reward also signals the beginning of a period in which reward is unlikely, but the length of the period of nonreward is less predictable. The pause after each reward is shorter and the overall rate of responding between rewards is steadier than in fixed schedules. Because responding is more uniform under variable interval schedules, they are often used for training as a preliminary to some other treatment, such as a test for stimulus generalization (Thomas, 1993) or the effects of drugs (Schaal, McDonald, Miller, & Reilly, 1996).

Actually, animals must always stop pressing the lever or pecking the key, briefly at least, to consume a reward so there is always some pause after each reward. After that, pauses and acceleration depend on the likelihood of the next reward.

Virtually all of the investigations of schedules of reinforcement have been conducted in a particular sort of experiment. In these experiments, the original conditioning consists of reward for each response. Then, the number of responses required for each reward is gradually increased to some intermediate number. After the animal reaches a reliable rate of responding for the intermediate schedule, the experimenters vary the schedule from day to day. Every time the experimenters change the schedule, they allow the animal some time to adapt and then, when the rate of responding seems to stabilize, they compare the rates induced by different schedules during these stable periods.

In most experiments each experimental subject goes through many shifts in schedule, cycling through the whole range of schedules many times. The results show that animals respond in characteristic patterns to each schedule regardless of the number of cycles or the number and type of other schedules in each cycle. That is to say, the effects of the schedules are localized and independent of each other. They look more like patterns maintained by the short-term effects of each reward than like the long-term effects of conditioning. They are at best only indirectly related to any basic laws of conditioning.

This book describes these four types of schedule for historic interest and also for reference so that readers can decode abbreviations such as "FR 10" and "VI 30" when they appear in professional descriptions of experimental procedure.

Time Schedules

Recently, experimenters have added two types of schedule that deliver rewards after a predetermined time, regardless of response. These are called *fixed time* and *variable time* schedules. In *interval* schedules, the first response after the end of a predetermined interval earns a reward. By contrast, in *time* schedules the apparatus delivers rewards precisely at the end of a predetermined interval whether or not the rat ever pressed the lever during the interval. Consequently, time schedules are noncontingent schedules. Strictly speaking, time schedules resemble classical conditioning more than instrumental conditioning. Yet, time schedules maintain robust rates of lever-pressing and key-pecking. If classical and instrumental conditioning are two distinct forms of learning suitable for two distinct forms of response, this finding is very puzzling. This book looks more closely at this puzzle and other puzzles like it in later chapters.

DISCRIMINATION

Animals must learn to discriminate between different stimuli as well as to generalize from one stimulus to another. They must be able to respond differentially, depending on the stimulus situation. Laboratory procedures for studying discrimination learning have used two basic procedures: *successive* and *simultaneous* presentation.

Successive Procedure

Successive discrimination is the most common discrimination procedure that experimenters use in the Skinner box. A single stimulus, usually a light or a sound, serves as S+ and a second stimulus serves as S–. The two stimuli appear one at a time in an unpredictable sequence and the apparatus delivers S* after responses to S+ and no rewards or less frequent rewards after responses to S–. The experimenter scores results in terms of the differential frequency or rate of response during the positive and negative stimulus periods. In the Skinner box for pigeons, visual stimuli are often projected directly on the key that the pigeons peck as in Hanson's experiments on the peak shift (chap. 13). Touch-sensitive video screens replace keys in many modern laboratories (Wright, Cook, Rivera, Sands, & Delius, 1988).

Simultaneous Procedure

In the simultaneous procedure, S+ and S– appear at the same time, usually side by side, and the subject chooses between them by responding to one side or the other. In a single-unit T- or U-maze, for example, one arm can be black and the other white. Experimenters prevent subjects from seeing into the goal boxes by placing curtains at the entrance to the goal boxes, or by making them turn a corner to enter the goal box (converting the T-shape to a U-shape as shown in Fig. 7.1). For half of the animals, white is S+ and black is S–, and for the other half black is S+ and white is S–. Reward is in the goal box at the end of the S+ arm and reward is absent from the goal box at the end of the S– arm. The experimenter alternates the left–right arrangement of S+ and S– in a counterbalanced and unpredictable sequence, and measures discrimination in terms of percentage choice of the S+ arm.

The diagram in Fig. 3.4 shows an automatic two-choice apparatus. Coate and R. A. Gardner (1965) designed this device to expose rats to visual stimuli projected on panels as the rats pushed the panels with their noses. Effective exposure is necessary, because rats are nocturnal animals with poor vision and they are much less interested in visual stimuli than the human beings who design the experiments.

In a Skinner box for pigeons there can be two keys—one green, the other red, for example—with the left–right arrangement of green and red alternated in a balanced but unpredictable sequence. An automatic device delivers rewards for pecking at the S+ key, but delivers no rewards or fewer rewards for pecking at the S– key.

Multiple Stimuli and Responses

Experimenters can present more than one S+ and more than one S–, or present more than one pair of stimuli to the same subject in the

6 INCHES

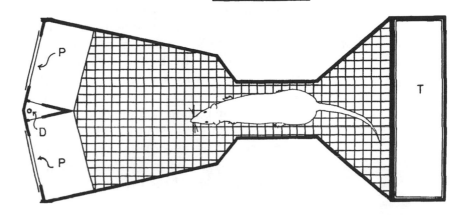

FIG. 3.4.   An automatic apparatus used by Coate and R. A. Gardner (1965) to study simultaneous discrimination. At the beginning of a trial the apparatus is dark. When the rat steps on the treadle (T) S+ and S– appear side by side projected on the plastic panels (P) by two projectors (not shown) just beyond the panels. When the rat pushes the panel lighted with S+, a dipper (D) delivers a drop of water and both projector lights turn off again. When the rat pushes the panel with S– the projectors turn off, but the dipper does not deliver any water. The rat can start the next trial by stepping on the treadle again. Copyright © 1997 by R. Allen Gardner.

same discrimination task depending on the experimental objectives (Coate & R. A. Gardner, 1964; R. A. Gardner & Coate, 1965).

REINFORCEMENT AND INHIBITION
VERSUS DIFFERENTIAL RESPONSE

In *reinforcement* theories, reward for responding to S+ builds up excitation for responding to S+ and nonreward builds up inhibition against responding to S–. As a result, the strength of the criterion response, R_c, to S+ is greater than the strength of R_c to S–. In a successive discrimination in the Skinner box, however, pigeons never just stand in front of the key, pecking it when S+ is lighted and waiting for S+ to reappear when S– is lighted. They engage in other behavior—preening, flapping their wings, walking about the box, and so forth—whether S+ or S– appears on the key. With discrimination training, they do more pecking when S+ is lighted and more other behaviors when S– is lighted. They seem to be learning one set of responses to S+ and a different set of responses to S–.

In a simultaneous discrimination, animals could be learning to approach S+ and avoid S−, or they could be learning two different habits. In an apparatus like the one in Fig. 3.4, the two stimuli appear side by side and there are only two possible spatial arrangements: S+ on the left and S− on the right, S+/S−, and S− on the left and S+ on the right, S−/S+. Instead of approaching S+ and avoiding S−, the animals could be learning to go left when they see the arrangement S+/S− and right when they see the arrangement S−/S+, as in a successive discrimination. Although this seems intuitively unlikely, several experiments indicate that rats and pigeons learn a simultaneous discrimination as two different spatial habits rather than as reinforcement of an approach to S+ and avoidance of S− (Pullen & Turney, 1977; Siegel, 1967; Wright & Sands, 1981).

SUMMARY

Instrumental conditioning is a versatile technique that has generated an enormous number and variety of learning tasks for laboratory studies. This chapter only introduces the most basic procedures and terms. Later chapters describe additional variations of this technique that experimenters have introduced for specific experimental problems. Later chapters also question the traditional claim that there are two principles of conditioning: one principle of conditioning by contiguity sufficient for classical conditioning, and a second principle of conditioning by contingency necessary for instrumental conditioning.

Mechanisms of Conditioning

THEORY AND EXPERIMENT

In the 1970s, the John Hancock insurance company erected the tallest building ever attempted in the city of Boston up to that time. They had to level a portion of historical Copley Square to make room for it, and this dramatically altered the historical neighborhood. Some grand old structures look puny and insignificant beside the new monster. Soon after it was completed, windows began to fall out of their frames in the upper stories. The sight of the modernistic marvel with random boarded patches where windows should have been, and with the sidewalk cordoned off below to protect pedestrians, must have given some satisfaction to the many enemies of the Hancock Tower. It certainly troubled the owners and builders and cost them a lot of money and prestige.

What went wrong with the Hancock Tower? Well, modern skyscrapers actually sway in the wind, and the upper stories sway considerably more than the middle stories. The structure must be able to withstand the force of the wind and materials must be flexible enough to stretch with the forces of distortion and then return to their original shape. In the Hancock Tower, the rigidity of the glass windows was improperly matched with the flexibility of their metal frames, so many of the windows just popped out when the wind blew.

Grand disasters like the John Hancock Tower seldom happen in modern times because scientists have mastered most of the physical principles of structural engineering and also because they usually test new design features as they are invented and before a new structure goes up. This is a basic principle of modern technology: First, the theory, next the laboratory tests, and only then the practical structure. But, the practical test is the object of all of the theory and laboratory testing that went before.

In ancient times, trial and error in architecture was costly and builders had to be conservative. It was too dangerous to try anything very far beyond the last successful design. The great cathedrals of Europe were marvels of engineering in their day and they were based on principles of physics that scientists and engineers had discovered. But, the buildings themselves were the laboratories and testing grounds for new principles.

The basic principles of conditioning and learning could yield immensely more profit than the grandest dreams of the most ambitious architects. Driving, reading, writing, athletics, computer repair and programming, problem solving in every field, require skills that must be learned. Scientists study elementary forms of conditioning and learning to discover the laws of all skilled behavior. The strategy of analyzing the complex phenomena of the practical world into relatively simple components in order to discover the most basic and most powerful laws of physics, chemistry, and biology, has paid handsomely in every field of modern life. This is the objective of the theories and experiments covered in this book.

This is why so many experiments concentrate on relatively simple animals and relatively simple learning tasks. The strategy is to discover the most basic principles and build step by step to the most complex forms of learning. This is a bottom-up strategy. The eventual objective is a practical outcome in the real world. Theories are about the real world and a theory fails in a fundamental way if it only works on paper or in a computer.

STIMULI AND RESPONSES

It should be clear, even from the brief reviews of experiments in chapters 1 through 3, that many quite different things are called stimuli and responses. Stimuli can be lights, sounds, pictures, songs, odors, tastes, an entire situation, electric shock, even time itself. Responses can be lever-presses, problem-solving, muscle twitches, glandular secretions, dilation of blood vessels, electrical impulses in a neuron, eyeblinks, even withholding response for a period of time.

Most experimenters write as if any reasonable reader must agree that they are correct in calling this or that in their experiment a stimulus and this or that other a response. By and large, reasonable readers do agree with the experimenters. The trouble comes when readers disagree in their interpretations. This section of the book defines stimuli and responses in terms of a general system that receives inputs from its environment and responds with outputs into its environment.

In modern times, computers as well as animals respond to stimuli and they also solve problems and modify their own behavior on the basis of past experience. Computers can do many things that once seemed to be exclusive abilities of living animals and even some things that seemed to be exclusively human abilities until quite recently. The complex behavior of humans and other animals challenges computer scientists the way flying birds once challenged engineers.

In the case of bird flight, biologists only discovered how birds fly after engineers discovered how to build machines that fly. To build flying machines, engineers had to master the same laws of physics that govern the flight of birds. In modern times, many scientists hope to discover how humans and other animals learn and think by study-ing computer science. Whether or not this is a sound strategy, the practical, bottom-up problem-solving approach of the engineer can be useful for defining biological problems.

Some version of the diagram in Fig. 4.1 appears in many textbooks on computer science. It is a good place to start talking about stimuli and responses. Let's call it the *E-S-Q-R paradigm*. The free-form

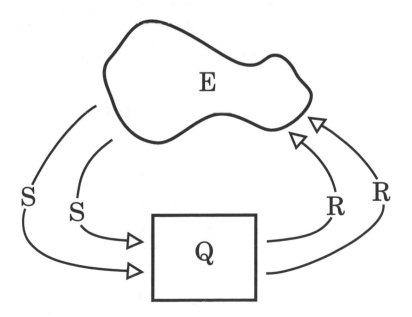

FIG. 4.1.   The E-S-Q-R paradigm. Copyright © 1997 by R. Allen Gardner.

figure represents the environment, E, and the box represents the system (a machine or an animal).

S stands for an *input* into the system. All inputs are stimuli and all stimuli are inputs. They come from the environment.

R stands for an *output* from the system. All outputs are responses and all responses are outputs. Outputs into the environment often change the environment, which may change the inputs from the environment, which may then change the outputs.

Q stands for the *state* of the system. In a digital computer, the state Q is the pattern of on–off switches at any given moment. Presumably, the state Q of a living animal is an analogous pattern of on–off elements in neural circuitry. The response to a given stimulus or input depends on the state Q of the system. At any given time, Q depends on the way the system was originally constructed and programmed and also on the past history of the system, which is written with many tiny on–off switches.

FOUR BASIC MECHANISMS

In roughly one century of theorizing about the basic mechanism of all learning, only four candidates have emerged. Considering the intelligence and knowledge of the theorists and the amount of thought and experimentation devoted to this question, the four mechanisms shown in Fig. 4.2 probably exhaust the possiblilities.

S-S represents conditioning by *contiguity* between two stimuli. By S-S contiguity, the dog associates an arbitrary stimulus S^a (such as a

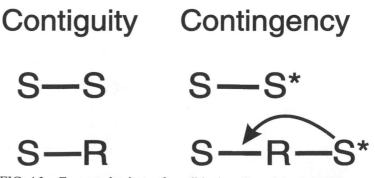

FIG. 4.2.   Four mechanisms of conditioning. Copyright © 1997 by R. Allen Gardner.

light or a tone) with another stimulus S^b (which could be food) because they have appeared together.

S-R represents conditioning by *contiguity* between a stimulus and a response. A dog makes the obligatory response of salivating to the food soon after hearing the tone S^a. This contiguity between tone and salivation associates salivation to the tone.

S-S* represents conditioning by *contingency* between a biologically significant stimulus, S* (such as food or painful shock), and the prior appearance of an S^a (such as a light or a tone). According to this mechanism the animal learns that S^a predicts S*. The symbol S* can refer to an appetitive S* such as food or an aversive S* such as painful shock. The difference between S-S* and S-S is that any two stimuli can be associated by S-S contiguity, but S-S* conditioning requires a biologically significant S* that the S^a predicts.

S-R-S* represents conditioning by *contingency* in which an S* is contingent on the performance of a particular response to an S^a. As shown in the diagram, the S* acts backward (arrow) to strengthen or weaken the S-R association. In the case of an appetitive S* like food, the effect is to strengthen the bond between the S^a and the response. In the case of an aversive S* like shock, the effect is to weaken the bond between the S^a and the response. In this mechanism, the S* is a *consequence* of the response to S^a; hence it is also called *learning by consequences*. Traditional theorists reserve this mechanism for instrumental conditioning.

Common Sense

Most students and former students have already thought about many of the questions in this book. After all, learning is the main business of a student. Informally, most students have already considered the four mechanisms on this list. Students memorizing the vocabulary of a foreign language usually spend some time with a paired list of English and, say, French words, reading them in pairs one pair at a time as if forming S-S associations. People have argued that S-S association will not work. You have to say the words as you read them, preferably out loud if you really want to learn to speak the foreign language. That would be an S-R mechanism. On the other hand, cognitive psychologists who stress the mental representation of stimuli in the brain tend to stress S-S association. There are cognitive sports psychologists who claim that even athletes like tennis players can improve just by playing moves "in their heads" (e.g., Savoy, 1993).

Mechanisms that include a special biologically significant stimulus (S*) start with the notion that learning tends to be biologically adaptive. According to S-S* contingency, an arbitrary stimulus, S^a, becomes associated with a biologically significant stimulus, S*, such as food or painful shock. In this cognitive view, the learner learns that the S^a predicts the S*. The S-R-S* version of this is that the learner learns that S* is contingent on a particular response, R^a, to the S^a. If the S* is appetitive, like food or water, contingency strengthens the association between S^a and R^a, thus increasing the probability that R^a is the response to S^a. If the S* is aversive, like painful shock, the contingency weakens the association, decreasing the probability that R^a is the response to S^a. In S* theories learning is always motivated, and this agrees with common sense.

Parsimony

Since each of the four proposed mechanisms of learning seems to have some merit in some situations, a reasonable student might ask why we cannot use all four principles and apply each to the learning situations that seem to fit best. The trouble with this strategy is that it is *unparsimonious*. Why limit the number of conditioning mechanisms to four? Why not add three, four, five, or any number of additional mechanisms as the need arises? Why not have mixed cases in which more than one mechanism applies at the same time? Common sense looks at each case of learning—memorizing French nouns, studying college economics, skating on ice, absorbing social values—one at a time and this allows the common sense interpreter to find a new mechanism or combination of mechanisms for each case. There are no limits to the number of mechanisms that can agree with common sense. There can be as many different mechanisms as there are different types of learning. Common sense is unparsimonious.

Many large organizations are governed in this way. Anyone who has ever dealt with tax laws, or welfare laws, or the U.S. Army has had firsthand experience with unparsimonious rules. Large organizations set down rules. As exceptions and unexpected cases arise, they add rules. To satisfy politicians, clients, and interest groups, they add still more rules. Eventually, there are so many rules that the rules start to contradict each other. The mass of rules becomes so entangled that it is extremely difficult, if not impossible, to tell which rule or which mixed set of rules applies in any given situation. Decisions have to be made on a case-by-case basis by bureaucrats. Soon, rather than government by laws we have government by bureaucracy, often with hideous consequences for citizens and clients.

Scientists apply the *principle of parsimony* to avoid this bureaucratic result of common sense. The objective is the smallest set of principles that cover the largest set of findings. Much of the difference between scientific discovery and bureaucracy depends on this strategy.

IMPLICATIONS

There are too many mechanisms in Fig. 4.2. The scientist who obeys the rule of parsimony must eliminate some of them, hopefully all except one. In this the scientist is like the detective who cannot solve the crime because there are too many likely suspects. Hunches, intuition, and common sense are helpful as a start, but, they tend to produce too many likely suspects in scientific work as in detective work. Fortunately, neither the scientist nor the detective needs to depend on hunches, intuition, and common sense. Both can find out more facts about the suspects and the crime.

In the classic detective story, for example, the wife of the murder victim may be a prime suspect. She was abused by her husband for years and she stands to inherit a great deal of money. The detective finds that the wife is frail, confined to a wheelchair, and left-handed. If the victim was bludgeoned to death by a tall, right-handed assailant, this eliminates the wife as a suspect.

In the same way, each of the proposed mechanisms in Fig. 4.2 has necessary implications that can be checked against the evidence of basic experiments in classical conditioning. By comparing these implications against the evidence, scientists can narrow the list of possibilities.

S-S CONTIGUITY

This principle is familiar to most readers because it is based on traditional philosophical and psychological notions about the association of ideas in the mind. Even though S-S association is firmly grounded in folk wisdom and cognitive psychology, the history of science teaches us that an idea can be repeated by wise folk for hundreds, even thousands, of years and still be quite false.

Introspective reports of human beings contain vivid descriptions of memory by the association of ideas or images in the mind. Is this evidence? Remember the blind and blindfolded students in Dallenbach's experiments. They reported vivid images of obstacles in their path, experienced as impressions on the skin of their faces. Yet, sound experiments described in chapter 1 revealed that personal impressions are as unreliable as any other kind of armchair philosophizing. The problem of this section of this chapter is to compare the implications of S-S association by contiguity with experimental evidence.

Pavlov argued for S-S contiguity. According to Pavlov, conditioning consists of a connection between the neural representations of two stimuli in the brain. In this view, a dog salivates to a tone as if it is the food, after associating the sound of the tone with sight of the food. Through conditioning, the tone becomes a substitute for the sight of the food. The principle of *stimulus substitution* was a fundamental part of Pavlov's theory and it is widely popular as this chapter is being written, in spite of the well-known, long-standing, contrary evidence reviewed here.

The mechanism of S-S contiguity has clear implications. How do these compare with the evidence accumulated in a century of research on classical conditioning?

Fractional Anticipatory Response

If the CS becomes a substitute for the UCS, then the dog should respond to the tone in the same way that it reponded to the food. As chapter 2 showed, however, a dog in Pavlov's procedure responds to the food in one way and to the light in a very different way. At best the CR is a fraction of the UCR to the food. This fact only appears when experimenters like Zener (1937) report learning in ethologically rich detail.

If it existed, stimulus substitution would be maladaptive under most natural conditions. It is adaptive to associate smoke with fire, but it would be maladaptive to respond to smoke as if it were the same as fire. It is adaptive to associate the word *apple* with apples, but it would be maladaptive to try to eat the word, or peel it and slice it.

Length of the Interstimulus Interval

If conditioning connects the CS and the UCS by contiguity alone, then closer contiguity should make easier and stronger connnections. Thus, a second implication of S-S contiguity is that the closer the contiguity in space and time the better the conditioning; the shortest possible separation should be the best. The shortest possible ISI is zero and this is called simultaneous conditioning. Chapter 2 describes the results of experiments that looked for the most favorable ISI. Although shorter intervals are generally more favorable than longer intervals, the most favorable ISI is much greater than zero. Indeed, the most favorable interval is long compared to the speed of neural conduction, at least three to four times longer than simple reaction time, and often longer than that. The offset is so much longer than necessary that it implicates some additional process beyond S-S contiguity.

Direction of the Interstimulus Interval

Sometimes in nature the effect of a variable is continuous over a wide range, but discontinuous at certain special points called *cusps*. A possible defense of S-S contiguity is that a simultaneous ISI is a special point. In this view, the sight of food overshadows the tone when both appear simultaneously. The sight of food is so exciting that the dog fails to notice the tone.

This version of S-S contiguity also implies that shorter ISIs should be more favorable than longer ISIs, even though the shortest possible intervals are unfavorable because of overshadowing. This allows for an offset between the CS and UCS, but still implies that the shorter the interval the greater the conditioning. Even allowing for overshadowing at the cusp of zero, S-S contiguity still implies that the ISI curve should be symmetrical: Short negative intervals (UCS before CS) should be as favorable as equally short positive intervals (CS before UCS). As the evidence reviewed in chapter 2 shows, however, the ISI curve is definitely asymmetrical. The ISI curves in Fig. 2.3 are typical. Instead of a cusp at zero, the curve is continuous with a maximum at about a half-second. Short positive intervals are plainly more favorable than short negative intervals.

Many experiments on length and direction of favorable intervals contradict the temporal implications of the S-S mechanism. These contradictions should eliminate S-S contiguity from the list of suspects in Fig. 4.2.

S-S* CONTINGENCY

Pavlov's basic theory can be preserved by claiming that a UCS such as food, shock, air puff to the eye, and so on, is a special biologically significant stimulus, an S*, while the CS is an arbitrary stimulus, an S^a. In this view, the arbitrary tone predicts the biologically significant food. By learning the contingency between S^a and S*, the dog can respond appropriately to the food before the food arrives. This S-S* contingency is also compatible with the finding that the CR is usually only a fractional part of the UCR. An animal can only profit from such a contingency, of course, if the S^a predicts food, shock, or air puffs. Thus, S-S* contingency is compatible with an offset between S^a and S* and the asymmetry of the ISI curve.

In this version of the traditional doctrine of the association of ideas, some ideas are more important than others. These privileged ideas are the UCSs of classical conditioning, while the lesser ideas are the arbitrary CSs. Conditioning takes place when a lesser stimulus predicts a privileged (biologically significant) stimulus, such as food or shock. There is a clear implication of this mechanism. If S-S* contingency is the mechanism of classical conditioning, then conditioning should be impossible without an S*. Before considering the evidence on this point, let us first consider the other mechanism of Fig. 4.2 that requires an S*.

S-R-S* CONTINGENCY

The ISI curve shows that S^a and S* need to be offset and that forward conditioning is much better than backward conditioning. Those facts agree with the principle of S* contingency. Even so, why should the most favorable ISI be so long, at least three to four times the length of simple reaction time? If the association of ideas takes place entirely within the brain, then it should be very rapid. Perhaps, the ISI must be long enough to permit the learner to make an anticipatory response before the S* arrives.

In classical conditioning, the experimenter presents the UCS after the CS regardless of anything that the subject does between CS and UCS. Nevertheless, the CR can alter the UCS when it arrives and this alteration can be a significant consequence: If the dog's mouth is wet with saliva when food arrives, the food will be easier to eat; if the college student's eye is blinking when the air puff arrives, the air puff will feel less irritating; defensive responses such as leg withdrawal and heart rate acceleration may reduce the pain of shocks; and so on, through any list of common UCSs. It is easy to think of a reasonable source of reward for anticipatory responses in just about any type of classical conditioning experiment.

If classical conditioning depends on the consequences of response during the interval between S^a and S*, that might very well require an appreciably long ISI. The process would require enough time for the animal to respond and then to receive and process information about the consequence of the response. This interpretation of the ISI curve would imply that, in spite of traditional views, both classical and instrumental conditioning are based on S-R-S* contingency.

A procedure called *omission contingency* tests this implication of S-R-S* contingency. The traditional distinction between classical and instrumental conditioning depends on the difference between obligatory association by contiguity and arbitrary association by consequences. In classical conditioning, salivation, leg withdrawal, eyeblink, and so on, are supposed to be obligatory responses to the S*, or anticipatory fractions of obligatory responses. In contrast, the responses in instrumental conditioning, pressing levers, running mazes, playing tennis, driving cars, and so on, are supposed to be arbitrary responses that become conditioned by the arbitrary rewarding effect of an S*.

If, in classical conditioning, food rewards salivation then it should be possible to condition both increases and decreases in salivation by arbitrarily altering the consequences. Under the standard procedure, S^a, say a tone, appears and then food appears whatever the dog does. Under the omission contingency, food follows tone, if and only if the dog fails to salivate. If the dog salivates before the food, the food is omitted. An omission contingency rewards the dog with food for withholding salivation immediately after the CS.

At first, under omission contingency, a dog salivates when the food appears and then salivates after the tone but before the food, as in ordinary conditioning. Under an omission contingency, however, the experimenter omits the food on those trials in which the dog salivates before the food. When food is omitted, the dog is on extinction and salivation decreases. When salivation after the CS decreases through extinction, lack of salivation satisfies the omission requirement and the experimenter delivers food again. After trials with food, salivation again increases, food is again withheld, and salivation again decreases. This can go on indefinitely.

Dogs seem to be unable to learn to withhold salivation in order to obtain food under conditions in which a strictly noncontingent procedure yields robust increases in salivation (Konorski, 1948; Sheffield, 1965). This result indicates strongly that the responses that increase in classical conditioning are obligatory rather than arbitrary. If salivation were an arbitrary response for a hungry dog, then experimenters could use food as an arbitrary reward to condition dogs either to salivate or to refrain from salivating (for replication, see Gormezano, 1965, on aversive conditioning of rabbits; Gormezano & Hiller, 1972, on appetitive conditioning of rabbits; and Patten & Rudy, 1967, on appetitive conditioning of rats).

ROLE OF S*

Hedonism, the pleasure principle, is deeply embedded in Western culture. Learning to seek pleasure and avoid pain appears in the Old Testament and the New Testament, in the writings of Freud and the writings of Skinner, in the profit motive and the criminal code. Can such a strong cultural tradition fail to agree with experimental evidence?

Higher-Order Conditioning

An obvious problem with the pleasure principle is that adult human beings and many other animals learn all sorts of things without eating, drinking, or escaping from pain. Obviously, arbitrary stimuli such as money and scores on exams are removed from any immediate satisfaction of biological needs by several steps at least. How can these arbitrary stimuli evoke pleasure and pain? In S-S* and S-R-S* theories of learning, Pavlov's principle of *higher-order conditioning* is supposed to bridge the gap between biological need and the arbitrary stimuli in daily life.

Experimenters have conditioned dogs to salivate at the arbitrary sound of a tone or the arbitrary lighting of a light by pairing the arbitrary stimulus with food. After conditioning a dog to salivate to a light, experimenters can try to condition the dog to salivate to a tone by pairing the light with a tone, that is, without pairing the tone with food. Pairing the CS of one phase of an experiment with a new CS in a second phase of the experiment is called *second-order conditioning*. Conditioning by pairing the CS of the second phase with still a third CS in a third phase, and so on, is called *higher-order* conditioning.

In higher-order conditioning, the first-order CS becomes a second-order UCS by pairing with the first-order UCS as shown in Table 4.1. By a series of intermediate CS-UCS steps, a still higher order CS becomes a UCS even though the original biologically significant UCS never appears after the first phase of conditioning. The whole system of CS-UCS pairs, each one built on the one before, depends on the initial pairing of the first arbitrary CS with a biological UCS. Higher order conditioning is vital to S* contingency. Without higher order conditioning, contingency could apply only to behavior that is directly and immediately associated with an S* such as food, water, or escape from pain.

TABLE 4.1
Second-Order Conditioning

Group	Phase I	Phase II	Phase III
1	L---S*	T---L	T Only
2	L---S*	L—T	T Only
3	L---S*	T/L	T Only

Table 4.1 shows the standard paradigm for second-order conditioning. Tone (T) is S^a and light (L) is S^b. In Phase I (Monday) all three groups are treated the same; a shock (S^*) follows the light. In Phase II (Tuesday) the groups are treated differently. For Group 1, the light follows the tone. For Group 2, the tone follows the light. For Group 3, both light and tone appear as often as for Groups 1 and 2, but they are unpaired. In Phase III (Wednesday) there is a test in which T appears alone for all three groups. Finally, there is a second parallel set of experimental groups (not shown in Table 4.1) in which the roles of T and L are reversed to show that S^a and S^b are arbitrary stimuli.

Groups 2 and 3 are *control groups* that receive the same amount of exposure to tone and light in Phase II as Group 1. For Group 2 the light precedes the tone and for Group 3 the sequence is random. These are both unfavorable temporal relations for conditioning an anticipatory response, as shown in Fig. 2.3 and in the section on backward conditioning later in this chapter. Groups 2 and 3 test for the effects of *habituation* and *sensitization* discussed in chapter 2. If the response of Group 1 in the test phase is greater than the response of Groups 2 and 3, then the experiment demonstrates second-order conditioning. The subjects in Group 2 should respond less than the subjects in Group 3 because Group 2 is a backward conditioning group.

Pavlov and others (Brogden, 1939a, 1939c; Murphy & Miller, 1957; Razran, 1955) tried using a CS from one experiment as the UCS in a second experiment with the same animal, but with limited success. In one of Pavlov's demonstrations the original CS was a metronome. When salivation to this CS was firmly established, a black square was presented briefly just before the metronome. On the 10th pairing of the black square and the metronome, there was a salivary response to the black square that was about half as strong as the response to the metronome. This is an example of second-order conditioning. Pavlov found third-order conditioning possible, but only with defensive reflexes such as responses to shock. He failed to establish any evidence for fourth-order conditioning in his laboratory (Pavlov, 1927/1960, pp. 34–35).

Evidence for second-order conditioning is acceptable, but unimpressive. Evidence for higher-order conditioning is weak at best. In Pavlov's experiments and others since, the higher order CRs had typically low amplitudes and long latencies, and soon faded out entirely. The evidence reviewed in chapter 2 shows that first-order classical conditioning is a versatile and powerful phenomoneon of learning. The weakness of evidence for higher-order conditioning contradicts Pavlov's principle of S* contingency as the mechanism of classical conditioning.

Preconditioning

By Pavlov's principle of higher-order conditioning, arbitrary stimuli such as praise and money acquire their motivating S* properties by a chain of associations that begins with a biologically significant UCS. The UCS is the anchor that secures the chain of stimuli and responses to biological motivation. This implies that conditioning must be impossible without an S*. This implication can be tested directly by reversing the procedure of Table 4.1 and pairing the arbitrary tone and light in Phase I (Monday) before pairing light and shock in Phase II (Tuesday). The shock cannot start the chain of association if it appears after the pairing of light and tone. Any conditioning that occurs in Phase I of the experiment clearly indicates that S* and hence S* contingency is unnecessary for classical conditioning. This experimental paradigm, called *preconditioning*, appears in Table 4.2. Notice how it reverses Pavlov's prescribed paradigm illustrated in Table 4.1.

In Table 4.2, tone (T) is S^a and light (L) is S^b. In Phase I (Monday) the groups are treated differently. For Group 1, the light follows the tone. For Group 2, the tone follows the light. For Group 3, both light and tone appear as often as for Groups 1 and 2, but they are unpaired. In Phase II (Tuesday) all three groups are treated the same; a shock (S*) follows the light. In Phase III (Wednesday) there is a test in which T appears alone for all three groups. Finally, there is a second parallel set of experimental groups (not shown in Table 4.1) in which the roles of T and L are reversed to show that S^a and S^b are arbitrary stimuli.

As in higher-order conditioning (Table 4.1) Groups 2 and 3 are control groups that receive the same amount of exposure to tone and light in Phase I as Group 1. They test for the effects of *habituation* and *sensitization* discussed in chapter 2. If the response of Group 1 in the test phase is greater than the response of Groups 2 and 3, then the experiment demonstrates preconditioning. By analogy with the usual training phase of classical conditioning, Group 2 is a backward

TABLE 4.2
Preconditioning

Group	Phase I	Phase II	Phase III
1	T---L	L---S*	T Only
2	L---T	L---S*	T Only
3	T/L	L---S*	T Only

conditioning group and the subjects in Group 2 should respond less than the subjects in Group 3.

In spite of the fact that it directly contradicts Pavlov's theory, preconditioning is easy to demonstrate experimentally. Brogden (1939b) published the first clear demonstration of preconditioning using dogs as subjects, buzzer and tone as S^a and S^b, and shock as S^*. There were earlier demonstrations of the same phenomenon (Bogoslovski, 1937; Cason, 1936; Kelly, 1934; Prokofiev & Zeliony, 1926), but these could be questioned by skeptics because they lacked necessary control groups. After World War II, several experiments confirmed and extended Brogden's (1939a) findings (Bahrick, 1952; Bitterman, Reed, & Kubala, 1953; Brogden, 1947; Chernikoff & Brogden, 1949; Coppock, 1958; D. Hall & Suboski, 1995; Hoffeld, Thompson, & Brogden, 1958; Karn, 1947; Seidel, 1958; Silver & Meyer, 1954; Tait & Suboski, 1972). The preconditioning procedure is the reverse of the higher-order conditioning procedure prescribed by conventional learning theories, yet preconditioning is not only possible but it is easier to demonstrate than higher-order conditioning.

Preconditioning should be impossible if classical conditioning depends on S^* contingency. The light and tone are arbitrary stimuli. Neither one can be privileged over the other because either one can serve as the preconditioning stimulus in Phase I of Table 4.2 as long as one starts before the other. Control Group 2 shows that the one that comes first in Phase I acquires the power to evoke the UCR in Phase III. Prediction of S^* is impossible in Phase I because the S^* appears for the first time in Phase II. Therefore conditioning is possible without any S^*. The evidence of preconditioning eliminates both S-S* and S-R-S* contingency as necessary mechanisms for classical conditioning.

A Hybrid Paradigm

A latter day revival of Pavlov's teaching stimulated a series of experiments on second-order conditioning (Hittesdorf & Richards, 1982; Holland & Rescorla, 1975; Leyland, 1977; Nairne & Rescorla, 1981; Rashotte, Griffin, & Sisk, 1977; Rescorla, 1979; Rescorla & Cunningham, 1979; Rizley & Rescorla, 1972). These latter day Pavlovians attributed the weakness of second-order conditioning in the experimental paradigm of Table 4.1 to extinction of the first-order CS in Phase II. To overcome this extinction, they inserted what they called "refresher" trials of light paired with shock just before the test trials. The refresher trials appear as Phase C in Table 4.3.

The trouble with the refresher Phase C is that it violates the operational definition of second-order conditioning. In Table 4.3,

TABLE 4.3
Hybrid Paradigm: Second-Order Conditioning With Refresher Trials

Group	Phase A	Phase B	PhaseC	Phase D
1	L---S*	T---L	L---S*	T Only
2	L---S*	L---T	L---S*	T Only
3	L---S*	T/L	L---S*	T Only

Phases A, B, and D are the same as Phases I, II, and III of the standard paradigm for second-order conditioning that appears in Table 4.1. At the same time, Phases B, C, and D are precisely the same as the standard paradigm for preconditioning that appears in Table 4.2.

We know from many other experiments using the standard paradigm of Table 4.2 that Phases B, C, and D produce strong evidence of preconditioning without Phase A. Meanwhile, experiments using the standard paradigm of Table 4.1 show that Phases A, B, and D produce, at best, weak evidence of second-order conditioning. The need for refresher Phase C in the hybrid paradigm only confirms the failure of the standard paradigm of second-order conditioning. On the evidence then, Phase A is weak or ineffective without the refresher trials of Phase C. Phase A probably had little or no effect on the conditioning shown in Phase D. All or nearly all of the test results in Phase D should be attributed to Phase B followed by Phase C, but this is precisely the standard paradigm of preconditioning.

If, as Pavlov taught, classical conditioning must be anchored by the original pairing of CS with UCS, then second-order conditioning should be robust and preconditioning should be impossible. Rather than adding support for the power of second-order conditioning, the need for refresher trials confirms instead the usual finding that second-order conditioning is weak in comparison with preconditioning. The results of the hybrid paradigm add to the weight of evidence against S* contingency as the mechanism of classical conditioning.

There is a lesson in experimental design to be learned here. The interpretation of experimental results depends on experimental operations. It is probably impossible to design a perfect experiment that controls for all possible variables. It is possible, however, to design experiments that answer specific questions. When an experiment jumbles together the defining operations of two opposing principles, as in the case of the hybrid paradigm of Table 4.3, then the experiment fails to answer any specific question about either principle. Taken together with the results of the sound paradigms of Tables 4.1 and 4.2, however, these experimental findings support the conclusion that conditioning is both possible and robust without any S* contingency.

A Misnomer

In classical conditioning, the experimenter only manipulates the Ss and the S*s, their pairing and their timing. This led Pavlov and latter day Pavlovians who followed him to describe classical conditioning in terms of stimulus associations, either S-S or S-S*. In preconditioning, the UCR cannot appear until Phase II, which is the first time that the UCS appears. For this reason Pavlov's followers usually called the experimental paradigm in Table 4.2 *sensory preconditioning* or *sensory conditioning*. The sensory label, however, fails to recognize the critical role of the control groups in defining the phenomenon. If all that happened in Phase I was that the subjects associated a tone with a light somewhere in their brains, then backward conditioning would be as easy as forward conditioning and the most favorable ISI would be very short, almost zero. In actual experiments, however, the control groups show instead that the offset between the arbitrary stimuli in Phase I is critical as in all classical conditioning.

The preconditioning experiments that have appeared so far have used constant ISIs, mostly in the range between 0.5 seconds and 5 seconds, which is a favorable range for aversive conditioning. These are surprisingly long units in neuroelectric time. The implications of the need for long ISIs appears earlier in this chapter and also in chapter 2. If ISIs of this length are necessary, it must be because something has to happen between S^a and S^b that is critical for conditioning; mere exposure to the stimuli is insufficient. Since the experimenter does nothing during the ISI, the critical thing that happens must be something that the subject does. The amount of time is long enough for the subject to make a response; indeed, it is long enough for three to four consecutive rounds of responses and stimuli. It is highly unlikely that preconditioning is based on sensory association. The success of the preconditioning paradigm is evidence for conditioning by S-R contiguity.

S-R CONTIGUITY

Experimental evidence eliminates three of the four prime suspects in Fig. 4.1. This leaves S-R contiguity as the only surviving possibility. As in any good detective story, it is insufficient to eliminate the other suspects. There must also be positive lines of evidence that implicate the remaining alternative. The comparison between Group 1 and Group 2 in preconditioning implicates S-R contiguity. Additional positive lines of evidence depend on an ethological alternative to S* contingency.

Sign Stimuli

Traditional learning theories are based on *hedonism*, the principle that pleasure and pain govern behavior. In this view, the S* is essential for learning because it causes pleasure or pain and the S^a becomes significant because it predicts the pleasure or pain of the S*. By contrast in ethology, S* is a *sign stimulus* that plays its vital role in behavior whether or not it evokes pleasure or pain. The essential property of a sign stimulus is that it evokes a response or a pattern of responses called an *action pattern*. In ethology what matters is what the S* makes the animal do rather than how good or how bad the S* makes the animal feel. An ethological S* acts forward rather than backward.

The three-spined stickleback, for example, is a traditional subject of ethological studies in the field and in the laboratory. The stickleback is a small fish commonly found in English streams and ponds. During the breeding season, male sticklebacks establish individual breeding territories which they defend vigorously against all other male sticklebacks.

How do these simple, little fish know that the invader is another male stickleback? Tinbergen noted that during the breeding season, the underside of males turns a fiery red color. To see if this is the cue that sets off territorial defense, Tinbergen placed individual males in laboratory fish tanks, gave them some time to establish themselves as territorial owners of the tanks, and then placed various objects in the tanks with the fish. The fish promptly attacked any red object. They usually ignored the same objects when they were painted some other color, even when the objects were exact replicas of living male sticklebacks, except for the color (Collias, 1990). Tinbergen also noticed that male sticklebacks living in tanks in front of the windows of the laboratory would launch furious attacks against the window side of their tanks when the fiery red vans of the Royal Mail Service rode past the windows (Tinbergen, 1953b, pp. 65–66). During the breeding season, the redness of objects that invade a territory is a sign stimulus that evokes attack from resident male sticklebacks.

Action Patterns

Ethological *action patterns* are true patterns in the sense that individual elements can vary while the pattern of behavior remains constant. Variations in the pattern of head-bobbing threat in different species of anoline lizards, for example, were first noted by Darwin. Within a species the extent and timing of the bobbing movements can vary significantly even though the species-specific pattern remains constant (Barlow, 1977). Birds weave string into their species-specific nests and sticklebacks threaten the red vans of the Royal Mail Service but we easily recognize the species-specific pattern of their behavior. These patterns appear in spite of variations in their elements. It is the patterns rather than the individual movements or muscle twitches that are constant in ethological action patterns.

TEMPORAL PATTERNS

The clue that points most directly to S-R contiguity as the mechanism of classical conditioning is the contrast between Group 1 and Group 2 in preconditioning. Why must one stimulus come before the other in classical conditioning and why such a long interval between stimuli? Clearly, something vital happens during the ISI. Since the experimenter does nothing during the ISI, the vital event or events must depend on something that the subject does.

Feedback Systems

The common combination of a furnace and a thermostat is a simple example of a machine that receives inputs from the environment and responds in a way that alters the environment, which in turn alters the input. When the temperature indoors drops below a set point, a switch is thrown that starts the furnace. When the heat from the furnace raises the temperature above another set point, the switch is thrown off, which stops the furnace. This is an effective way to keep the temperature of a home within a comfortable range. It is called a *feedback system* because the furnace cycles back and forth between on and off phases on the basis of information about cold and hot phases of the environment. Each change in input from the environment switches the machine back to the opposite phase. This feedback system is satisfactory for most homes and offices.

Thermostatic control by feedback is far from ideal, however. In most home furnaces, the fire cannot heat the house directly. It must first heat a chamber called the fire box. A second thermostat turns on the fan when the fire box reaches a suitable temperature. Otherwise, the fan would blow cold air into the house at first. The second thermostat keeps the fan blowing over the hot fire box after the fire goes out and until the fire box cools below another set point. There are better and worse systems, but all systems involve appreciable time lags of this sort. The result, as most people who live with similar systems know, is that there are appreciable fluctuations in the temperature of the house. Sometimes it is hotter and sometimes colder than desirable.

Feed Forward Systems

It would be much better to place the thermostat outside of the house. Then, the signal would arrive at the furnace when the outside temperature fell below a set point, but before the inside temperature had the chance to fall in response to the outside temperature. The furnace action would then be ahead of the environment. Similarly, the outdoor thermostat could turn the furnace off when the outside temperature was rising, thus predicting a rise in indoor temperature and again allowing the furnace to get ahead of the environment. In a truly efficient system, the rate of rise and fall in the outdoor temperature would control the amount of furnace action. Such a system would be a *feed forward* system and it would keep the indoor temperature much more constant.

To deliver the amount of heat required to compensate for any predicted drop in temperature, a feed forward system would have to take into account the individual size and furnishings of each house, the number of residents and their activities at any time, and so on. Even though it would keep people more comfortable, a feed forward system is too expensive to be cost-effective for most families and offices, so far. There are industrial situations such as oil refineries, however, where a small deviation from the required temperature can create a very expensive mess. Relatively simple, feed forward systems are cost-effective in many complex and demanding industrial applications.

Machines that fit the E-S-Q-R paradigm are devices that synchronize themselves with the environment. A machine that responds to what has just happened can be useful, but a machine that responds to what is about to happen is much better. If the environment fluctuates in predictable cycles, machines can respond to what is about to happen. In modern times, machines can learn regularly repeating cycles and program themselves to anticipate the environment.

Living systems also respond to regularly repeating cycles in the environment. New England maple trees transplanted to California lose their leaves at about the same time as their conspecifics back in New England, as if in sympathy, even though winters are much milder in California. The trees are responding to changes in the proportion of daylight to darkness because that predicts temperature changes back in New England. Most species of animals come into breeding condition when changes in the day–night cycle predict favorable weather for breeding and raising their young. There are long seasonal cycles and shorter daily cycles. In the jet age, many human beings experience jet lag when suddenly transported to a point on the globe that is out of sync with the cycle of night and day back home.

There are also shorter cycles. Pavlov's dogs could anticipate food fairly accurately when it regularly arrived 10, 20, or even 30 minutes after the onset of a CS. Human beings often estimate intervals of 10, 20, or 30 minutes with reasonable accuracy without consulting external clocks. There must be internal cycles of physiological events that permit animals to "tell time." Indeed, a tone or a light evokes a whole series of responses in most animals including human beings. With dogs in the harness of a conditioning experiment, for example, the onset of a sound evokes heart rate and breathing rate changes. Slightly later, the head and ears orient toward the source of sound. Depending on what the dog sees or hears next, other responses follow, including a general damping of the physiological responses and return to a relaxed posture if no particular stimulus follows. Quite regular patterns of this sort appear in all of the animals studied and these could easily mark the time between the onset of the CS and the beginning of the UCR, or the time between any two arbitrary stimuli, S^a and S^b.

Anticipatory Responses

Anticipation seems to imply a cognitive, *top-down* principle whereby complex decisions in the brain result in commands to lower motor centers. On the contrary, however, relatively simple, *bottom-up*, feed forward systems can control temperature under the complex and demanding conditions of an oil refinery. Many common biological action patterns also depend on relatively simple, bottom-up, feed forward anticipation.

To jump, human beings and other animals must extend their leg muscles, but they cannot extend their leg muscles without first flexing them. Jumping is impossible without anticipatory leg flexion. To throw a ball or to hit it with a racket, athletes must swing an arm forward, but swinging forward is impossible or very weak without first swinging backward. These are only simple cases; almost any significant act consists of a series of movements that must be made in sequence. When serious athletes and musicians practice, they practice the rhythmic sequences of their performances; the more complex the sequences the more they must practice them.

Backward Conditioning

When the UCS comes before the CS, the ISI is negative and the procedure is called backward conditioning. If, as Pavlov and so many latter day Pavlovians have insisted, the CS must be a signal that predicts the UCS, then backward conditioning should be impossible.

Until quite recently, there was virtually unanimous agreement that backward conditioning is impossible.

In spite of the traditional view, a series of modern experiments have demonstrated robust backward conditioning (Ayres, Axelrod, Mercker, Muchnik, & Vigorito, 1985; Ayres et al., 1987; Keith-Lucas & Guttman, 1975; Spetch, Wilkie, & Pinel, 1981; Van Willigen et al., 1987). The result is easy to demonstrate experimentally. The secret is in the number of trials. Backward conditioning readily appears after only one presentation of CS and UCS and within the first few trials (Heth, 1976). With repeated trials, the almost universal procedure since Pavlov, backward conditioning disappears and a negative ISI usually reduces responding.

It makes little difference what the ISI is within the first few trials. All intervals seem to be equally favorable if the CS and the UCS are not too far apart. Pavlov and his students and practically everyone else in this field until recent times believed that the first few trials represented unreliable performance, which gradually stabilized to form the traditional curve relating ISI to strength of conditioning. The stable curve that they got after dozens, often hundreds, of trials was the true curve for them. If the CS is acting as a signal for the coming of the UCS, then conditioning should be stronger as the time between CS and UCS gets shorter up to some relatively brief interval, and then decline steeply to a level near zero when the CS comes after the UCS.

RHYTHMIC PATTERNS

Modern experiments on backward conditioning show that the typical ISI curve shown in Fig. 2.3 only appears after many trials. Why is repetition so important? It is misleading to think of the dog in Pavlov's experiment in abstract terms, either responding or not responding. As we have seen in Zener's rich descriptions, live dogs in an actual experiment do much more than salivate or stop salivating. They fidget and stretch and scratch themselves and even fall asleep in the harness between trials.

"Between trials" is the critical concept. From the dog's point of view the experimental period is punctuated by the UCS and the CS, probably mostly by the UCS. Each appearance of the UCS is also a signal that the UCS, be it food or shock, will not appear for a while. Even when the time between trials varies randomly, the UCS is still unlikely to be followed immediately by a second UCS. So, the dog is free to stretch and scratch and so on, for a little while at least. If that is what the dog is doing when a backward CS arrives, then that is the response that gets conditioned to the CS by S-R contiguity. If the only CR that the experimenter measures is salivation or leg withdrawal, then increases in another response appear on the record as decreases in the CR. The result looks as though a backward ISI depresses or even inhibits conditioning. When experimenters measure other responses, however, it becomes clear that the backward CS is evoking other conditioned responses (Janssen, Farley, & Hearst, 1995).

The traditional ISI curve requires many trials because the dogs must learn the rhythm of the experimental procedure. By definition, only repeating temporal patterns can form rhythms. That is why the traditional curve fails to appear after only one or a very few trials. Backward conditioning is only "backward" if the experiment only measures a single type of response and that is an anticipatory response such as salivation or leg withdrawal. When UCSs follow each other at intervals in a rhythmically repeating pattern, then each UCS ends just before the beginning of an interval without any UCS. Responses, such as fidgeting or relaxing, that appear during the interval after a UCS become conditioned to a CS that appears during that interval. This conditioning is as "forward" as the conditioning of anticipatory responses to a CS that appears just before the UCS.

Delay Conditioning

Longer delays between CS and UCS further illustrate the role of temporal patterns in conditioning. Pavlov discovered delay conditioning in the following way. After conditioning dogs to salivate with an interstimulus interval of about 2 seconds between a metronome CS and food UCS, he increased the ISI to 6 seconds. At first the dogs salivated within 2 seconds of the metronome as they had with the original ISI. With repeated trials, the dogs salivated later until they were salivating about 4 seconds after the CS, just before the time that the food arrived with the new ISI. Pavlov repeated this process, gradually increasing the interval, in some cases increasing it to 30 minutes. Each time Pavlov increased the interval, the dogs at first salivated just before the time that the food used to arrive and then adjusted to the new rhythm so that again they were salivating just before the new arrival time.

Delay conditioning shows that time can serve as a stimulus. Most animals can judge intervals of time, on the basis of regularly repeating physiological cycles. Outside the laboratory, dogs must synchronize their behavior to the critical events of daily life. In the conditioning laboratory, dogs synchronize themselves to the rhythm of the experimental procedure. When the CS is reliably related to the time of arrival of the UCS, then the CS helps the dog to synchronize his behavior. If the food regularly arrives a fraction of a second after the CS, then the dog salivates almost immediately after the arrival of the CS. If the food regularly arrives 10 minutes after the CS, then the dog salivates about 10 minutes after the CS and does something else while waiting. The dog is always responding to the food or to the absence of food.

The early experiments that failed to show backward conditioning only measured CRs that appeared within a short time after the CS, usually about half a second, seldom more than one second. This is because these experimenters always defined the CR as a response to the CS, rather than as a response to the food. Figure 2.2 is typical of most conditioning records in showing that the latency of the CR is significantly longer than the latency of the OR or the UCR. This is only slow if the CR is supposed to be a response to the CS. As an anticipatory response to the UCS, the CR is well timed. An anticipatory response to the UCS would be ill timed indeed if it appeared 10 or 20 minutes before the UCS.

S-R SEQUENCES

Conditioning is a mechanism that synchronizes the animal to its environment. If food regularly follows a stimulus like a light, then the animal can salivate at a favorable time. If the food follows very soon after the light, then the dog can start salivating right away. If the food follows 20 minutes after the light, then the animal can salivate about 20 minutes after the light and do other things in the interim. Viewed in this way, conditioning permits human and nonhuman animals to get in step with the regularly repeating events of their lives (see also Akins, Domjan, & Guitiérrez, 1994; Kehoe, P. S. Horne, & A. J. Horne, 1993; Kehoe, P. S. Horne, Macrae, & A. J. Horne, 1993). This section shows how conditioning by S-R contiguity can accomplish this.

Most, probably all, stimuli evoke a series of reactions that appear in a regular pattern. Each response alters the external or internal environment in some way. Increases in breathing or heart rate create stimuli. Looking toward the source of the light or turning the ears in that direction also create new stimuli, and so on. The stimulus created by each response is the stimulus that evokes the next response in the chain. Different initiating stimuli (lights, tones, shocks) initiate distinctively different S—R chains, which could serve as timing devices in temporal conditioning. Animals could use this feed forward mechanism to anticipate future events.

Simultaneous conditioning, when CS and UCS start at the same time, is very difficult if not impossible. The most favorable ISIs are a half a second or more. Simple reaction times are between one eighth and one sixth of a second. An ISI of half a second allows enough time for three or more units, of the form: S_0—R_0—S_1—R_1—S_2—R_2—S_3—R_3.

Figure 4.3 illustrates a chain of S—R units that might be evoked by a light. The illustrations in the remainder of this chapter show only three links in a chain. That is an arbitrary number chosen for convenience of illustration. There is time for at least three such links in the ISI (as explained in chap. 2). Very likely there are more than three links in most cases of conditioning.

Figure 4.4 shows the same type of chain initiated by a light in Fig. 4.3 with a similar chain initiated slightly later by a shock. The links in the shock chain could be a startle posture followed by a sharp rise in breathing and heart rate, followed by agitation, followed by relaxation, and so on. In Fig. 4.4, S_2 in the light chain comes just before R_1 in the shock chain. In this way, the chain initiated by the light could mark the time that R_1 in the shock chain usually happens. There is a hollow line drawn between S_2 of the light chain and R_1 of the shock chain to indicate conditioning. According to this view, R_1 (from the shock chain) is conditioned to S_2 (from the light chain) by S-R contiguity, alone. Once evoked, however, R_1 of the shock results in S_2 of the shock, which in turn evokes the rest of the shock chain. In this way, a part of the shock chain is evoked whenever the light chain is evoked.

The alternative is the S-S* view that the response to the shock becomes conditioned to the light because the arbitrary stimulus of the light predicts the arrival of the biologically significant shock. But, as the preconditioning experiments demonstrate, conditioning can occur between two arbitrary stimuli in Phase I of preconditioning before the experimenter introduces any biologically significant S*.

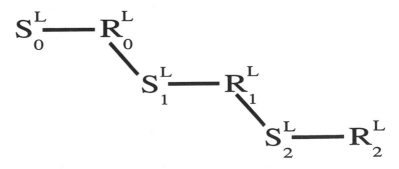

FIG. 4.3.   A chain of S—R links initiated by a light. Copyright © 1997 by R. Allen Gardner.

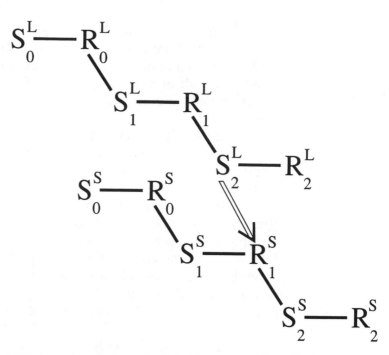

FIG. 4.4.   A conditioned S—R link between a light and a shock. Copyright © 1997 by R. Allen Gardner.

Figure 4.5 shows how the same process could take place with a tone and a light without any privileged, biologically significant stimulus, such as painful shock. With S-R contiguity, all that is necessary is a regularly repeating temporal pattern. An earlier link in one chain can always be conditioned to a later link in another chain. Perhaps, this is because an earlier S-R link is stronger than a later link; an R_1 in the chain that starts earlier is always stronger than an R_2 in the chain that starts later. The hollow line between S_2 in the tone chain and R_1 in the light chain represents the conditioned link between the two chains.

The alternative to this view is the S-S contiguity view that any two stimuli can be associated by contiguity. But, if this is true, why do the two stimuli have to be offset by an ISI as long as one half of a second? Unlike the S-S mechanism, the S-R contiguity mechanism is compatible with the need for a forward interval of at least a half second between S^a and S^b.

Now, the conditions in Fig. 4.5 are the conditions of Phase I of the preconditioning paradigm pairing a tone and a light before introducing any S^*, and the conditions in Fig. 4.4 are the conditions of Phase II, which is when the experimenter first introduces S^*.

Figure 4.6 puts together all three phases of the preconditioning experiment to show how the tone could evoke the shock by a condi-

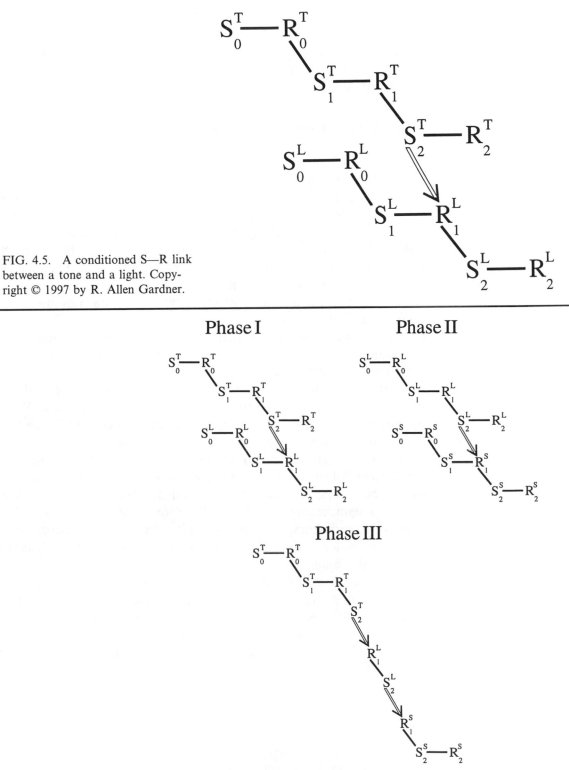

FIG. 4.5. A conditioned S—R link between a tone and a light. Copyright © 1997 by R. Allen Gardner.

Phase I

Phase II

Phase III

FIG. 4.6. Conditioning by contiguity in the preconditioning paradigm. Copyright © 1997 by R. Allen Gardner.

tioned link between the tone chain and the light chain followed by a conditioned link between the light chain and the shock chain—even though the tone and shock never appeared together.

Contrast With Stimulus Substitution

The S-R mechanism frees conditioning from Pavlov's principle of stimulus substitution. In everyday life, stimulus substitution would inevitably lead to maladaptive behavior. It may be adaptive to begin salivating to S^a if food is coming in about half a second. And, it may also be adaptive to begin salivating to S^b if S^a is coming in half a second. But, a point must come when there is an S^n that actually predicts that food will not arrive for some time. That is, it is adaptive for a dog to begin salivating when it is just about to eat, but it would be maladaptive for a dog to begin salivating at the beginning of a hunt or on first detecting prey.

Guests dining at their favorite restaurant may very well begin salivating when their waiter brings their food to the table. Should they begin salivating before that? Should they salivate when they see the waiter go to the kitchen with their orders? Should they salivate when the waiter writes their orders? When they read the menu? When the hostess seats them? When they enter the restuarant? When they drive into the parking lot? When they see the resaurant down the street? When they start out from home? When they decide to go out for dinner? All of these stimuli certainly predict a good dinner, but most occur at inappropriate times for salivation. In fact, most of them predict a significantly long interval before the arrival of food. Not only the experimental evidence, but also the common sequences of learned behavior in daily life contradict Pavlov's principle of higher-order conditioning.

The mechanism of S-R contiguity outlined here shows how the learner can make appropriately different responses to different stimuli in a predictable sequence. This mechanism can extend forward and backward in either direction and it can incorporate new links into established sequences. In the view of this book, that is the function of conditioning.

SUMMARY

Scientists are looking for the most basic unit of learning, the atom of conditioning. With this basic unit they can build up a system that applies to all forms of learning, to training, teaching, and even problem-solving strategies. In a century of research and theorizing, four basic mechanisms emerged as candidates for this role in classical conditioning, and these four probably exhaust the possibilities. These mechanisms are S-S, S-S*, S-R, and S-R-S*.

This chapter considers a mass of evidence from studies of the ISI. These studies show that, after repeated pairing, the most favorable interval between CS and UCS is long in neural time and asymmetrical; CS before UCS. These abundantly documented findings should eliminate one candidate, S-S.

The three remaining candidates each make use of the ISI. The S-S* mechanism needs the interval so that CS can signal the coming of UCS. The S-R-S* mechanism needs the interval so that the animal can do something that the S* can reward—something that increases the pleasure or decreases the pain of the S* when it comes. The S-R mechanism also needs the interval for the animal to make a response, but an S-R mechanism avoids the need for contingent pleasure or pain.

The evidence of omission experiments and preconditioning experiments eliminates S* contingency as necessary for classical conditioning. This should eliminate S-S* and S-R-S* as candidates.

According to S-R contiguity, it is a stimulus and a response that must be paired. The dog in Pavlov's experiment first salivates after food arrives. With repeated feeding, the dog starts to salivate before the food arrives. If the tone precedes the food by a favorable interval, then the procedure induces the dog to salivate soon after the tone. According to S-R contiguity, the salivation becomes conditioned to the tone because it occurs soon after the tone. That contiguity alone is sufficient for conditioning. With S-R contiguity alone, an animal can synchronize its behavior to rhythmically repeating events in its environment.

There is a fifth mechanism, R-S* contingency, first proposed by Skinner (1938), that continues to receive some support (Mackintosh, 1983; Rescorla, 1987). The R-S* mechanism is only appropriate for instrumental conditioning, so this book deals with it in later chapters concerned with the mechanisms of instrumental conditioning.

CHAPTER 5

Reinforcement Versus Expectancy

Possibly the longest running dispute in the psychology of learning concerns two principles: response contingent reinforcement and cognitive expectancy. Do rewards and punishments automatically stamp in the association between stimuli and responses? Or, is much if not all of learning a matter of building up cognitive expectancies about future events? During the middle of this century, this dispute flared up to the point where almost all experimenters seemed to be involved in one way or another. For about 30 years laboratories seethed with activity and the quality of research and argument yielded a rich harvest of solid findings. This chapter considers the theoretical roots of the dispute and some of the lasting findings and insights that came out of it. The basic questions remain, but significant advances in operational definition and experimental design grew out of this dispute.

RESPONSE CONTINGENT REINFORCEMENT

S-R-S* Contingency

In this book the expression S-R-S* represents conditioning by *contingency* in which an S* is contingent on the performance of a particular response to a particular stimulus. In Fig. 4.2, the S* acts backward to strengthen or weaken the S-R association. In the case of an appetitive S* like food, the effect is to strengthen the bond between an arbitrary stimulus, S^a, and an arbitrary response, R^a. In the case of an aversive S* like shock, the effect is to weaken the bond between S^a and R^a. Learning, according to this principle, is brought about by the automatic effect of an S* on an arbitrary response to an arbitrary stimulus. The principle is called the *law of effect*. In this view, the association between S^a and R^a is arbitrary in the sense that any response can be conditioned to any stimulus by the arbitrary action of the law of effect.

According to the law of effect:

1. Motivation is necessary for learning.
2. Animals learn a response to a stimulus (with the understanding that there can be patterns of responding and patterns of stimulation).
3. The motivational consequences (rewards, punishments) of a response to a stimulus determine whether or not learning takes place.

The S-R-S* formula seems to be designed for a single, highly simplified form of laboratory learning. How can reinforcement theorists adapt this principle to more complex, sequential behavior such as playing a game of tennis, speaking a foreign language, or managing a business?

Goal Gradient

Often, particularly in the Skinnerian tradition, the response in instrumental conditioning is treated as a single *act* ending in a reward. Many of the facts about common forms of instrumental learning, however, indicate that this view is oversimplified and misleading. The instrumental response always requires a series of movements. Even in a straight alley, rats make a series of running responses that take them from the start box to the goal box segment by segment. The advantage of studying rats in mazes is that experimenters can monitor progress through each segment of the maze. Hopefully, this information can reveal the way individual units fit into a skilled sequence. This could be the bridge relating simple conditioning to more complex behavior.

A bottom-up view of the process leads to questions such as, why rats take shorter rather than longer routes through a maze, why they eliminate some blind alleys before others, and why mazes with different patterns vary in difficulty. The answers to these questions become more reasonable when we analyze the act in terms of its component segments and the stimuli that begin and end each segment.

Given enough trials, rats solved mazes as complicated as the Hampton Court maze in Fig. 3.2. This is a challenging problem for conditioning theory. On the first trial, and many others, rats made many errors and went down many blind alleys, eventually getting to the food at the goal. If the food rewards the whole performance, then the food in the goal box must reward errors as well as correct turns. How can rats improve under those circumstances? The obvious answer is that they get the food sooner and with less effort when they make correct turns. But, in a maze as complicated as the Hampton Court maze, how can rats remember all the turns they made on each trial and compare time and effort on different trials?

In multiple-unit mazes such as those at the bottom of Fig. 3.3, distance from reward is a critical variable. Rats usually master the choices that are closer to the goal box before the choices that are farther from the goal box. There is also a clear-cut speed gradient; in general, rats run faster as they near the goal. This phenomenon is called the *goal gradient*, or *delay-of-reinforcement gradient*. C. L. Hull, one of the two or three most influential learning theorists of the 20th century, formulated a goal gradient principle as follows: "The mechanism . . . depended upon as an explanatory and integrating principle is that the goal reaction gets conditioned the most strongly to the stimuli preceding it, and the other reactions of the behavior sequence get conditioned to their stimuli progressively weaker as they are more remote (in time or space) from the goal reaction" (1932, pp. 25–26).

Figure 5.1 is a diagram of Hull's analysis of an act into segments. In a maze or runway, each segment contains somewhat different stimuli. That is, each segment of the runway looks a little different from the others because it has a slightly different pattern of stains, knotholes, nails, bolts, temperature gradients, light gradients, and so on. As rats run through a maze, each stimulus becomes a stimulus for running to the next segment until they get to the goal box, which

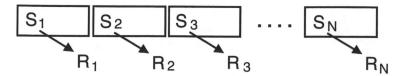

FIG. 5.1. Stimuli and responses of a serial act in C. L. Hull's (1932) theory. Each response R_1, R_2, R_3, . . . R_N moves the animal from one external stimulus S_1, S_2, S_3, . . . S_N to the next. Thus, each segment of a maze contains somewhat different stimuli and running moves the animal from segment to segment. Copyright © 1997 by R. Allen Gardner.

presents stimuli for approaching the food dish and eating. The goal gradient principle says that these S-R connections are stronger or weaker depending on whether they are closer or farther from the reward. Hull's system is a bottom-up system, working step by step through each unit of a series of stimuli and responses.

Learning the Shorter Path to a Goal

If there is more than one path to the goal box, as in the maze plan of Fig. 5.2, animals learn to take the shorter path. According to the goal gradient principle, the responses involved in a correct run should, therefore, be stronger, as illustrated in Fig. 5.2. More generally, animals should learn to take the shortest of several alternative paths to a goal.

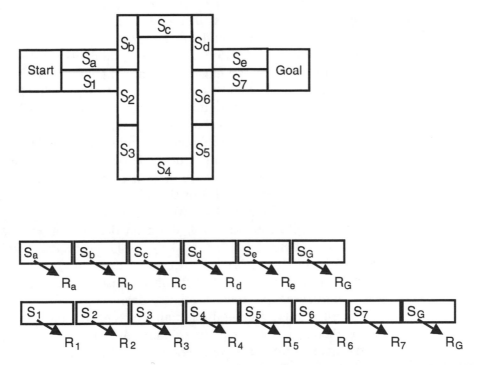

FIG. 5.2.   Preference for the shorter of two alternative paths according to C. L. Hull's (1932) goal gradient principle. The upper diagram represents a maze with a shorter path of five arbitrary units from start to goal, and a longer path of seven equivalent units. The stimuli associated with each unit form a series S_a to S_e for the shorter path and a series S_1 to S_7 for the longer path. There are two corresponding series of responses to each unit: R_a to R_e for the shorter path and R_1 to R_7 for the longer path. According to the goal gradient principle, the closer to the goal the stronger each S-R link in these chains. S_a-R_a is closer to the goal than S_1-R_1. Therefore, after an equal number of runs through both paths, S_a-R_a will be stronger than S_1-R_1 and the animal will enter the shorter path. Copyright © 1997 by R. Allen Gardner.

Order of Elimination of Blinds

A similar application of the goal gradient principle predicts the backward order of elimination of blinds in maze learning. Performance in a multiple-unit maze is a more complicated case of learning the shortest route to a reward. Errors, such as entries into blind alleys and retracings, are all rewarded eventually, but a correct run is rewarded sooner. To illustrate, suppose that entering a blind alley adds 5 seconds to the time required to run the maze, and therefore, 5 seconds' delay of reinforcement. Consequently, a correct response is always rewarded 5 seconds sooner than an error. Suppose that, after a correct choice at the last choice point, it takes 5 more seconds to reach the food in the goal box. Then a correct choice is rewarded after 5 seconds and an incorrect choice is rewarded after 5 seconds plus 5 seconds or 10 seconds. Suppose further that, after a correct choice at a point in the middle of the maze, it takes 50 seconds to get to the goal box. In that case, a correct choice would be rewarded after 50 seconds and an incorrect choice after 55 seconds. Suppose finally that, after a correct choice at the first choice point at the beginning of the maze, it takes 100 seconds to reach the goal box. In that case, a correct choice would be rewarded after 100 seconds and an incorrect choice after 105 seconds.

In most psychophysical dimensions, relative differences are more important than absolute differences. Accordingly, in Hull's theory, the difference in habit strength depends on the ratio of delays. For the last choice point in the hypothetical example, the ratio of delay would be $(10 - 5)/10 = 5/10$. For the middle choice point the ratio of delay would be $(55 - 50)/50 = 5/50$, and for the case of the first choice point $(105 - 100)/100 = 5/100$. If difficulty depends on relative delay, then the last choice point before the goal should be the least difficult because the relative delay is greatest and the first choice point after the start should be the most difficult because an incorrect choice at that point causes the smallest relative delay.

Experimental tests in multiple-unit mazes have roughly agreed with this prediction but other factors complicate the picture. Mechanical inertia favors a forward-going tendency, and centrifugal swing favors running off at a tangent after a turn to take the opposite turn at the next choice point. Rats also tend to orient in the direction of the goal box, or sometimes their home cages, leading them into blinds that point in certain directions. Finally, they tend to make *anticipatory errors,* that is, to make the response that is correct at the last choice point—just before the reward—too soon. Because of these factors rats seldom eliminate blinds in a perfect backward order and the usual result is only a rough approximation.

The goal gradient principle predicts that the correct turn at the last choice point in a multiple-unit maze will be learned first and best. Once learned, however, the last response will tend, on the basis of stimulus generalization, to appear at other choice points, that is, in anticipation of the final choice point. Whether such anticipation aids or interferes with learning the maze depends on the maze pattern.

Figure 5.3 is a drawing of a maze used by C. L. Hull (1939, 1947), and Sprow (1947) to study patterns of error in a linear maze. The upper panel of Fig. 5.4 shows how the correct path through the maze may require either a series of identical responses (homogeneous case) or a series of different responses (heterogeneous case). In the homogeneous case, anticipation is always correct and aids learning, while in the heterogeneous case anticipation is always an error and interferes. There are also *perseverative errors* when the learners repeat their previous choices. In the homogeneous case, perseveration is always correct and aids learning, while in the heterogeneous case, perseveration is always an error and interferes. Both anticipation of later responses and perseveration of earlier responses interfere with learning in the heterogeneous maze, so the middle of the maze should be more difficult than the beginning and the end. The lower panel of Fig. 5.4 shows that the pattern of errors agrees with the expected sources of error.

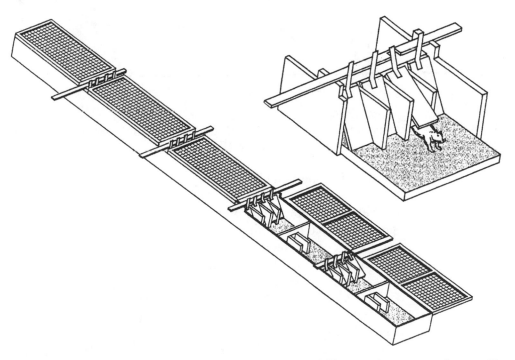

FIG. 5.3. Maze used by C. L. Hull (1947), and Sprow (1947) to study patterns of error. From Sprow (1947).

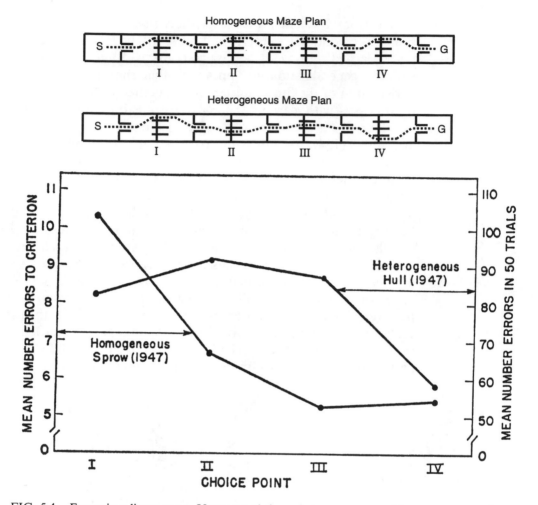

FIG. 5.4. Errors in a linear maze. Upper panel shows heterogeneous and homogeneous pathways. Lower panel shows experimental results. From Eprow (1947).

Speed-of-Locomotion Gradient

The same reasoning that predicts the order of elimination of blinds applies to speed of running. The goal gradient alone leads us to expect faster running as the animal approaches the goal. Once again, there are mechanical factors that influence the actual gradient. In a straight alley, in particular, rats that build up their speed as they run must decelerate somewhat before they get to the end of the alley or else they will crash into the end wall. Results of a typical experiment appear in Fig. 5.5.

Figure 5.5 presents data obtained by Hull (1934) on the time spent by rats in various segments of a 40-foot straight runway. As expected, the animals ran slowest in the early maze sections and progressively

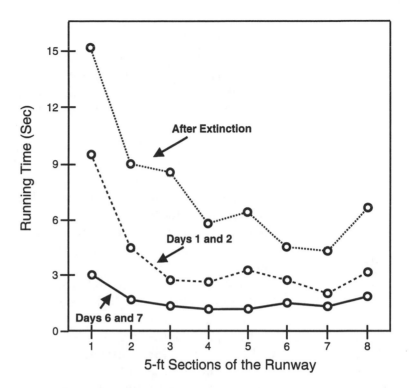

FIG. 5.5.   Speed of locomotion gradient in a 40-foot runway. Running time in each successive 5-foot section early in training, late in training, and during extinction. From C. L. Hull (1934).

faster as they approached the goal, slowing up slightly in the final segment. Late in training the curve flattens because running times are reaching the absolute limit of zero. The top curve shows how the gradient continued, even accentuated, during extinction. Later, Drew (1939) showed that the gradient occurs in many situations and becomes more pronounced under massed as compared to distributed practice.

The goal gradient principle is only an illustrative sample of the way a representative bottom-up theory can work to describe specific results of specific experiments. Hull (1952) constructed an elaborate theoretical system which involves many additional functions that are far beyond the scope of this book.

COGNITIVE EXPECTANCY

Theories of cognitive expectancy differ from theories of response contingent reinforcement in that learning is perceptual and top-down rather than motor and bottom-up. Human and nonhuman animals learn to expect events. Their perception of the situation determines what they do. Rewards and punishments cannot strengthen or weaken responses, directly. Perception of rewards and punishments creates *expectancies*. An executive entity at the top of the system commands the lower motor entities according to these perceived expectancies. Cognitive theories are top-down systems.

Learning, according to expectancy theory, consists of perceiving a stimulus and its significance. With experience in a T-maze, a rat perceives that the food is at the end of one arm. If the rat is hungry, this expectancy motivates running down that arm of the maze. The rat "sees" that such and such a stimulus followed by such and such behavior leads to the goal box. In this way, the rat forms a *cognitive map* or representation of the maze somewhere in its brain. The executive entity in the brain uses this cognitive map to direct the motor entity to the reward.

Expectancy theory accounts for all of the findings covered by the goal gradient principle. With a cognitive map of the maze, rats can select the shortest path to the food in the goal box. Rats run faster as they approach the goal because the expectancy of reward is greater, and so on. Top-down principles of cognitive expectancy seemed to predict some additional findings that contradict the bottom-up principles of response contingent reinforcement, and this is what took the dispute out of the debating halls and into the laboratories.

Unrewarded Trials

If all that rats learn by exploring the maze is a cognitive map, then a rat should learn just as much whether or not it is hungry and whether or not there is food in the goal box. According to cognitive expectancy theory, food makes a hungry rat take the shortest path to the goal box because the executive center at the top evaluates the expected value of the available actions and commands lower, motor centers to respond appropriately. Cognitive expectancy theory distinguishes between the motivated performance that appears in the maze and the cognitive learning that governs performance.

A rather straightforward experiment should reveal whether reward in the goal box is necessary for learning or only necessary for performance. Rats in one group run through the maze as usual with reward in the goal box on every trial starting with Trial 1. Rats in a second group run through the maze for the same number of trials but without reward in the goal box during Phase I. Both reinforcement theory and expectancy theory predict that only the rewarded group should improve during Phase I. According to expectancy theory, however, both groups should learn the same amount during Phase I because learning is the cognitive result of experience in the maze. What the unrewarded group learns in Phase I remains *latent*, however, until the experimenter puts food in the goal box and shows the rats in this group that it is worthwhile to proceed to the goal box by the shortest route.

To test this prediction, both groups find food in the goal box during Phase II of the experiment. Phase II tests whether the previously unrewarded group profited from their *latent learning* during Phase I. According to cognitive expectancy theory, both groups should perform equally well during Phase II because both groups learned roughly the same amount during Phase I.

According to reinforcement theory, on the other hand, the unrewarded group learns nothing during Phase I because they receive no rewards. Without an S*, there is no strengthening of the association between S^a and R^a. Therefore, the performance of the experimental group should start at about the same level as the performance of the control group when they first found food in the goal box.

Tolman and Honzik (1930) was one of the first experiments to test for latent learning after unrewarded trials. Tolman and Honzik ran hungry rats in a 14-unit maze like the one shown in Fig. 5.6. They used this fairly elaborate, complex maze, reasoning that a more complicated maze would require a better cognitive map and thus amplify the difference between learning by cognitive expectancy and learning by response contingent reinforcement.

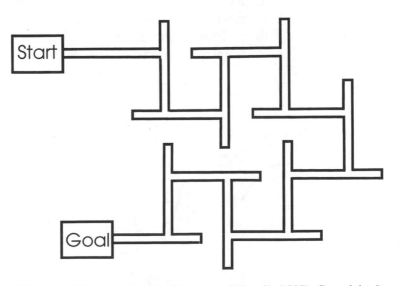

FIG. 5.6.   The maze used by Tolman and Honzik (1930). Copyright © 1997 by R. Allen Gardner.

In the Tolman and Honzik experiment, one group found food in the goal box at the end of the maze on every trial beginning with the first trial. This is, of course, the usual procedure. This group showed a steady decline in errors throughout the experiment, which is, of course, the usual finding. The second group never found any food in the goal box and performed much more poorly than the first group throughout the experiment, as any theory would expect. The critical third group ran the maze from beginning to end without finding any food in the goal box for 10 trials. Then, on the 11th trial and every trial after that, they found food in the goal box.

Figure 5.7 shows the results, which are typical of many similar studies using the same design to test for latent learning. The third, latent learning group performed very poorly for the first 11 trials. After their first reward at the end of the 11th trial, however, the latent learning group improved rapidly, so rapidly that on the very next trial, the 12th trial, they actually equaled the performance of the group that found food in the goal box starting from Trial 1. After a single food reward, the experimental group performed just as well as the first control group did after 11 food rewards. Indeed, in Tolman and Honzik (1930), the experimental group slightly outperformed the control group from the 12th trial onward.

Soon, many other experimenters replicated the basic results of the Tolman and Honzik (1930) experimental design (see Kimble, 1961; MacCorquodale & Meehl, 1954; for extensive reviews). Sometimes the latent learning groups took more than one trial to overtake the animals that were rewarded throughout, but a very few rewarded trials were always enough to bring the latent learning groups up to the performance of animals that had been rewarded many more times for running in the same maze. We cannot doubt the reliability of this

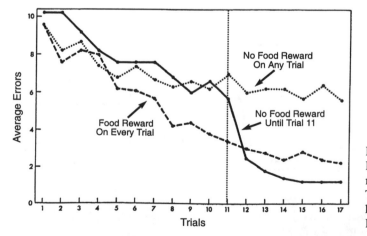

FIG. 5.7.   Results of Tolman and Honzik (1930). A sharp drop in errors on Trial 12 after first reward on Trial 11 seems to indicate latent learning during the first 10 trials. From Tolman and Honzik (1930).

experimental finding, but does that mean that there can be significant, even dramatic, amounts of instrumental learning without any reward? Is learning a cognitive phenomenon that depends on exposure to the stimulus situation, while reward only provides the incentive for performance?

Karn and Porter (1946) entered this arena after several additional experiments had thoroughly replicated the main results of Tolman and Honzik (1930). Karn and Porter replicated the main conditions but they asked additional questions. They looked at their subjects as living animals that learn many things in the course of an experiment, more things than the plan of the maze and the location of food. By broadening the scope of their experiment beyond the traditional dispute between reinforcement and expectancy, Karn and Porter discovered more about living animals. Just as the warring parties in the dispute ignored the nature of their living subjects as irrelevant to theory, so Karn and Porter showed that the dispute was, itself, irrelevant to essential aspects of a learning situation. Karn and Porter were among the first to discover important features of a learning situation that the grand theorists usually ignore, features that have more direct implications for human and nonhuman learning outside of the laboratory. This book describes and discusses this particular experiment in detail because its implications extend far beyond the latent learning dispute that inspired it.

Karn and Porter (1946) used the special maze illustrated in Fig. 5.8. It is called a *Dashiel maze* after its inventor, John Dashiel. The distinctive feature of a Dashiel maze is that, if an animal is put into the maze in compartment A and finds food in compartment C, then there are many paths that all lead to food. At most of the choice points in this maze animals can choose between four alternative alleys, two leading toward the goal box and two leading away from the goal box. Responses that lead toward the goal box count as correct responses; those leading away count as errors. Correct and incorrect responses in a Dashiel maze depend on orientation toward the goal, which should make it especially appropriate for studying cognitive maps.

Table 5.1 outlines the design of Karn and Porter's (1946) experiment. In this experiment, Phase III was the usual training condition for maze learning. Rats were deprived of food for 23.5 hours each day, and then, once each day they were placed in the maze in compartment A and left in the maze until they found food in compartment C where they ate for 1 minute from a dish of bread soaked in milk (a preferred food for laboratory rats). During Phase III, each animal ran through the maze for one trial a day until it reached a criterion of two successive errorless runs.

FIG. 5.8.   Plan of the Dashiel maze used by Karn and Porter (1946). Copyright © 1997 by R. Allen Gardner.

TABLE 5.1
Experimental Design of Karn and Porter (1946)

Group	Phase I 6 days No deprv No Maze	Phase II 5 days 23.5 hrs deprv No Food in Maze	Phase III To Criterion 23.5 hrs deprv Fed at C	Results Trials to Criterion
1	Handling	In at A Out at C	In at A Out at C	3.83
2	Handling	In at Random Out at Yoked Time	In at A Out at C	7.25
3	Handling	In Plain Box Out at Yoked Time	In at A Out at C	8.25
4	Handling	(Omitted)	In at A Out at C	8.66
5	(Omitted)	(Omitted)	In at A Out at C	10.25

The purpose of the experiment was to compare the effects of different kinds of preliminary training that the rats received before Phase III, including Tolman and Honzik's preliminary trials without reward. The number of trials that each group took to reach the criterion of two successive errorless trials in Phase III measured the effects of these different earlier treatments.

Group 5 is like the group that Tolman and Honzik (1930) rewarded on every trial starting with the first trial, and Group 1 is like the latent learning group that had a series of unrewarded trials before finding reward in the goal box. Once each day in Phase II, which lasted for 5 days, the animals in Group 1 were placed individually in the maze in compartment A and then left in the maze until they reached compartment C where they were confined for 1 minute and then removed from the maze. After 5 days of Phase II, Group 1 began Phase III, which was the same as Phase II except for the food reward in compartment C. The first experience that Group 5 ever had in the maze was the rewarded treatment of Phase III—they never experienced Phase I or Phase II. Group 1 and Group 5 of Karn and Porter (1946) replicated the procedure of Tolman and Honzik (1930).

The results, shown in the last column of Table 5.1, also replicated the findings of Tolman and Honzik; once they found reward in the goal box, Group 1 learned much faster than Group 5. According to cognitive expectancy theory, this demonstrates that Group 1 learned a cognitive map of the maze during Phase II and used it to reach the goal box after they found food there. If contingent rewards such as food and water are necessary to stamp in S-R connections, then Group 1 should have performed at about the same level as Group 5 because their rewarded treatment in Phase III was identical.

The remaining three groups of the experiment show how experimental controls separate out critical components of a main result. The difference between Karn and Porter (1946) and Tolman and Honzik (1930) offers a classic lesson in operational definition. During Phase II, the experimenters recorded the time that each animal in Group 1 took to get from compartment A to compartment C each day. According to cognitive expectancy theory, the animals of Group 1 spent this time learning a cognitive map of the maze. Each animal in Group 1 was then paired with a particular animal in Group 2. On each day of Phase II, each animal in Group 2 was placed in the maze at random either in compartment A, in compartment B, in compartment C, or in compartment D according to a table of random numbers, and then taken out of the maze wherever it happened to be after it had spent the same amount of time in the maze as its yoked mate in Group 1.

This is called a *yoked control*. In each yoked pair, both animals spent the same amount of time in the maze. The only difference between them was that the yoked animal in Group 1 had to get from compartment A to compartment C on every trial before the experimenter would take it out of the maze. According to cognitive expectancy theory, the animals in Group 2 had just as much opportunity to form a cognitive map of the maze as their yoked mates in Group 1 because both groups spent the same amount of time exploring the maze and neither got any food reward during Phase II. If that is all there is to maze learning, both groups should have performed equally well in Phase III. As Table 5.1 shows, however, Group 1 performed much better than Group 2. This is a puzzle for both cognitive theory and reinforcement theory. Both groups got the same amount of exploration and neither got any food. According to expectancy theory both should have learned the same amount, and according to reinforcement theory neither should have learned anything. The results seem to refute both theories.

The advantage of Group 3 over Group 5 is also puzzling. The animals in Group 3 were taken out of their home cages once each day and brought to the maze room where they spent their yoked time in a plain, wooden box that was made of the same material and built as a duplicate of the starting box of the maze. In Phase III, Group 3 took more trials to reach criterion than either Group 1 or Group 2. This is only reasonable, because Group 3 never had any experience with the maze before Phase III. But, Group 3 still learned the maze faster than Group 5. Both reinforcement theories and expectancy theories depend on experience in the maze, so neither theory can cope with the difference between Group 3 and Group 5 because neither group had any prior experience in the maze.

In Phase I, which lasted for six days, the experimenters handled each of the animals in Groups 1, 2, 3, and 4 once each day. The five days of *handling* was the only difference between Group 4 and Group 5, and yet Group 4 mastered the maze faster than Group 5. Again, neither expectancy theory nor reinforcement theory can cope with the difference between Group 4 and Group 5 because neither group had any prior experience in the maze.

A procedure like Phase I in Karn and Porter (1946) became a standard procedure after the results of this and similar experiments conducted at about the same time. In most experiments with nonhuman subjects, the animals live in cages and the experimenters must take them out of their cages and bring them to the testing apparatus (which is often housed in a different experimental room) and then bring them back to their cages after testing. This is a disturbing experience for animals that have never before been handled by human beings. Modern experimenters take their animals out of the cages and handle them once a day for at least one week before the start of an experiment. When laboratories can afford the luxury of a breeding colony, human beings handle the animals from birth and this is an important part of the colony procedure. An animal that arrives in the maze stressed and agitated by its first experience with a human handler is definitely a different learner from an animal that is tame and calm when it enters the maze (Morato & Brandão, 1996).

The need for preliminary taming by handling was not generally appreciated at the time of Tolman and Honzik's (1930) experiment. One of the pitfalls of abstract theorizing is that theorists and experimenters often think of their subjects as furry little test tubes and forget that they are talking about live animals that respond to everything they experience, not just to rewards and punishments and cognitive maps. Handling the animals in Group 4 helped them learn the maze faster, even though handling is irrelevant both to response reinforcment and to cognitive expectancy. Karn and Porter (1946) showed that handling plays a role in maze learning even if it plays no role in abstract theories.

Rats have to get used to a schedule of feeding once a day for only half an hour and few experimenters appreciated this at the time of the Tolman and Honzik (1930) experiment. As Table 5.1 shows, another difference between Groups 1, 2, and 3 and Groups 4 and 5 was that Groups 1, 2, and 3 got five days of adaptation to the schedule of 23.5 hours of deprivation and 0.5 hours of eating at the same time each day, while Groups 4 and 5 both got their first experience with food deprivation when they started rewarded training in the maze during Phase III. We can see from Table 5.1 that a large portion of the difference between Group 1 and Group 5 depended on differences in adaptation to the experimental conditions—handling, deprivation schedule, maze environment, and so on—quite apart from any difference between cognitive expectancy or contingent reward.

From the point of view of cognitive expectancy theory, the most perplexing finding in the Karn and Porter study is the advantage of Group 1 over Group 2 in Phase III. In Phase II, both groups spent the same average amount of time in the maze so both had the same opportunity to form cognitive maps, and also the same amount of time to become adapted to the maze environment. The difference was that the animals of Group 1 always started at compartment A and ended at compartment C, while the animals in Group 2 were placed in the maze at random and taken out wherever they happened to be at the end of their yoked study time. How can we explain this finding within either theory?

Suppose that the rats were unhappy in the maze or preferred being put back in their home cages or suppose that they enjoyed handling after they got used to it. During Phase II, the sooner the animals in Group 1 found their way to compartment C, the sooner they got out of the maze and back to their home cages, and during the trip they got handled by their familiar experimenter. Perhaps, getting out of the maze and getting handled by the experimenter was their reward and that is why they performed better than the animals in Group 2. Looking at Fig. 5.7, we see that the animals in the unrewarded conditions of the Tolman and Honzik (1930) experiment also improved. Many other replications of the Tolman and Honzik experiment confirmed this result. Indeed, in some of these experiments (e.g., Meehl & MacCorquodale, 1951) the so-called "unrewarded" animals performed almost as well as the rewarded animals before receiving the first reward. Perhaps, all of the so-called "unrewarded" groups in Tolman and Honzik type latent learning experiments got rewarded for finding their way to the place where the experimenter took them out of the maze and handled them.

It certainly is reasonable to say that there are lots more ways of rewarding rats—or human beings for that matter—than by giving them food or water. While this move does get reinforcement theory out of trouble here, there is a heavy price. Reinforcement theorists must now admit that they have no independent operational definition of reward. They found out that being picked up out of the maze and handled was an incentive only after many experiments demonstrated learning without any other incentive. The value of a scientific theory lies in telling us more than we know already. Saying that the rats must have been reinforced because they learned and then saying that whatever they got must have been a reinforcement only tells us what we already know. They might as well say that the rats learned because they learned.

Some experimenters tried to measure the reward value of picking rats up out of the goal box and handling them. In these experiments, rats were taken out of a T-maze and handled after they reached the goal box at the end of one arm, but only confined briefly after they reached the goal box at the end of the other arm. In one experiment, the rats learned to go to the handling goal box, in a second experiment they learned to go to the confinement side, and in the third experiment they ran equally often to both sides (Candland, Faulds, Thomas, & Candland, 1960; Candland, Horowitz, & Culbertson, 1962; Sperling & Valle, 1964). If we follow the line of argument that whatever the rats learned must have been rewarding, then we have to say that handling was rewarding in the first experiment, punishing in the second experiment, and neutral in the third. That sort of theory cannot tell us anything in advance. It only gives us names for whatever we happen to find—after we find it.

Saying that taking a rat out of the maze and putting it back in the home cage is rewarding also removes the difference between cognitive expectancy and response reinforcement. This is because cognitive expectancy theory always predicts the same thing as response reinforcement theory when there is any incentive to get somewhere or do something. All of those experiments and all of those arguments only proved that latent learning experiments of this type cannot distinguish between cognitive expectancy and response reinforcement. Allowing theorists to invent incentives after the results are in is like giving them blank checks to pay for their mistakes.

The inconclusive results of experiments on latent learning after unrewarded trials teach valuable lessons in operational definition. First, many aspects of experimental treatment have crucial effects on learning quite apart from the hypothetical effects of stimulus response habits or cognitive expectancies. Theories about the behavior of live animals rather than furry test tubes must take these effects into account. That is the ethological view. Second, there is a serious weakness in both reinforcement theory and expectancy theory. Neither theory has a suitable operational definition of reward or punishment that is independent of the learning already observed in past experiments. Later chapters of this book return to both of these themes.

Free Exploration

In this type of latent learning, the experimenter places a hungry rat in a multiple-unit maze like the one in Fig. 5.6 and then goes home for the night. In the morning the experimenter places the rat in the start box and feeds it when it reaches the goal box. Animals in the control group spend the night in the same experimental room in a different apparatus, say a plain box, a simple straight alley, or a rectangular arrangement of four straight alleys. In most of these experiments, the animals that explored the maze during the night performed nearly perfectly when they ran the maze for rewards in the morning. The animals in the control groups performed like naive animals on the first trials of the usual experiment (see Kimble, 1961; MacCorquodale & Meehl, 1954; for extensive reviews). This certainly looks like learning without any possible source of reward. Or does it?

After several reports of latent learning following free exploration, some experimenters became curious enough to stay in the laboratory and watch the animals to see what they did during the night. They found that the rats spent a lot of time exploring the maze from one end to the other, as ethologists would expect of animals that normally live in burrows. The exploration was far from random, however; the rats soon started to avoid the blind alleys and spend more and more time in the true path running between the start box and the goal box. After a while each animal spent most of its time in the true path and very little time in the blind alleys. They found the true path and practiced running in this path without any food reward or any other help from the experimenters who never even touched the rats during the study periods. Where is the reward here and where is the expectancy?

MacCorquodale and Meehl (1951) reasoned as follows. Rats like to run freely through the maze, especially rats that live in small cages. They prefer the true path because it lets them run more freely. They avoid the blind alleys because these are confining. So far, all we have is another post hoc (after the fact) explanation of what we know already. But, MacCorquodale and Meehl went a step farther and formulated the following hypothesis. If rats avoid blind alleys because they are confining, then narrower alleys should be more confining than wider alleys. The effect should depend on the width of the alleys. Accordingly, they built mazes with narrower alleys and found that the narrower the alleys the more the rats avoided the blind alleys during free exploration. This is a classic example of a theoretical explanation that generated a prediction which was confirmed experimentally.

Notice that the fresh thinking of MacCorquodale and Meehl started when experimenters became curious about what the animals were doing during the periods of free exploration. Then they approached learning as ethologists. Parties to the latent learning dispute who were only interested in the final scores on test trials were content to go home for the night and forget about the animals till testing time in the morning.

By watching the animals as well as theorizing about them, MacCorquodale and Meehl discovered an unexpected incentive that favors the true path of the maze over the blind alleys. That is certainly a step up from saying that rats learn because they learn, but it opens up the possibility of an unlimited number of similar sources of reward that can appear unexpectedly in any learning situation. Without a rule that tells us in advance what will be rewarding and what will not be rewarding, reinforcement theorists are a long way from giving us a useful theory. And once again, after the source of incentive has been found, cognitive expectancy theories predict the same result that response reinforcement theories predict.

Irrelevant Drive

In this type of latent learning, experimenters deprive rats of one incentive, say water, and satiate them for another, say food. In Phase I, they typically run the rats in a T-maze with water in both goal boxes and food in only one of the two goal boxes. With equal experience in both goal boxes, the animals get to see that there is food in one goal box but not in the other. They never eat, however, because they are not hungry. After many such trials, the experimenters satiate the animals for water and deprive them of food for Phase II. If the rats now go to the food side, then they demonstrate latent learning because we cannot say that they were reinforced with food in that goal box if they never ate there. Or can't we?

Once again, reinforcement theory turns out to be more complicated than people thought. When animals learned without eating, reinforcement theorists were quick to point out that the rats may have received *secondary* or *conditioned reinforcement* from the sight or the smell of food. Secondary or conditioned reinforcement is an integral part of reinforcement theory. We know that animals have to learn to recognize food. Therefore the sight of laboratory food is a learned or derived secondary reward rather than a primary reward based directly on eating. The concept of stimuli that acquire the power of reinforcement is extremely important and chapter 7 considers this concept in detail.

Reinforcement can explain any result of learning from experience with irrelevant drive. When animals learned even though they never ate during the exploratory phase, their reward could have been the sight or the smell of food. At the same time, when animals failed to learn from the sight of uneaten food in these experiments—that is, when rats now satiated for water and deprived of food continued to run equally to the food and the nonfood side—this also confirmed reinforcement theory because lack of latent learning always confirms reinforcement theory.

According to expectancy theorists, when rats failed to learn to go to the food side, it was because they were so thirsty that they failed to notice the food; they were literally blinded by their thirst. Several experiments attempted to avoid this objection by ensuring that the rats would *attend* to the food.

Walker (1948), for example, used the maze plan in Fig. 5.9 to test for latent learning about food by thirsty rats. In Phase I, Walker deprived rats of water and let them eat all they could in their home cages. In the maze, if they ran to the water goal box, he stopped them there and let them drink. If they ran to the food side, he let them continue past the food goal box until they got to the water goal box

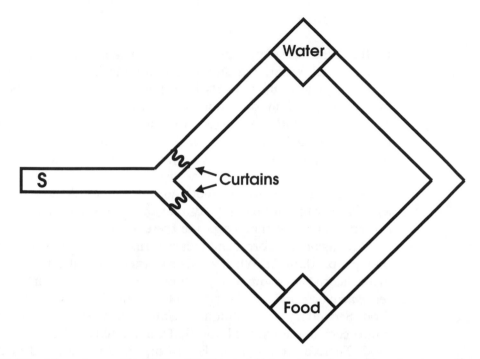

FIG. 5.9.   Maze plan used by Walker (1948) to test for latent learning. In Phase I, rats were deprived of water and satiated for food. In Phase II, they were satiated for water and deprived of food. From Walker (1948).

from the other direction, and then stopped them and let them drink. Doors at key points in the maze prevented the animals from retracing their steps. Walker made sure that the animals would have equal experience with both goal boxes by blocking one arm occasionally so that they had to go the other way. To make sure that the rats experienced the food, Walker piled it up in the food goal box so that they had to climb over the food on their way to the water.

In spite of experiments like Walker's the results remained inconclusive. Once you grant the possibility that rats can be so blinded by thirst that they fail to notice food, then nothing really guarantees attention. At the same time, once you grant the possibility that the sight of food can be secondarily reinforcing without eating, then secondary reinforcement becomes indistinguishable from cognitive expectancy.

Experiments with irrelevant drive in Phase I yielded positive results that demonstrated latent learning and negative results that demonstrated absence of latent learning in roughly equal proportions. Since both sides of the dispute had an explanation for both positive and negative results, both sides could claim victory but neither side was actually supported. The dispute over this type of experiment revealed the importance of the concepts of secondary reward and attention. These concepts play parallel roles and predict parallel results in both types of theory. Yet, without clear operational definitions that tell us in advance just when an animal has received secondary reward or when an animal has paid attention, both reinforcement theory and expectancy theory fail as theories. Chapter 7 takes up the problem of secondary reward in detail.

SUMMARY

The latent learning controversy frustrated those who looked for a crucial experiment that could prove that response reinforcement theory fits the evidence better than cognitive expectancy, or vice versa. The rest of us can still profit from these experiments because they were good experiments. In their attempts to design rigorous experiments that would define the difference between reinforcement and expectancy, experimenters discovered serious logical defects in both theories. The chief problem is the lack of an operational definition for either primary or secondary reward. This problem is the subject of chapter 7.

Many important aspects of animal learning, such as the need to tame animal subjects and accustom them to the regimen of deprivation, came to light only when the latent learning controversy forced all sides to scrutinize every possible flaw of these experiments. All in all, the controversy enriched experimental method and enriched our understanding of the learning process.

Notice how experiments can discover much more about animal behavior by bottom-up experiments than by debating the grand hypotheses of top-down theories. When experiments on the value of unrewarded trials separated out aspects of experience in a maze, they found that adaptation to the learning environment is at least as important as incentive and reward. This is a general principle of all learning, directly applicable to human learning in factories and classrooms. It is a valuable principle whatever the fate of the controversy between the grandest theories of reinforcement and cognition.

In studies of free exploration, experimenters who were only interested in grand theories went home for the night and left the rats to study on their own. The only thing that interested these experimenters was the scores on tests in the morning. When experimenters who were interested in live animals started watching the animals, they discovered that rats gradually learned to keep to the true path of a maze without any input from the experimenter. They discovered something about rats in mazes that was quite beyond the imagination of the grand theorists.

CHAPTER 6

Sequence and Anticipation

Many critical analyses in this book depend on sequences of stimuli and responses that arise from experience with an S* and must anticipate the S* for conditioning to be effective. These sequences are the basis of the analyses of preconditioning in chapter 4 and of goal gradient effects in chapter 5. The existence of sequences of stimuli and responses and also *response-produced stimuli* is based on actual observation rather than on speculative theory. This chapter describes two case histories in which conjectures about anticipatory links in a sequence led from academic debates about top-down contingency to bottom-up observations of actual behavior.

LATENT EXTINCTION

According to response reinforcement theory, rats learn to turn right or left at the choice point of a T-maze because they receive reward in the goal box at the end of the arm. The S^a is the stimulus situation at the choice point and the R^a is the turn, right or left. We know the response is arbitrary because the experimenter randomly assigns half the rats to one group and the other half to a second group. The first group gets rewarded for turning right and the second group gets rewarded for turning left. In response reinforcement theory, animals learn the turn at the choice point because they receive reward in the goal box after they make an arbitrarily correct turn. According to cognitive expectancy theory, animals learn to expect food in one goal box or the other. They can learn this without making any turns at all.

There is the same contrast in extinction. According to response reinforcement theory, failure to find food in the goal box extinguishes the chain of responses that leads to the goal box. According to cognitive expectancy theory animals discover that the goal box contains food during acquisition and that it is empty during extinction. During extinction they stop making the turn because expectancy of food extinguishes. One way to test this contrasting view of extinction would be to train the animals with food reward in the usual way and then extinguish the expectancy without extinguishing the turning response.

To make this test, Deese (1951) trained 20 rats to go to the left side of a T-maze and 20 other rats to go to the right side for food reward. After six days of training at four trials per day, the 40 rats were going to the rewarded side on about 90% of the trials. On the seventh day, Deese extinguished all of the animals in the usual manner. They ran in the maze as before, but without food in the goal box. Extinction reduced the preference for the formerly rewarded side to 50%, which is the same as zero preference.

Half of the animals received special experience just before the start of extinction. Deese placed each of these rats in the empty goal box four times for one minute each time with one minute between each exposure to the empty goal box. The results of Deese's (1951) experiment and a similar experiment of Seward and Levy (1949) were clear. The animals that spent time in the empty goal box before making the correct turn for themselves extinguished the correct response much more rapidly than animals without this preextinction experience. In fact, the experimental animals that experienced nonresponse extinction extinguished almost immediately, while the control groups took many trials to extinguish. This looks like a clear-cut case of learning by perceiving without responding. Or does it?

Segments of a T-Maze

Deese's typical version of cognitive expectancy views a run through a T-maze as one of two acts, a right turn or a left turn with food at the end of the rewarded alternative. In those terms, there cannot be a response in nonresponse extinction because a rat that the experimenter places in the goal box cannot perform the *act* of making the formerly correct turn at the choice point. Popular as this view may be among traditional theorists, it is an unrealistic view of behavior that distorts and obscures vital details. More realistic and more informative pictures emerge from more detailed descriptions.

This section first analyzes the sequence of stimulus-response units in an act such as running to the goal box of a T-maze. Next the analysis zooms in on the sequence of stimulus-response units between entering a goal box and seizing a reward and between pressing a lever and seizing a reward.

Chapter 5 began with Hull's analysis of a maze into a series of segments as shown in Figs. 5.1 and 5.2 and the experiments on the goal gradient that confirmed his analysis. Figure 6.1 recasts Hull's S-R diagrams of Figs. 5.1 and 5.2 into the S-R chain diagrams of Figs. 4.3 through 4.6. All of these diagrams express the fact that every response changes the stimulus situation in some way. As a rat runs through a maze, each movement changes the stimulus situation. Each section of the maze is a little different: There are different spots on the floor, different imperfections in the walls, different lighting from outside the maze, different gradients of warmth and sound from the room outside the maze, and so on. Running from one section to another ends the stimulation from one section and exposes the animal to the stimulation in the next section.

The advantage of the system shown in Fig. 6.1 over Hull's in Figs. 5.1 and 5.2, is that it emphasizes parallels: (a) parallels between maze learning and classical conditioning described in Figs. 4.3 through 4.6, and (b) parallels between maze learning and other sequential patterns of response such as lever-pressing and key-pecking described in detail in later chapters of this book.

In Fig. 6.1, S_1, S_2, S_3, ... S_n represent the stimuli in each section of the maze, while R_1, R_2, R_3, ... R_n represent the response of running in each corresponding section of the maze. The break between S_3—R_3 and S_n—R_n (indicated by dots ...) means that the diagram can stand for any arbitrary number of maze units. Also, R_1, R_2, R_3, ... R_n

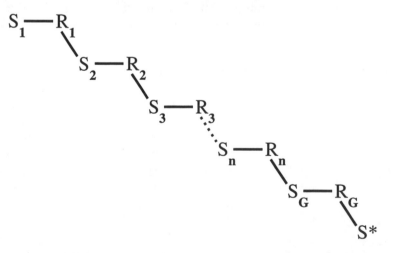

FIG. 6.1. Chain of S-R units in a runway or a T-maze. Copyright © 1997 by R. Allen Gardner.

could represent running straight on in a straight alley runway, or they could represent turning right or left at successive choice points in a multiple-unit maze, and S_1, S_2, S_3, . . . S_n could represent the stimulus situation at each corresponding choice point. As in Hull's analysis, S_G represents the stimulus situation at the entrance to the goal box and R_G represents the response of entering the goal box and getting the reward. For simplicity at this point in the analysis, everything that happens after the rat enters the goal box and finds the food is represented in Fig. 6.1 as S^*.

Figure 6.2 is a diagram representing a segmental analysis of a T-maze. The diagram arbitrarily divides each arm into three segments: R_1, R_2, and R_3 for the right arm and L_1, L_2, and L_3 for the left arm. Both arms have a compartment at the end. The compartment at the end of the right arm contains the food dish and it is labeled G for goal box. The choice point where the rat must enter one arm or the other is labeled C. At that point, the rat either responds to the stimuli in R_1 by entering R_1 or responds to the stimuli in L_1 by entering L_1. There are two chains like the one in Fig. 6.1, one starting with a right turn and the other with a left turn. In S-R-S* theories, only one of the chains is rewarded because the rat only finds food in the goal box at the end of the right arm. Consequently, only the response of turning right to enter the first segment of the right arm in response to the choice point stimuli is part of the rewarded chain.

Segments of a Goal Box

Latent extinction depends on what happens when the rats are placed directly in the goal box without running there on their own. In the cognitive expectancy view, they just sit in the goal box either eating the

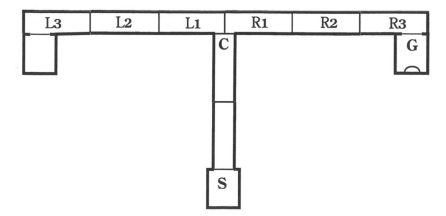

FIG. 6.2.   Segmental analysis of S-R units in a T-maze. Copyright © 1997 by R. Allen Gardner.

food and forming expectancies of reward or experiencing the empty goal box and forming expectancies of nonreward. Experimenters who have enough ethological interest in living animals to observe their experimental subjects in the goal box describe sequences of stimulus-response units. The first stimulus is the entrance to the goal box and the first response is entering. Once in the goal box, rats see the food dish and respond by approaching the food dish. At the food dish, they find food and respond by eating. Then, in S-R-S* theories, the stimulus effects of eating provide the S* that reinforces the whole chain that began when the rat left the starting box and includes the right turn at the choice point. This is still a very simplified version of what actually happens, but it is sufficient for the present analysis. Figure 6.3 is a diagram of this simplified version of the behavior chain in a goal box.

According to the goal gradient principle, the first thing a rat learns is to find food in the food dish at the back of the goal box. This is the strongest response. Next the rat learns to go straight to the food dish after entering the goal box; next to enter the goal box, and so on. Placed in the goal box with an empty dish, rats in a latent extinction experiment get immediate and concentrated extinction of the last response, approaching the food dish. Extinction of the anchor point in the chain of responses is the most important factor in extinction. This view of latent extinciton has specific experimental implications.

Several experiments tested for the implications of this bottom-up view of latent extinction (see Coate, 1956; and Kimble, 1961; for detailed reviews). In one type of experiment (Moltz, 1955; Moltz & Maddi, 1956), two groups of rats spent time in the goal box without finding food. One group found the usual food dish in the goal box, but it was empty. The second group found an empty goal box containing

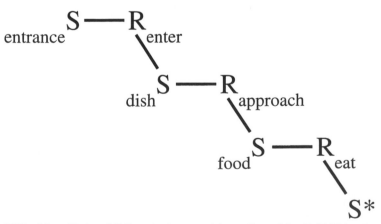

FIG. 6.3. Chain of S-R units in a goal box. Copyright © 1997 by R. Allen Gardner.

neither food nor food dish. The extinction test, running the maze from start to goal without food reward, was carried out in the usual fashion; both groups found the usual food dish, but it was empty. The group that had found an empty food dish in the goal box during preextinction, extinguished the turning response at the choice point much more rapidly. Moltz reasoned that the response of approaching the food dish is what extinguishes in so-called "nonresponse" extinction. In this way, confinement in the goal box with an empty food dish extinguishes the anchor point and weakens the whole chain. If the food dish is absent, a rat cannot extinguish the response of approaching the food dish, which preserves the vital anchor and increases resistance to extinction.

Coate (1956) devised an ethologically more explicit demonstration of the response in nonresponse extinction by constructing a modified Skinner box. In Coate's experiment, the apparatus delivered pellets into a food dish, as usual. Instead of placing the food dish inside the box, however, Coate placed the food dish outside the box. Rats could reach the food by poking their heads through a hole in the wall under the lever. There was a curtain over the hole that prevented the rats from seeing the food before they poked their heads through the curtain. The food magazine, an apparatus that delivered pellets one at a time into the food dish, sounded a distinct click each time it operated.

Coate first conditioned the animals to poke their heads through the hole when they heard the click of the magazine. They could poke their heads through the hole at any time, but they only found food after hearing the click, and soon poked only after a click. Next, Coate trained the rats to press the lever which operated the food magazine on a VI 36 schedule of food reward. During training, the rats pressed the lever at the usual high rate generated by VI 36 schedules; they would stop pressing the lever when they heard the click, then poke their heads through the hole, and then eat the pellets they found in the food dish. After six days of this training, Coate divided the rats into two matched groups on the basis of their rate of lever-pressing during acquisition. That is, performance during acquisition was nearly equal for both groups.

For the next three days, all of the animals received preextinction in the original apparatus with the lever removed to prevent any preextinction of lever-pressing, itself. During preextinction, the experimental group heard the click of the food magazine at roughly the same rate that they had heard it during training, but the magazine never delivered any pellets. The control group spent the same amount of time in the apparatus, but the food magazine never operated and never made a single click when the control group was getting their preextinction. When they heard the clicks, the experimental group poked their heads through the hole, at first, but soon extinguished

TABLE 6.1
Design of Coate's (1956) Preextinction Experiment

	Experimental Group			Control Group		
Magazine Training		Click	Food		Click	Food
Lever Training	Lever	Click	Food	Lever	Click	Food
Preextinction		Click				
Test	Lever	Click		Lever	Click	

that response. Without the stimulus of the click, the control group rarely poked their heads into the hole. Coate then extinguished both groups with the lever present and with the food magazine operating on the VI 36 schedule, but the magazine was empty so that it only made clicks and never delivered pellets. The design of Coate's experiment appears in Table 6.1. The results were clear. The experimental group that received preextinction of the clicks extinguished very rapidly compared to the control group.

Coate's (1956) result together with the results of Moltz (1955) and Moltz and Maddi (1956), who induced latent extinction in a T-maze like Deese's as well as in a straight-alley runway, clearly implicate the response to the food dish as the significant factor in latent extinction. The extinction was latent only when experimenters refused to look at the actual behavior of the living animals. When experimenters like Coate observed and recorded what the animals were doing during latent extinction, they saw manifest rather than latent extinction. Responses to particular stimuli extinguished before their eyes. Coate, Moltz, and Moltz and Maddi all interpreted their results in terms of secondary reward. They reasoned that the food dish in the mazes and the click of the food magazine became secondary or conditioned rewards by association with the food. It is this secondary reward effect that extinguished in nonresponse extinction according to reinforcement theory. Chapter 7 takes up the question of secondary reward and discriminative stimuli in great detail.

Studies of latent extinction stimulated experiments that separated out parts of the chain of responses leading up to reward. Although bottom-up systems had assumed the existence of such chains for a long time, the evidence appeared when the latent learning controversy challenged these assumptions.

DRIVE DISCRIMINATION

Obviously, animals must be able to tell whether they are hungry or thirsty, otherwise they might eat when they were thirsty and drink when they were hungry, which would be clearly maladaptive. That said, what is the role of learning? Can animals learn to go to a particular place to eat when hungry and to a different place to drink when thirsty?

To answer this question, Kendler (1946) deprived rats of both food and water at the same time and gave them equal experience running in both arms of a T-maze. At the end of one arm there was food to eat and at the end of the other there was water to drink. In this phase of the experiment the animals were both hungry and thirsty, but they found food in the goal box on the food side and found water in the goal box on the water side. On 2 test days, Kendler deprived the animals of only one incentive, either food or water on alternate days, and gave them a single test trial on each test day. On thirsty days 98% of them ran to the water side of the maze and on hungry days 73% ran to the food side. Clearly, the animals learned which side had food and which side had water and responded appropriately on test days.

Contingencies were the same on both sides during training because the animals were both hungry and thirsty and received either food or water on every trial. They received reward for going right just as often as they received reward for going left. Contingent reinforcement theory seems to say that they should have gone equally to both sides on the test days. Does Kendler's experiment prove instead that the rats had expectancies or images of food and water in their minds to guide them in their choices? Did cognitive images dance in their heads like visions of sugar plums on the night before Christmas?

The trouble with expectancies is that they are confined to the minds of learners, unobservable by definition and knowable only by their end effects. Kendler attributed his results, instead, to anticipatory responses and *response-produced stimuli* that were observable in principle, although they had not yet been observed when he wrote.

During the training phase of Kendler's experiment, the rats always ate in the goal box at the end of one arm of the T-maze and drank in the goal box at the end of the other arm. Kendler reasoned that *prefeeding responses,* like salivation, became conditioned to stimuli in the arm on the food side and *predrinking responses,* like licking, became conditioned to stimuli in the arm of the water side. Anticipatory eating and drinking responses like all responses must themselves produce stimuli which become part of the stimulus complex in each arm. These are the response-produced stimuli discussed in chapter 4 and earlier in this chapter and illustrated in Figs. 4.3 through 4.6 and Figs. 6.1 and 6.3. When the animals ran in the food arm, they experienced the stimulus complex of the food arm of the maze plus stimuli produced by prefeeding. When they ran in the water arm, they experienced the stimulus complex of the water arm plus stimuli produced by predrinking.

During the test phase of Kendler's experiment, hunger made prefeeding responses more likely on hungry days and thirst made predrinking responses more likely on thirsty days. As a result, when the animals found themselves at the choice point on hungry days, prefeeding responses evoked stimuli for running in the food arm, while on thirsty days predrinking responses evoked stimuli for running in the water arm. Notice that this is a bottom-up, feed forward principle. Hunger evokes prefeeding and thirst evokes predrinking.

The alternative, as usual, is cognitive expectancy. Animals ran to the food side when they were hungry because they had learned to expect food there. They ran to the water side when they were thirsty because they had learned to expect water there. This is the same as saying that the animals learned to go to the food side because they learned to go to the food side, and likewise, that they learned to go to the water side because they learned to go to the water side. As usual, cognitive expectancy only restates the results of the experiment after the results are in. At the time, the trouble with Kendler's line of reasoning was that anticipatory eating and drinking responses in the arms of a T-maze existed only as conjectures in Hull's theory. They had never been observed in any experiment. Unlike the expectancies of Tolman's theory, however, anticipatory eating and drinking are in principle observable.

Deaux and Patten (1964) used the device in Fig. 6.4 to observe predrinking responses directly as rats ran freely through a straight-alley runway.

At first, as Fig. 6.5 shows, the rats licked the tube at roughly the same low rate in all segments of the alley. In later trials, however, they licked more, and as they ran, the closer they came to the goal box the more they licked just as Hull and Kendler predicted many years earlier. The curves in Fig. 6.5 directly confirm Hull's and Kendler's conjecture about anticipatory responses conditioned to stimuli that regularly appear before an S*. Deaux and Patten's findings confirm by direct observation the chains of stimuli and responses discussed in chapter 4 and earlier in this chapter and illustrated in Figs. 4.3 through 4.6 and Figs. 6.1 and 6.3. Cognitive expectancies remain unobserved.

Other modern, ethologically rich observations of behavior in the Skinner box also confirm the existence of fractional anticipatory responses. Using high-speed motion picture photography and video-tape of pigeons in a Skinner box, Jenkins and Moore (1973) recorded the precise form of each key-pecking response. Sometimes the pigeons in this experiment were deprived of food and rewarded with grain,

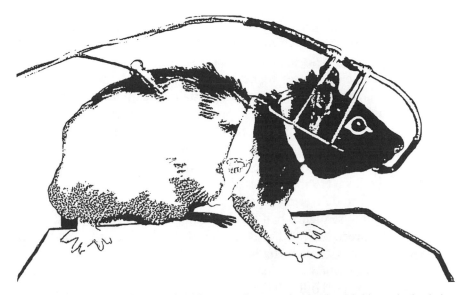

FIG. 6.4. Rats in Deaux and Patten (1964) wore a harness that held a drinking tube in their mouths. Each lick at the end of the tube activated an electronic device called a lickometer, which recorded all licks, but delivered water only when the rat was in the goal box. Copyright © 1964 by Psychonomic Society, Inc. Adapted by permission.

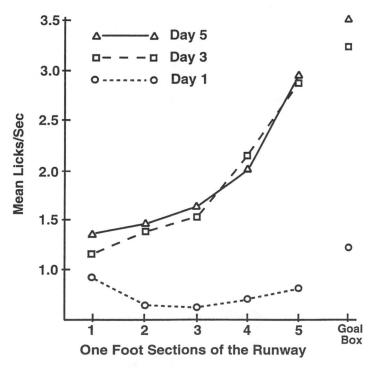

FIG. 6.5. Anticipatory licking in a runway. From Deaux and Patten (1964). Copyright © 1964 by Psychonomic Society, Inc. Adapted by permission.

and sometimes they were deprived of water and rewarded with water. Jenkins and Moore found that, when pecking the key for grain, pigeons held their beaks in a shape and pecked with a force related to the responses made in eating grain. At the same time they found that key-pecking for water partially resembled drinking. This is exactly what should happen if prefeeding becomes conditioned to a key in the Skinner box that regularly precedes eating, and predrinking becomes conditioned to a key that regularly precedes drinking.

In a series of experiments described in detail in chapter 8, Timberlake (1983) delivered a small steel ball into a Skinner box just before delivering a pellet of food or a drop of water. After repetition of the sequence ball-food or ball-water, his rats handled the ball when it preceded food and mouthed it when it preceded water with responses that partially resembled their responses to the food or the water when these came.

J. H. Hull (1977) made videotape records of rats pressing levers; sometimes Hull deprived the rats of food and rewarded them with pellets of food and sometimes he deprived them of water and rewarded them with drops of water. The tapes showed frontal views of the rats pressing the levers, but the animals were out of view when they lowered their heads to eat or drink their rewards. After watching live rats eat and drink, six students viewed the tapes and judged when the experimental rats were pressing for food and when for water. The inexperienced students were correct in 96% of their judgments. Clearly, stimuli that regularly precede S* in instrumental conditioning evoke distinctive *fractional anticipatory responses,* and animals incorporate these anticipatory responses into instrumental behavior such as running in mazes, pecking keys, and pressing levers (see also J. H. Hull, Bartlett, & Hill, 1981).

CONDITIONED REJECTION

Fractional anticipatory responses also play a role in avoiding poisons. Poisonous plants and animals taste bad, usually bitter. It is a good defense against predators. Usually, poisonous plants and animals also look conspicuous. Fiery reds are common and so are showy patterns like the distinctive orange and black wings of the Monarch butterfly. Monarch butterflies eat milkweed plants, which contain a cardiac poison. Birds will die of cardiac arrest if they eat too much Monarch butterfly. Fortunately, the poison tastes so bad that they usually spit out the first mouthful and vomit up anything they may have swallowed. Just the taste of the wings as the bird first catches a Monarch is so bad that birds usually quit right there and release the victim.

This is a better defense than killing a predator with poison. First, many Monarchs escape with minor injury that way. More important, the last thing that a bird sees as it spits out whatever got into its mouth is the orange and black pattern of Monarch wings. The next time that bird sees the same distinctive stimulus, it spits before it bites, or perhaps it hesitates just long enough for a Monarch to escape (Brower, 1984, 1988). In this way, one taste of one Monarch defends many other Monarchs from that bird. Death would accomplish the same thing, of course, but a live bird feeds on other species of bugs that often compete with Monarchs for food. That bird also competes with other birds that prey on Monarchs. Thus, a live predator that has been conditioned to reject Monarchs is better than a dead predator, for the overall survival of Monarchs.

Conditioned rejection is also good for the overall survival of the predator. If poisonous food has a distinctive taste, an animal can spit it out immediately without serious consequences. If poisonous food also looks or smells distinctively different from other foods, an animal can learn to reject it before retasting it. Viceroy butterfies are a different species from Monarchs that have very similar orange and black patterns on their wings. Brower also demonstrated that birds that had tasted a single Monarch in the laboratory not only rejected all other Monarchs but also rejected Viceroys.

Sooner is better than later for conditioned rejection. Extended trials of repeated experience to build up statistical contingencies of reinforcement or expectancy would cost animals more discomfort and more danger of serious consequences than immediate conditioning in a single trial.

In an extensive series of laboratory studies of conditioned *taste aversion,* experimenters have made rats sick with poisons, usually lithium chloride, and experimentally paired poisoning with an innocuous novel taste such as water sweetened with saccharine. After recovering from the illness, rats get a choice between two water bottles, one with the experimental flavor and the other with plain water or with a control flavor. Conditioned rats drink dramatically less of the experimental flavor. Only one trial is sufficient for this form of conditioned rejection. In agreement with the evidence on single trial conditioning in chapter 4, temporal relations between the CS and the UCS are much more variable than expected from traditional Pavlovian principles (Domjan, 1980).

Most early studies of conditioned taste aversion only measured the amount that the rats drank from the experimental and control drinking bottles. Modern studies take advantage of inexpensive videotape recording to observe what the animals actually do when they reject fluids

(Meachum & Bernstein, 1990; Parker, 1988; Parker, Hills, & Jensen, 1984; Zalaquette & Parker, 1989). Usually, experimenters administer poison directly by intraperitoneal injection. The resulting illness evokes characteristic behavior in rats, such as rubbing their bellies on the ground or stretching their limbs. These are unconditioned responses to this sort of poisoning. Later, the experimental flavors evoke fractions of these unconditioned responses including responses that are appropriate to a poisonous taste in the mouth, such as rubbing their chins against the floor or gaping their mouths open; these are conditioned responses to otherwise innocuous flavors. It is easy to see how these conditioned responses reduce drinking so dramatically. Modern ethological observations certainly vindicate Kendler's and Hull's early conjecture that choices depend on anticipatory responses to food and water that appear before actual eating or drinking.

Before the current movement to study conditioned rejection through direct observation, Rescorla (1987) proposed a return to traditional cogntive speculation. Where Deese (1951) rewarded rats in the goal box for turning right or left in a T-maze, Colwill and Rescorla (1985a, 1985b, 1986) rewarded rats for pressing levers or for pulling chains in a modified Skinner box. They rewarded one response, either lever-pressing or chain-pulling, with saccharine-flavored food pellets and rewarded the other response with ordinary food pellets. Then, instead of nonresponse extinction as in Deese (1951), they paired the saccharine flavor with lithium poisoning. In an extinction test conducted after poisoning, the rats markedly reduced either lever-pressing or chain-pulling, depending on which had formerly earned saccharine-flavored pellets. Just as Deese attributed nonresponse extinction in a T-maze to loss of cognitive expectancy in the goal box, Rescorla (1987) attributed selective extinction after poisoning to a cognitive factor called "devaluation."

Rescorla's (1987) analysis depends entirely on Skinner's (1938) distinction between elicited and emitted responses. There Skinner (1938, p. 20) maintained that in classical conditioning, which he renamed *Type S* or *respondent conditioning,* there is always a stimulus, UCS, that initially *elicits* a particular response, UCR. In instrumental conditioning, on the other hand, responses such as pressing a lever seemed to Skinner to appear spontaneously—to be *emitted* without an initiating stimulus. He renamed this *Type R* or *operant conditioning.* Skinner argued throughout his long life that, if operant responses are emitted, then the proper formula for contingent reinforcement is R-S* rather than S-R-S*. Rescorla's version of this principle is: "According to this third view . . . the basic structure of instrumental learning is response-reinforcer [that is, R-S*] in nature" (1987, p. 120).

In a long life of writing on this subject, Skinner offered only one argument to support his R-S* formula for instrumental conditioning. This was his personal inability to identify or even to imagine a stimulus for lever-pressing or key-pecking. For decades his followers subscribed to this view without producing any other evidence. In scientific circles this is called the argument from "lack of imagination." In this case, there cannot be a stimulus for the response in instrumental conditioning because B. F. Skinner and his followers cannot imagine such a thing. As most readers should know, the history of modern science is largely a history of discoveries that were once beyond the imagination of innumerable learned, even distinguished, scholars.

In the case of the R-S* formula, plain facts must replace Skinner's imagination. Rats do not press the air in the Skinner box; they press the lever. Pigeons do not peck the air in the Skinner box either; they peck the key. Taken literally, the R-S* formula implies that pressing and pecking randomly increase with reinforcement and only lead to lever-pressing and key-pecking accidentally when these stimulus-independent responses happen to engage the levers or keys of an operant conditioning chamber.

In the case of the Colwill and Rescorla experiments, the R-S* formula implies that rats emit lever-pressing and chain-pulling into the air and these responses engage the lever or the chain, adventitiously. Clearly, rats respond to levers by pressing and to chains by pulling. This is impossible unless levers and chains have stimulus differences. Colwill and Rescorla (1986) attempted to answer this objection with a Skinner box that contained neither a chain nor a lever, but only a single rod suspended from the ceiling. For half of the rats in this experiment, pushing the rod to the right earned saccharine-flavored rewards and pushing it to the left earned unflavored rewards. For the other half the left–right contingency was reversed. After the experimenters paired saccharine with lithium chloride, the rats markedly reduced either the right or the left movement of the rod, whichever had earned saccharine-flavored rewards. Colwill and Rescorla argued that there was only one stimulus, the single rod, that could precede right and left pushes; hence their results implicate an R-S* formula rather than an S-R-S* formula.

Like their lever-pressing versus chain-pulling experiments, the single-rod experiment of Colwill and Rescorla (1986) demands that the rats emit right and left pushing responses at random and only engage the rod by chance. After the alleged cognitive devaluation of saccharine by pairing with lithium chloride, the rats emit less of one response than the other. This blinkered view may appeal to experimenters who refuse to look at the rats in the box while they theorize about increases and decreases in a single index of response. Worse still, this restrictive view cannot cope with sequential behavior. Applying the R-S* formula to experiments with single-unit T-mazes like Kendler (1946) or Deese (1951), we have to say that there is only one stimulus, the single choice point, and rats make correct choices by emitting either right or left turns at that single choice point. But, what can we say of mazes with multiple sequences of choice points as in Tolman and Honzik (1930), shown in Fig. 5.6. Rats cannot respond correctly in a maze with a sequence of choice points if they only learn one response for one type of reward as in the R-S* formula. The only way that they can learn to go to the right at certain choice points and to the left at certain others is by responding to stimulus differences that distinguish one choice point from another. The R-S* formula is trapped in the Skinner box and cannot cope with the vast amount of animal behavior that involves sequences of appropriately different responses to different stimuli.

In the case of conditioned taste aversion, conditioned rats continue to drink. They even continue to drink from drinking bottles that are identical to the drinking bottles that they reject. They only reject drinking bottles that taste of the experimentally flavored liquid. Birds that have tasted Monarch butterflies continue to attack and to eat butterflies. They only reject butterflies that look like Monarchs. Perhaps the most characteristic feature of conditioned rejection is that it is stimulus specific.

Rescorla's (1987) analysis of conditioned taste aversion is a return to Skinner's (1938) behaviorism and Deese's (1951) cognitivism. This is an honorable tradition that continues to attract supporters. This book would rather point readers toward modern ethological and ecological studies of taste aversion. With inexpensive videotape recording, experimenters can look into the conditioning chamber and observe what the animals are doing. They can supplement a traditional single index like lever-pressing or key-pecking with rich descriptions of ongoing behavior. They can discover new patterns of behavior and open up the field to new interpretations of earlier research. For example, by watching the animals she injected with different poisons, Parker (1993, 1996) found different patterns of response to injection, to the place paired with injection, and to the taste paired with injection. She also found different patterns of response that depended on whether the drug was a nauseating emetic like lithium chloride or a psychoactive drug like lysergic acid diethylamide (LSD). Parker also showed how ethological patterns of response have significant implications for human problems such as anorexia and drug addiction.

SUMMARY

Modern ethological observations reveal that fractional anticipatory responses play a vital role in common forms of sequential behavior. Unlike the hypothetical mechanisms of reinforcement and cognition, fractional anticipatory responses appear in direct observations of actual animals. Detailed observations of reward and extinction in T-mazes, runways, and Skinner boxes as well as conditioned rejection of poisons show the same pattern of conditioned anticipatory responses.

These direct ethological observations contradict the traditional view that classical and instrumental conditioning represent distinctly different forms of conditioning. Clearly, instrumental conditioning is impossible without regularly repeating sequences of stimuli and responses followed by an S*. A distinctive arbitrary stimulus, S^a, always precedes the S* at the end of a chain of instrumental responses and this pairing of S^a and S* plays a vital role in instrumental conditioning (Bolles, 1988; Plonsky, Driscoll, Warren, & Rosellini, 1984). This vital pairing also satisfies the defining operations of classical conditioning. Instrumental conditioning is impossible without the defining experimental operations of classical conditioning.

Apart from procedural differences, is there any value to the traditional distinction betweeen classical and instrumental conditioning? The next chapters pursue this question as it arises in the study of several basic phenomena of conditioning and learning.

CHAPTER 7

Feed Forward Versus Feed Backward

The typical reader of this book is a human being who hopes to learn something by reading it. Human readers are seldom hungry or thirsty when they read and learn. Eating and drinking during reading is more likely to distract than to fix human attention on a book. The traditional experiment on rat or pigeon learning submits the learners to severe deprivation to make them hungry or thirsty and rewards their primary needs with food or water. Meanwhile, human beings learn a great deal every day without any deprivation of food or water or any other *primary need* and without immediate, or even prompt, *primary reward*. Indeed, human beings probably learn better when they are comfortable and well fed. Rats and pigeons, dogs and cats, not to mention cows and horses, and pigs and chickens, learn all sorts of things without being hungry and without prompt primary reward. What could the traditional theory of learning by contingent reinforcement possibly have to do with the bulk of human and nonhuman animal learning?

The traditional answer to this question is the claim that there are secondary or conditioned rewards, such as money and praise, that serve as surrogates for primary rewards, such as food and drink, as a result of past association. Without experimental evidence to support this claim, the traditional theory is irrelevant to most of the learning of live human and nonhuman beings. The purpose of this chapter is to take a hard look at the experimental evidence for this claim.

OPERATIONAL DEFINITION

As chapter 5 showed, decades of debates and experiments on the question of latent learning failed to produce an operational definition of S*, the foundation concept of the *law of effect*. In the course of the dispute, it became clear that whenever animals learned, reinforcement theorists could find an S* that reinforced the learning—but only post hoc, after the fact. At the same time, whenever reinforcement theorists found an S* that could reinforce learning, cognitive theorists easily reinterpreted it as an incentive that governed performance rather than learning. Both contingent reinforcement and cognitive expectancy share the same post hoc position. Perhaps, the following example explains why post hoc explanations are unacceptable in modern sciences.

Suppose that you met a distinguished psychologist who specialized in the theory of coin behavior. Suppose that the coin psychologist invited you to toss a coin and then predicted that the coin would land with its head up or its tail up, unless it happened to balance on its edge. Every time the coin landed head up, the coin psychologist could explain that this meant that the coin wanted to land head up more than tail up. Every time the coin landed tail up, the coin psychologist could explain that this meant that the coin wanted to land tail up more than head up. It might take many tries before the coin balanced on its edge, but when it did the coin psychologist could explain that this meant that the coin wanted both head and tail up equally. Clearly, you could not win any bets with the help of coin psychology, because the theory never tells you anything in advance.

You might argue that everyone knows that coins cannot have wants. Suppose we humored you on this (you really have no proof; it is just an assumption) and asked you how you know that food-deprived rats want to eat food. If you answered that you know that they want to eat food because they eat it, and that when they stop eating food that means that they stopped wanting to eat, you would be agreeing with traditional cognitive psychology, but your theory would be exactly the same as the theory of coin psychology. You would be saying that the animal must have wanted to eat, because it ate. This is why both hedonistic reinforcement theories and hedonistic cognitive theories must find an operational definition of pleasure and pain. Otherwise, they tell us nothing in advance, like the coin psychologist.

The notion of reward and punishment as a principle of learning appears throughout the history of Western civilization, since biblical times at least. The *law of effect* is so ancient and so deeply ingrained in Western culture that many readers will be surprised to find that it has ever been questioned. Progress in modern science largely depends on demanding evidence in place of faith in tradition.

The first formal expression of the modern law of effect appears in the writings of Thorndike.

> The Law of Effect is that: Of several responses made to the same situation, those which are accompanied or closely followed by satisfaction to the animal will, other things being equal, be more firmly connected with the situation, so that, when it recurs, they will be more likely to recur; those which are accompanied or closely followed by discomfort to the animal will, other things being equal, have their connections with that situation weakened, so that, when it recurs, they will be less likely to occur. The greater the satisfaction or discomfort, the greater the strengthening or weakening of the bond. (1911, p. 244)

This is the commonsense view that pleasing consequences strengthen responses and displeasing consequences weaken responses. More recent statements of this principle differ chiefly in substituting other terms (reward, reinforcement, drive-reduction, homeostasis) for satisfaction and annoyance.

There have been many attempts to find an operational definition of satisfaction and annoyance. Thorndike tried the following: "By satisfying state of affairs is meant one which the animal does nothing to avoid, often doing such things as to attain and preserve it. By a discomforting or annoying state of affairs is meant one which the animal commonly avoids and abandons" (1911, p. 245).

Other definitions emphasized the tension-reducing character of reinforcement. They pointed out that an animal in a problem box or maze is aroused, restless, hypertensive, until food appears. After ingesting food, an animal becomes relaxed and quiescent. Many writers have described the end of goal activity to be the reaching of a state of "complacency" similar to that which Cannon (1932) called "homeostasis." T. L. McCulloch (1939) proposed that reward may be effective because it causes the disappearance of restless, excited behavior. C. L. Hull's principle of drive-reduction is similar.

So far all attempts at operational definition have failed. The following definition written by Morse and Kelleher (1977) is typical. Note that this definition appeared in the *Handbook of Operant Behavior,* considered one of the most authoritative reference books in the Skinnerian (also called behaviorist) tradition:

The increased occurrence of responses similar to one that immediately preceded some event identifies that event as a *reinforcer* ... the decreased occurrence of responses similar to one that immediately preceded some event identifies that event as a *punisher* ... There is no concept that predicts reliably when events will be reinforcers or punishers; the defining characteristics of reinforcers and punishers are how they change behavior. Events that increase or decrease the subsequent occurrence of one response may not modify other responses in the same way. (p. 176)

With this statement, Morse and Kelleher seem to concede (a) that it is impossible to say in advance which events will reinforce or punish which responses, and (b) worse still, that the reinforcing effect of any particular event on any particular response may or may not predict the effect of that same event on a different response. In other words, all that the language of reinforcement theory has to offer is names for things that we know already, as in coin psychology.

The basic lack of an operational definition of primary reinforcement is sometimes obscured by describing an S* as a "biologically significant stimulus." This seems obviously true in cases where hungry animals receive pellets of food, but what about the latent learning experiments in which rats seemed to learn the path to the goal box for the reinforcement of being taken out of the maze?

There are other interesting cases. Kish (1955), for example, reported the first of a series of experiments demonstrating that mice pressed a lever more when the only contingent stimulus was a brief lighting of a lamp. When the response failed to change the light, extinction set in. Kish and others (J. F. Hall, 1976, pp. 238–239; Kimble, 1961, pp. 254–256; Kish, 1966; Osborne & Shelby, 1975) called this *stimulus change reinforcement* because either light on or light off increased lever-pressing. All this tells us, however, is that light change must have been a reinforcer because lever-pressing increased. Without some independent way of specifying in advance which effects will be reinforcing and which will not, this circularity must continue.

Reports that direct *brain stimulation* reinforces lever-pressing and maze-running are supposed to prove that there are specific *pleasure centers* in the brain. This is the same sort of post hoc reasoning. How could anyone have known that these consequences reinforce before they saw the experimental results? And, what good does it do if someone tells us that these are cases of reinforcement after we already know that the rats learned? This chapter considers how the concept of secondary or conditioned reward can offer an experimental way out of this problem. The next section of this chapter looks at the operational definition of secondary reward.

DEFINING SECONDARY REWARD

Even though the operational definition of primary reinforcement may always elude us, *secondary* or *conditioned reward* may be easier to define in terms of experimental operations. The following typical definition appears in Hulse, Egeth, and Deese (1980), a highly respected review of this field:

> A conditioned reinforcer is a neutral stimulus that acquires the functional properties of a primary reinforcer by being paired with a primary reinforcer or with another conditioned reinforcer . . . conditioned reinforcers are stimuli that acquire the power to reinforce by being paired with other stimuli that already possess the power to reinforce (p. 52). (Note that Hulse et al. uses the term *neutral stimulus* where this book uses the term *arbitrary stimulus*.)

Actual experiments can fulfill this definition without defining primary reward in advance. All we need is agreement that a particular stimulus has the power of primary reinforcement. This has always been easy. Everyone who believes in primary reinforcement agrees that food is a primary reward for lever-pressing. Given that agreement, we can pair an arbitrary stimulus, S^a, with food and then test whether this S^a then functions as a secondary reward, S^r. Now we have an operational definition of secondary reinforcement. With this definition we can find out whether there is indeed a class of phenomena that fit this definition or whether, instead, the definition specifies a scientifically empty class, like unicorns.

Before reviewing the evidence, consider why the Hulse et al. definition is both typical of all published definitions of secondary reward and also why it is the only possible definition of secondary reward. To begin with, a primary reward must be a stimulus. This is true because the only way that information enters a nervous system is in the form of stimuli or inputs. Consequently, the only way that a nervous system can tell that it has been reinforced is by receiving a reinforcing stimulus.

The fact that the actual reinforcing stimulus often originates inside the animal may obscure this slightly. Dryness of the throat and salinity of the blood are signals of thirst. Levels of sugar in the blood and contractions of the stomach are signals of hunger. The basis of primary reinforcement must be sensory, even if the sensors are monitoring conditions inside the animal.

To serve as a surrogate for primary reward, a secondary reward must also be a stimulus. If the secondary reward acquires its surrogate power by conditioning, it must be by S-S* conditioning—that is, by Pavlovian higher order conditioning. The trouble with this source of secondary reward is the evidence reviewed in chapter 4 that Pavlovian higher order conditioning is difficult to establish in experiments and also weak and easily extinguished. This chapter describes the parallel problem with experimental attempts to fulfill the operational definition of secondary reward.

Magazine Clicks

The following experiment by Bugelski (1938) is often cited as evidence for secondary reward in the Skinner box. Bugelski first rewarded rats with food pellets for lever-pressing. Then he divided the animals into two groups for extinction. For both groups the food magazine, the device that holds the pellets and drops them into the food dish, was empty during extinction. Bugelski extinguished the experimental group with the lever still wired to the food magazine so that the magazine continued to operate making its usual audible clicks without delivering any pellets. Bugelski extinguished the control group with the lever disconnected from the magazine so that they received neither clicks nor pellets when they pressed the lever. The experimental group made many more responses under extinction than the control group. Since the test was conducted without any primary reward, the clicks alone must have maintained performance. Is this evidence for secondary reward?

Although some textbooks continued to cite Bugelski (1938) as evidence for secondary reward right up to the 1990s (e.g., Schwartz & Reisberg, 1991, p. 154), most modern critics reject this evidence for the following reason. The Bugelski experiment only demonstrates transfer from one stimulus situation to another. All things being equal, transfer from a training situation to a testing situation depends on the similarity between training and testing conditions. College students, for example, who memorize a list of words in one room recall more of the words on the list when tested later in the same room than when tested in a different room. Similarly, rats conditioned to press a lever in one Skinner box in one room make more responses in an extinction test carried out in the same box and the same room, than in a test carried out in a different box in a different room. If there is a special light in the box and it is lighted during training, then there are more responses in an extinction test carried out with the light on than with the light off (Thomas & Morrison, 1994). In the Bugelski experiment, the clicks are part of the stimulus situation during training. Therefore, we must expect more responses during extinction with clicks than without clicks based on stimulus transfer whether or not there is any such thing as secondary reward.

The Bugelski (1938) experiment fails to demonstrate secondary reward for a significant reason. The clicks in this experiment only *maintain* responding in extinction, but secondary rewards must *reinforce* new learning. Consequently, the only appropriate test is one in which the secondary reward acquired in one learning situation reinforces new responses in a new situation. Once again, the discipline of operational definition reveals critical implications of a scientific notion

New Learning

Saltzman (1949) was the first experiment that fulfilled the defining operations of secondary reward. Saltzman's apparatus consisted of two separate parts, a straight alley and a single-unit U-maze as shown in Fig. 7.1. The purpose of the straight alley was to establish a distinctive goal box as a secondary reward, by associating it with food in Phase I. The purpose of the U-maze was to measure the secondary reward value of the distinctive goal box as the only incentive for new learning in Phase II.

In Phase I, all rats found food in one of two distinctive goal boxes at the end of the straight alley. One goal box was painted black and the rats had to climb over a low hurdle to enter it. The other goal box was painted white and the rats had to climb down to a lower level to enter it. Two groups, the continuous reward group and the control group, received exactly the same treatment during Phase I. Over a 5-day period they found food in the same distinctive goal box, either the black one or the white one, on every trial for 25 trials. A third group, the partial reward group, also received 25 rewarded trials during Phase I, but, in addition, they received 14 nonrewarded trials in the same distinctive goal box. These nonrewarded trials appeared haphazardly in the series but were always preceded and followed by a rewarded trial. A fourth group, the differential reward group, received the same treatment as the partial reward group except that on all rewarded trials the food was in one of the distinctive goal boxes, either the black one or the white one, and on all nonrewarded trials they were detained briefly in the other distinctive box.

In Phase II, all of the rats received 15 test trials in the U-maze. All groups except the control group found the black goal box at the end of one arm of the U-maze and the white goal box at the end of the other. This was counterbalanced so that the goal box associated with reward in Phase I was at the end of the left arm for half of the

Phase I
Runway

Phase II
Maze

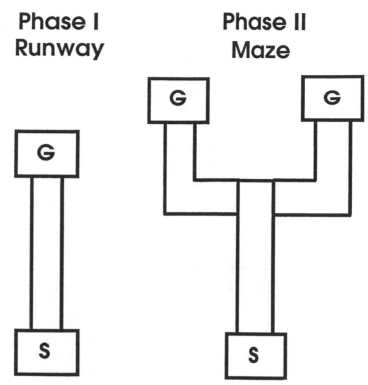

FIG. 7.1. Typical apparatus used in demonstrations of secondary reward. Rats run first to distinctive goal boxes in the runway, next to the same goal boxes in the U-maze. S indicates start boxes; G indicates goal boxes. Copyright © 1997 by R. Allen Gardner.

animals and at the end of the right arm for the other half. The control group found one of two new identical gray goal boxes at the end of each arm of the U-maze. The animals in the experimental groups never received any food during Phase II. Their only incentive for choosing one arm or the other of the U-maze was to get to the goal box that had contained food during Phase I. The control group found food in one of the new gray boxes in one arm or the other of the U-maze; for half of the animals this was the left arm and for the other half this was the right arm.

The U-shape of the maze prevented the animals from seeing either of the distinctive goal boxes until after they made their choice. Experimenters frequently use U-mazes for this purpose. Gates were lowered behind the animals to prevent retracing.

The Saltzman experiment fulfills the operational definition of secondary reward. During Phase I, an S^a was associated with an S^*. During Phase II, the animals learned a new response in a new apparatus without any primary reward, so the only possible source of reinforcement was the S^a.

Results were as follows. In the 15 trials of Phase II, the control group was rewarded with food in fresh new goal boxes and chose the rewarded side on an average of 10.0 trials. The continuous, partial, and differential reward groups chose the side leading to the goal box in which they had received reward during Phase I on an average of 8.3, 9.0, and 10.7 trials, respectively. Since there were 15 trials in all, and since the U-maze is a two-choice situation, the average level of choice expected by chance would be one half of 15 or 7.5. Other experimenters have replicated the general results of Saltzman's (1949) experiment, although some have failed to replicate them. In general, however, a good argument for a weak positive result can be sustained from the existing evidence (see J. F. Hall, 1976, pp. 246–254, for an extensive review).

You might at first suppose that, if the experimental groups were learning the correct path in the U-maze because they were secondarily rewarded by the distinctive goal box, they could easily have improved further and raised their performance higher above chance, if only Saltzman had given them more trials. The reason that Saltzman and others ended the experimental tests when they did, however, was that the secondarily rewarded rats were showing signs of extinction. Performance was declining rather than improving. This is a problem that cannot be avoided because tests of the power of secondary reward to reinforce new learning must be carried out without any primary reward.

The principle of secondary reward supports a heavy burden in response reinforcement theories. It is supposed to account for the bulk of human learning as well as a huge amount of learning by nonhuman beings, which also occurs without any primary reward. Secondary reward is supposed to account for the value of money and prestige, love of home and love of country. Secondary rewards, such as money, are supposed to be more powerful and more resistant to extinction than food and water. How can secondary reward that is too weak to support robust amounts of behavior in the Saltzman type of experiment carry the immense theoretical load assigned to it in reinforcement theories? Evidence for secondary reinforcement must be strong, precisely under extinction conditions. Chapter 4 already considered a similar requirement and a similar failure of evidence for higher-order conditioning.

Partial Reward

Zimmerman (1957, 1959) proposed that the problem was one of weak resistance to extinction after 100% reinforcement. He reasoned that other demonstrations of secondary reward found weak evidence because they failed to use Skinnerian schedules of reinforcement. Since schedules of partial primary reward generate much higher rates of responding and much greater resistance to extinction, they should generate more robust effects of secondary reward.

Zimmerman's (1957) demonstration used a procedure like the one in Coate (1956). Chapter 6 describes how Coate designed a special Skinner box to measure lever-pressing and food-finding separately. Coate's apparatus delivered food pellets into a dish that was outside of the box. Rats reached the food by poking their heads through a hole in the wall of the box. There was a curtain over the hole so that the rats could not see the food until they poked their heads through the curtain.

Using a similar apparatus, Zimmerman first trained rats to find water by putting their heads through an opening in the box when they heard a buzzer. There was no lever in the box during this phase of the experiment. To discourage the animals from waiting near the opening, Zimmerman sounded the buzzer only when they were in some other part of the box. Soon the rats rushed to the opening as soon as they heard the buzzer. Next, he set the mechanism so that it delivered water only half the time when the buzzer sounded, but haphazardly so that the rats could not tell in advance when they would find water. The animals continued to rush to the water opening every time they heard the buzzer. Gradually, Zimmerman increased the ratio to 10 buzzes for each water reward. The animals continued to rush to the watering place every time they heard the buzzer.

In Phase II of this demonstration, Zimmerman introduced a lever into the box for the first time, and wired the lever to the mechanism in such a way that each lever-press sounded the buzzer although the rat only found water once on the average for every 10 buzzes. The animals soon began to press the lever and then go to the opening when they heard the buzzer. Gradually, Zimmerman increased the requirement so that the rats had to press the lever more and more times before they heard the buzzer. As in the case of the buzzer, he required a variable and random number of presses for each buzz. Eventually, the animals were pressing the lever an average of 10 times for each time that the buzzer sounded. Water followed the buzzer after 1 out of 10 buzzes, so the rats were pressing the lever about 100 times for every tiny drink that they got. They also demonstrated robust resistance to extinction. Reasoning that the buzzer was secondarily reinforcing lever-pressing, Zimmerman concluded that partial primary reinforcement could generate robust amounts of secondary reinforcement.

That delivering rewards for a fraction of the responses rather than for every response generates higher rates of responding and greater resistance to extinction, is probably the most well-documented phenomenon in all of experimental psychology. But this is the opposite of what should happen if rewards such as food reinforce responses such as lever-pressing. That is, if food reinforces lever-pressing, how is it possible for 10% reinforcement to be more reinforcing than 100% reinforcement? If the buzzer acquires its secondary reinforcing power by association with food, then how could a buzzer that was paired with food only 10% of the time acquire more power than Saltzman's distinctive goal boxes that were paired with food 100% of the time? This additional demonstration that partial reward is more reinforcing than 100% reward is actually an additional embarrassment to reinforcement theory.

This is a good place to point out the advantages of referring to the food, water, and other commodities dispensed in these experiments as rewards rather than as reinforcements. The statement that 10% reinforcement is more reinforcing than 100% reinforcement is a contradiction in terms. This useage "does violence to language" because it uses the same word in two contradictory senses in the same argument. Using words in this way can only lead to confusion. Distinguishing between rewards and their theoretical reinforcing effect avoids the problem. In this book commodities such as food, water, and so on, that the experimenter delivers are *rewards* and the effect of rewards on learning is *reinforcement*.

It is illogical to say that fewer reinforcements are more reinforcing than more reinforcements, but it is logically possible for fewer rewards to be more reinforcing than more rewards. The argument that reward refers to the intentions of the trainer and reinforcement refers to what happens to the trainee, favors the terminology used in this book. By separating rewards—what the experimenter does that is contingent on what the animal does—from reinforcement—the theoretical effect of what the experimenter does—we can evaluate the theory objectively.

Zimmerman's (1959) demonstration carried his argument a step further. The apparatus in the second demonstration appears in Fig. 7.2. It consisted of a 9-inch-square starting box with a 4-inch-wide door that opened onto a 40-inch-long alley which ended in another door that opened into a 4-inch by 12-inch goal box. In Phase I, the

FIG. 7.2. Apparatus used by Zimmerman (1959). Copyright © 1997 by R. Allen Gardner.

rats first found food in the goal box after running from the start box through the alley to reach the goal box. Next, Zimmerman kept the door leading from the start box to the alley closed until he sounded a buzzer. At that point, the start box door opened and the rats could run through the alley to the goal box. At first, they found food in the goal box on every trial, but later Zimmerman reduced the schedule to the point where they found food less than one out of every four times that they got to the goal box.

In Phase II, Zimmerman introduced a lever into the start box and never again put any food in the goal box. Thus, the animals had to learn to press the lever for secondary reward without any primary reward. Now Zimmerman arranged the contingencies so that when a rat pressed the lever, the buzzer sounded and the start box door opened. The rats quickly learned to press the lever and then ran out into the alley as before. Gradually, Zimmerman raised the ratio of responses to buzzes to 20 to 1 (FR 20).

Zimmerman found that the animals pressed the lever at high rates that are quite comparable to rates found in similar experiments when the apparatus delivers primary food rewards. But they never received any food reward for pressing the lever. Indeed, they only received the buzzer as a secondary reward for 1 out of every 20 times that they pressed the lever.

Zimmerman (1959) included two important control groups. Control 1 received the same treatment as the experimental group during both Phase I and Phase II, with one exception. The buzzer never sounded during Phase II. Control 2 received the same treatment as the experimental group during Phase II, including the buzzer, but they received no treatment at all during Phase I. That is, they never found any food in the goal box at the end of the alley.

These two control groups served an essential function. Rats and many other animals tend to explore new openings. A very effective type of mouse trap consists of an opening into a mouse-sized tunnel. Mice that enter the tunnel are trapped there. It is a very effective trap with the attraction of the open tunnel as the only bait. The opportunity to run through the door and explore the runway could have been rewarding all by itself. Because the control groups also ran out into the alley, they controlled for the effect of opening a door and letting rats run into an alley. The control groups did press the lever but much less than the experimental group. Even if a run in the alley was a primary reward, the experimental group still pressed the lever much more than control rats that only received that primary reward.

Zimmerman interpreted his 1957 experiment as a demonstration of the power of partial secondary reward. Zimmerman (1959) reported another result that alters this interpretation, however. The response of running in the alley extinguished during acquisition of the response of pressing the lever. At first, the animals ran through the alley all the way to the empty goal box. Gradually, they began to slow down as they approached the goal box to the point where they stopped before they entered it. They stopped sooner and sooner until they ran out only a short distance into the alley and waited for Zimmerman to pick them up and return them to the start box. Thus, at the same time that the goal box and the later segments of the alley were losing their secondary reward value, the secondary reward value of the buzzer was effective enough to increase the rate of lever pressing. In fact, lever-pressing only declined after the rats stopped running out into the alley at the sound of the buzzer.

Now, if the power of secondary reward depends on S-S* contiguity, then the goal box and the last segments of the alley should have acquired more secondary reward than the buzzer. Food, when present, was contiguous with the goal box in space and time. The buzzer sounded before the door to the alley opened, long before the food in time, and far away from the food in space. Yet, at the same time that the goal box was losing its power to reinforce, the buzzer was gaining power, at least according to the theory that attributes reinforcing power to these stimuli. At this point it may be helpful for readers to review the section on Latent Extinction in chapter 6 that analyzes S-R units in a T-maze.

Interstimulus Interval

Schoenfeld, Antonitis, and Bersh (1950) attempted to demonstrate secondary reward in the following way. They delivered food one pellet at a time in a Skinner box with the lever removed. To be sure that a 1-sec light stimulus would be maximally associated with the food, they watched each rat take each pellet and only lighted the light at the moment when a rat put the food in its mouth. Next, they replaced the lever and lighted the light every time that a rat pressed the lever, but never delivered any more food to the rats in the box. A control group of rats had the same conditions except that they never experienced any pairing of light and food. Schoenfeld et al. found no difference between the experimental and control groups.

After this failure to demonstrate secondary reward, Schoenfeld et al. remembered Pavlov's much replicated discovery that simultaneous presentation of CS and UCS yields very weak classical conditioning or none at all. If, secondary rewards acquire their reinforcing power by classical conditioning, then simultaneous presentation of light and food was a mistake. All that trouble to light the light at just the moment that the rats started eating only made sure that the light appeared at an unfavorable time for classical conditioning. This set the stage for the next experiment.

Bersh (1951) systematically varied the ISI between the lighting of the light and the delivery of the food pellets in a Skinner box. In Phase I, Bersh paired light with food with no lever present. Rather than waiting and watching to see what the rats did, Bersh set the mechanism to deliver light and food, automatically. The light always stayed lighted for 2 seconds after the apparatus delivered each pellet into the food dish, regardless of what the rat did. Bersh divided the rats into six groups that differed in the interval between the onset of the light and the delivery of the food. The intervals were 0.0 seconds, 0.5 seconds, 1.0 seconds, 2.0 seconds, 4.0 seconds, and 10.0 seconds. In Phase II, the lever was present but lever-pressing only lighted the light; no food was delivered. Figure 7.3 shows the results of Bersh's experiment. Just as in so many other classical conditioning experiments, the most favorable ISI was a half a second.

Bersh (1951) concluded that the light had acquired secondary reinforcing power, and that the most favorable ISI for the pairing of primary and secondary rewarding stimuli was the same as the most

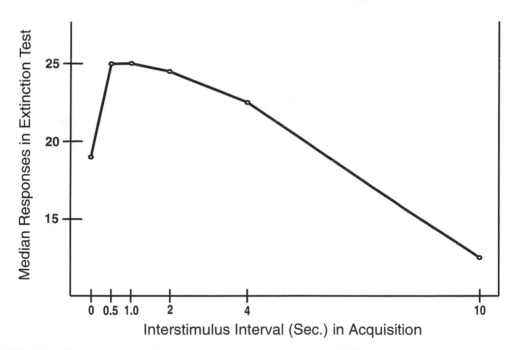

FIG. 7.3.   Secondary reward during extinction as a function of ISI during training (after Bersh, 1951). Lever-pressing in the first 10 minutes of extinction depends on the light-food interval in acquisition: light then food without lever during acquisition; lever then light without food during testing. Copyright © 1997 by R. Allen Gardner.

favorable interval in classical conditioning. From the point of view of reinforcement theory, the trouble with this finding is that the light was supposed to acquire its secondary reinforcement power by S-S* contiguity. But the shorter the ISI the closer the contiguity. Hence the findings (a) that simultaneous presentation of light and food is unfavorable, and (b) that one half second is the most favorable interval directly contradict the notion that S-S* contiguity is the mechanism of secondary reinforcement. Chapter 4 discusses how these same findings contradict the notion that S-S* contiguity is the mechanism of Pavlovian conditioning. Once again, the time interval strongly implicates some response to the S^a as the basis of the experimental results—something that the animal does between the onset of the S^a and the onset of the S*.

Summary

Secondary reward (S^r) plays a vital role in theories based on response contingent reinforcement. It is supposed to link laboratory studies of hungry and thirsty rats and pigeons rewarded with food and water to the vast amount of learning by comfortable, well-fed human and nonhuman animals in their everyday lives outside of the laboratory. It is also supposed to account for the incentive value of arbitrary symbols such as money. The operational definition of secondary reward avoids the central weakness of all S-R-S* theories: their inability to provide an operational definition of primary reinforcement that is independent of its effects on conditioning.

The best existing research shows that the amount of S^r that can be demonstrated experimentally is rather weak. The phenomena that appear in the laboratory seem entirely too weak to bear the theoretical burden placed on S^r in response contingent reinforcement theories. The effects that appear under laboratory conditions seem very different from the effects specified by the theories.

Demonstrations of an S^r effect have succeeded only when the interval between the S^r and the S* was long enough for the subjects to make some anticipatory response to the S*. In chapter 6, when experimenters such as Coate (1956) and Zimmerman (1959) observed and reported responses to the S^r, they found that the effect involves a distinctive response that the subject makes to the alleged S^r.

S-R CONTIGUITY

In reinforcement theories, an S^r acquires secondary reinforcing power by classical conditioning. Chapter 4 reviews the evidence against an S-S or an S-S* mechanism of classical conditioning. The favorable

ISI in classical conditioning must be long enough to permit the subject to make an anticipatory response to the S*. The length and asymmetry of the ISI supports an S-R contiguity mechanism of classical conditioning. According to S-R contiguity, if a human or nonhuman animal can be induced to make some response shortly after an S^a (usually within one half second), then that response will be conditioned to the S^a. This chapter considers the possibility that instrumental conditioning also depends on the mechanism of S-R contiguity.

S-R Chains in a Skinner Box

Figure 7.4 analyzes the series of stimuli and responses that occur in a Skinner box in detail. This diagram and similar diagrams in chapters 4 and 6 rely on the fact that every response of a human or nonhuman animal has some stimulus effect. When people walk, receptors in all of their joints send back new information about the movement and position of the joints, the resistance and angle of the ground, balance with respect to gravity; their eyes send back information about the passing visual scene, and so on. In the same way, as a rat runs through a maze, each movement changes the stimulus situation. Figure 7.4 describes some details of the series of movements and movement-produced stimuli in a Skinner box, but it is still a simplified description.

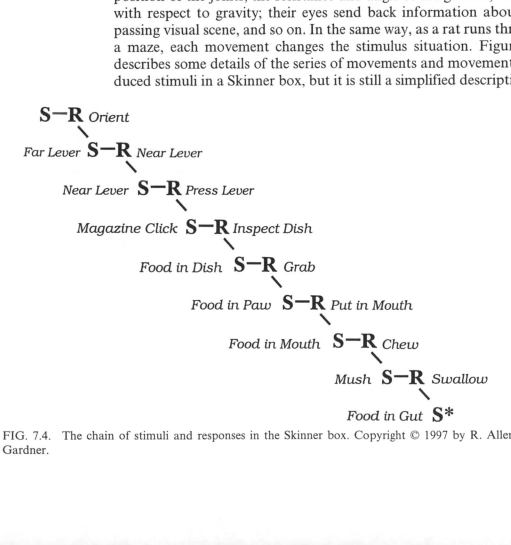

FIG. 7.4.   The chain of stimuli and responses in the Skinner box. Copyright © 1997 by R. Allen Gardner.

Figure 7.4 represents lever-pressing in the Skinner box as a chain of stimuli and responses. The food gets into the gut after it is swallowed. It is swallowed after it reaches the proper mushy consistency in the mouth. It becomes mush after it is chewed. It is chewed after it is put into the mouth. It is put into the mouth after it is in the paws. It gets into the paws after it is grabbed from the dish. It is grabbed after it is found in the dish. It is found in the dish after the rat inspects the dish. The rat inspects the dish after hearing the click. The rat hears the click after pressing the lever. The rat presses the lever after seeing that the lever is near. The rat sees that the lever is near after approaching the lever. The rat approaches the lever after seeing that the lever is far. The rat sees that the lever is far after orienting its head and eyes around the box. The rat orients after the experimenter places it in the box.

Preliminary Training

Most textbooks describe instrumental conditioning in the Skinner box as though the experimenter puts a hungry rat in the box and then waits for the first response, which causes the apparatus to deliver food or water reward. This procedure may work, but virtually all experimenters divide the procedure into steps. First, the experimenter adapts a rat in its home cage to eat the kind of food that the apparatus will deliver during conditioning. Next, the experimenter adapts the rat to eat small pellets of this food in a Skinner box from which the lever has been removed. A delivery mechanism, called a *food magazine,* delivers the pellets one at a time and makes a sharp click each time it operates (see Fig. 7.5).

The sharp click of the magazine is critical. Early Skinner boxes used inexpensive mechanical technology. Modern electronic technology provides a number of improved ways of delivering food, including a mechanism based on silent laser disk technology. Experimenters report little or no conditioning with silent food magazines unless they add some distinctive sound between the lever-pressing response and the appearance of the food (Bolles, 1988; Plonsky et al., 1984).

Some experimenters watch the rat carefully during *magazine training* and wait until the animal has moved away from the food dish before they operate the magazine with a remote switch. They fear that, otherwise, the rats might get conditioned to wait at the food dish for the pellets to appear. Soon, the animals learn to run to the dish when they hear the click of the magazine. That is the procedure that Skinner recommended, and the procedure of Zimmerman (1957; chap. 6). In the automatic procedure, the experimenter sets the apparatus to deliver

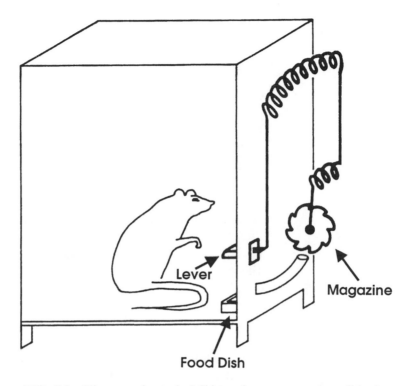

FIG. 7.5.   Diagram of a typical Skinner box or operant conditioning chamber showing the Lever that a rat must press, the Magazine that makes a sharp noise as it delivers food to a chute, and the Food Dish that receives the food inside the chamber. Copyright © 1997 by R. Allen Gardner.

pellets automatically at irregular intervals and this procedure also conditions rats to rush to the food dish when they hear the sound of the magazine delivering food. The automatic procedure obviously saves a lot of experimenter time. Coate (1956; chap. 6) used such an automatic procedure in his experiment on latent extinction.

Traditionally, the next step in the procedure is to replace the lever in the box and *shape* the rat to approach the lever and press it. The experimenter watches the animal carefully and operates the magazine (thus producing a click followed by a pellet) whenever the rat comes closer to making the desired response; in this case pressing the lever. The rat has already been conditioned to inspect the dish at the click of the magazine, grab each pellet when it appears in the dish, pop the pellet in its mouth, and eat. Gradually, the rat becomes conditioned to press the lever. Chapter 8 discusses an automated procedure, called *autoshaping,* that works as well and and saves a great deal of experimenter time. For the discussion in the present chapter, *manual shaping* and autoshaping have equivalent effects.

S-R-S^r

According to S-R-S* theory, the click of the magazine serves as an S^r that rewards the rat for pressing the lever. The close association of the click with food pellets during magazine training established the association between click and food. Rats have to learn to eat the pellets in the first place, so the sight of the pellets must itself be an S^r. If the sight of the pellet became an S^r by contiguity with a previously conditioned S^r or S*, then the sound of the magazine can become an S^r by contiguity with the sight of food.

What is the S* that makes the sight (or smell) of the pellets into an S^r? Experimenters have conditioned rats to accept or reject foods on the basis of arbitrary tastes and colors. Where is the S* in that case? And certainly, human beings accept and reject food arbitrarily on the basis of learned tastes and sights. Perhaps it is the feel of the food in the stomach that finally must be the S*. Reinforcement theories have so far failed to produce an operational definition that specifies the original S* in advance for any case of learning. Fortunately, for the purposes of the discussion in this chapter, all we have to assume is that the final S* happens somewhere between the sight of the pellet in the dish and the sensation of food in the gut. The feel of food in the gut is the last possible stimulus that could serve as an S*; Fig. 7.4 labels this stimulus as the S*. Whichever stimulus we choose as the theoretical final S*, however, the result is the same as long we choose a stimulus that comes later than the sight of the pellet in the dish. The stimulus that comes just before the S* becomes the first S^r by S-S* contiguity, then the stimulus just before that becomes the second S^r by S-S* contiguity with the first S^r, and so on to the begining of the chain. Each stimulus becomes an S^r by contiguity with the S^r that follows it and each S^r rewards the response that it follows.

Zimmerman (1959) raises doubts here. In that experiment, the S^r at the end of a runway was the goal box that was closely contiguous with the only food that rats received. Yet, at the same time that the response of running to the goal box was extinguishing, presumably because the empty goal box was losing its power to reward running, a buzzer that signaled the opening of a door to the runway continued to enhance lever-pressing. The stimuli in the goal box were much closer in space and time to food than the buzzer. How could the closer goal box lose its S^r power before the buzzer lost its S^r power?

DISCRIMINATIVE STIMULUS: S^d VERSUS S^r

Feed Forward Versus Feed Backward

Traditionally, secondary reward is a feed backward concept in which the stimulus consequences of behavior act backward to reinforce past S-R connections. According to this description, each S-R unit in Fig. 7.4 is rewarded by the appearance of the stimulus that begins the next unit in the series. The S^d is a feed forward concept in which the stimulus consequences of behavior feed the animal forward from one action to the next. According to this description, each S-R unit starts with an S^d and ends when the next S^d starts the next S-R unit. What matters is not the positive or negative effect of the S^d on the S-R unit that just happened, but rather the response that the S^d evokes next; not how the S^d makes learners feel after the last response, but what it makes them do next.

Have you ever wondered why everything you lose is always in the last place you look for it? The reason, of course, is that you always stop looking as soon as you find it. But, you do more than stop looking. When you find your lost car keys after a long search, for example, you take the keys out to start the car. Finding the keys ends the search because the keys are a stimulus for the next thing you do. This is the feed forward principle. The response that produced the S^d is always the last response made in the stimulus situation before the S^d appeared. This is because the S^d always evokes the next response in the chain.

Conditioned Eating

Like most other baby mammals, rat pups try putting just about everything in their mouths. It is a way to learn the difference between food and nonfood. When they chew food, it turns into mush and they swallow it. Other materials—pebbles, twigs, sawdust, sand, and so forth—are difficult or impossible either to chew or to swallow, and the pups soon spit them out. Consequently, the last thing they do to food in their mouths is chew because chewing turns food to mush, and they swallow it. The last thing they do to other objects, say pebbles or sawdust, is spit them out. Soon they drop nonfood objects before putting them in their mouths and may not pick them up at all. This is how conditioned eating could take place by S-R contiguity alone. The sight and smell of food becomes a discriminative stimulus for grabbing the food and putting it in the mouth.

Magazine Click as S^d

For a rat that enters a Skinner box, the sight and smell of familiar laboratory food is an S^d for grabbing. The feel of food in the paws is an S^d for popping the food in the mouth. The taste and feel of food in the mouth is an S^d for chewing. And finally, mush is an S^d for swallowing. Swallowing is the last response after feeling mush in the mouth, because after the rat swallows, the mush is gone. Chewing is the last response after feeling food in the mouth, because after the rat chews, the food turns to mush and mush is the S^d for swallowing. Putting the food in the mouth is the last response after feeling food in the paws, because after the rat puts the food in its mouth, the food is gone from the paws. Grabbing the food in the dish is the last response after seeing the food in the dish, because after the rat picks up the food it is gone from the dish.

Conditioning the rat to inspect the dish after each click of the magazine is only one simple step further. The experimenter places the rat in the Skinner box with the lever removed and delivers pellets of food by operating the magazine. Whenever the rat inspects the dish about one half second after hearing the magazine click, it finds food in the dish. That is the last response to the click because the next stimulus is the sight of the pellet, which is the S^d for grabbing the food and removing it from the dish.

At first, of course, the rat may take longer than one half second to inspect the dish. In those cases, some extraneous stimulus—say a creaking sound in the woodwork, an odd smell, or a slight change in temperature—may be the last stimulus before the rat finds food in the dish. Next time that extraneous stimulus appears, the rat will inspect the dish because that was the last response to the extraneous stimulus. Most of the time that the rat inspects the dish after an extraneous stimulus, however, there is no food in the dish. This gives the rat time to do something else, say scratch itself, rise up on its hind legs, or clean its whiskers. These extraneous responses become the last thing the rat did after extraneous stimuli. The only stimulus that is always the last stimulus before the response of inspecting the dish is the magazine click because, if the rat inspects the dish at that time, it always finds the S^d for grabbing the pellet and that initiates the rest of the chain.

When the rat is inspecting the food dish promptly after each magazine click, the experimenter inserts the lever in the Skinner box and after that each food delivery is contingent on lever-pressing. If the rat approaches the lever and presses it, then that will be the last response to the lever, because the next stimulus will be the magazine click, which is now the S^d for inspecting the dish. After inspecting the dish, the rat finds a pellet, which is the S^d for grabbing. After grabbing the pellet, the rat finds food in its paws, which is the S^d for putting food in its mouth. After putting the food in the mouth, the rat finds food in its mouth, which is the S^d for chewing. After chewing, it finds mush, which is the S^d for swallowing. After swallowing, the food is gone. If the rat does anything else near the lever—say scratch, rise up, or clean its whiskers—the stimulus situation remains the same. So, the rat goes on to do other extraneous things and none of them remains the last response for long. Only pressing the lever becomes the last response to the lever, because after the rat presses the lever, the magazine clicks and this sets the chain of responses in motion once more.

Viewed in this way, instrumental conditioning in the Skinner box is an inefficient kind of classical conditioning. In classical conditioning, the experimenter would place the rat in a harness in front of the food dish and arrange for a response, such as salivation to appear about one half second after a stimulus such as a magazine click. In the usual classical conditioning procedure, food evokes salivation, but inspecting the dish can serve just as well as the UCR evoked by magazine clicks. In the classical conditioning procedure, the experimenter makes sure that the CS and the UCR evoked by the UCS appear on every trial. In the Skinner box, the experimenter makes sure that the sight of the lever is paired with the sound of the magazine whenever the rat presses the lever. When the rat presses the lever, the pairing of lever and magazine click is the same as in classical conditioning. The rat makes many other extraneous responses, such as sniffing in corners, rearing up on its hind legs, exploring the box, and so on. Extraneous behavior postpones lever-pressing and clicks, wasting the rat's time compared with classical conditioning in which the experimenter schedules each trial. But the procedure is only inefficient from the point of view of the rat. From the point of view of the experimenter, it is much easier to set the apparatus to pair lever with clicks and let the rat present its own trials at its own pace. This is a powerful reason for the popularity of the Skinner box. It is a very convenient and efficient conditioning apparatus from the point of view of the experimenter.

Token Rewards for Chimpanzees

The stage is now set to consider the most famous of all demonstrations of secondary reward. Cowles (1937) and Wolfe (1936) demonstrated that chimpanzees could learn to use poker chips to operate a vending machine that dispensed grapes, and then learn to pull a lever (much like a Nevada slot machine lever) to earn poker chips, which they could insert into a slot to operate a vending machine. Textbooks and teachers often cite this result as a demonstration that the value of money depends on secondary reinforcement.

In later experiments, Kelleher (1956, 1957a, 1957b, 1958a, 1958b) replicated and extended Cowles' (1937) and Wolfe's (1936) findings. Basically, Kelleher taught two young male chimpanzees first to get grapes by operating the vending machine with poker chips, and then to earn poker chips by pressing a telegraph key. Kelleher next varied the schedules of poker chip reward for key-pressing. When the chimpanzees were working for poker chips, he lighted a white earning light; when they could spend their poker chips, he turned off the earning light and lighted a red spending light.

Time has to be divided into earning periods and spending periods in this experiment. If Kelleher had allowed the chimpanzees to press the key to earn poker chips and then let them spend each poker chip in the vending machine as soon as they received it, the demonstration would be much less significant. Without the division into earning and spending periods, Kelleher's procedure would only be an example of a chain of responses starting with a key-press, followed by a poker chip, followed by picking up the chip and putting it in the slot, followed by receiving a grape. This is practically the same thing as the chains analyzed by the goal gradient principle for rats in mazes discussed in chapter 5. The only difference is that chimpanzees have hands that they can use to manipulate objects so that they can execute chains of movement that are superficially more complex than the chains of running executed by rats in mazes. Other attempts to demonstrate an S^r effect through complex chains of reinforcement schedules in a Skinner box fail for the same reason (e.g., Jacob & Fantino, 1988). An S^d can maintain an earlier link in a chain by feeding forward to the next link without feeding backward to reinforce the link that it follows.

By lighting one light to signal working periods and a second light to signal spending periods, Kelleher produced a much more interesting situation, something much more like a chimpanzee working to earn poker chips in order to spend them later. Human beings also work during designated times, and spend during other, quite separate, times. Even street vendors who get paid in coins, transaction by transaction, normally collect the coins during designated earning times and spend the money later.

The rate at which Kelleher's chimpanzees worked at pressing the key depended on the schedule of poker chip reward. Like many human factory workers, however, they got to a point where each chimpanzee worked at a stable rate for a given schedule of payment so that it took about the same amount of time, about 4 hours, each day for them to earn the allotted number of poker chips, about 50 chips, depending on the condition. Consequently, they could have been working for a stable period of time or for a stable number of chips. The spending light came on after about the same amount of working time either way. Note that this is because of the stable rate of working maintained by a stable schedule of reward (see chap. 3).

Kelleher's chimpanzees lived in rather boring cages when they were not serving in experiments. The experimental enclosure was larger and more interesting. At the beginning of the experiment, the chimpanzees naturally spent a certain amount of time running, jumping, climbing, playing with the apparatus, and otherwise enjoying the place before they settled down. This period of playfulness before settling down to work persisted through hundreds of hours of experimental sessions. At the beginning of each session, the chimpanzees took between 20 and 40 minutes before they pressed the key for the first time. The next key-press came a little sooner, the next sooner, and so on, faster and faster until they reached their top speed usually with a spurt at the end of the earning period.

Kelleher (1958b) reasoned that this pattern of results could be interpreted in either of two ways. First, if the poker chips acted as secondary rewards, then the pause at the beginning of each session might be the result of lack of reward. The first chip rewarded the first few responses, which reinforced key-pressing so that responding increased, which resulted in more rewards, which further increased responding, and so on until the chimpanzees reached their top speed.

Perhaps the poker chips acted, instead, as discriminative stimuli. As chips collected in a pile beside the lever, the steadily growing pile was a kind of clock telling the chimpanzees how close they were coming to the end of the earning period and the beginning of the spending period with its delicious grapes. At the beginning of the session with no pile at all, a chimpanzee could see that spending time was a long way off. Even after accumulating a few chips he could see that grape time was still far away. He might respond more than he had at the start, but still sluggishly. As the pile grew, he could tell that spending time was getting closer and this stimulated him to press faster and faster until the end spurt when the pile was highest. In the secondary reward description, the poker chips act backward to reinforce what the chimpanzee had done before. In the discriminative stimulus description, the poker chips act forward to stimulate the next thing the chimpanzee does.

With this in mind, Kelleher tried the following ingenious test. He put 50 poker chips in the experimental enclosure before each chimpanzee arrived for his daily session. If the poker chips were acting as response contingent secondary rewards (S^r), then the chimpanzees would be finding a large heap of free S^rs as they entered the enclosure. The free chips would then reward the beginning laziness and playfulness, and reward this behavior at a better rate than key-pressing ever had. If the chips were S^rs, the chimpanzees should take much longer to settle down to work, or they might never settle down to work at all. If the pile of chips was acting as a discriminative stimulus, however, we would expect just the opposite. The chimpanzees would arrive to find the clock set ahead telling them that they were near to spending time. If the chips were S^ds the chimpanzees should begin at their high middle-of-the-session rate, immediately, and improve from then on as more chips piled up.

Kelleher's results were decisive. When the chimpanzees found the pile of free chips, they omitted their usual 20- to 40-minute period of no responding. They went directly to work pressing the key at a high rate.

Kelleher's experiment tests whether the pile of poker chips acts *backward* as an S^r to reward the chimpanzees for pressing the key, or acts *forward* as an S^d to stimulate them to press the key more rapidly. When the chimpanzees got a pile of poker chips for doing nothing, they immediately started to press the key rapidly as if the pile of chips stimulated them forward to intense activity rather than rewarding them backward for doing nothing.

Money Feeds Forward

The poker chip experiments originally aimed to support the traditional view that money is an S^r that controls human beings by feeding backward to reward past behavior. Suppose, however, that the poker chip experiments had been designed to investigate the role of money, to discover something new rather than to shore up traditional beliefs. What would these experiments teach us then? Do Kelleher's experiments with chimpanzees agree with the role of money in human life?

When a customer purchases a pair of shoes at a store, the customer pays before taking the shoes out of the store. Rather than rewarding the store for giving up the shoes, the customer pays first and takes possession later. The money feeds forward to induce the cashier to give up the shoes.

The cashier puts the money in a safe place, or stores the credit card receipt. Most cashiers never spend the money they receive in the name of the store. The owner, who may also be the cashier, seldom spends the money soon after earning it. Usually the owner deposits the money in a bank and only much later spends the money credited to the store from checks and credit cards. When the owner spends the money it induces someone else to give up a purchased item or to perform a service.

When the owner pays the cashier, people say that the owner is rewarding the cashier for past service. But why should the owner pay the cashier for work done last week or last month? When owners fail to pay in real life, there is usually little or nothing that a worker can do about it except to refuse to return to work. Owners pay up promptly, because prompt payment induces workers to return to work. Salaries also feed forward.

CHAPTER 8

Contiguity Versus Contingency

Since Skinner invented the procedure in the 1930s, armies of experimenters have conditioned hordes of rats and pigeons to press levers and peck keys in Skinner boxes. The success of this procedure is supposed to support traditional, almost biblical, faith in reward and punishment. This chapter reviews the modern evidence that bears on this ancient belief.

SHAPING AND AUTOSHAPING

Instrumental conditioning in the Skinner box is easily and cheaply automated, which makes it cost-effective and popular with experimenters. The most inefficient step in the procedure used to be the wait for the first response. Without some intervention from the experimenter, a great deal of waste time often elapsed before a naive rat or pigeon first pressed the lever or pecked the key. Some impatient experimenters smeared the lever with moist food to induce the first lever-press. Skinner (1953) described the orthodox technique as follows:

> We first give the bird food when it turns slightly in the direction of the spot from any part of the cage. This increases the frequency of such behavior. We then withhold reinforcement until a slight movement is made toward the spot. This again alters the general distribution of behavior without producing a new unit. We continue by reinforcing positions successively closer to the spot, then by reinforcing only when the head is moved slightly forward, and finally

only when the beak actually makes contact with the spot. . . .

The original probability of the response in its final form is very low; in some cases it may even be zero. In this way we can build complicated operants which would never appear in the repertoire of the organism otherwise. By reinforcing a series of successive approximations, we bring a rare response to a very high probability in a short time. . . . The total act of turning toward the spot from any point in the box, walking toward it, raising the head, and striking the spot may seem to be a functionally coherent unit of behavior; but it is constructed by a continual process of differential reinforcement from undifferentiated behavior, just as the sculptor shapes his figure from a lump of clay. (pp. 92–93)

Obviously, human and nonhuman animals learn many things every day on their own without the intervention of dedicated shaping that Skinner prescribed. The only reasonable claim that anyone could ever make for shaping is that it is efficient, speedier, longer lasting, in some practical way superior. There is only one way to establish such a claim, however, and that is an experimental comparison between the prescription and an alternative. In a long lifetime, Skinner never attempted any experimental comparison that could compare his prescribed methods with alternatives. After decades, a comparison did emerge when more adventurous experimenters deviated from accepted wisdom in an attempt to save themselves a little time.

Manual shaping is obviously labor intensive. Inevitably, experimenters began to look for labor-saving devices. In 1968, P. Brown and Jenkins reported a truly economical procedure, which they called autoshaping. They lighted up the response key for a pigeon in a Skinner box for 8 seconds. At the end of that time, an automatic device turned off the key light and delivered food no matter what the pigeon did. If the pigeon pecked the key while it was still lighted, the device turned off the light and delivered food, immediately. In either case, after an intertrial interval, the key was relighted and the cycle repeated. Soon, pigeons were pecking the key on their own. Autoshaping was as effective as Skinner's laborious manual procedure.

The discovery of autoshaping generated a large volume of research that replicated and extended the early findings in great detail. Later experiments induced robust rates of pecking with food delivered only at the end of the light-on period, independently of anything that the pigeon did. D. R. Williams and H. Williams (1969) showed that they could maintain key-pecking if they only delivered food when pigeons failed to peck the key—that is, when they *omitted* food every time the pigeon pecked the key. In this *omission contingency,* free food evokes robust rates of pecking, at first. As a result of the negative contingency, the more the pigeons peck the less food they get. As food is omitted, pecking declines. When pecking declines, food is again delivered, pecking recovers, food is again omitted, and so on, indefinitely. Overall, this procedure maintains a robust rate of key-pecking.

Under the omission contingency, hungry pigeons behave as if they are trying to *avoid food.* When food stops they rest content, as if a painful stimulus has been removed. When food appears again, they hasten to make responses that stopped food in the past (see Schwartz & Gamzu, 1977, for an extensive review). This experimental result of omission contingency indicates that key-pecking in the Skinner box is an obligatory response like salivation in Pavlovian conditioning (as explained in chap. 4) and raises fundamental questions about the traditional distinction between classical and instrumental conditioning.

SUPERSTITION

The elaborate manual shaping—so carefully described and so painstakingly followed by Skinner and a generation or two of his faithful followers—was entirely unnecessary. Its popularity among experimenters could serve as a striking human example of what Skinner called *superstitious* behavior and described as follows:

> If there is only an accidental connection between the response and the appearance of a reinforcer, the behavior is called "superstitious." We may demonstrate this in the pigeon by accumulating the effect of several accidental contingencies. Suppose we give a pigeon a small amount of food every fifteen seconds regardless of what it is doing. When food is first given, the pigeon will be behaving in some way—if only standing still—and conditioning will take place. It is then more probable that the same behavior will be in progress when food is given again. If this proves to be the case, the "operant" will be further strengthened. If not, some other behavior will be strengthened. Eventually a given bit of behavior reaches a frequency at which it is often reinforced. It then becomes a permanent part of the repertoire of the bird, even though the food has been given by a clock which is unrelated to the bird's behavior. Conspicuous responses which have been established in this way include turning sharply to one side, hopping from one foot to the other and back, bowing and scraping, turning around, strutting, and raising the head. (Skinner, 1953, p. 85)

The concept of superstitious behavior plays a central role in the traditional view of key-pecking as *arbitrary behavior* reinforced by feeding rather than *obligatory behavior* evoked by feeding. Skinner published only one report of any research observations to support the highly interpretive term, *superstition*, and that (1948) report never mentions any direct observation of a single adventitious conjunction between response and food. In a long lifetime, Skinner never reported any further direct observations of any such adventitions conjunction between response and reward. Nor, as late as 1997, has anyone else ever reported any direct observations that support Skinner's purely speculative interpretation. Nevertheless, adventitious reinforcement survives as an argument for the arbitrary effect of reinforcement together with the suggestion that it is the mechanism of human superstitious ritual. Skinner's "superstition" lived on for many years without any supporting evidence and in spite of the following contradictory evidence.

Staddon and Simmelhag (1971) published the first, fully reported, description of what hungry pigeons actually do when they receive noncontingent food at intervals. After repeated, noncontingent delivery of food, all of Staddon and Simmelhag's pigeons developed the same habit—pecking at the wall above the food hopper. This is a sign of an obligatory as opposed to arbitrary effect of food arriving at intervals. Most of the pecking occurred just before each delivery of food. This is what we would expect if pecking is a *prefeeding response* evoked when food is about to arrive, just as salivation is a prefeeding response in Pavlovian conditioning.

Staddon and Simmelhag (1971) also reported other stereotyped behaviors, such as wing-flapping and circling movements, with individual variations from pigeon to pigeon. These resembled Skinner's descriptions of individually stereotyped behaviors that he called superstitious. Individual variation is a sign of arbitrary as opposed to obligatory effects. These arbitrary variations appeared, however, early in the intervals long before food delivery so they could hardly depend on adventitious conjunction between the responses and food. Other experimenters soon replicated Staddon and Simmelhag (e.g., Fenner, 1980; Reberg, Innis, Mann, & Eizenga, 1978; Timberlake & Lucas, 1985).

EARNING VERSUS FREE LOADING

In the traditional view, lever-pressing and key-pecking entail *arbitrary work* that rats and pigeons perform in order to earn food or other necessities of life. The *biological utility* of the incentives must justify the *biological effort*, because animals would not press the bar or peck the key if they had an easier way to get the incentives. This proposition seemed so obvious to so many that no one thought to test it empirically before G. D. Jensen's (1963) experiment on *free feeding*. Jensen was the first to offer rats a choice between pellets of food that they could earn by pressing the lever in the usual way, and a heap of identical pellets free for the taking from a convenient food dish.

Soon, many other experimenters replicated Jensen's findings with pigeons as well as with rats. With an abundant supply of free food in front of them in the food dish, most animals earn some food by pressing the lever or pecking the key. Under some conditions, animals earned as much as 90% of the food they ate. So much for the cognitive interpretation that rats press the lever because images of food make them expect that lever-pressing brings them food.

It is tempting to suppose that operant conditioning turns rats into lever-pressing machines so thoroughly conditioned that they go on pressing the lever even when there is free food in front of their faces. Further experiments showed, however, that from their first experience in a Skinner box animals begin to press levers and peck keys if there is free food continuously available, and they acquire the habit of pressing levers and pecking keys before they have had any opportunity to receive reward for responding. Hungry animals press levers and peck keys even when the consequences of work are negative; that is, when they abandon the heap of free food to work at the lever or the key, they lose time that they could have spent eating (see extensive reviews in Inglis, Forkman, & Lazarus, 1997; Osborne, 1977, 1978).

AVOIDING FOOD

In 1951, Breland and Breland first described a kind of show business based on techniques they had learned as junior associates of B. F. Skinner. The Brelands taught chickens to bat baseballs and parakeets to ride bicycles; and some 38 different species acquired a wide variety of unlikely skills, which they displayed in museums, zoos, fairs, department stores, and—the ultimate achievement—television commercials. The popularity of the animal actors combined with the practical effectiveness of the conditioning techniques resulted in a profitable business. There were some failures, not random failures, but patterns of failure that plainly contradicted the behavior theory behind their otherwise so successful program of conditioning. The Brelands referred to these patterns as *misbehavior* (Breland & Breland, 1961).

In one display that the Brelands planned for the window of a savings bank, a pig picked up large wooden coins from a pile and deposited them in a "piggy bank" several feet away. After shaping with a single coin placed farther and farther from the bank, the pig progressed to four or five coins picked up and deposited one by one to earn each small portion of food. It was a textbook example of ratio reinforcement (chap. 3) and most pigs acquired it rapidly. Instead of improving with practice, however, performance deteriorated day by day. The pigs continued to pick up the coins readily enough, but they were slower and slower to deposit them in the bank. On the way to the bank, they would drop a coin and root it along the ground with their snouts, pick it up and drop it again, often tossing it in the air before rooting it along the ground once more. Pig after pig indulged in more and more rooting and tossing until they delayed the delivery of food, indefinitely.

Raccoons failed in a similar way. Adept at manipulating objects, raccoons quickly learned to grasp and carry wooden coins and even to insert them into a slot. But, after a few rewards the raccoons seemed unable to let the coins out of their grasp. They kept on handling and rubbing the coins and dipping them in the slot as if washing them. Given two coins, a raccoon would rub them together over and over again like a miser. Raccoon misbehavior looked very much like the manipulatory behavior raccoons normally direct toward naturally occurring portions of food—they handle and rub foods that have husks and shells, and even pull prey such as crayfish out of pools. Similarly, wild and domestic pigs kill small rodents by rooting and tossing them before eating them.

In the Breland failures, animals first had to direct responses that resembled *prefeeding* toward objects that resembled food. Then they had to stop prefeeding the token food before they could receive actual food. The Brelands tried making their animal actors hungrier, reasoning that this should increase the incentive value of food. If, instead, "misbehavior" consists of obligatory components of prefeeding evoked by a conditioned connection between the tokens and the food, then it should increase with increased hunger. This is precisely what the Brelands report; the hungrier they were, the more the animals persisted in "misbehavior" that postponed food.

Rodents also manipulate their food before eating it. Timberlake and his associates (Timberlake, 1983, 1986; Timberlake, Wahl, & D. King, 1982) placed rats in a specially designed Skinner box without the usual lever, and dropped a 5/8-in. steel ball into the box through a hole in one wall. Unimpeded, the ball took 3.1 seconds to roll down a groove in the slightly inclined floor and pass out of the box through a hole in the opposite wall. The experimenters also dropped pellets of food one at a time into a food dish located to one side and above the exit hole. Under some conditions the food arrived at the same time as the ball, under others it was delayed for a measured period of time, and under still others food was delayed until the ball rolled out of the box.

The rats handled, mouthed, and carried the ball as if it were a seed or a nut in a shell. They dug at the entry hole during the delay between the sound of the dispenser and the entry of the ball, even though this tended to delay the ball by blocking the hole. When food was delayed until the ball dropped through the exit hole, the rats continued to handle the ball, thus blocking its progress, preventing its exit, and postponing the food. Under experimental conditions in which food arrived before the ball rolled out of the box, most of the rats formed a habit of carrying the ball to the food dish or otherwise blocking its exit and later resumed handling the ball after they had consumed the food. They persisted in this even though it lengthened the intertrial interval, thus delaying the next feeding.

In the usual Skinner box for rats, the lever is the only graspable, movable object, hence the only available target for the prefeeding manipulatory behavior of these animals. Lacking a manipulatory appendage, pigeons peck at targets with their beaks, and the most prominent target in the Skinner box for pigeons is the lighted key. The box used by Staddon and Simmelhag (1971) had no key, but their pigeons pecked at the wall above the food bin, anyway. If conditioned pecking were based on a kind of *stimulus substitution* in which the pigeons pecked at random spots of dirt or other imperfections that resembled grains of food, then we would expect them to peck at the floor. Random spots on the floor of the chamber should resemble grain as much as random spots on the upright walls, and downward pecking should resemble normal feeding behavior more than horizontal pecking. Why should pigeons peck at spots on a wall? Unlike precocial birds such as chickens that feed themselves from the first, the young of altricial birds such as pigeons are fed by their parents. The young of altricial birds solicit food by pecking upward at a parent's beak and crop (Lehrman, 1955).

The misbehaviors of the Breland pigs and raccoons and the Timberlake rats are components of prefeeding in these species. They were evoked by stimuli associated with feeding. When food appeared, the animals interrupted the prefeeding they were directing at the tokens, in favor of consummatory responses directed at the food. The prefeeding responses only became "misbehavior" when the animals had to interrupt them before the food appeared.

In the Skinner box, rats and pigeons interrupt lever-pressing and key-pecking to consume food. They also mix eating with prefeeding, as when heaps of food are already available in free feeding experiments. But, they drift into "misbehavior" when they have to stop key-pecking or lever-pressing to get food, as in the omission contingency. It is then that their responses postpone rather than hasten the arrival of food.

These observations suggest a recursive program that ends with a test. Fresh inputs initiate the next loop in the program. Without fresh inputs the loop repeats. Prefeeding behavior such as lever-pressing and key-pecking is mixed with feeding proper under conditions in which heaps of free food are already available. This suggests a recursive program of the form:

$$\text{Feed} \rightarrow \text{Manipulate} + \text{Eat} + \text{Feed}$$

The Brelands describe how easy it was to teach chickens to pull in a loop of string or wire, a simple feat that was extremely difficult for pigeons. Unlike pigeons, chickens in a farmyard get much of their food by scratching in the earth for worms. In one of their displays, the Brelands wanted a chicken to stand still on a platform for 12–15 seconds, waiting for food. They found that about 50% of their chicken performers began to shift from place to place on the platform while scratching vigorously at the floor beneath them. The resourceful Brelands labeled the platform "dance floor" and had the chickens start a "juke box" by pulling a loop. They then required the chickens to stand on the platform (thus depressing a switch) for 15 seconds and called this show "The Dancing Chicken." They estimated that in the course of an average performing day, each chicken made more than 10,000 useless scratching responses when all they had to do was to stand still on the platform for 15 seconds at a time. Audiences were amazed to see how a behaviorist could get an animal to dance to any tune through the power of positive reinforcement.

CONSTRAINTS AND CONTINGENCY

The Skinner box was supposed to be so *arbitrary* that the *obligatory*, species-specific aspects of rat and pigeon behavior would be minimal, just as civilized life was supposed to be so artificial and arbitrary that human behavior must be virtually free of *biological constraints*. But, rats and pigeons stubbornly refuse to leave their ethology behind when they enter the Skinner box. Lever-pressing and key-pecking were supposed to represent arbitrary work that rats and pigeons would only perform for food and water rewards. Instead, food and water evoke and maintain these particular responses without any contingency at all. Indeed, under a wide range of conditions, positive and negative contingencies are irrelevant to learning. The Brelands discovered analogous phenomena in a wide range of animal species under a wide range of conditions. We cannot dismiss these findings as artifacts peculiar to the behavior of rats and pigeons in a Skinner box.

In response to this mounting evidence, defenders of the law of effect retreated to the position that the arbitrary effects of consequences must operate within limits imposed by certain species-specific constraints. This is known as the "constraints on learning" approach (Hinde, 1973; Shettleworth, 1972). The constraints are said to be evolutionary adaptations for vital functions such as feeding, courtship, and defense.

Like the law of effect, the constraints position is a traditional view with a long cultural history. For example, in the film classic, *The African Queen* (Huston & Agee, 1951), Katharine Hepburn plays a devout missionary in Africa in the early 1900s. To Humphrey Bogart, who plays the rough operator of a tramp riverboat, she preaches, "Nature, Mr. Allnutt, is what we were put in this world to rise above." Echoing the missionary tradition in recent times, Skinner (1977) wrote, "Civilization has supplied an unlimited number of examples of the suppression of the phylogenic repertoire of the human species by learned behavior. In fact, it is often the very function of a culture to mask a genetic endowment" (p. 1007).

The missionary tradition supposes a fundamental conflict between the civilizing effect of learning and the brutalizing effect of biology. This supposed conflict separates learning from biology. Nevertheless, the learning of living animals, whether human or nonhuman, can only be a biological phenomenon. The laws of learning must emerge from more general laws of ethology. The rest of this chapter develops this theme to resolve the supposed conflict between learning and ethology.

Meanwhile, the constraints in actual experiments are hardly constraints on learning because learning is abundant in these experiments. A much better name would be "constraints on the law of effect." So much ethologically based learning by contiguity appears in these experiments that it is difficult to see anything that remains to be learned by contingency. This raises a fundamental question of experimental operations. The answer to this question is the subject of the next section of this chapter.

YOKED CONTROL

Responses that seem to be reinforced by the contingent delivery of food or water are evoked by these incentives without any contingency at all. In that case, how much of the results of instrumental conditioning can we attribute to the effect of response contingent reinforcement? The experimental answer to this question is straightforward. It requires two conditions. Under one condition, C, incentives are contingent on some criterion response. Under the second condition, Y, the same number of incentives are delivered, but independently of the criterion response. In virtually every experiment that used this design to test for contingency, regardless of the response measured and regardless of the species, whether human or nonhuman, the contingent subjects responded more than the yoked subjects. This result seems to confirm the principle of S-R-S* contingency. Nevertheless, this experimental design contains a fatal error that vitiates the results. So many experimenters and commentators have failed to appreciate this error that students and nonspecialists often miss the problem at a first reading. Because the error has profound implications for any theory of learning, this chapter analyzes the yoked control for contingency in great detail.

Experimental Design

The two Skinner boxes shown in Fig. 8.1 are identical except that the lever of box C operates both food magazines, while the lever of box Y is not connected to either magazine. Both magazines dispense pellets of food when rat C presses his lever, but neither magazine operates when rat Y presses his lever. Thus, C's feeding is contiguous with and contingent upon his lever-presses, while Y receives the same number of pellets at the same time intervals but Y's feeding is independent of his lever-presses. The difference between C's responses and Y's responses should measure the difference between contingent and evocative effects of the incentives. This general procedure can be adapted to use with any criterion response and any method of dispensing incentives.

Perhaps the error of the yoked control appears more clearly in the design shown in Fig. 8.2, which represents two college students C and Y participating in a word recognition experiment. They sit in separate rooms at identical terminals. Each subject reports by speaking into a microphone. Immediately after subject C says "Ready," identical target words appear on both screens, and immediately after C reports a word both screens black out, but nothing that subject Y says has any effect on either screen. As a result, the target words will usually appear when C is attending to her screen. Sometimes, Y will also be attending to her screen, but many trials will begin at times when Y is paying no attention to the screen, whatever. On the average trial, then, Y's attention will be lower than C's, and C will report more correct words than Y does. C will have the same advantage if the

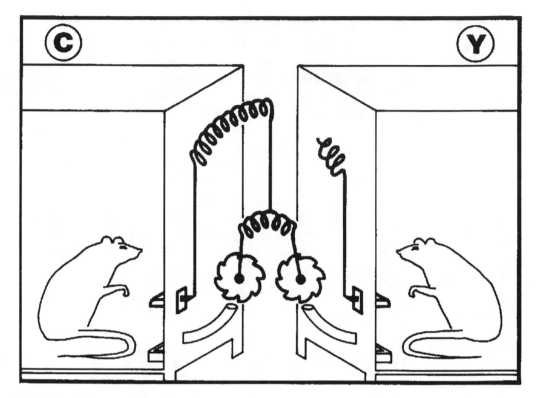

FIG. 8.1. Diagram of a yoked control experiment for measuring the effect of contingency in the Skinner box. C is the contingent condition and Y is the yoked control. Copyright © 1997 by R. Allen Gardner.

experiment is converted from word recognition to word learning by requiring C and Y to memorize the words. But, we cannot attribute C's superiority in either case to the rewarding effect of her control over the screen.

The yoked control is an *ex post facto* design. The classical example of this error (discussed in Underwood, 1957, pp. 97–99) is a study of the effects of time spent in the Boy Scouts on later participation in community affairs. The study found that youths who had joined the Scouts and remained Scouts for an average of 4 years later participated in more community activities than other youths who had joined the Scouts at about the same time but quit in an average of 1.4 years. The authors concluded that the additional years in the Boy Scouts increased the amount of community involvement when the youths became adult citizens.

The Boy Scout study proves nothing of the kind. The quitters were different from the stickers at the time that they quit. That is why they quit. It is a mistake to attribute later differences to participation in the Boy Scouts because the two groups were different before the

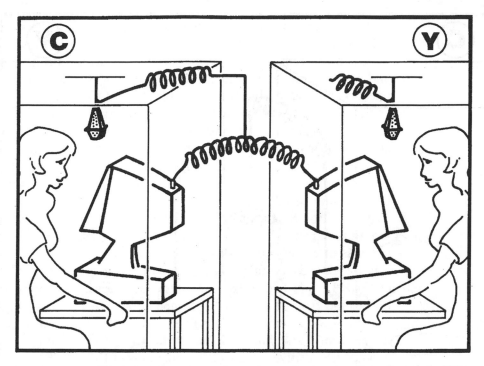

FIG. 8.2.   Diagram of a yoked control experiment for measuring the effect of contingency on word recognition. C is the contingent condition and Y is the yoked control. Copyright © 1997 by R. Allen Gardner.

differential conditions had any chance to act on them. Once experimenters select subjects on the basis of past behavior, they cannot logically attribute subsequent differences in behavior to later conditions imposed by the experiment.

Subject Selection

A sound experiment assigns subjects to different conditions in an unbiased way. Suppose that an experiment aims to test the relative effectiveness of praises and insults on college students memorizing lists of words in a special laboratory. Suppose further that in the praise condition the experimenter praises the subjects every time they are correct and in the insult condition the experimenter insults the subjects every time they make an error. In a sound experiment, the experimenter must assign students to the two conditions at random. One way to do this would be to toss a coin each time a new student arrived in the laboratory, and then to assign a student to the praise condition whenever the coin came up heads and to the insult condition every time the coin came up tails. This would be *unbiased selection*.

An example of *biased selection* would be to assign the subjects to conditions on the basis of arrival time. One way to do this would be to assign the first 20 volunteers who arrived to the praise condition and the second 20 to the insult condition. This would be biased selection because early volunteers are different from latecomers—otherwise all students would arrive at the same time. If personal characteristics that lead to early instead of late arrival also affect ability or effort to learn, then the difference between the two groups on the memorization task could depend on difference in personal characteristics between early and late arrivers, rather than the relative effects of praise and insult.

In the Boy Scout study, the stickers received 4 or more years of scouting and the quitters received less than 1.4 years of scouting, but this was after the scouts themselves decided to stick or to quit. The Boy Scout study would come closer to the yoked design illustrated in Figs. 8.1 and 8.2, if experimenters had allowed the boys to apply for release from the Scouts and then forced them all to stay in for the full 4 years whether they liked it or not. This, more rigorous, design would still fail to demonstrate that volunteering to stay enhances the positive effects of membership in the Boy Scouts. Just as in the original study, quitters are different from stickers. Otherwise, all the scouts would quit or all would stick. This basic difference between the two types of scout can account for any difference that appears later. Scouts who stayed in voluntarily might as adults participate in more community affairs than the scouts who were forced to stay. But, that could only be a further consequnce of the personal differences that made stickers ask to stick and quitters ask to quit.

Readiness

The E-S-Q-R paradigm in Fig. 4.1 shows how response outputs depend on the interaction between stimulus inputs and the state Q of an animal or a machine. Remember from chapter 4 that the state Q depends partly on the original design of the animal or machine and partly on past history. A state Q is a state of readiness to respond in certain ways to certain stimuli.

In Fig. 8.1, food always arrives when rat C has just pressed his lever—that is, when he is engaged in that particular prefeeding behavior. By definition this means that his current state, Q (E-S-Q-R paradigm of chap. 4), makes pressing more likely, that he is *ready* to press.

A rat in a Skinner box that has just pressed the lever is in a different state from a rat that has just done something else—otherwise, they would both have done the same thing. The first rat was ready to press; the second rat was ready for something else. If the experimenter delivers a pellet at this moment, the procedure is biased because, at this moment, the contingent rat is more ready to press than the yoked rat. In the same way, the contingent student in the word recognition task was, on average, more ready when she said "Ready," than she would be at other times.

Conclusion

Yoked control experiments always confound contiguity with contingency when the reinforcing stimulus, S*, either evokes or inhibits the to-be-conditioned response. The source of confounding cannot be eliminated by more powerful procedures or more precise instruments. All conceivable versions of the yoked control for response contingent reinforcement suffer from the same *ex post facto* error.

The principle of response contingent reward and punishment is an intuitively attractive hypothesis that agrees with an everyday, commonsense view of learning that has appealed to parents, teachers, animal trainers, moralists, and psychologists for centuries. Nevertheless, for those who judge scientific merit on the basis of experimental operations rather than on the basis of intuition or common sense, a principle without any possibility of operational definition is also without any scientific merit.

LEARNING WITHOUT HEDONISM

If we can dispense with response contingent reinforcement, then we can also dispense with much of the clutter of a learning process based on experienced or expected pleasure and pain.

Bioassay

Consider the following version of the experiment in Fig. 8.1. Suppose that instead of delivering pellets of food into a dish, the apparatus delivers doses of a drug directly into the bloodstream by means of a fistula (a surgically implanted tube). The doses are small enough to metabolize rapidly, hence their effect is transitory and brief. Let us further suppose that there is a drug, Epsilon, that has only one effect on rats: It excites feeding behavior.

The rats are yoked in pairs as before, so that both receive an injection of Epsilon when rat C presses his lever, but neither is affected when rat Y presses his lever. When C presses his lever, he receives a dose of Epsilon, which excites his feeding behavior. Since manipulation is one of his feeding behaviors, that bout of lever-pressing will be prolonged. Sometimes Y will also be pressing his lever when Epsilon is released into his bloodstream, but often he will be in some other part of the Skinner box engaged in some other behavior, altogether. Consequently, rats in Condition C will, on the average, press the lever more times than rats in Condition Y.

Since we know that Epsilon is limited to one effect—the excitation of feeding behaviors—we can resist the temptation to conclude that Epsilon is a positive reinforcer. But we only have this advantage in thought experiments. Real experiments are performed to determine the effects of unknown drugs. An actual bioassay experiment that used the traditional definition of reinforcement (chap. 7) and failed to take into account the logical fallacy of the yoked control would have to conclude that Epsilon was a positive reinforcer.

In fact, bioassay experiments with analogous designs frequently appear to support the claim that electrodes implanted in certain regions of the rat brain deliver "reinforcing brain stimulation." The argument for this claim begins with the assumption that lever-pressing is arbitrary work that rats shun unless we pay them for it with food or some other commodity. It follows that, if contingent brain stimulation increases lever-pressing, it must have some value for the rat, hence the stimulated region is a "pleasure center." As we have seen, however, feeding evokes lever-pressing. It is more parsimonious to conclude that stimulation of certain regions of the rat brain evokes manipulation just as feeding does. The experimental result would be the same.

If reinforcing brain stimulation is a way of paying the rat with the pleasurable result of eating, then we would expect eating, itself, to decline and even stop entirely when brain stimulation is freely available. Indeed, we might expect some rats to starve to death under these conditions. Nevertheless, when food is freely available and brain stimulation is also freely administered by the experimenter, rats eat more rather than less food (Mogenson & Cioé, 1977, pp. 581–584). This is the opposite of what we would expect if brain stimulation is a substitute for the pleasure of eating. But it is just what we should expect if electrical stimulation delivered to certain regions of the brain evokes a repertoire of obligatory feeding behaviors that includes both eating and manipulation. In that case, when there is food and no lever, brain stimulation should evoke eating, and when there is a lever but no food, brain stimulation should evoke lever-pressing. When both are available, brain stimulation should evoke a mixture of feeding and prefeeding just as food does (see also Stewart, De Wit, & Eikelboom, 1984).

Inhibition and Competition

Consider one more variant of the yoked control experiment. Once again paired rats receive injections of a drug by means of a fistula. This time, however, the drug is Iota, which has only one effect on rats: It inhibits feeding. The subjects are yoked in pairs as before, so that both rats receive Iota when rat C presses his lever, but neither gets any Iota when rat Y presses his lever. When C presses his lever, he receives a dose of Iota that inhibits his feeding. Since manipulation is one of his feeding behaviors, that bout of lever-pressing will be shortened. Sometimes Y will also be pressing his lever when Iota is released into his bloodstream, but often he will be in some other part of the Skinner box engaged in some other behavior which may or may not be part of a rat's feeding behavior.

On the average, doses of Iota will depress C's lever-pressing more than Y's. If we did not know that Iota has only one effect—the inhibition of feeding behavior—we might conclude that Iota was aversive. For, if lever-pressing is arbitrary work that increases with pleasureable consequences and decreases with painful consequences, then Iota must be a punisher, and a site of brain stimulation that has the same negative effect must be a "pain center." Only the omniscience of the thought experimenter or the logical analysis of the yoked control can protect us from this error.

Suppose that instead of inhibiting feeding behavior, Iota excites a repertoire of *nonfeeding behavior* that is incompatible with lever-pressing. Doses of such a drug or stimulation of such a brain site would also interrupt bouts of lever-pressing. In the same way, doses of Epsilon or stimulation of an Epsilon brain site would interrupt bouts of nonfeeding behavior. An inhibitory process based on negative consequences is only required in a system that requires an excitatory process based on positive consequences. The result is a cumbersome, top-down system in which each response is governed by a separate pair of opposing excitatory and inhibitory processes. All that a living animal requires, however, is circuitry that can select now one response and then another.

The carrot and the stick move the donkey forward when the carrot is applied to the front and the stick is applied to the rear of the donkey. If the stick is applied to the nose of the donkey, then the donkey moves backward even if the stick is applied as a punishment for moving backward. Whether applied to the front or to the rear, the stick has a feed forward effect. Aversive stimulation depresses feeding behavior by evoking responses that are incompatible with feeding. In aversive conditioning with shock as in appetitive conditioning with food, the responses that are conditioned are the responses that the S* evokes. Aversive conditioning is also independent of the contingency between response and S*, and robust conditioning develops even when this earns more pain. Chapter 10 considers the problem of aversive conditioning.

Feedback Versus Sign Stimuli

The prototypes of what Norbert Wiener called *cybernetics* were two-phase systems such as thermostats, in which one of two possible inputs maintains the current output (positive feedback) and the second possible input switches the device back to the alternative phase (negative feedback), thus limiting fluctuations in temperature (discussed in chap. 4). Modern computers are multiphase systems that perform a given operation until a test is passed. This initiates the next operation, and so on. A computer can go through many operations before it repeats the first operation. Indeed, it may never return to the logical state that initiated the first operation. The pulse that ends one operation initiates the next. It feeds forward rather than backward, like the *sign stimuli* of classical ethology. In the case of a male stickleback, for example, establishing a territory and building a nest are not rewarded by the appearance of a gravid female. Instead, the swollen abdomen of the female is a sign stimulus that initiates courtship. Courtship is not rewarded when a female deposits eggs in the nest; instead, the clutch of eggs is a sign stimulus that initiates fanning and nest tending.

Highly artificial sign stimuli can evoke genuine, species-specific patterns of behavior. Remember Tinbergen's description of the male sticklebacks in his laboratory that attempted to attack Royal Mail vans passing by the windows, even though the only stimulus that a van shared with an intruding male stickleback fish was its fiery red color (chap. 4).

According to S-R contiguity, an S* serves to evoke obligatory responses rather than to reinforce arbitrary responses. The stimulus feeds forward rather than backward. The rats studied by Timberlake and his associates manipulated small steel balls almost indefinitely until pellets of prepared grain arrived. Under comparable conditions, rodents manipulate a seed until they find a suitable place in the husk to break open. This is the S* for breaking open the husk. If a rat finds a kernel of food in the husk, this is the S* for consuming the kernel, and so on (Lawhon & Hafner, 1981; Weigl & Hanson, 1980).

The sight of food evokes prefeeding responses, such as salivation. If an arbitrary stimulus, such as a tone, appears when the subject is salivating, the tone later evokes salivation before food appears. A vast number of experiments demonstrate that this procedure is sufficient for conditioning. Is it necessary to introduce an additional feed backward mechanism by which positive or negative consequences reinforce or weaken the connection between stimulus and response? Are there economic advantages to a feed backward mechanism of learning with all of the cumbersome, prespecified, top-down mechanisms that it entails? If not, the additional burden handicaps both organism and robot in a competitive world. A feed forward model of the learning process offers a more practical alternative that is also more consistent with the experimental evidence (see also, R. A. Gardner & B. T. Gardner, 1988a, 1988b, 1992).

AUTONOMOUS ROBOTS

Recent advances in robotics are beginning to offer attractive alternatives to traditional learning theories, alternatives that are even more simple-minded than Hull's model and behave even more intelligently than Tolman's. To be autonomous a robot must operate under unpredictable conditions on its own without any human supervision. So far, successful autonomous robots follow basic ethological principles.

Top-Down Robots

In traditional philosophy, information coming in from the senses must be represented in the brain in some reduced shadowy form, as in Plato's parable of the cave. In this view, human beings must decide what to do next from moment to moment by looking at these shadows of the outside world, often called *representations*. Sadly, many modern attempts to build *autonomous robots* have used this ancient model of how a nervous system governs behavior. In traditional robotics, a central processor receives information from sensors and constructs a reduced model of the present state of the world. The central processor then uses this model to decide the robot's next move and commands the motors accordingly. After the next move, the world outside changes, which changes the inside model of the world and causes the machine to reevaluate the new situation and decide once again on the next move after that. This conception of a central processor that governs behavior by receiving and processing information from sensors and then transmitting commands to motors is, of course, the top-down model of cognitive psychology.

So far, top-down robots have performed rather poorly. Imagine a top-down robot trying to maneuver through a corridor in a building. Each time it moves, the information coming in changes and alters the model of the world stored inside. Each time someone or some object in the corridor moves, this also changes the information and alters the model. To receive and process all of this information, the onboard computer must have a fairly large capacity. Even if it only has to proceed through the corridor avoiding obstacles, the onboard computer has to do a lot of computation. If the robot has additional tasks to perform (and why ever would anyone send it into the corridor or out into space to move around without doing anything?), it has to have still greater capacity. This requires a rather large onboard computer to process the information rapidly. Otherwise, the robot could only move at a snail's pace. A large computer that computes with reasonable speed has to have a large power source in the form of large, heavy batteries. This means large, heavy wheels and motors to carry the onboard computer even before the engineers add the hardware that does the jobs required by the mission.

As late as 1997, the best top-down robots were so large and so cumbersome and their processing was so slow that the fastest of them were still too slow to do any practical work. Some engineers continue to design larger top-down robots with larger onboard computers in the hopes that larger computers may eventually process the information fast enough to become practical. There is always hope that miniaturization may someday make top-down robots more practical. Meanwhile, existing top-down robots are so large and so expensive that it would be impossible to send more than one at a time on a space mission, say to the moon. And, if one bearing or one spring failed, the whole robot would be lost and the mission would fail with it.

Bottom-Up Robots

More recently, engineers lead by Brooks (1990) of MIT shifted their attention to *bottom-up* models that need little or no central processing. Suppose that the diagram in Fig. 8.3 represents an egg-shaped robot equipped with two light-sensitive units at its front end and two motor-driven wheels at its rear end. In this illustration, the light sensor on the left side of the robot is wired to the wheel motor on the right of the robot and the light sensor on the right is wired to the wheel motor on the left of the robot. This is called *contralateral* connection.

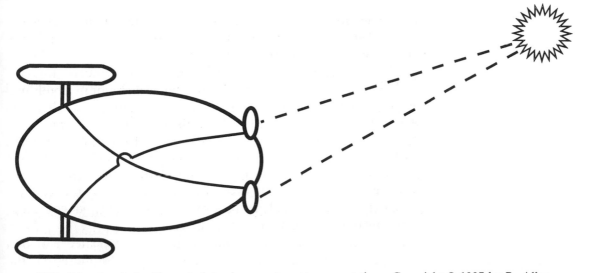

FIG. 8.3. A robot with contralateral sensor-to-motor connections. Copyright © 1997 by R. Allen Gardner.

The star-shaped object in the diagram represents a source of light. When the light is closer to the sensor on the left, more power goes to the wheel on the right and less power to the wheel on the left. As a result, the robot moves toward the light. When the light moves, the robot follows, eventually colliding with the light. Notice that the robot can follow the light faithfully without any central processor to compute where the light is or the speed and direction of the light's movement, or where the robot is and the speed and direction of its own movement. The robot never has to compute anything and evaluate the results in order to decide what to do next. All it has to do is respond directly to the relative amount of light reaching its sensors.

Bottom-up robots have been around for some time. By the time of the Korean War, the U.S. military had already developed a system like the one in Fig. 8.3 to operate heat-seeking missiles. Heat-seeking missiles are fired at enemy aircraft, but they only have to get near enough to sense the heat of the enemy's engines. With more than two pairs of jets, the heat-seeking missile can maneuver in three dimensions and track the enemy engine no matter what evasive action the pilot may take. Eventually, the missile collides with the enemy engine and destroys it.

It is a simple, cheap, and effective design that operates without a central processor. It never has to know anything about the location or the movements of a target, it never has to know anything about its own location or movements, either, and it never has to create a model of the world outside in order to decide what to do next. In fact, it never makes any specific response to any specific stimulus. It only responds to relative stimulation. To people who do not know how these robots work, they seem very clever. To the first pilot who was pursued and shot down by a heat-seeking missile, the robot must have seemed devilishly clever, indeed.

In Fig. 8.3, the connections between the sensors and the motors are contralateral, and the robot always moves toward the light. Suppose the connections are *ipsilateral,* instead—that is, the sensor on the left wired to the motor on the left and the sensor on the right wired to the motor on the right. With ipsilateral connections, the robot should always turn away from the light. If the sensors have wide-angle reception, like the eyes of many animals such as rabbits, the ipsilateral robot not only turns away from the light, but continues to move away until it gets to a dark place.

The behavior of the robot would be more complicated if it had another pair of sensors, say a pair of odor sensors. Suppose that the light sensors have ipsilateral connections to the motors and the odor sensors have contralateral connections. Then the robot would track odors in the dark and avoid light in general. With a little adjustment, the robot would approach when an odor is relatively strong and light is relatively weak. Such a robot would even dither a bit when attraction to the odor conflicted with repulsion from the light. In close cases, the robot would seem to be having trouble deciding what to do next. Brooks (1990) has already tested a robot that runs away from the light and into the darkest corner it can find, when it hears a loud sound. It then stays in the dark until an interval of quiet time has passed.

In recent times, engineers have used the simple principle of direct response to relative stimulation to produce more ingenious robots. Horswill and Brooks (1988), for example, mounted two small television cameras on a small robot about 2 feet long, and wired the robot (as in Fig. 8.3) to follow small solid objects about the size of a baseball. The vision of the cameras is very crude compared with the vision of most vertebrate animals, but they can sense simple objects and direct the robot motors to follow the objects. When someone dangles a ball on a string near this robot, the robot chases it like a kitten.

The robot also has sonar units that sense obstacles and it is wired to avoid obstacles before collision. If the ball moves over an object like a chair but still remains in view, then the robot goes around the chair. If a large object, like a utility cart, gets between the robot and the ball, the cameras lose sight of the target. The robot then remains oriented toward the last place where it detected a ball and stays oriented in this direction for a while. If the obstacle moves away soon enough, the robot picks up the target again and continues to follow it. If the obstacle remains in place too long, then the robot begins to wander randomly until it finds another target.

Again, this simple, autonomous robot can navigate around obstacles and deal with a wide variety of unpredictable situations without any cognition at all. It only has to make relative responses to relative sources of stimulation. Bottom-up robots can do without any internal representation of the outside world because they respond directly to the world, itself. They operate without constructing an internal model, because they use the world as a model of itself.

Building From the Bottom Up

Autonomous robots of the Brooks type are designed from the bottom up. The most basic element in the design is the system that avoids obstacles. The engineers perfect this system first. Next, the engineers design and perfect a simple system that makes the robot wander. This is necessary for situations in which the robot reaches a blank wall or some other obstacle. Without a spontaneous wandering system, it would continue to rest at a safe distance from the obstacle.

The next layer of the system begins to direct the robot. With two cameras, the robot can have depth perception to detect openings such as doorways and to go through them. One of Brooks' requirements for bottom-up robots is that they can operate in a natural and unpredictable environment, such as the lobby outside his MIT lab where people come and go and move carts and furniture at unpredictable times. After entering a doorway, a robot called Herbert seeks out desk-size objects and approaches them. When Herbert is close enough, it passes a laser beam over the top of a desk till it detects an object like a soda pop can. Herbert's arm then reaches out, grabs the can, and hefts it. If the can is heavy, Herbert replaces it. If the can is light, Herbert takes it away and deposits it in a recycling bin down the hall.

Bottom-up robots only need simple computers, so the robots can be quite small, often only about 1 foot long. Because they are so small and so cheap to build, a rocket ship to the moon could carry 100–200 of them. Any that failed to operate could be left behind with little loss. The odds are high that many of them would perform well enough to assure the success of a mission.

Bottom-Up Learning

Suppose that Herbert's laser beam can scan only to the right or to the left. Suppose further that 80% of the empty cans in this environment are on the right and only 20% are on the left. To profit from this contingency, all Herbert would need is a circuit that prevented immediate repetition, right or left, but ensured repetition after a delay, say till the next desk.

This would guarantee that at the next desk, Herbert would beam in the same direction that was successful at the last desk. On average, Herbert would find a can on the first try 80% of the 80% of the time that the cans were on the right and 20% of the 20% of the time that cans were on the left. That is 64% plus 4% or 68% of the time, which is distinctly better than 50%. This could be improved by allowing a cumulative effect of repeated success in one direction. This would dampen the effect of infrequent instances of left-lying cans. By contrast, engineers could burden Herbert with onboard computing facilities that recorded past right and left successes and computed the contingencies. When Herbert had enough data to conclude that beaming to the right was the best strategy, the robot could beam to the right at every desk. That would increase performance to 100% of 80% or 80% success, only a modest improvement over 68%.

The practical advantages of a simple-minded, *win-stay* system increase if there are three or more alternatives, as when cans can have right, center, and left or still more different positions (R. A. Gardner, 1957, 1961). An onboard computer that had to compute all of the contingencies would have to take into account an $N \times N$ matrix of reaches, successes, and failures. The last-trial-only learning system would only have to record the last successful reach. While modestly less accurate than a system that computed exact probabilities, it would make up for this by responding immediately to the prevailing contingency. Herbert could respond to changes in the right–left distribution of cans on desks without waiting until new instances averaged out the old computations, a serious problem in practical applications of neural network computing (Kosko, 1993, pp. 331–369).

With this bottom-up learning mechanism, Herbert could benefit from experience without discriminating correlation from causation and without evaluating, computing, or storing positive and negative hedonic contingencies. Herbert could use the recent history of the world as a model of the future and respond directly to that.

SUMMARY

Abundant evidence reviewed in earlier chapters shows that S-R contiguity is sufficient for learning. Ethological evidence shows that lever-pressing and key-pecking in the Skinner box or operant conditioning chamber are obligatiory behaviors evoked by food or water. They persist even when the contingency between responses and incentives is negative. The idea that lever-pressing and key-pecking are arbitrary behaviors that animals only perform for contingent food or water has caused much confusion. Analysis of the yoked control experiment shows that, when food or water evokes a response, then it is impossible under any conceivable experimental arrangements to measure any additional effect of contingency beyond the well-established evidence for contiguity.

This chapter goes on to show how relatively simple, feed forward, ethological principles fit the facts of conditioning without recourse to cumbersome, hedonistic, feed backward principles of contingency. This chapter ends by contrasting the practical failures of top-down robotics with the practical successes of bottom-up robotics. A foraging robot with a simple, low-powered, bottom-up mechanism could learn much more cheaply and efficiently than a foraging robot that had to compute actual contingencies. The simpler, bottom-up system is also more flexible so that its advantages increase with complexity and natural fluctuations in practical foraging problems.

CHAPTER 9

Appetite, Aversion, and Conflict

Throughout the 20th century, the concept of motivation has served three functions in most psychological theories: 1) driving behavior, 2) directing and selecting behavior, and 3) rewarding behavior. With respect to the driving or energizing function, conventional psychological theory maintained that active behavior requires internal motive force. According to this view, an animal that was satiated for all incentives—hunger, thirst, sex, warmth, etc., would become completely inactive and probably fall asleep—unless aroused by pain or threat of pain. With respect to the directing and selecting function, in order to eat when hungry and drink when thirsty, an animal must be able to tell when it is thirsty and when it is hungry. Otherwise, animals would drink when hungry and eat when thirsty, which would certainly be an awkward state of affairs. With respect to the rewarding function, if learning depends on contingent reinforcement then motivation determines learning, because motivation determines reward and punishment.

Earlier chapters of this book considered difficulties with the traditional view of contingent reinforcement as the basis of learning. This chapter considers further difficulties with the traditional view and shows how modern developments replace the Greek notion of motive force with the feed forward principles of appetite, aversion, and conflict.

MOTIVE AND DRIVE

In classical times, Greek scientists noted that celestial bodies move in circular patterns, with our earth at the center. Terrestrial bodies move downward by themselves, but human beings and beasts of burden have to push, pull, and carry inanimate objects. Human beings move by themselves, which classical philosophers attributed to divine gifts of internal power. Other animals move by themselves, endowed with a kind of robotic internal force that also required divine intervention. This model of motive forces remained essentially in tact through Descartes' time. It was late in the 18th century that chemists discovered the relationship between combustion and animal energy and only early in the 20th century that the chemistry and biology of this relationship reached its modern form (Mendelsohn, 1964).

The most dramatic technological advances of the 19th century were steam engines that did useful work, and actually moved themselves in contraptions called locomotives. The terms *motivation* and *drive* express the concern with sources of motion that comes down to us from classical Greece. During the first half of the 20th century, a series of influential studies seemed to support the traditional energizing view of drive. Animals, mainly rats, lived in an apparatus which consisted of a running wheel and a counter that recorded revolutions of the wheel. Animals lived in the wheel for days, sometimes without food, sometimes without water, and sometimes without either food or water.

The experimenter or a technician visited the apparatus regularly each day to record the number of revolutions on the counter. With so little effort required, experimenters could keep squads of these inexpensive devices running at the same time. Without a learning or perceptual task to be disturbed, they could set up the running wheels anywhere in the laboratory without the bother of isolating the subjects from visual and auditory disturbance. These *activity wheel* studies all showed the same pattern. Activity increased with hours and days of deprivation up to some maximum and then declined, presumably because the animals weakened from lack of food or water (Morgan & Stellar, 1950, pp. 368–381; Reed, 1947). This seemed to confirm the notion that deprivation causes an increase in drive and drive increases output. This steam engine model of motivation appears in the work of such diverse theorists as Freud, Hull, Skinner, and Tinbergen and remains influential at this writing.

Irritability

The energy output of 19th century steam engines made a great impression on psychologists of the early 20th century because this was the most dramatic technological advance of those times. The most dramatic advances of recent times have to do with systems that process information and govern energy. Modern psychobiologists can see that living animals make their way in the world by responding appropriately to external stimulation. Life depends more on government than on release of animal energy.

In a landmark experiment, Campbell and Sheffield (1953) studied the interaction between activity and external stimulation. First, they isolated their rat subjects in a special insulated cabinet that they placed in a soundproofed room. They further isolated the rats from disturbing stimuli by keeping them in the dark and running a fan that made the same steady hum all day long. They housed each rat separately in a specially designed activity cage, which had a round floor balanced on a central point. Silent mercury switches at four opposite points of the floor recorded all movements that tilted the cage in any way. The animals must have gotten some stimulation from their own movements. Apart from that their stimulus environment was virtually constant, with one exception. For 10 minutes every day, a timer automatically turned on the lights and turned off the fan. Water was always available to the rats from a drinking tube. For 4 days, food was also constantly available and then for 3 days all food was withdrawn.

The results in Fig. 9.1 show that activity depended on stimulation. During the 10 minutes of stimulus change each day (upper curve), activity was much higher than during the 10-minute constant period before stimulus change (lower curve). During the control days before food deprivation, activity remained fairly constant whether we look at the higher level evoked by stimulus change or the lower level during constant stimulation. During the days of food deprivation, activity remained virtually constant during the 10-minute periods of constant stimulation, but rose dramatically with each day of deprivation during the 10-minute stimulus change periods. Without stimulus change, increased hunger failed to increase activity. Increased hunger only increased responsiveness to stimulation—that is to say, it made the animals more *irritable.*

We can see now why hunger seemed to have a general energizing function when animals lived in running wheels in busy laboratory rooms. Hunger made them more and more responsive to the noises and sounds around them. The running wheels themselves made noise, so that running caused noise that stimulated more running. When Campbell and Sheffield kept the level of stimulation in the rooms nearly constant, and at the same time kept the activity cages themselves silent, the level of activity remained nearly constant even though the level of hunger rose with each passing day. Activity rose with hunger only when the experimenters changed the sounds and the sights that stimulated the rats. These results contradict the notion of

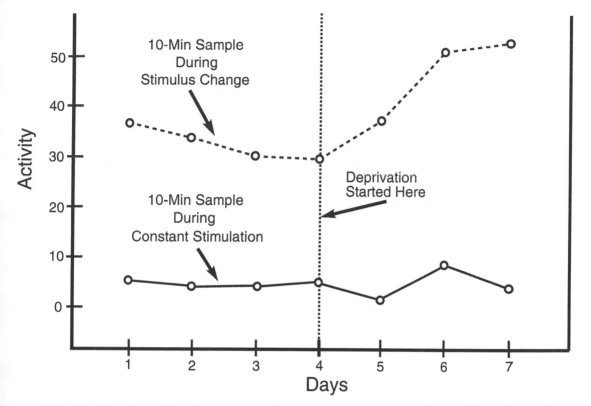

FIG. 9.1.   The effect of deprivation on activity in response to a stimulus change. From Campbell and Sheffield (1953).

hunger as energizing motivation. They show instead that hunger made the animals more responsive to changes in stimulation. Irritability together with the directing and selecting function of drive is enough to account for all evidence that activity or energy output rises with increases in deprivation (see review by Hall, 1976, pp. 212–213).

Campbell and Sheffield's discovery that hunger increases irritability rather than energy output applies directly to the phenomenon called *stimulus change reinforcement* (Kish, 1966; Osborne & Shelby, 1975). Kish (1955) was the first to show that if lever-pressing caused changes in illumination, mice increased their lever-pressing. He and many others interpreted this as reinforcement by stimulus change (chap. 4). Suppose, however, that Campbell and Sheffield had arranged their stimulus change experiment somewhat differently. Suppose that instead of fixed periods of stimulus change, they wired the apparatus so that each small amount of activity started a brief stimulus change. We can see from the results they obtained in Fig. 9.1 that each brief stimulus change would evoke activity, which would cause the apparatus to deliver more stimulus change, which would evoke more activity, and so on. This version of the Campbell and Sheffield experiment would seem to show that contingent stimulus change reinforces general activity. We already know from Campbell and Sheffield's results, however, that stimulus change feeds forward to activity without any contingency at all. Just as in the other cases of stimuli that evoke responses in chapter 8, we cannot attribute this result to contingent reinforcement.

How Many Drives?

Early theorists such as Hull, Skinner, and Freud claimed to be biological and materialistic because they assumed a small number of primary drives—hunger, thirst, sex, and a very few others. Secondary drives were supposed to develop by association with primary drives just as second-order conditioning and secondary rewards were supposed to develop by association between an arbitrary S^a and a biological S^* (chaps. 4 and 7). In this view, an infant loves its mother because she brings food, drink, and warmth. In this way, the sight and sound of mothers become incentives that motivate behavior. In humans, her praising voice becomes a reward, her scolding voice, a punishment. Eventually, the sight and sound of other women who resemble her become rewarding or punishing, and so on.

Modern studies, however, reveal a wide variety of incentives that cannot be traced to a history of conditioning with one of the traditional short list of primary drives such as hunger or thirst. Monkeys, for example, are good at solving mechanical problems because they spontaneously manipulate objects such as sticks and straw (Westergaard, 1988; Westergaard, Greene, Babitz, & Suomi, 1995). In a particularly revealing study, H. F. Harlow, M. K. Harlow, and Meyer (1950) left mechanical latches (Fig. 9.2) in cages and showed that monkeys would work the latches open without any extrinsic reward. The latches were mounted on a wall of their cages and nothing else opened when the monkeys undid the latches. The monkeys acted as if the latches, themselves, evoked manipulation.

Later, H. F. Harlow (1958) showed that infant monkeys became attached to artificial dolls if the dolls had the right sort of cloth texture. They preferred a familiar cloth-covered doll to an equally familiar wire-covered doll, even when they got all of their food from the wire doll. After they became attached to a cloth doll, just the sight of the doll could comfort them even when they could only see the doll through a window.

It may be a small step to add a need for contact comfort to the list of primary motives, but a need to manipulate hardware on a wall

FIG. 9.2.   Latches evoke manipulation and unlatching in H. F. Harlow et al. (1950). Copyright ©
1950 by Harlow Primate Laboratory, University of Wisconsin. Reprinted by permission.

begins to stretch the concept of primary biological needs. This sort
of motivational psychology says that monkeys manipulate hardware
on the wall because they need to manipulate hardware on the wall.
Why not say they manipulate because they manipulate?

Evocative Stimuli

The latch problems of Harlow et al. (1950) evoked manipulation and
the cloth dolls of Harlow (1958) evoked cuddling. The evidence indicates that you love your mother when you are an infant because
her skin and her voice evoke cuddling, which is certainly a materialistic
discovery.

From a feed forward point of view, motivation is responsiveness
to stimuli. In *Alice in Wonderland,* Alice keeps finding cakes labeled
"eat me" and liquids labeled "drink me." She cannot seem to resist
orders to eat or drink even though she is always sorry afterward. In
a feed forward system, instead of inside forces that push there are
outside stimuli that pull—drink me's, eat me's, cuddle me's, unlatch
me's, and so on. It is very hard to resist touching newly painted walls,
fences, and furniture in spite of warning signs and memories of past
disasters. Wet paint seems to say "touch me."

Selection

A working prototype of a modern robot cleans floors without human guidance and, when its batteries are low, seeks out specially designed power outlets to recharge the batteries by itself. While not yet commercially successful, the technology for mass producing such devices is already commonplace. When a meter attached to the batteries reads above a certain point, the robot cleans the floors; when the meter reads below that point, the robot goes to the nearest outlet and recharges its batteries. Early models had only two motives, but more could be added according to the same principle. They could, for example, grease their own bearings or chase off intruders.

The onboard computer regulates the robot; it does not drive it. Some tasks might require small, delicate movements. The robot would have to carry out such tasks with a low energy output no matter what the level of need of its batteries, its designer, or its present owner. A robot that had to operate at high energy levels when needs were high and low energy levels when needs were low would be unsuitable for many economically significant tasks.

Robots function quite well so long as their prevailing state (Q in the E-S-Q-R paradigm of chap. 4) determines their response to prevailing stimulation. They function without liking clean floors and charged batteries or disliking dirty floors and weak batteries. An engineer who added likes and dislikes to the system would be adding to the burdens of the onboard computer. Unless likes and dislikes added some economic advantage, robots governed by pleasure and pain would disappear from the commercial marketplace. In the same way, unless the likes and dislikes frequently imputed to living organisms add ecological advantages, it is prudent to assume that they cannot survive in evolutionary competition. To keep an animal alive, motivational states only have to increase and decrease the probabilities of competing responses in a way that selects now one type of behavior, now another.

Summary

In a feed forward system, the effect of hunger and thirst is to increase feeding and drinking behavior and decrease other types of behavior. Rather than eating harder or drinking harder, animals eat or drink more exclusively when they are hungry or thirsty. In the same way, hormonal chemistry can increase responsiveness to sexual stimuli and lower responsiveness to other types of stimulation, such as food and even lectures and textbooks.

AVERSION

To make its way in the world, an organism must obtain food, water, and other goods. It must also escape and—preferably—avoid injury, poison, and other bads. A significant portion of the behavior of human beings and other animals consists of responses to pain or to the threat of pain. In human behavior, we see some of the most dramatic examples of persistent responses that have plainly negative consequences. When human responses to stress persist in spite of their negative consequences, we call them maladaptive and, if the consequences are serious, some even recommend psychotherapy.

This is why so many psychologists are so interested in studies of aversive conditioning in nonhuman animals. Some of the classic symptoms of anxiety resemble conditioned defensive behavior that is evoked in anticipation of impending painful experience. Other symptoms, such as eating and drinking disorders, resemble conditioned consumatory behavior that is evoked in the aftermath of painful experience. Experimenters have justified a great deal of outright torture of captive animals in the name of this cause.

Defensive Aggression

The notion that animals approach appetitive stimulation and withdraw from aversive stimulation is deeply ingrained in Western culture, but it hardly exhausts the ethological possibilities that we find in nature. For example, chapter 2 described how flocks of smaller birds can drive off larger predators by aggressive mobbing. Wild rodents, like squirrels and rats, nest in burrows that shelter them from predators as well as from weather. Some predators, like snakes and weasels, invade burrows and prey on rodents. An invader in the burrow is a highly aversive stimulus, but rodents approach rather than retreat. Ethological observations record a species-specific defensive approach: chest pressed against the floor of the burrow and forelimbs outstretched, hurling loose dirt from the floor at the face of the invader. With luck, the dirt obstructs the passage enough to halt the invasion. Dirt in the face should also feed the predator forward to nonfeeding behavior, so that the predator withdraws.

Pinel, Mana, and Ward (1989), Pinel, Symons, Christensen, and Tees (1989), and others reviewed by them, studied this phenomenon in the laboratory. If there is hurlable material on the floor, such as sawdust, rodents hurl it. If not, they assume the characteristic posture and make the characteristic forelimbs movements anyway. Animals that have lived in the wild are more likely to engage in this form of defensive aggression (Heynen, Sainsbury, & Montoya, 1989).

Pinel, Mana, and Ward (1989) placed rodents in a U-shaped burrow. Instead of an invader, the experimenters placed a wire coiled around a small stick that was horizontally mounted on the back wall of one arm of the U. In the course of exploring the burrow, each rat eventually touched the coil and received a painful shock. Each rat immediately retreated to the middle section of the U, but soon returned, chest to the floor and forelimbs throwing sawdust or imaginary dirt at the coiled wire. Rather than avoiding the place where they were shocked, as we would expect from the pleasure–pain principle, rats spent most of their time in the shock section of the U. As usual, what a stimulus makes an animal do is much more significant than what a stimulus makes an animal feel—whether the feeling is pleasure or pain.

Suppression and Induction

In traditional systems of excitation and inhibition, appetites excite and aversions inhibit. In the feed forward analysis of this book, motivation makes animals selectively irritable—that is, more responsive to certain stimuli than to others and more likely to make certain responses than others. Painful shocks suppress eating by positively evoking aversive responses that are incompatible with eating rather than by inhibiting eating.

After an interruption, many forms of behavior resume with increased vigor. When they have free access to food, animals tend to consume a stable amount of food per hour or per day. After a period of deprivation, they tend to consume more than usual at first and then resume their stable rate of consumption. They overcompensate for the deprivation.

That animals should need food seems fairly obvious, but the biological significance of much behavior remains obscure. *Dreaming* is a good example. Human beings dream for a portion of each night of sleep. We can tell when they are dreaming by *rapid eye movements* (REM), when the cornea moves under closed eyelids, and correlated with self-reports of dreaming. There are cycles of REM and non-REM sleep throughout the night, and individual human beings tend to dream for a stable portion of each night of sleep.

Experimenters have deprived subjects of REM sleep for several consecutive nights by waking them whenever REM started. On nights that follow nights of REM deprivation, subjects overcompensate with more than the usual amount of REM before returning to their usual amount of REM sleep (Vogel, 1975). To say that they have a need to dream is imminantly reasonable, but only tells us that they must have a biological need to dream because they dream. The supernormal increase in dreaming after *dream deprivation* is like the supernormal increase in feeding after food deprivation.

Stimuli that evoke incompatible responses also interrupt ongoing behavior. Painful electric shock evokes a pattern of behavior that is incompatible with feeding, and the interruption is followed by a supernormal increase in feeding in the aftermath of the shock (Tugendhat, 1960).

Rhythmic Patterns

In Pavlov's laboratory, when the interval between the conditioned stimulus and the food

> . . . is short, say 1–5 seconds, the salivary reaction almost immediately follows the beginning of the conditioned stimulus. On the other hand, in reflexes which have been established with a longer interval between the two stimuli the onset of the salivary response is delayed, and this delay is proportional to the length of the interval between the two stimuli and may even extend to several minutes. (Pavlov, 1927/1960, p. 88)

Presumably, *temporal conditioning* is possible because there are biological rhythms which correlate with time so well that animals can use them as stimuli. The cyclically repeating events of a conditioning experiment—a constant stimulus that begins each trial, followed by the S*, followed by an intertrial interval—are favorable conditions for temporal conditioning.

Temporal conditioning also appears in the Skinner box. If the apparatus delivers food at intervals, then the distribution of responses varies accordingly. Lever-pressing or key-pecking is absent soon after each delivery of food and begins again later on, reaching its peak toward the end of each interval, just before food usually arrives. This pattern appears whether or not the delivery of food is contingent on responding (Staddon & Simmelhag, 1971; Zeiler, 1968). The absence of lever-pressing and key-pecking immediately after receiving food is called the *postreinforcement pause*.

During the postreinforcement pause, subjects engage in *nonfeeding* behavior such as grooming or preening (Anderson & Shettleworth, 1977; Shettleworth & Juergensen, 1980). If there is a drinking tube in the chamber, rats drink during the pause in lever-pressing and, as conditioning progresses, they may drink three or four times as much as normal (Falk, 1971). This overdrinking is called *polydipsia*. If, instead of a drinking tube, there is a second (suitably restrained) pigeon in the chamber, the subject pigeon attacks it vigorously during the pause in key-pecking, beginning these attacks with elements of the classic, ethological, agonistic pattern; including swaying head-lowered approach, deep-throated growls, and wing striking (Azrin, Hutchinson, & Hake, 1966). Such nonfeeding behaviors, often called *adjunctive behaviors,* are evoked by the schedule of widely spaced food delivery; they fail to appear when food deliveries are frequent and they cease when food deliveries are stopped (Cohen & Looney, 1984).

An S* evokes some responses and suppresses other incompatible responses. When an S* ceases or is consumed, other responses recover, often at a supernormal level in the aftermath of the S*. If there are repeated, spaced intervals between deliveries of S*, then an S* itself becomes a stimulus for a period without any S*. As the animal synchronizes its behavior to the rhythm of the spacing, the animal makes prefeeding or preshock responses late in the interval when an S* is imminent, and makes otherwise incompatible responses early in the interval when an S* is unlikely to appear (Janssen et al., 1995).

An S^a that appears late in the interval is contiguous with prefeeding or preshock behavior, and an S^a that appears early in the interval is contiguous with nonfeeding or nonshock behavior. Consequently, prefeeding and preshock responses become conditioned to an S^a that precedes the S*, and nonfeeding or nonshock responses become conditioned to an S^a that follows the S*. In this way, the responses that become conditioned to the S^a depend on the phase of the inter-S* interval.

In a feed forward system, differentiation between the pre- and post-S* phases of the trial cycle should appear only after a certain amount of repetition of the cycle. At first, food should only evoke consummatory responses, and shock should only evoke defensive responses. With very few trials there should be little difference between the responses paired with an S^a that occurs before S* and the responses paired with an S^a that occurs after S*—perhaps no difference in response at all after only a single trial. Thus, backward conditioning should be roughly the same as forward conditioning after a single trial (chap. 4). With repetition of the trial cycle, the suppression and induction effects should condition opposite responses in the pre- and post-S* phases.

Avoidance

Painful electric shocks delivered through a grid in the floor of the conditioning chamber evoke running and jumping in many animals. If the shock ceases as soon as they respond, animals learn to run or jump more quickly. This is called *escape.* They also readily learn to run or jump during a *warning interval* that precedes shock. In a highly effective procedure, animals avoid shock altogether if they respond before the end of the warning period. This is called *avoidance.* It seems clear that the reward for escape conditioning is that pain stops when shock stops. But, what is the reward for avoidance?

A series of pioneering experiments by Solomon and his associates established the basic phenomena of avoidance conditioning. The subjects were usually dogs trained to avoid shock in a two-compartment apparatus. The conditioned stimulus, signaling the onset of a strong shock, was a change in illumination and the lowering of a door, permitting the dog to jump over a shoulder-high hurdle and get into the other compartment. A favorable warning interval between the onset of the warning signal and the onset of shock is about 10 seconds. Jumping the hurdle to the "cold" compartment escapes shock in the early stages of conditioning. The dogs avoid the shock entirely when they jump before the end of the warning interval.

Figure 9.3 shows the responses of a typical subject. Note that:

1. After seven trials with latencies longer than 10 seconds, the dog responded soon enough to avoid the shock on Trial 8 and every trial after that.

2. Instead of extinguishing in the absence of any addititional shocks, the dog improved its performance throughout 32 remaining trials, improving rapidly at first and then more slowly, producing the usual negatively accelerated learning curve. In fact, after 10 successive avoidances the dog responded so promptly that it never received another shock.

3. Signs of fear such as increased heart rate and breathing rate tend to appear during the first three or four trials of avoidance conditioning followed by marked decrease later in learning. During later trials, animals appear to be quite calm in the experimental apparatus. Liddell (1956) found this same calmness in the laboratory chamber when he conditioned sheep with electric shock. In his experiments, Liddell often shocked the same individual in the same laboratory chamber for several years. Ethologically interested in his animals, he continued to observe them outside of the laboratory. He reported dramatically disturbed behavior in the pasture and the barn after long periods of aversive conditioning with shock (1956, pp. 51–67).

4. Vigorous hurdle jumping persists for hundreds of trials, which completes the picture of the problem confronting the reinforcement theorist attempting to account for the facts of avoidance learning.

How is such rapid and persistent conditioning possible with so little reward or punishment? At first, the principle of persistence after

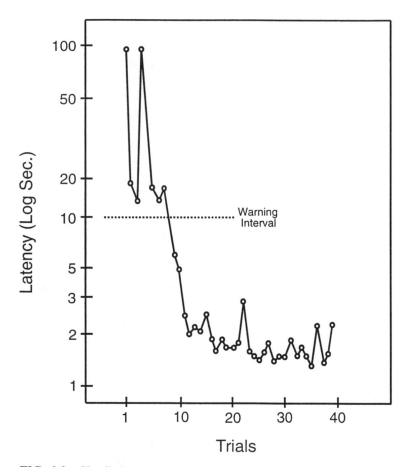

FIG. 9.3. Hurdle-jumping avoidance by a dog. From Solomon and Wynne (1953).

partial reward (chap. 11) seemed to account for the persistence of conditioned avoidance. According to this view, conditioned avoidance resists extinction, because it gets intermittently reinforced by occasional lapses and consequent punishments during acquisition. Typically, however, as in Fig. 9.3, there is shock rewarded by escape from shock on every trial until the first avoidance. From then on dogs avoid all shocks. Persistent avoidance develops without any period of intermittent reward.

Solomon and Wynne (1953) proposed an elaborate *two-factor theory* to explain avoidance conditioning. The main elements of this theory are similar to Mowrer's (1960) two-factors. *Fear* becomes conditioned to the warning signal by stimulus-response contiguity. After that the animal escapes from the fear evoked by the warning stimulus. But how does conditioned fear, itself, resist extinction? This is a puzzle, since second-order conditioning is so weak and easily extinguished under laboratory conditions (chaps. 4 and 7). Nevertheless, versions of this two-factor theory remain popular among those who would preserve reinforcement theory at all costs (e.g., Schwartz & Reisberg, 1991, pp. 139–153). The problem with theories of conditioned fear is that the fear in these theories is an entirely hypothetical phenomenon that exists only to fill the gaps between reinforcement theory and the results of experiments. By adding new imaginary phenomena to account for each new experimental finding, reinforcement theories weaken their claim as down-to-earth, hardheaded scientific formulas and lose much of their credibility.

Compatibility

Defensive responses evoked by painful shock are incompatible with feeding. Since lever-pressing is a feeding behavior, it should be very difficult to condition a rat to press a lever to avoid shock. Meyer, Cho, and Wesemann (1960), for example, failed to obtain any appreciable amount of lever-pressing for the reward of shock avoidance under a variety of procedures that would have been quite favorable to condition running or jumping. D'Amato and Schiff (1964), using a similar procedure, gave rats 60 trials per night for a total of 123 nights or 7,380 trials of avoidance conditioning, altogether. And still, half of their subjects failed to develop any appreciable level of avoidance responding. Results of this kind were the point of departure for Bolles' influential discussion of species-specific defense reactions in aversive conditioning (Bolles, 1970).

These studies used a discrete trial procedure—warning signal, followed by scheduled shock or avoided shock, followed by intertrial interval. In D'Amato and Schiff (1964), the intervals between shocks were about 3 minutes; in Meyer et al. (1960) the interval between shocks was about 1 minute; and both used a 5-second *warning interval*. These are favorable intervals for conditioning rats to run or jump to avoid shock. Reasoning that the association between warning and shock should be stronger if the onset of the warning signal were closer to the onset of the shock, Meyer et al. tried still shorter warning intervals but only obtained still less lever-pressing during the warning interval. Greater suppression is what we would expect, of course, if anticipatory defensive responses are conditioned to the warning signal while components of feeding behavior (e.g., lever-pressing) are suppressed by defensive responses (see discussion of conditioned emotional response, CER, in chap. 2). In that case, the closer the warning signal to the shock, the more the defensive effect should suppress feeding.

Apparently, D'Amato and Schiff did not record responses between trials—that is, between each shock and the next warning signal. Meyer et al. did record intertrial responses, and they reported "[intertrial] bar-pressing rates that often reached extremely high values. There were many instances, in fact, of rates above two thousand per hour; had these rates been evenly distributed in time, at least a third of all the subjects would have shown us ultimately perfect avoidance. We obtained, instead, a suppression of the rate when the warning stimulus came on" (p. 226). Again, intertrial lever-pressing is what we would expect if components of feeding behavior that were suppressed during the warning interval recovered at a supernormal level during the intertrial interval.

The longer the warning interval the more the onset of the warning signal predicts an interval without shock. Longer warning intervals should evoke less defensive behavior and permit more lever-pressing. The onset of very long warning intervals should seem like signals of safety and actually induce lever-pressing. Berger and Brush (1975) lengthened the warning interval and that is precisely what they found. The longer the warning interval the more often their rats avoided shock by pressing the lever. This increased as they lengthened the warning interval from 20 to 30 and even to 60 seconds. As we would expect—if lever-pressing is suppressed by signals close to shock and enhanced by signals remote from shock—most of the lever-pressing appeared shortly after the onset of the warning signal. The warning signal tells the subject that shock will not come for 20, 30, or 60 seconds. Denny (1971) discusses in detail a great deal of related evidence on the temporal distribution of defensive and nondefensive responses together with a theory that also attributes the observed distribution of responses to theoretical phases of relief and relaxation in the aftermath of shock.

Operant Avoidance

Skinner's operant procedure (chap. 3) has neither trials nor intertrial intervals. The delivery of S* punctuates conditioning sessions according to a schedule that is contingent, noncontingent, or partially contingent on a criterion response such as lever-pressing or key-pecking. Sidman (1953) introduced an avoidance procedure for rats in which painful electric shocks are the S* and each lever-press lengthens the interval between shocks. A clock delivers shocks at the end of shock-shock intervals and response-shock intervals. If the animal presses the lever or pecks the key, the next shock comes at the end of the response-shock interval, typically 20 seconds. If an animal fails to respond after a shock, the next shock comes at the end of the shock-shock interval, typically 5 seconds. Consequently, the shorter the interval between responses the fewer the shocks. If an animal always responds within the response-shock interval, it never gets any shock at all. The vast number of successful experiments that have used variants of this method proves that Sidman's procedure is highly effective for conditioning rats to press levers with shock as the S* (see Hineline, 1977, 1981, for extensive reviews of this literature).

Where defensive responses, such as running and jumping, serve to avoid or postpone shock, animals respond most frequently at times when shock is imminent. By contrast, in Sidman's operant procedure rats characteristically press the lever in bursts in the aftermath of each shock and make the majority of their responses early in the intervals between shocks when there is little or no probability that shocks will occur (Ellen & Wilson, 1964; Forgione, 1970; Herrnstein & Hineline, 1966; R. W. Powell, 1972; R. W. Powell & Peck, 1969; Sidman, 1958). This distribution of responses is clearly shown in Fig. 9.4 (Powell & Peck, 1969, p. 1059). Just as in the discrete trials procedure, lever-pressing and key-pecking in Sidman's procedure appear in the aftermath of shock as if evoked by the absence of shock (R. A. Gardner & B. T. Gardner, 1988a, pp. 140–142).

Two Ways to Abolish Contingency

From a feed backward point of view, rats press levers and pigeons peck keys in operant avoidance because this earns them lower probabilities of shock. That is the role of contingency in operant avoidance. From a feed forward point of view, on the other hand, shock evokes lever-pressing and key-pecking as Powell and Peck (1969) plainly showed, regardless of any contingency. In a feed backward system, responses extinguish when contingency is abolished. There are two ways to abolish contingency in operant avoidance: 1) the experimenter continues to deliver shock no matter what the subject does or, 2) the experimenter stops delivering shock altogether no matter what the subject does. The results of this comparison are decisive. In Sidman's procedure, lever-pressing persists indefinitely when the apparatus continues to deliver noncontingent shocks, particularly if the number and spacing of the shocks is roughly the same as it was in the contingent phase of the experiment (Hineline, 1977, pp. 377–381).

In Herrnstein and Hineline (1966), for example, a typical subject that received noncontingent shocks continued to press the lever for 170 daily sessions of 100 minutes each, making about 20,000 responses before meeting the criterion of extinction. Other experimenters, per-

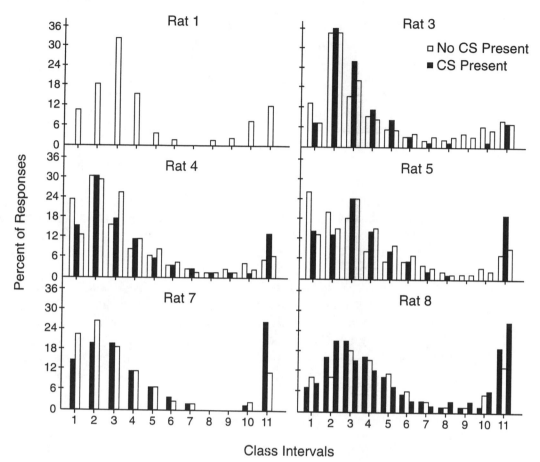

FIG. 9.4. Shocks evoke lever-pressing in Sidman's procedure. Shocks lasted for 0.5 seconds and the intershock period was 5 seconds, yielding a regularly repeating cycle of 0.5 seconds each. Interval 1 is the interval of 0.5-second shock and Intervals 2–11 are the intervals without shock. Most lever-pressing appeared during Interval 1 and the immediately following intervals as if evoked by the shock. There was another peak in response in the last 0.5-second interval before shock, which is where we would expect anticipatory responding in classical conditioning. From R. W. Powell and Peck (1969). Copyright © 1969 by the Society for the Experimental Analysis of Behavior, Inc. Adapted by permission.

haps because they were less persistent than Herrnstein and Hineline, failed to find any appreciable drop in responding after less extended but still reasonably long periods of noncontingent shock. Under the same conditions, indeed in the same experiments, when shock ceased entirely, lever-pressing ceased abruptly (Hineline, 1977, pp. 377–381). Clearly, shock evokes operant responding in Sidman's procedure regardless of contingency.

In aversive conditioning with shock as in appetitive conditioning with food, the responses that become conditioned are the responses that an S* evokes. At the same time that it evokes certain responses an S* suppresses other responses, which recover in the aftermath of S*. If an S* repeats at intervals, then the repeating cycles evoke different responses during different phases of a cycle. The S* evokes the responses, but the responses become conditioned to arbitrary stimuli that are correlated, either positively or negatively, with S*. The arbitrary conditioning of response to stimulus depends on the temporal contiguity between arbitrary stimulus and evoked response. Conditioning is independent of any change in contingency that the experimenter arranges between response and S*.

Earning Pain

In a feed forward system, responses become conditioned to an arbitrary stimulus regardless of any contingency between the responses and any S*. If this is true, then lever-pressing and key-pecking will become conditioned to an S^a that appears in the aftermath of shock, even if responses earn more shocks at other times. This is just what happens in Sidman's operant avoidance procedure. Lights and tones that signal relatively shock-free periods evoke lever-pressing and key-pecking even when the apparatus delivers more shock for more responses—that is, even though the animals earn many additional painful shocks if they respond during shock-free periods (Badia, Coker, & Harsh, 1973; Badia, Culbertson, & Harsh, 1973; E.T. Gardner & Lewis, 1977; Hineline, 1977, pp. 393–398). Thus, in aversive conditioning with shock as in appetitive conditioning with food, rhythmic temporal patterns control conditioning, even when responding has negative consequences for the well-being of the subject.

The positive effects of shock parallel the negative effects of food (see Avoiding Food, chap. 8). These effects are only paradoxical, however, if learning depends on contingencies between responses and feelings of pleasure or pain. The paradox vanishes when we look directly at the responses that an S* evokes instead of trying to imagine the feelings that it might cause.

Summary

The traditional association of appetites with positive approach and aversion with negative withdrawal ignores prominent ecological and ethological aspects of behavior such as defense and aggression. In a feed forward system, stimuli evoke responses and responsiveness depends on the state, Q, of a human or nonhuman animal. Hormonal balance and depletion of resources as well as repeated experience determine responsiveness to particular stimuli. This system can deal with all aspects of motivation without making subjective conjectures about the experience of pleasure and pain. Specifically, it provides a rule for conditioning that fits the facts of experiments. Yes, the results of many experiments seem to agree with the notion that contingent pleasure and pain govern learning. These experiments all fail to evaluate the role of contingency because they fail to compare contingency with noncontingency. Experiments that actually compare contingency with noncontingent control conditions repeatedly show that contingency is irrelevant to conditioning whether the S* is food or painful shock.

CONFLICT

Traditional views of motivation are weakest when they attempt to deal with conflict between motives. This section describes recent developments in computer science that offer a means of dealing with the problem of confict within a feed forward system.

Homeostastis

Cannon (1932) introduced the term *homeostasis* to apply to the self-regulation of vital constants in living systems. In this view, such values as temperature, hydration, saline and sugar in the bloodstream, and so on, have critical *set points* that a living organism must maintain to stay alive. Behaviors such as seeking shelter from the sun and foraging for food are an extension of physiological homeostasis. The traditional analogue of a homeostatic system is the regulation of temperature in a home by a thermostat (chap. 4).

Many successful industrial systems incorporate automatic devices, called *comparators,* to maintain vital set points. A thermostatic comparator, for example, responds to a temperature sensor by heating up the system when temperature falls below a set point or cooling it down when temperature rises above another set point. Comparators appear schematically in traditional theories (Plooij & Rijt-Plooij, 1994, pp. 359–361; Staddon, 1983, pp. 66–69) that attempt to use control theory to model behavior.

Set points and comparators are unlikely models for living animals, however, because they are designed for artificial systems that depend on outside supplies of vital resources. The thermostat in a home works well as long as someone pays for unlimited amounts of energy from external suppliers. When the price of energy rises, many homeowners allow the temperature to fall or rise to uncomfortable levels in preference to uncomfortably empty refrigerators or idle automobiles. Set points fail to control artificial systems when critical needs compete for limited resources.

The traditional analogy between home thermostats and body temperature fails because living systems must balance conflicting needs, or die. Body temperature drops when perspiration evaporates on the body surface, but this cooling device is strictly limited. Perspiration leads to dehydration, and dehydration leads to death. A live animal must replace the water lost in perspiration fairly soon. Finding water usually demands movement, energy expenditure, and further increases in temperature. Finding water often brings risk of death from predators that wait for prey at watering places. Autonomous systems must resolve conflicts.

Robots in Conflict

Figure 9.5 is a modified version of the robot vehicle of Fig. 8.3. In this case, the connections between the light sensors and the motors are ipsilateral so that the robot automatically avoids light and rests in dark places. In Fig. 9.5, there is an additional chemical sensor with contralateral connections to the motors so that the robot approaches chemicals that smell like fuel. An autonomous robot might need to approach sources of fuel to replenish its onboard stocks and yet avoid light because of enemy surveillance. A successful autonomous robot would have to make different decisions at different times depending

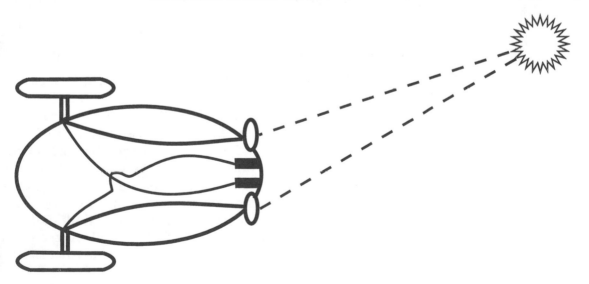

FIG. 9.5.   A robot with contralateral connections between chemical sensors and motors and ipsilateral connections between light sensors and motors approaches chemicals and avoids light. Copyright © 1997 by R. Allen Gardner.

on the amount of light and the depletion of onboard fuel, just as a living animal must balance danger of predation against depletion of onboard stocks of energy.

The two conflicting motives in Fig. 9.5 underestimate the number of conflicting motives in a moderately useful autonomous robot and certainly underestimate the number of conflicting motives in a moderately complex animal. Under natural conditions, a best or even a relatively favorable balance of motives shifts constantly with shifts in external and internal conditions. The robot vehicle in Fig. 8.3 works well without a central processor. The robot in Fig. 9.5 needs a central processor to resolve conflict.

FUZZY CONTROL

Recent industrial developments require systems that are much more sophisticated than comparators. Fuzzy controllers are simple, effective, and economical systems currently in use under demanding industrial conditions. Fuzzy controllers can balance multiple conflicting demands in situations of flux and change that resemble the problems of living animals under natural conditions. In the following example, two computer scientists in the Research and Technology division of Boeing Aircraft Company, Kipersztok and Patterson (1995), solved a modern industrial problem with an intelligent fuzzy controller. Their solution offers a practical model for analogous problems faced by living animals.

Fuzzy Logic

To readers schooled in traditional Greek logic, *fuzzy logic* seems to be a contradiction in terms. By Aristotle's law of the excluded middle, things must belong either to A or to not-A. They cannot belong partly to A and partly to not-A at the same time. Aristotle's laws of logic are so deeply entrenched that the notion of fuzzy categories sounds downright illogical. On the other hand, the natural world of daily experience appears in shades of gray, described in overlapping, continuous variables rather than sharp divisions. To traditional logicians, this only shows that daily experience is inferior to logical ideals. In this time-honored view, a truer picture of nature will emerge when we obey Plato's injunction to carve nature at the joints—that is, into mutually exclusive categories.

Following this Greek prescription, many social scientists and philosophers pursue endless searches for the dividing lines between intentional and unintentional, conscious and unconscious, human and nonhuman, and so on. Meanwhile, the natural sciences that have progressed since classical times soon discarded Aristotle's mutually exclusive categories in favor of continuous variables. Fuzzy, overlapping categories are hardly new. What is new is the discovery that artificial computer systems work well with fuzzy categories. Not only that, but computer systems based on fuzzy categories are simpler, cheaper, and easier to program than traditional systems (Kosko, 1993; McNeill & Freiberger, 1993).

Parallel Processing

Boeing's control problem arose from the introduction of a massive *parallel processing system* to solve massive computational needs of this huge organization. Most computers solve problems sequentially, one step after another, the way human beings solve problems with pencil and paper. Even though individual steps may require only a fraction of the power of a large computer, the whole system must wait for the results of each step in a sequential procedure. More recently, computer scientists discovered how to program computers to divide large problems into individual parts and process the parts simultaneously, in parallel. *Parallel processing* dramatically increases efficiency in many common industrial and research applications. One of the advantages of parallel processing to a very large organization such as Boeing is that individual computers can be connected to work together in a network even though they are located in separate offices and laboratories scattered throughout an enormous facility. This reduces the idle evening and weekend time of many systems at the facility. Kipersztok and Patterson set up just such a massive parallel processing system for Boeing.

Queuing

An enormous organization consumes an enormous amount of computing power. At Boeing there are massive amounts of data to analyze regarding the aerodynamics and braking mechanisms for jumbo jets. Logistical problems of supply, storage, and shipping have to be solved. Global market trends have to be anticipated. These examples only suggest the enormous computer needs at Boeing. After consolidating scattered individual systems into one massive parallel processor, Kipersztok and Patterson had to decide how to assign priorities to the jobs that colleagues submitted to the new supersystem. Just as with living animals in nature, conflict arises because there are many jobs to accomplish with limited resources. In industrial situations, this sort of problem is called *queuing*.

First come, first serve is a common queuing strategy, but it has many drawbacks in serious industrial situations. Suppose that the system is already processing many jobs simultaneously, but without fully occupying its resources. The next job submitted is so large that it requires more of the system than the total amount of resources that are currently idle. The large job must wait until there are enough available resources to serve its needs. Suppose that it takes a long time for enough of the smaller jobs in progress to finish and free the needed resources. In the meantime, quite large amounts of computer resources remain idle waiting until the system can accommodate the large job. This is obviously wasteful. Suppose that the system manager lets smaller jobs take advantage of idle resources while the large job continues to wait. This strategy could make the large job wait indefinitely even though the large job may be much more important to Boeing than many of the smaller jobs. To recognize this economic priority, the system manager should suspend enough smaller jobs in process to accommodate an important large job, but then how to decide which jobs to suspend? That is, how to resolve conflicts that arise when many tasks compete for limited resources?

At the outset, Kipersztok and Patterson could specify the most important variables in their queuing problem, they knew that the problem has a mathematically optimum solution, and they knew that between them they had more than enough mathematical skills to solve it. Unfortunately, they could also estimate that it would take them many months, certainly more than a year, probably more than two years, to solve a problem involving so many complex interacting variables. From the point of view of Boeing Aircraft, that would be impractical. First, it would cost at least two years' salary for two senior computer scientists. Second, the expensive super parallel processor would have to limp along inefficiently while it waited for the solution. Worst of all, things change swiftly both in computer science and in the aircraft industry. While Kipersztok and Patterson labored at the mathematical problem, many vital factors would probably change, making their solution obsolete before they found it.

The problem is very similar in evolutionary biology. Given enough time and generations some species can emerge perfectly adapted to any ecosystem. Adaptation fails, however, if it takes too many generations to produce the optimal solution for a particular ecological problem. Ecosystems are inherently unstable. If it takes too long to emerge, the optimal species will be perfectly suited to an ecosystem that is long gone.

With a fuzzy controller, Kipersztok and Patterson produced a practical solution to the queuing problem in a matter of weeks, without even breathing hard. The secret of fuzzy systems is that they produce good practical solutions without attempting to find optimum solutions. This strategy permits them to take advantage of crude, but effective, devices. In nature, species only have to survive. Crude devices will serve because optimality is unnecessary. This is a signficant similarity between fuzzy systems and living animals.

Control Problem

Figure 9.6 is a schematic diagram of the controller that Kipersztok and Patterson (1995) developed. New jobs arrive unranked in the queue at the left of the diagram. The fuzzy controller assigns priorities to the jobs in the incoming queue on the basis of their resource requirements and the current availability of resources in the network. This creates a new queue with jobs ranked for priority. The controller allows the jobs in the ranked queue to enter the network for processing until the resources that remain are insufficient to accommodate the highest ranking job in the queue. At that point the controller ranks the jobs in process in the network and suspends enough lower ranking jobs in process to accommodate the highest ranking jobs that remain in the queue. When all of the jobs in process outrank all of the jobs in the queue, and idle resources are insufficient to accommodate the

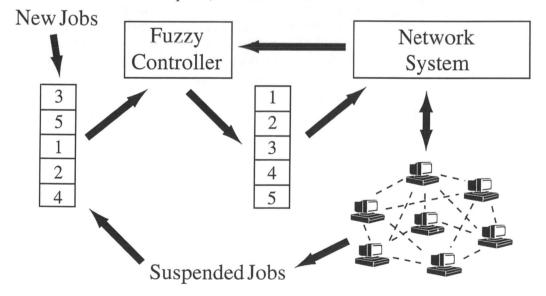

FIG. 9.6.   Overview of an intelligent controller for network queuing. From Kipersztok and Patterson (1995). Copyright © 1997 by R. Allen Gardner.

highest ranking job that remains in the queue, the system is stable and the controller rests.

The controller automatically resubmits suspended jobs to the queue along with new jobs and assigns priorities to the jobs in the newly formed incoming queue. As the network completes jobs in process, more resources become available, and the ranking of jobs in the waiting queue changes along with the ranking of jobs remaining in process in the network. Thus, the fuzzy system is continually reevaluating priorities, submitting waiting jobs, and suspending jobs in process. Like a living animal its needs and resources are constantly in flux.

Fuzzy Solution

The controller uses the requirements of jobs and the availablilty of resources to assign priorities. Two major requirements for the Boeing system are the number of machines and the communication load requested by a job. Communication is critical in parallel processing because the separate units that are working on separate parts of the same problem must communicate with each other and different jobs require different amounts of communication.

In general, the less that a job requires in the way of resources, the higher its priority. The weight of each requirement in assigning priority depends on the current availability of that resource. Kipersztok and Patterson constructed the matrix shown in Table 9.1 to assign weights to the factor of requested machines under different conditions of available machines. The matrix is simple and straightforward. The first row in Table 9.1 applies when the number of available machines is very high. In that situation, the number of machines requested by a new job is less significant and usually has a relatively low weight, but this weight increases with the number of requested machines. The last row applies when the number of available machines is very low.

TABLE 9.1
Matrix for Assigning Weights to the Number of Machines Requested

	Demand				
Availability	*VL*	*L*	*M*	*H*	*VH*
VH	VL	VL	L	M	H
H	L	L	M	H	VH
M	M	M	H	H	VH
L	H	H	H	VH	VH
VL	VH	VH	VH	VH	VH

Note. VL = very low, L = low, M = medium, H = high, and VH = very high.

In that situation, even the requirements of a small job may be too high to begin processing. Each cell in the matrix generates an inference rule. The cell in the second row and the third column generates the rule, "If available machines is high and requested machines is medium, then weight is medium."

The matrix is as easy to construct as it appears in this brief description. Some matrices are better than others and some are worse, of course, so expertise and familiarity with the system helps, but the first matrix only needs to be a starting point. It is so easy to change all or part of any matrix that system managers can later adjust, indefinitely.

This ease of adjustment makes fuzzy controllers even more suitable as models of evolutionary adaptation. Designers have tested fuzzy systems by deliberately introducing erroneous inference rules or removing several rules entirely. The controllers continue to function although they limp along less efficiently (Kosko, 1993, pp. 339–361). On the positive side, this same property of fuzzy systems allows computer scientists to improve on their first attempts and to modify each part of the system easily and quickly as conditions change. This crude but powerful property of fuzzy systems is a promising model for rapid adaptation to dynamically changing natural ecosystems. A fuzzy system could survive without achieving the optimal solution to a unique, and very likely transient, ecological situation.

Each cell in the matrix of Table 9.1 represents a fuzzy category without sharply defined boundaries. A particular value of available or requested machines can belong partly to one category and partly to an adjacent category. In these common cases of overlap, the fuzzy system assigns a crudely defined intermediate weight to the output. These outputs combine with the outputs of other matrices in higher order matrices, which produce fuzzy outputs of the combinations. Eventually, the system converts the combined fuzzy weights to crisp values that determine the ranking of each job waiting in the queue and each job in process in the network. Again, the fuzzy system converts fuzzy values to crisp values by crude but effective approximation rather than by precise mathematical modeling.

Kipersztok and Patterson could have developed a precise mathematical equation for the output of Table 9.1 by dint of thorough experimentation with the system and elaborate mathematical modeling. The fuzzy matrix describes the main features of the problem in an intuitively reasonable and direct way, saving computer scientist time, calendar time, and computer resources. The advantage of the fuzzy system mutiplies as the system combines more and more complexly interacting factors to assign priorities. Without attempting to produce optimum results, fuzzy systems settle for good practical results. They exchange optimality for practical savings in time and effort.

The system designer must also define the degree of overlap between fuzzy categories, and the different boundaries can overlap in different ways. The details of these and other technical steps in constructing a fuzzy controller are beyond the scope of this book, but they are as simple and straightforward as described here. All of the details of Kipersztok and Patterson's controller appear in their 1995 article. At this writing, Kosko's (1993) book on fuzzy systems is a serious, yet accessible, technical introduction and many excellent new books on this subject will certainly appear soon. Kipersztok and Patterson (1995) used available commercial software to translate the crude rules into a working fuzzy controller.

Biological and Industrial Priorities

Assigning priorities on the basis of available resources and projected needs has clear parallels to the way living animals and autonomous robots must resolve conflicts. Kipersztok and Patterson had to incorporate factors into their industrial application that increase the resemblance to living animals under natural conditions. The system had to include, for example, a weight for economic importance to the health of the Boeing Aircraft Company. The most efficient controller would still fail if it failed to relate priority of a job to Boeing's profits. Kipersztok and Patterson also had to be sure that the system would eventually run every job submitted to it. To do this, they introduced an aging factor that adds priority to a job according to the time it spends waiting in the queue. Living animals can also tolerate moderately critical needs for limited periods without serious consequences. An animal, for example, can survive at moderately higher than normal internal temperatures for a while. Eventually, however, the animal must do something to lower temperature, such as rest or seek shelter from the sun, even if it must suspend other critical activities.

Summary

This section considered the modern view of motivation as jobs to be done with limited resources. The problem is one of balanced control rather than maxium output of energy. Limited resources create conflicts which must be resolved. Increasingly, modern industrial systems also focus on control, which makes them increasingly resemble living systems. Fuzzy systems like living systems deal with job requirements and resources that are in a constant state of flux. Fuzzy systems are valuable in modern industry because they are simple and inexpensive, which makes them easy to improve and to modify rapidly as conditions change. This is a valuable property for a living system in an evolving natural world. Fuzzy logic of continuous overlapping categories is also a more appropriate way to describe nature, including the behavior of human and nonhuman animals.

CHAPTER 10

Excitation, Inhibition, and Competition

Chapters 2 and 3 outline the defining operations of *experimental extinction* in the procedures of classical and instrumental conditioning. Other chapters, such as chapter 7, illustrate the use of extinction in particular experiments. The defining operations of secondary reward in chapter 7, for example, require measurement under conditions of extinction for primary reward. Extinction is an interesting and important phenomenon in its own right, however, and this chapter concentrates on the problems that the phenomenon of extinction presents for contingent reinforcement theory and cognitive expectancy theory, and also offers an alternative in terms of feed forward contiguity.

Figure 10.1 represents a typical experiment. In acquisition on Monday, S* always follows each correct response. In extinction on Tuesday, S* never follows any response. The third panel of Fig. 10.1 shows two alternative ways of treating the subject on Wednesday after extinction on Tuesday. The lower curve, labeled "Extinction 2," shows a second session of extinction without S*. The upper curve, labeled "Reacquisition," shows a session with S* again as on Monday. In a second session of extinction, the response tends to fall faster than in the first session and to fall to a lower level. In reacquisition, the response tends to rise faster than in the initial phase of acquisition, and to rise to a higher level.

In traditional theories, rewards strengthen and punishments weaken responses, but why should responding weaken during extinc-

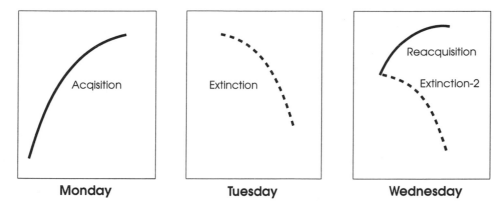

FIG. 10.1.   Acquisition, extinction, reacquisition, and extinction 2. Copyright © 1997 by R. Allen Gardner.

tion? Why should something as neutral as nothing at all have a weakening effect? The only possibility within a reinforcement theory is some *inhibitory* process arising from nonreward.

A theory that attributes conditioning to a positive process of reinforcement must also include a negative process of inhibition. Otherwise, all learning would be permanent. The negative effect of aversive consequences is a source of inhibition that could weaken a learned response. That would be punishment. In reinforcement theories, the effect of an aversive S* is the reverse of the effect of an appetitive S*. But, extinction by the absence of any consequences requires still another source of inhibition.

In cognitive expectancy theories, the solution seems easier, at first. If the animals increase responding during acquisition because they expect S*, then they must decrease responding during extinction because they cease to expect S*. By this time readers should see that this is an empty explanation, because it is only a different way of saying that responses go up during acquisition and go down during extinction. The problem with expectancy theory becomes even more obvious in spontaneous recovery.

Spontaneous recovery is the most significant and least expected phenomenon shown in the third panel of Fig. 10.1. At the beginning of Wednesday's session, there is less responding than there was at the beginning of extinction on Tuesday, but at the same time more responding than there was at the end of extinction on Tuesday. This increase in responding after a day of rest without any intervening experience in the experimental apparatus is called spontaneous recovery. Virtually all other experimenters since Pavlov replicated his discovery of spontaneous recovery. Can either reinforcement theory or expectancy theory cope with this finding?

According to reinforcement theory, the response went up on Monday because it was reinforced and down on Tuesday because of it was not reinforced. What happened to the inhibition of nonreinforcement overnight between the end of Tuesday's extinction and the beginning of extinction 2 or reacquisition on Wednesday? Why is the recovery incomplete? In expectancy theory, the response went up on Monday because the animal learned to expect S* and down on Tuesday because the animal learned not to expect S*. In that case, what happened to the negative expectancy overnight? Why did only part of the positive expectancy recover? Spontaneous recovery seems to defy common sense. Yet, it is one of the most well documented phenomena in all of psychology.

HULL'S EXCITATION AND INHIBITION

Hull's (1952) book is still the most complete and successful theory of reinforcement that we have at this writing, which is really not very high praise. The reinforcement mechanism in Hull's theory is the *drive reduction* that results when a hungry animal eats or a thirsty animal drinks. Drive reduction builds up *habit strength,* the association between a stimulus and a response that leads to drive reduction. Hull's symbol for habit strength is $_sH_r$ and its value depends on a complex set of contributing variables that we can ignore here. Habit strength, in conjunction with a few more variables that need not concern us here, determines *excitatory potential* or $_sE_r$, the effective strength of the response that determines actual performance. In Hull's system of symbols, a term with both s and r subscripts represents the relation between a particular stimulus and a particular response. Thus, $_sH_r$ represents the habit strength or positive conditioned effect of drive reduction on the association between a particular S and a particular R while $_sE_r$ represents the effective strength after factoring several other variables into the equation. Effective strength is the actual result measured in a particular experiment.

Two Kinds of Inhibition

The inhibitory effect of nonreward enters Hull's equation in two forms. First, the theory assumes that every response produces an inhibitory reaction that opposes immediate repetition of that response. Immediate repetition is, indeed, difficult for human and nonhuman animals. As well practiced as you may be in signing your name a particular way, you will find it hard to write your signature the same way over and over again without pausing for rest. Almost any habit breaks down with enough immediate repetition. Living systems seem to have a built-in resistance to exact repetition that ensures response variability.

There is an easy way to demonstrate this resistance. Roll up a sheet of paper and, choosing a suitably friendly and cooperative subject, pretend to strike someone across the eyes with the rolled-up paper. Come as close as you can without actually striking the person. Most people will blink the first time you do this. Repeat the pretend strike a few times. Most people will soon stop blinking even when the paper almost hits them in the eyes. Let your subject rest for 20 or 30 seconds and then repeat. Most people will blink again after this short rest indicating that the inhibition was transitory.

In Hull's system *reactive inhibition* is the mechanism that prevents immediate repetition; its symbol is I_r, and it specifically inhibits the particular response that was just made. During conditioning, Hull's I_r grows with each repetition. As long as there is positive drive reduction (e.g., from food or water reward) to build up more $_sH_r$ with each response, the net effect on $_sE_r$ is an increase. Hull's I_r dissipates with rest (like fatigue), which raises $_sE_r$, but it also has drive properties that are reduced by rest. That is, the presence of I_r is aversive and the reduction of I_r is rewarding (like the reduction of thirst or hunger). This drive reduction reinforces the habit of not making response r to stimulus s, which produces a negative habit called *conditioned inhibition* and its symbol is $_sI_r$. Conditioned inhibition is like habit strength (or conditioned excitation) in that it is relatively permanent.

The following formula expresses this part of Hull's theory.

$$_sE_r = {_sH_r} - I_r - {_sI_r}$$

The theory assumes (a) that I_r builds up with repetition and dissipates with rest, and (b) that I_r has drive properties. Rest reduces I_r, which reinforces rest or nonresponding. This reinforces the habit of not making this response, $_sI_r$. The formula is straightforward and consistent with the rest of the theory. It says that the effective strength of the response r to the stimulus s equals habit strength minus temporary reactive inhibition minus relatively permanent conditioned inhibition.

Returning to Fig. 10.1, Hull's equation describes acquisition, extinction, and spontaneous recovery in the following way. During acquisition on Monday, both $_sH_r$ and I_r increase, but $_sH_r$ builds up faster than I_r, so responding increases. On Tuesday, S* stops, which stops the increase of $_sH_r$, but I_r continues to increase every time the subject repeats response r to stimulus s. When I_r builds up enough, responding stops momentarily, which dissipates I_r. This reduces reactive inhibition and reinforces the subject for not making response r to stimulus s, thus adding to conditioned inhibition, $_sI_r$.

This description agrees with the usual record of individual performance during extinction. Both in acquisition and extinction, individual records show bursts of responding punctuated by pauses. In acquisition, the pauses get shorter and the bursts get longer. In extinction, the pauses get longer and the bursts get shorter. Complete extinction is one long pause. The average curves of responding for a group of subjects show smooth increases and decreases, because the bursts and pauses occur at different times for different subjects.

As for spontaneous recovery, all of the reactive inhibition dissipates during the overnight rest between Tuesday and Wednesday. The $_sI_r$ cannot increase, however, because the subject only experiences the stimulus situation s in the experimental apparatus. So, the subject cannot receive any reward for not responding to s. Consequently, there is a big increase in responding between the end of Tuesday's session and the beginning of Wednesday's session because all of the I_r is gone. Recovery is incomplete, however, because the relatively permanent conditioned inhibition that developed during extinction on Tuesday depresses responding. If the procedure on Wednesday is another session of extinction, then more $_sI_r$ will build up so that there will be less spontaneous recovery on Thursday, and so on, until extinction is complete.

Hull's reactive inhibition and conditioned inhibition are straightforwardly consistent with the rest of the theory, and the result does account for all of the facts of the usual experiment. Unfortunately, the theory requires as many principles as there are facts to account for. Habit strength, reactive inhibition, and conditioned inhibition account for acquisition, extinction, and spontaneous recovery, but a theory that is as complex as the phenomena it describes is hardly an improvement over a list of the phenomena. One way to remedy this situation is to apply the principles to predict new phenomena. By predicting new phenomena, a theory proves its value because it tells us something more than we knew without the theory.

Massed and Distributed Practice

Hull's reactive inhibition and conditioned inhibition apply directly to perceptual-motor learning of all kinds. During World War II, and for decades afterward, learning theorists actively engaged in applied research on training both in military and civilian situations. It was a practical and profitable application of experimental psychology and occupied a great deal of the graduate curriculum. Psychologists studied the development of skills such as gunnery and machine operation and also devised tracking tasks and precise motor tasks such as picking up small pins with a forceps and placing them into small holes. This period corresponded with the period of Hull's greatest influence.

The principle of *massed versus distributed practice* emerged from research on perceptual-motor skills. In massed practice, for example, a trainee might practice for 45 minutes and rest for 15 minutes. In distributed practice, the trainee might divide the same hour into three periods of 15 minutes of practice and 5 minutes of rest. In task after task, distributed practice proved superior to massed practice in perceptual-motor learning. This is precisely what should happen if Hull was correct about reactive inhibition. That is, frequent rests should allow I_r to dissipate without developing $_sI_r$. With distributed practice, skill, or $_sH_r$, should develop faster because so little I_r can accumulate. With massed practice, on the other hand, I_r should accumulate and skill should develop slower. With more I_r there should be more pauses, leading to more of the relatively permanent conditioned inhibition, $_sI_r$, and relatively permanent impairment of skill.

Experimenters discovered that performance often declined during massed practice and then improved after a rest. They called the improvement in skilled performance that comes from rest, alone, *reminiscence*. After a series of highly massed periods of practice, reminiscence produces the paradoxical finding that losses in performance appear during practice and gains appear after rest without practice. This is precisely what should happen if there is a process such as reactive inhibition that grows during practice and dissipates during rest. And, of course, reminiscence looks just like spontaneous recovery. In spite of this agreement, permanent effects of Hull's hypothetical $_sI_r$ on perceptual-motor skills have been difficult (perhaps impossible) to demonstrate (Irion, 1969, pp. 5–9).

There are many ways of distributing practice in different tasks. A good theory should provide a set of rules that predict the best way to distribute practice on each new task in each new applied setting—or at least, the best distribution in many new tasks in many new settings. There have been many attempts to set up such rules, but up to the time of writing this book all have failed. The best, or even a relatively more favorable, way to distribute practice must always be determined separately for each new task. Common sense about the similarity between a new task and other, better known, tasks remains more effective than any direct application of existing theory. Nevertheless, the finding of a robust phenomenon that resembles reactive inhibition in entirely new types of behavior supports Hull's basic concept. Perhaps, by expanding the basic concepts to accommodate competition among incompatible responses, future theorists will apply Hull's principles more successfully.

RESISTANCE TO EXTINCTION

Just as the level of responding never starts at absolute zero at the beginning of acquisition, it never returns to absolute zero at the end of extinction. Fortunately, long before absolute zero, relative measures of resistance to extinction are quite sensitive to different conditions of acquisition.

Virtually all experimenters measure resistance to extinction in terms of some arbitrary criterion. In Skinner boxes, experimenters have measured frequency of lever-presses in a fixed amount of time under extinction conditions, and number of lever-presses before a criterion period of time, say 10 minutes without a response. In straight alleys, experimenters have measured running speed during a fixed number of extinction trials and number of trials before the first trial in which a rat took longer than a fixed amount of time, say 2 minutes, to run a short distance.

In many situations, measures of response in acquisition reach a limit so that groups that acquired the same response under different conditions appear to be equal. Late in acquisition, rats may be running as fast as they can so that there is no room left for improvement in speed. In two-choice situations, such as a T-maze, the best that a subject can do is to choose the rewarded alternative on every trial. In these cases, resistance to extinction provides a sensitive measure of differences that cannot appear during acquisition. Experimenters have rarely questioned the widely held belief that resistance to extinction measures the strength of conditioning, which for many is the same as strength of reinforcement. Overtraining and partial reward, however, are two well-documented situations in which resistance to extinction actually decreases with increases in reward. Resistance to extinction after overtraining is the subject of the next section of this chapter. Resistance to extinction after partial reward is the subject of chapter 11.

OVERTRAINING

If some reward reinforces a response, then more rewards should have more reinforcing effect. After many trials of rewarded running in a straight alley, however, both the running speed maintained by reward and the resistance to extinction decrease with further rewarded trials (Birch, Ison, & Sperling, 1960; Prokasy, 1960). If both running speed in acquisition and resistance to extinction measure strength of association, how could additional rewarded trials produce lowered speed and faster extinction?

To his credit, Hull's reinforcement theory actually predicted this paradoxical result. A central principle of the theory assumes that there is a limit to habit strength, $_sH_r$. According to this principle, the negatively accelerated learning curve (largest gains early in conditioning and decreasingly smaller gains later in conditioning as in Fig. 1.1) that appears in most experiments arises from the fact that gains in habit strength are proportional to the difference between the current level and the maximum level possible. There are large gains early in acquisition because there is so much room for improvement; smaller and smaller gains late in acquisition because there is much less room left for improvement.

As $_sH_r$ increases, responding increases and this produces more reactive inhibition, I_r. As I_r increases, the subject takes more rests to dissipate I_r, and this produces more conditioned inhibition, $_sI_r$. Early in conditioning, $_sH_r$ builds up faster than $_sI_r$ because the strength of conditioning is far from the maximum; but late in conditioning, $_sH_r$ grows more slowly because it is closer to the maximum. Eventually, $_sI_r$ builds up faster than $_sH_r$ and subtracts more and more from effective performance leading to actual decreases late in acquisition. That Hull's theory of excitation and inhibition predicted this unexpected, even paradoxical, effect of increased reward before it was discovered is a very strong point in favor of the theory.

SUMMARY

Hull's theory is the reinforcement theory that comes closest to accommodating the paradoxical effects of nonreward in extinction and spontaneous recovery. Unfortunately, Hull's theory only accomplishes this by adding several layers of complexity, which makes it less parsimonious and less intuitive than more popular treatments such as Skinner's. To Hull's credit, his principles predicted some unexpected findings in both animal conditioning and human perceptual-motor learning.

COMPETING RESPONSES

Much of the difficulty with traditional theories, such as Hull's, arises from the practice of recording a single index, such as lever-pressing or salivation. All that can happen in such a record is that the index goes up or it goes down. With only two outcomes, the only possible theoretical factors are opposing forces of excitation and inhibition.

Considering More Than One Response

When experimenters actually look at their learning subjects, they see a population of responses. A *criterion response* R_c such as lever-pressing must be one of the responses in this population, otherwise conditioning is impossible. Figure 10.2 is a diagram of the usual observation. The broad, relatively flat curve represents a population of responses before conditioning, R_1, R_2, ... R_n, which includes R_c. The tall, relatively steep curve about R_c represents the distribution of this same population of responses after conditioning. During conditioning, the experimenter presents S* and then R_c increases together with a relatively few other responses. This increase in a small set of responses depresses the rest of the responses in the original population because competing responses are mutually exclusive—that is, the subject can make only one of these responses at any given time.

Traditional reinforcement theories treat the strength of each response in the population as an independent function of excitatory factors and inhibitory factors. This is a necessary characteristic of any theory that describes conditioning and learning as the building up of association between response and stimulus. In that case, the only way that a conditioned response can decline is by some process of weakening. Otherwise, all conditioning would be permanent. The

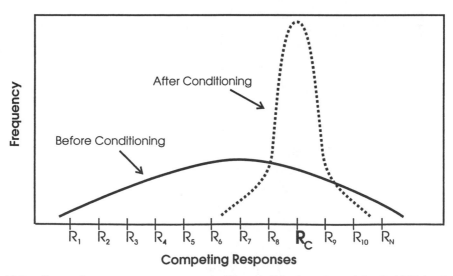

FIG. 10.2. Competing responses before and after conditioning. Copyright © 1997 by R. Allen Gardner.

actual strength of response, then, must be some positive function of excitation minus some negative function of inhibition as in Hull's $_sE_r$ that equals $_sH_r$ minus $_sI_r$ and I_r. Furthermore, each competing stimulus-response pair must have its own equation balancing its own $_sH_r$ against its own $_sI_r$ and I_r. In such a system, the response that appears at any moment would be some complex result of all of these separate equations. This a very cumbersome way to describe the situation. It would also be a very cumbersome way for a nervous system to deal with the situation, because it would demand needlessly expensive use of limited nervous tissue; first to keep track of all of the positive and negative values, and then to compute the result.

At any given time, all mutually exclusive responses in a population must compete with each other. Even though many experimenters measure the frequency of only one criterion response, such as lever-pressing, they are necessarily measuring the relative frequency of all other responses, indirectly. Saying that pauses in lever-pressing measure the response of not lever-pressing only dodges the question of what rats actually do when they are not lever-pressing.

Food evokes feeding. One of the feeding responses that food evokes in the Skinner box is lever-pressing. In a sense, the mechanism that evokes feeding responses inhibits nonfeeding responses, but it is simpler to describe the mechanism as one of switching among a set of alternatives. When someone switches channels on a television set, we could say that they are exciting one channel and inhibiting each of the others, but that is a cumbersome way to describe the situation. If the television set tunes in only one channel at a time, then a positive description of the position of the switch is a complete description of the situation.

During acquisition, rats press levers in bursts and pauses. Even when animals are very hungry and very well trained and every press is rewarded with food, they often pause to do other things. During pauses in lever-pressing, rats in a Skinner box groom their whiskers, scratch themselves, sniff the air, rear up on their hind legs, explore the box, and so on.

At the start of extinction, when food stops rats continue to press the lever as before. Indeed, they press at a higher rate without the interference of food to eat. Since nothing about the stimulus situation changes and there is a built-in biological resistance to immediate repetition, the rat eventually varies its response. This built-in tendency to vary responses when the stimulus situation remains the same is also the basis for Hull's reactive inhibition. In a feed forward analysis, the effect of variability is to get the rat to make some other response to the lever. The rat makes this other response, but without an S^d for the next response in the chain (as in Fig. 7.4), that new response gives way to still another new response, and so on. Eventually, the rat moves away from the lever, and that becomes the last response in that stimulus situation. When the rat returns to the lever, he does the last thing he did when he last approached the lever. If he pressed the lever last time, he presses it again. During extinction, successive bouts of lever-pressing give way to other responses sooner and sooner, without food to evoke feeding behavior. Thus, bursts of lever-pressing become shorter and pauses filled with other responses become longer.

Acquisition on Monday looks the way it does in Fig. 10.1 because there is a shift from the broad, flat curve to the narrow, steep curve of Fig. 10.2. That is, in acquisition on Monday the range of responses narrows to the criterion response, R_c, and a few similar responses. Extinction on Tuesday looks the way it does in Fig. 10.1 because there is a shift from the narrow, steep curve back to the broad, flat curve of Fig. 10.2. That is, there is a shift from concentration on a few responses in acquisition to a broad range of responses. But, what happens on Wednesday? A feed forward system copes with these findings without invoking either excitation or inhibition—and also without invoking either positive or negative expectancies. The stimulus situation at the start of Wednesday's session is more like the stimulus situation at the start of Tuesday's session than at the end of Tuesday's session. So, the rat starts off responding more like it did at the start of Tuesday's session, but there is some effect of Tuesday's extinction and the rat responds at a somewhat lower level.

If extinction continues, then the stimulus situation gets more like the end of Tuesday's session and lever-pressing goes down while other responses go up. Thursday, the stimulus situation at the start is even less like the start and more like the end of Wednesday so lever-pressing falls off further and more quickly in favor of other responses. If instead of more extinction, Wednesday is a day of reacquisition, then the stimulus situation is much more like the situation on Monday and the rat behaves more and more like it did on Monday. Remember also, that part of the stimulus situation in acquisition is the stimulus of actual food, which we know evokes lever-pressing without any contingency at all. Food stimuli are absent in extinction and present in acquisition and reacquisition.

Two-Choice Situations

The difference between feed forward contiguity and feed backward contingency appears more clearly when there are two or more alternative responses. In a Skinner box with two levers, A and B, the experimenter can reward all responses to lever A and never reward any response to lever B. Rats quickly come to press A almost all of the time and hardly ever press B. In a reinforcement theory, this is because positive reinforcement builds up for pressing A and negative inhibition builds up for pressing B. In a feed forward theory, an S^d, such as the click of the food magazine, always follows pressing lever A, which makes pressing the last response to lever A. Pressing B never changes the stimulus situation so the rat makes other responses to B and these become the last responses to that lever (chap. 8).

Suppose that during extinction, the experimenter stops rewarding for A presses and starts rewarding for B presses. In a reinforcement theory, the rat would have to press A without reward repeatedly until enough inhibition developed to overcome the excitation of all of the reward previously received for pressing A. Enough inhibition would have to develop to weaken A presses to the already weakened level of B presses before the animal could make the first B press. Then, the rat would have to make enough rewarded B presses to overcome the inhibition generated by the earlier period of nonreward and build up enough reinforcement to press lever B most of the time.

In a feed forward theory, on the other hand, nonreward for pressing A means that there is no click S^d for making the next response in the chain. Consequently, the rat continues to press A until the built-in tendency to vary results in different responses to lever A. Eventually, one of these responses will be turning away from A and that will become the last response to A. The rat only has to make one rewarded B press to make that the last response to lever B before the click S^d evokes the next response in the chain. The switch from pressing A to pressing B should be fairly quick and there should be little or no spontaneous recovery. In fact, the classical extinction curves shown in Fig. 10.1 are only found in experiments with only one lever or key or only one criterion response, such as salivation or galvanic skin response. With rewarded alternatives, extinction is very rapid and spontaneous recovery is negligible.

Perhaps the following example can make this more clear. Our family lived in the same house in Reno for 13 years before we sold the old place and moved to a new home. The first leg of the drive home from the university where we both worked was the same for both places until we came to a critical intersection. At that point, the driver should turn right to head toward the old place or continue straight through the intersection to head for the new place. For 13 years we had turned right at that intersection. As you would expect, we made the old right turn several times during the first few weeks after moving to the new place. But, we made very few of these perseverative errors considering the thousands of times that we had practiced that right turn at exactly that intersection for 13 years. The number of errors we made and the number of trials that it took to learn to drive straight through the intersection every time without turning right required nothing remotely related to 13 years of reward for getting home after turning right.

Competition and Contingency

In Fig. 10.2, the curve labeled "before conditioning" represents a population of responses under stable conditions. Changes in conditions change the distribution. If, for example, the experimenter attaches a running wheel to the Skinner box, then the frequencies of all responses from grooming whiskers to drinking water will decrease. This decrease in other frequencies must occur because it takes time for a rat to run in a running wheel and this subtracts from the time that the rat can spend on other responses. Removing the running wheel, or blocking its movement with a bolt, will have the opposite effect. The time that the rat spent running in the wheel will now be distributed among the other possible responses. This is a result of basic physics and arithmetic.

Ignoring the problem of response competition, Premack (1965) proposed the results of a new type of experimental operation as evidence for the strengthening effect of response contingent reinforcement. Premack's proposal fails precisely because it fails to control for response competition, but it is an instructive failure.

Premack (1959) tested first-grade children (average age 6.7 years) one at a time in a room that contained a pinball machine and a candy dispenser. The candy dispenser only dispensed a new piece of candy after a child ate the previous piece. Premack first measured the amount of time that each child spent at each of the two competing activities during a 15-minute sample. In a second 15-minute sample taken several days later, Premack divided the children into two groups. For half of the children, the pinball machine was locked until a child ate a piece of candy. After a bout of pinball, the machine was locked again until the child ate another piece of candy, and so on. For the other half, the candy dispenser was locked until a child played pinball, and locked again until the child played pinball again, and so on.

As expected from Fig. 10.2, eating candy increased when Premack blocked pinball playing, and playing pinball increased when Premack blocked candy eating. As Fig. 10.2 also indicates, the more time the children had spent at an activity during the first sampling period the greater the effect when Premack restricted that activity during the second sampling period. That is, if they had spent more time eating candy than playing pinball in the first period, then restricting candy in the second period increased pinball more than restricting pinball increased eating. Premack amplified the effect of blocking by measuring time spent rather than frequency. Restricting the higher probability activity frees more time for the lower probability activity and thus has a greater effect on the result.

Premack (1962) went on to demonstrate a similar result with rats drinking and running in a Skinner box. He manipulated the relative amount of time spent at each activity in a sampling period by earlier depriving the rats of water and giving them free access to running or depriving them of running and giving them free access to water. In a second sampling period, restricting access to the activity that consumed more time in the first period had a greater effect than restricting access to the activity that consumed less time in the first period.

On the basis of this type of experiment, Premack proposed the following as a principle of reinforcement: Making access to a higher frequency activity contingent on performance of a lower frequency activity reinforces the lower frequency activity. Thus, drinking can reinforce running and running can reinforce drinking depending on which one is more frequent under prevailing conditions.

In these experiments, however, one activity is made contingent on another by blocking the contingent activity until the subject performs the target activity. Obviously, blocking one activity frees time for other activities apart from any hypothetical effect of contingency. The direct effect of competition is more than hypothetical; Dunham (1972), Harrison and Schaeffer (1975), and Premack (1965) all demonstrated in experiments that blocking either competing activity increases the other activity without any contingency whatsoever. Indeed, the effect of noncontingent blocking in these experiments leaves very little room for any additional effect of contingency. If there is any residual effect of contingency apart from the effect of competition, it must be very small, too small to justify any major principle of reinforcement.

The detective must show that a prime suspect could be responsible for the crime. A good detective must also eliminate other prime suspects. In the case of Premack's proposal for a new principle of contingent reinforcement, response competition is an obvious, likely, emprically supported, and more parsimonious suspect for the factor that is responsible for the experimental results.

Summary

Contingent reinforcement must describe the strength of each response as the combined effect of positive excitation and negative inhibition. This response by response analysis seems appropriate when experimenters only measure a single response that can only increase or decrease. The weakness of this analysis becomes clear in more complex experiments that measure extinction, spontaneous recovery, or response competition.

CHAPTER II

Reward Versus Nonreward

In the world outside the laboratory, 100% reward and 100% punishment must be very rare, if they exist at all. In buying radios or fruit, planning careers or weekends in the country, practicing tennis strokes or studying textbooks, hardly anything succeeds or fails every time. Even perfectly correct responses only earn rewards some of the time, often after long periods of persistence with little or no reward. Experiments on the effects of consequences that are only occasionally rewarding or punishing are more ecologically valid and relevant to life outside the laboratory than any other kind of research on learning.

OPERANT PROCEDURE

In the Skinner box, the subject operates the lever or key in bursts interspersed with pauses. During pauses the subject engages in other kinds of behavior. Usually responses are measured in frequency per unit time (number of responses in say 60, 30, or 10 minutes) or rate of responding (per hour, per minute, per second, etc.). By contrast, the procedure in a straight alley or T-maze is called *discrete trials* because the beginning of each trial is controlled by the experimenter and the latency or amplitude of response is measured separately on each trial.

Some experimenters have used discrete trials procedures in a Skinner box. These experimenters mount the lever on a contraption that inserts and withdraws the lever from the box. The apparatus measures the latency between each insertion and the first response. After each response, the lever is withdrawn until the beginning of the next trial. In a discrete trials procedure, the experimenter controls the beginning of each trial, and in an operant procedure, the subject controls the frequency and rate of a series of responses.

Partial Reward During Acquisition

Skinner first introduced operant procedures in the 1930s and soon reported the now well-known fact that, in operant procedures, rats and pigeons maintain a robust rate of responding when only a small fraction of their responses receive contingent reward. This was an impressive finding when most psychologists taught that all learning depended on the reinforcing effects of response contingent rewards and punishments. Recognizing that a mixture of reward and nonreward is also much more typical of the world outside of the laboratory, Skinner and his followers promoted this as a special virtue of operant conditioning. But, the finding that responding goes up as contingent reward goes down actually reverses the principles of Skinner's theory and the whole family of reinforcement theories.

Innumerable experiments have replicated the effects of partial or intermittent reward in operant conditioning. Rate of responding increases as rate of reward decreases down to some very low rate of reward. The smaller the number of responses that actually get rewarded, the greater the rate of responding. At some point the animals get so few rewards that responding begins to decrease but still stays higher than responding with 100% reward. Eventually, if there are hardly any rewards at all, extinction sets in, but vigorous rates of responding can be supported by schedules that require more than 100 responses for every bit of food reward (Catania, 1984, pp. 161–164).

The superiority of low levels of reward appears only in extremely constrained training situations, as in a Skinner box, a prison, a mental hospital, or other similarly constrained environments. Even in a Skinner box, the availability of only two alternative responses dramatically alters the situation. If there are two levers or two keys and one pays off every time while the other pays off only some of the time, rats and pigeons soon respond only to the one that pays off every time. Similarly, if both levers or keys pay off only part of the time, but one pays off more often than the other, rats and pigeons learn to respond more to the one that pays off more frequently.

Now that autoshaping, freefeeding, and misbehavior are well documented and the ethology of operant conditioning is also well documented (chap. 8), it is easier to understand the effects of partial reward in operant conditioning. To begin with, we know now that food evokes lever-pressing and key-pecking in the Skinner box without any contingency at all. After a stimulus situation becomes a feeding situation through association with feeding, rats and pigeons and many other animals persist in *prefeeding* behavior between each S*. Food actually interferes with prefeeding under these conditions because the animals have to stop prefeeding in order to eat the food. The less food they get, the less that feeding interrupts prefeeding. Of course, if there are too few S*s then at some point there is too little association with feeding and this produces extinction.

Extinction After Partial Reward

Because animals stop to eat when they find food, they have more time for lever-pressing and key-pecking when the apparatus delivers less food. More lever-pressing or key-pecking under lower rates of reward could only mean that fewer rewards interferes less than more rewards. Consequently, experimentally sound tests of the difference between partial and 100% reward must measure differences in extinction.

Skinner soon demonstrated that after partial reward, lever-pressing and key-pecking are more resistant to extinction than after 100% reward. If resistance to extinction measures the strength of conditioning, then we must conclude that less reward is more reinforcing than more reward. But, this is the opposite of the principle that the strength of conditioning depends on response contingent reward. Skinner and his followers seem to avoid the antireinforcement implications of this major finding by attributing it to the superiority of operant procedures over other kinds of conditioning. It is certainly true that the most dramatic demonstrations of the positive effects of partial reward have appeared in the Skinner box, but the finding that less reward is more reinforcing than more reward remains the strongest evidence against all theories based on response contingent reinforcement.

Amount of Practice

Greater resistance to extinction after partial reward in a Skinner box is confounded with *amount of practice*. That is, in a Skinner box the fewer rewards they get, the more lever-pressing or key-pecking responses the animals must make per reward. Consequently, experimental subjects practice the criterion response many more times during acquisition or maintenance under partial reward schedules. Therefore, as far as operant conditioning is concerned, the additional practice alone should create greater resistance to extinction. Consequently, the operant procedure is poorly suited for comparing the effects of different rates of reward.

DISCRETE TRIALS

The chief apparatus used to study partial reward with discrete trials has been the straight alley, in which speed of running from start to goal box measures response strength. The positive effects of partial reward contradict reinforcement theory even more clearly in discrete trials experiments. Also, behavior outside the laboratory is more like the discrete trials procedure. Human beings and other animals tend to make discrete responses in nature. They seldom repeat the same response over and over again the way rats press levers and pigeons peck keys in the Skinner box.

According to reinforcement theory, 50 trials of reward strengthens by a positive process of reinforcement and 50 trials of extinction weakens by a negative process of inhibition. Partial reward intersperses 50 trials of nonreward with 50 trials of reward during acquisition. To be consistent, reinforcement theory should predict that the effect of the 50 nonrewarded trials must subtract in some way from the 50 rewarded trials. If the strengthening effect of reward is greater than the weakening effect of nonreward, then partially rewarded subjects should still improve with practice, but their improvement should be less than the improvement of subjects that get 50 trials of reward without any negative effects of nonreward.

The earliest experiments with discrete trials controlled for total number of rewards but confounded percentage of rewarded trials with total number of trials. Table 11.1 shows how a typical experiment would start with Phase I consisting of 50 trials at 100% reward for all conditions and end with Phase III consisting of an extinction test for all conditions. In Phase II, the partial reward condition receives 50 rewarded trials randomly mixed with 50 nonrewarded trials, while

TABLE 11.1
Comparing Partial With 100% Reward in a Discrete Trials Procedure

Conditions		Phase I	Phase II	Phase III
Partial Reward	50%	50R	50R + 50NR	Ext
Control 1	100%	50R	50R + 0NR	Ext
Control 2	100%	50R	50R + 50R	Ext

Note. R = rewarded trials, NR = nonrewarded trials.

the Control 1 condition receives the same number of rewarded trials without any nonrewarded trials. The surprising finding (for those who believed in reinforcement based on response contingent reward) was that the additional 50 unrewarded trials in the partial condition not only failed to subtract from the effect of the 50 rewarded trials, but actually added resistance to extinction.

Experiments like Karn and Porter (1946) discussed in chapter 5 showed that total amount of experience in an experimental situation is critical. This could be the advantage of partial reward in any experiment that failed to equate total number of trials. That is, if the 100% reward group got 50 rewarded trials and the 50% reward group got 50 rewarded trials plus 50 nonrewarded trials, then the 50% reward group got twice as many trials in the apparatus as the 100% reward group. Later experiments remedied this problem by comparing groups that had the same number of trials, one with 100% reward, others with 50% reward or less. This is illustrated by Control 2 in Table 11.1, which received 50 rewarded trials plus 50 more rewarded trials in order to equate total number of trials with the partial condition. In these comparisons, partially rewarded groups virtually always have more resistance to extinction than a 100% rewarded group. This result contradicts the implications of contingency theories more directly and more clearly than the original findings. If resistance to extinction measures strength of conditioning, then this must mean that 100 rewards are less reinforcing than 50 rewards minus 50 nonrewards.

Even the complex twists and turns of Hull's reinforcement theory, with its two types of inhibition (described in chap. 10), cannot cope with the positive, apparently strengthening, effects of nonrewarded trials when they are interspersed with rewarded trials during acquisition in a discrete trials procedure. This has to be a major problem for reinforcement theories, because partial reward in a discrete trials experiment resembles learning in the world outside the laboratory more than any other laboratory procedure.

Generality

A series of proposals that might preserve reinforcement theory in the face of the paradoxical effects of partial reward have appeared over the years. The next section discusses two prominent examples, the discrimination hypothesis and the frustration hypothesis. Kimble (1961, pp. 291–320) and Hall (1976, pp. 281–297) review a larger sample.

When these proposals led to experiments, they extended the generality of the phenomeon. To test a hypothesis about massed and distributed practice, Weinstock (1954, 1958) compared 100% reward with partial reward for rats running in a straight alley for 300 trials at the rate of only *one trial per day*. If, as some said, the extinction effect depends on massed practice (V. Sheffield, 1949), then Weinstock's extreme distribution of practice should wipe out the difference between 100% reward and partial reward. In both experiments, Weinstock demonstrated much greater resistance to extinction after partial reward. This finding after such an extreme degree of spacing between trials killed off the Sheffield hypothesis along with a number of other once popular artifactual explanations of the partial reward extinction effect. For example, partial reward animals are hungrier on the average than 100% animals on any given trial after the first trial. All of the animals get to eat their full daily ration after training each day and are equally hungry on the first trial of each day. Since 100% animals get food reward on every trial they must be less hungry than the partial animals after the first trial. With only one trial per day, however, all animals get only first trials so all are equally hungry on every trial.

Crum, Brown, and Bitterman (1951) varied *delay of reward* to test an aftereffects hypothesis. Instead of a mixture of rewarded and nonrewarded trials, they varied the delay of reward so that one group received immediate reward on all trials and the other received immediate reward for half of their trials and reward delayed by 30 seconds for the other half. Crum et al. became the first to demonstrate that delayed reward has the same effect as nonreward in a discrete trials procedure. Note that in partially delayed reward, the 50% animals get rewarded every trial also so they begin each trial after eating just as many rewards as the 100% animals.

Discrimination

A popular explanation of the superiority of partial reward as an experimental artifact is the *discrimination hypothesis*. The difference between extinction and partial reward is less than the difference between extinction and 100% reward. During extinction after 100% reward, an animal should be able to tell immediately that reward has stopped completely. After acquisition with relatively few rewards per trial, it should take longer for an animal to detect the fact that reward has stopped. At a low rate of reward, say one reward for every ten trials, randomly interspersed with unrewarded trials, it might take more than twenty unrewarded trials to detect the shift to extinction.

There must be some truth in the discrimination hypothesis, but it is a very limited explanation. To begin with, discrimination only applies to laboratory conditions in which there is a shift from acquisition to extinction. Outside the laboratory, payoffs are not so neatly divided into periods of acquisition and extinction. If the whole phenomenon were only an artifact of the difference between acquisition and extinction under laboratory conditions, then it would be much less interesting. In addition, the discrimination hypothesis only applies to the effect of partial reward on resistance to extinction. Evidence later in this section shows that partial reward also leads to stronger responding during acquisition, even in discrete trial conditions when the effect in acquisition cannot be attributed to some artifact of operant procedures.

Early experimenters assumed that 100% reward was necessary for the beginning of acquisition. They virtually always began experiments with a series of 100% reward trials for all groups as shown in Table 11.1. After an initial phase of acquisition at 100% reward, they divided subjects into groups that received various percentages of rewarded trials. Usually, there was only a short partial reward phase in these experiments before extinction of all groups. A brief partial reward phase seemed appropriate because experimenters assumed that the partial reward groups would fall behind during acquisition. They feared that after a long series of partially rewarded trials the performance of the partial groups would fall significantly far behind the performance of the 100% groups. This would create difficulties in statistical comparisons during the extinction phase. That is, experimenters wanted the groups to be equal or nearly equal just before the start of extinction.

The assumption that partial reward during acquisition must retard performance remained untested for many years. Later, however, Capaldi, Ziff, and Godbout (1970) demonstrated successful, actually robust, acquisition in the runway when conditioning began with one or even a few unrewarded trials. Weinstock (1954, 1958) and Goodrich (1959) demonstrated that, after a substantial number of trials, partially rewarded rats ran *faster* than 100% rewarded rats during acquisition even with discrete trials. This result eliminates all of the proposed explanations that invoke an artifact of measuring performance during extinction. It also makes the phenomenon more general, hence more generally interesting. A true advantage of partial reward during acquisition indicates that it could be a useful training technique outside of the laboratory.

Frustration

Amsel (1958, 1962, 1992, 1994) proposed that the paradoxically positive effects of partial reward arise from the frustration that rats feel when they arrive at a formerly rewarding goal box and find it empty.

Amsel proposed that the frustration of not finding S* in a formerly rewarding goal box evoked a *frustration response.* The first effect of frustration is disruptive. During extinction, therefore, the frustration response should accelerate the decline in running. Under partial reward schedules, however, rats often receive reward for running after finding the goal box empty—that is while experiencing the stimulus aftereffects of frustration. When they make disruptive responses that slow them down, they get to the goal box later and rewards (when present) are delayed. Frustration also *energizes.* When the energizing effect of frustration is channeled into more intense running, animals get rewarded faster. Gradually, according to Amsel's theory, the partially rewarded animals become conditioned to run faster under the influence of frustration.

The 100% animals experience frustration for the first time on the first trial of extinction. They only experience extinction, so they only show the disruptive effects of frustration and they extinguish rapidly. The rapid running habits that the partially rewarded rats learned during acquisition transfer readily to the frustrating experience of extinction and they continue to run rapidly for many trials.

According to Amsel's frustration hypothesis, the empty goal box is *aversive.* This agrees with the informal observations of many experimenters. After many trials of feeding in the goal box, rats become agitated when they find the goal box empty. They often scream out in the empty goal box and they can be difficult to handle. Prudent experimenters wear protective gloves on extinction days.

To test for the aversiveness of the empty goal box in extinction, Adelman and Maatsch (1955) ran rats in a straight alley for food reward and then extinguished them by three different procedures. One group received a normal extinction series in which they were confined in the empty goal box for 20 seconds after running through the alley. A second group was allowed to jump out of the empty goal box, thus escaping from the frustration of nonreward. The animals in the third group were allowed to escape from the empty goal box by running back into the alley. Adelman and Maatsch called this group the "recoil" group. Results of this experiment in terms of running time appear in Fig. 11.1. Allowing the jump group to escape from the empty goal box maintained running in extinction at the same level as food reward in acquisition.

Adelman and Maatsch (1955) and many others have explained the performance of the jump group in terms of the reward of getting out of the frustrating goal box. In a feed forward system, the chain of responses that got them to the goal box should be maintained by any strong response that is the last response to the goal box, whether the

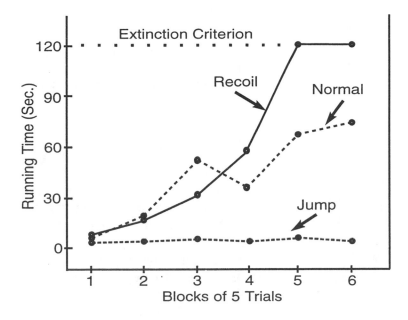

FIG. 11.1. The effect of three different treatments in the goal box during extinction. From Adelman and Maatsch (1955).

rats promptly find and eat food, or promptly jump out of the box. Adelman and Maatsch also rewarded the recoil group with escape from the frustrating goal box, but that group actually extinguished faster than the normally confined group. Feed forward theory would predict faster extinction in the recoil group because that group gets to run back through the maze in the wrong direction. Consequently, the last thing that they did when they were in the maze near the goal box was to run back away from the goal box. Conditioning them to run back should slow their forward movement, considerably, on the next trials.

Because Amsel's frustration energizes, partially rewarded rats should run faster during acquisition as well as during extinction. Weinstock (1958) and Goodrich (1959) confirmed this prediction when they ran rats under partial reward for an extended series of trials. This makes Amsel's frustration hypothesis superior to hypotheses such as the discrimination hypothesis that only account for superior resistance to extinction.

Hall (1976, pp. 291–297) reviewed evidence for and against Amsel's account of partial reward and found evidence both for and against the frustration hypothesis, which remains the most successful account that is compatible with response contingent reinforcement. Amsel (1992, 1994) summarized frustration theory in more detail and in the light of more recent experiments. This chapter presents only the basics of the theory and the evidence. Amsel's frustration hypothesis is notable because it has interesting implications for life outside the laboratory. Learning to persist in the face of frustrating nonreward and to channel the tension into productive behavior would be a very useful skill.

The frustration hypothesis shares a basic weakness with all explanations based on inferences about pleasure and pain. Consider the defining operations of frustration. An empty goal box, by itself, cannot arouse frustration. Animals must experience the pleasure of food in the goal box before the empty goal box arouses the displeasure of frustration. Compare this with the defining operations of *secondary reward*. In the case of S^r the goal box is neutral by itself, but acquires positive value when animals experience the pleasure of food there. Eventually, the empty goal box becomes an S^r that rewards the animals for running.

How can the same empty goal box have a pleasurable secondary rewarding effect that maintains responding in extinction and, at the same time, have an aversive frustrating effect that disrupts responding in extinction? The problem here is that both secondary reward and frustration are based on projection of subjective human feelings of pleasure and frustration into the minds of rats and pigeons. Both of these cognitive, hedonistic notions are reasonable. The trouble with this sort of subjective, projective reasoning is that it can and often does lead to flatly contradictory conclusions. The feed forward principle, by contrast, predicts behavior by observing what the subject does rather than imagining how the subject might feel.

WHAT IS WRONG WITH 100% REWARD?

The superior performance of partially rewarded animals in an apparatus like the straight alley flatly contradicts traditional reinforcement theory. This is because 100% reward should always be the best possible schedule. Any rate of reward that is less than 100% should add less reinforcement and more inhibition than 100% reward. All reinforcement accounts of this phenomenon must then account for the superior effects of partial reward as an experimental artifact that distorts the true difference between 100% and partial reward. This chapter has taken up two of these artifactual accounts: discrimination between acquisition and extinction, and Amsel's frustration hypothesis. Both attempt to explain why 100% reward really would be superior if it were not for some experimental artifact that distorts the picture.

And yet, all of the animals that serve as subjects in these experiments evolved in a world in which 100% reward is rare and partial reward, even sparsely distributed partial reward, is common. From an ecological point of view, there is something basically wrong-headed about a theory that treats the most unlikely condition found in nature as the normal case and the most common condition found in nature as the artifact. This wrong-headedness is even more serious if you want to apply the results of laboratory experiments to practical situations in the outside world.

Feed forward theories are based on switching between alternatives rather than positive strengthening through reinforcement and negative weakening through inhibition. In a feed forward theory, if 100% animals run slower than 50% animals, it must be because they are doing something else that interferes with running. The feed forward principle tells us to look for a disadvantage of 100% reward in terms of competing responses. What could this be?

Anticipatory Goal Responses

If the S* is food, and the criterion response, R_c, is a prefeeding response, then partial reward only increases the amount of prefeeding, because animals repeat *anticipatory prefeeding responses* until they get an S^d that evokes a feeding response. Foraging in burrows and fields is also a prefeeding response of rats; that is why it is so easy to train hungry rats to run in alleys with food incentives. Running through a maze or an alley and finding food in the dish at the end of the goal box involves a more extended and heterogeneous sequence of responses than pressing a lever over and over again. In this sense, rats running in mazes or straight alleys are much more like human beings practicing *skilled sequences* of behavior. In skilled behavior, the timing of each step in a sequence is critical. Anticipatory behavior disrupts the sequence and skill deteriorates.

Consider the case of a tennis player winning a match against a relatively inferior opponent. Becoming more and more confident, the tennis player starts to imagine jumping over the net at the end of the match to shake hands with the defeated opponent and accept the congratulations of the crowd. Distracted from the game at hand, the tennis player starts to miss shots and loses the match. Anticipation of reward disrupts the skill.

In the film, *Behavioral Development of the Cross-Fostered Chimpanzee Washoe,* there is a scene showing Washoe when she was about 3 years old stacking 1-inch children's building blocks. At that time, Washoe had become fairly good at stacking these blocks. She could build towers of up to 12 blocks fairly easily (our limit was 10 blocks). Essentially, Washoe taught herself to build these towers after we showed her that it could be done. Challenged by the task itself, she needed no external reward. During the filming Susan, then a graduate student and firm believer in Skinnerian reinforcement, started to tickle Washoe as a reward. Tickling seems to give infant chimpanzees more pleasure than just about anything else you can do for them. In the film, you can see Washoe stacking about four blocks rather carelessly with her eyes shifting from the blocks to Susan, and then starting to giggle in anticipation of the tickling. She starts to jump up and down and cover the most ticklish spots on her body. Actual stacking stops prematurely after only a few blocks and Washoe even knocks over the small tower in her anticipatory excitement.

Anticipatory behavior like this seems to appear when rats run in mazes and straight alleys. Figure 5.5 (discussed in chap. 5 in connection with the goal gradient phenomenon) is a plot of running time in a straight alley and shows rats actually slowing down as they near the goal box. This is the typical finding when experimenters compare running near and far from the goal box. Goodrich (1959) replicated this finding and found that hungry rats slowed down considerably as they entered the goal box. Very likely, behavior in the goal box consisted of responses, such as seeking out the food dish and preparing to eat, that disrupted the full-speed-ahead running in the alley. It seems likely that if this prefeeding behavior appeared too early in the sequence, it would slow the rats down earlier in the alley.

Goodrich (1959) compared 100% reward with 50% reward and found that both groups slowed dramatically when they entered the goal box and approached the food dish at the end of the goal box. This is what we would expect if there is prefeeding behavior in the goal box that interferes with rapid running. Goodrich's 100% animals reached the food dish faster than his 50% animals. This is what we would expect if the 100% animals made the terminal responses faster than the 50% animals. Meanwhile, Goodrich's 100% animals ran slower in the alley than his 50% animals. This is what we would expect if the 100% animals were making more anticipatory goal responses in the alley. The terminal responses that they had learned so well with 100% reward interfered with running in the rest of the straight alley. Could this be the advantage of partial reward in skilled sequences of behavior that require different responses at different points in a sequence?

Chen and Amsel (1980) used conditioned taste aversion to study the effect of anticipatory goal responses in a runway. Chapter 6 described the evidence that after experimenters pair a flavor with illness induced by injections of lithium chloride rats reject the experimental flavor. Further evidence discussed in chapter 6 identified fractional anticipatory responses to the illness as the mechanism of rejection. Conditioned responses are most pronounced when the rats taste the experimental flavor, but these fractional anticipatory responses also interfere with a well-practiced predrinking response such as lever-pressing. Deaux and Patten (1964), as illustrated in Fig. 6.4, showed how anticipatory licking in a straight alley increases with 100% reward at the end of the alley.

In a feed forward system, it is anticipatory goal responses that slow the 100% animals in the runway and speed them up in the goal box, just as Goodrich (1959) found. After conditioned taste aversion, anticipatory licking should evoke anticipatory rejection, which should interfere with running. In a feed forward system, 50% reward markedly reduces, even eliminates, anticipatory goal responses in the alley. Conditioned taste aversion should then cause much slower running after 100% reward than after 50% reward.

Chen and Amsel (1980) tested this implication of feed forward by training thirsty rats to run in a straight alley with vinegar-flavored water in the goal box. Half of the animals received 100% reward and half 50% reward. After 30 trials in the alley, the experimenters paired vinegar-flavored water with illness by injecting half of the animals in each group with lithium chloride. For the control half of each group of rats, they paired vinegar-flavored water with an injection of a neutral saline solution. Next they ran all of the rats in the alley under extinction. These animals never received any water, flavored or unflavored, in the alley again. Figure 11.2 shows that both groups of 100% animals extinguished much faster than both groups of 50% animals, which is the usual effect of 50% reward. Illness paired with the flavor of the rewards hastened the extinction of the 100% group without affecting the extinction of the poisoned 50% group. This is just what we would expect if 100% reward induces much more *anticipatory drinking* in the alley than 50% reward. Indeed, Chen and Amsel's results suggest that after 50% reward there may be hardly any anticipatory drinking to interfere with the habit of running in the alley.

Anticipatory Errors

In a feed forward system, the trouble with 100% reward is that terminal goal responses are learned too well. The advantage of the partially rewarded animals is that they concentrate on running and make fewer anticipatory goal responses in the alley. Ecologically significant skills outside the laboratory usually consist of a series of responses that must be made in a correct sequence and with correct timing. If 100% reward induces anticipatory errors, then partial reward is more appropriate for learning skilled sequences.

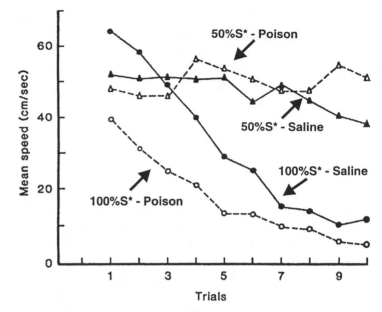

FIG. 11.2. Extinction in a straight alley after 100% and 50% reward. Vinegar-flavored rewards were paired with illness-inducing poison or neutral saline. Reprinted with permission from Chen, & Amsel, (1980). Copyright © 1980 by American Association for the Advancement of Science. Reprinted with permission.

The linear maze (discussed and illustrated in chap. 5, Figs. 5.3 and 5.4, in connection with the goal gradient phenomenon) is a way to observe anticipatory goal responses, directly. As a first step in testing this hypothesis, R. A. Gardner and Gamboni (1971) ran two groups of thirsty rats with water reward in a similar linear maze illustrated in Fig. 11.3. For one group, All Same, all four correct choices were the same, LLLL for half of the animals in the group and RRRR for the other half. For a second group, Terminal Opposite, the first three choices were the same but the terminal choice was opposite, LLLR for half the animals and RRRL for the other half. Figure 11.4 shows that the results were very similar to results found in earlier experiments (illustrated in

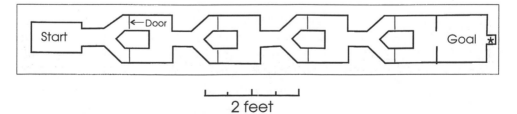

FIG. 11.3. Diagram of the linear maze used by R. A. Gardner and Gamboni (1971) and Gamboni (1973). Copyright © 1997 by R. Allen Gardner.

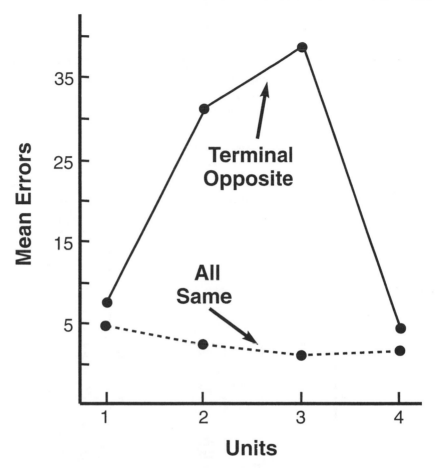

FIG. 11.4.   Mean errors at each choice point in a linear maze, as in R. A. Gardner and Gamboni (1971). Copyright © 1997 by R. Allen Gardner.

Fig. 5.4). The All Same group performed uniformly well in all four units of the linear maze, while the Terminal Opposite group performed about as well as the All Same group in the unit closest to the goal box, but made many anticipatory errors in the earlier units. That is, the Terminal Opposite group made anticipatory left errors when the correct terminal choice was left and anticipatory right errors when the correct terminal choice was right. Figure 11.4 also shows that anticipatory errors depended on distance from the reward. The closer to the terminal unit the greater the amount of anticipatory error.

After Gardner and Gamboni (1971) replicated earlier work with 100% water reward in the new apparatus, Gamboni (1973) studied the effect of partial delay of reward on anticipatory responses. Gamboni varied partial delay of reward rather than partial nonreward to take advantage of the technique discovered by Crum et al. (1951) and discussed earlier in this chapter. With partial delay of reward rather than partial nonreward, all animals in all groups are equally thirsty throughout each day's series of trials, which eliminates that possible source of bias.

Gamboni (1973) gave five groups of rats either 100%, 75%, 50%, 25%, or 0% immediate rewards and delayed rewards on the rest of their trials. Delayed reward consisted of 30 seconds of confinement in the goal box before access to the drinking cup.

Figure 11.5 shows that the more often the animals received immediate reward the fewer the errors they made in the fourth and last

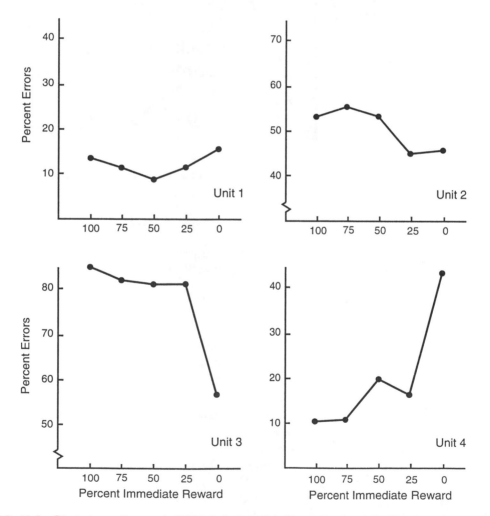

FIG. 11.5.   Percentage of errors in Units 1, 2, 3, and 4. From Gamboni (1973). Copyright © 1973 by the American Psychological Association. Adapted with permission.

unit before the reward. In the second and third units, this pattern was reversed. The more often the animals received immediate reward the more errors—now anticipatory errors—they made in the two units before the last unit, and this anticipatory effect was more marked in the unit closest to the last unit. Figure 11.6 shows percentage of anticipatory errors for the first three units combined. The curve is flat for the first unit shown in Fig. 11.5. Delay of reward failed to affect the unit farthest from reward.

These results confirm the notion that partial reward improves learning and performance when the task consists of a sequence of responses. Immediate 100% reward at the end of a sequence strengthens the later responses in the sequence to the point where they anticipate and interfere with earlier responses in the sequence.

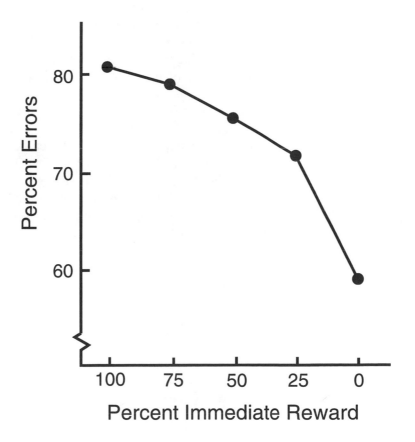

FIG. 11.6.   Percentage of anticipatory errors in Units 1–3. From Gamboni (1973). Copyright © 1973 by the American Psychological Association. Adapted with permission.

SUMMARY

The superiority of partial reward over 100% reward in both acquisition and extinction contradicts both contingent reinforcement theory and cognitive expectancy theory. In early experiments it seemed as if the superiority of partial reward only appeared in extinction, and early writers attributed the partial reward extinction effect to artifacts of experimental extinction. Later experiments demonstrated that partial reward is also superior during acquisition. It is a general phenomenon rather than a laboratory curiosity. Amsel's extension of Hull's theory by means of a frustration principle is the most successful attempt so far to explain the superiority of partial reward in both acquisition and extinction within traditional reinforcement theory.

The defining operations of Amsel's frustrating stimuli, however, are the same as the defining operations of secondary rewarding stimuli within the same theory. The two effects of the same experimental operations are clearly contradictory and this indicates that there must be some flaw in the reasoning. As usual, the error arises from basing theoretical principles on slippery foundations, such as subjective, projective notions of how human theorists would feel if they were rats in a maze.

The last section of this chapter describes a feed forward, contiguity interpretation of the effects of unrewarded trials. This interpretation emerges from experiments and direct ethological observations described in earlier chapters. Because feed forward conditioning takes place without building up habit strength or expectancy, it avoids the need for an inhibitory mechanism to counteract excitation. A feed forward system also offers a much simpler and more realistic way to deal with competing responses. It indicates, and experimental results confirm, that the positive effect of less frequent and less immediate reward depends on the disruptive effect of reward on sequential skill. This result has implications for learning skills in practical applications. The more frequent, the more immediate, and the more intense the end reward, the more reward should interfere with skilled sequences in practical situations.

CHAPTER 12

Places, Paths, and Bearings

Tolman argued that the Skinner box and the straight-alley runway make animals look stupid because they give them only stupid things to do. He designed his experiments to show how intelligent they could be when psychologists give them intelligent things to do. Probably the most productive line of research that Tolman inspired began with the argument about just what a rat learns in a maze. His notion of cognitive maps that guide the behavior of human and nonhuman animals influenced theory and research throughout the 20th century. This chapter introduces modern studies of foraging and orientation that offer us more ethological and more intelligent alternatives to the traditional cognitive map.

PLACE LEARNING VERSUS RESPONSE LEARNING

Chapter 5 described in detail how early reinforcement theorists such as Hull explained maze learning as a series of links in a chain of stimuli and responses ending with reward in the goal box. According to early cognitive theories on the other hand, rats learn a *cognitive map* of the maze—start box, choice point, end boxes, runways, and (when *extramaze* cues are available) the room that houses the maze. When rats learn that food is in the goal box at the end of the right arm of a T-maze, then they naturally go to the right at the choice point because that is the shortest route to the food. Rather than strengthening a chain of stimuli and responses from choice point to choice point, experience in the maze teaches cognitive rats where the food is and how to get there.

Rats could find the food in the usual maze either way: by learning to go to the place where the food is or by learning to make correct turns at each choice point. Tolman, Ritchie, and Kalish (1946) wanted to find out whether rats learn to return to the same place regardless of the responses it takes to get there, or instead, learn to repeat the same turns at each choice point. They designed the *cross-maze* shown in Fig. 12.1 to define the difference between place learning and response learning. This maze has two goal boxes, G1 and G2, as in the usual T-maze, but it also has two starting boxes, S1 and S2. When the experimenter always rewards a rat in the same place, say G1, then the rat must make right turns after starting at S1 and left turns after starting at S2. When the experimenter always rewards a rat for making the same turn, say a right turn, then the rat must run to G1 after starting at S1 and to G2 after starting at S2. If rats naturally learn to return to the same feeding place, as cognitive theorists claimed, then it should be easier for them to learn to return to the same goal box on every trial, even when they must take different paths from different starting places. If rats naturally learn to repeat the same response at the same choice point, as reinforcement theorists claimed, then it should be easier for them to learn to repeat the same turn on every trial, even when the same turn leads them from different starting places to different feeding places.

Each of the rats in this experiment started equally often from S1 and S2 in an alternating sequence, which was S1, S2, S2, S1, S1, S2

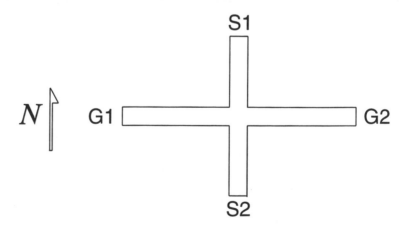

FIG. 12.1. Plan of the cross-maze used by Tolman et al. (1946) to compare place learning with response learning. Copyright © 1997 by R. Allen Gardner.

on odd days and S2, S1, S1, S2, S2, S1 on even days. The place learning group always found food in the same goal box. For half of the place group this was G1, and for the other half this was G2. An animal in the place group that always found food in G1 got there by turning right when starting from S1 and by turning left when starting from S2. An animal in the place group that always found food in G2 got there by turning left when starting from S1 and by turning right when starting from S2.

The second group, the response learning group, always found food after making the same turn at the choice point. For half of the response group this was a right turn, and for the other half this was a left turn. An animal in the response group that always found food after a right turn found food in G1 when starting from S1 and in G2 when starting from S2. An animal in the response group that always found food after a left turn found food in G2 when starting from S1 and in G1 when starting from S2.

If animals learn where the food is, then place learning should be easier than response learning. If, instead, animals learn to make right or left turns in response to the stimuli at the choice point, then response learning should be easier than place learning. The results of the first experiment by Tolman, Ritchie, and Kalish were decisive. All of the animals in the place group reached the learning criterion of 10 successive correct choices within 18 trials and all but three of them reached this criterion within 12 trials. Meanwhile, only three of the animals in the response group reached criterion within 72 trials.

All of the animals in the place group quickly learned to run to the rewarded place, and most of the animals in the response group soon ran exclusively to one of the goal box places, even though this strategy earned food reward on only 50% of the trials. Chapter 11 reviews the mass of evidence that 50% reinforcement builds up very strong habits. Place learning is such a dominant mode of learning that nearly all of the animals formed a place habit in both groups.

Later experimenters varied conditions to discover what stimuli the animals used to find their way back to the same place each time. The basic procedure started with a large experimental room, say ten to twenty times the size of the cross-maze in Fig. 12.1 in which there might be windows in the south wall, a door opening on to a hallway in the north wall, the rack of home cages along the east wall, and sinks and storage shelves on the west wall. Overall, the experimental rooms were unevenly lighted and unevenly heated and ventilated. Thus there were many *extramaze* stimuli to tell the rats where they were in the room. These experiments demonstrated that rats use cues to place and direction in a room rather than right and left turns. They can use right and left turns, but they only use turns when experimenters block out all other information (see Restle, 1957, for a detailed review).

Cognitive theories are top-down theories. They demand some sort of executive entity in the brain that receives inputs transmitted upward from the sensory systems, studies fresh inputs and stored memory, makes decisions, and then sends commands downward to the motor systems. Reinforcement theories seem less mentalistic but reinforcement theories are top-down theories, also. That is, first some central executive entity must decide that the animal has been reinforced, that the S that followed the R was, indeed, an S* or an S^r. Second, after a period of trial and error, some executive entity must store information about the contingency between S* and R and, if there is a contingency, then how large a contingency. Then the executive entity must command motor systems to make Rs. Place versus response experiments demonstrate conclusively that the dominant mode of the information and the commands is in terms of places and goals rather than specific stimulus-response units. Until the development of modern robotics (chaps. 7 and 9), the only sort of system that could handle such information seemed to be a top-down cognitive system using entities like cognitive maps.

The trouble with the cognitive map has always been that it seems to dodge the question of maze learning. For example, if rats use cognitive maps, where are those maps and who looks at them? If there is a little cognitive rat inside who looks at the cognitive map, then we only have a new set of puzzles about the cognition of the little rat inside of the big rat. Saying that the little cognitive rat inside "naturally" or "obviously" takes the shortest route tells us nothing about how any actual rat chooses any actual route. To the hardheaded theorists of the first half of this century, the only scientific alternative to cognitive maps seemed to be some version of the *goal-gradient* mechanism of chapter 5 that analyzes a runway or maze into many small segments, each providing its own stimuli and each requiring its own responses.

SPONTANEOUS ALTERNATION

On the first trial in a simple T-maze, about half the rats find food in the first goal box that they enter. What would you expect a rat to do on the second trial if, on the very first trial, it ran through the maze and found food at the end of the right arm? It seems as though both reinforcement and cognitive theories should predict that, while the effect of a single reward on the first trial might be small, the rat should be somewhat more likely to repeat the rewarded choice. A very large number of experiments, however, contradict this implication of both reinforcement and expectancy theories. After finding reward on the first run through a T-maze, rats mostly run to the opposite arm on the second trial. This powerful phenomenon is called *spontaneous alternation.* Depending on various conditions, 90% or more of the turns on Trial 2 can be in the opposite direction to the turn on Trial 1, whether or not the animal found reward on Trial 1 (see Dember & Richman, 1989, for extensive discussion).

From an ethological and ecological point of view, alternation is a highly appropriate strategy for an animal that lives by foraging for food. This is the first time that the animal explored this particular territory. If the animal can remember that it found food on the right, then it must also remember that it consumed the food that was there. So, on the second trial, it would be a good strategy to strike out in a new direction. If the animal found the first goal box was empty from the start, then it is even more sensible to try the left arm on the next trial.

Montgomery (1952) and Glanzer (1953) compared place alternation with response alternation in cross-mazes like the one used by Tolman et al. (1946) and illustrated in Fig. 12.1 to study place versus response learning. They started the rats alternately at start boxes S1 and S2 and fed them at goal boxes G1 or G2, whichever the rats chose on the first trial. They next gave the rats a second trial starting from the opposite start box. On the second trial, the rats could alternate places or they could alternate responses. They found that rats alternate places rather than turns on Trial 2 just as they learn places rather than responses in maze-learning experiments.

Intramaze Stimuli Versus Extramaze Stimuli

Walker, Dember, Earl, and Karoly (1955) pointed out that place in the room in the Montgomery and Glanzer experiments was confounded with place in the maze in an apparatus like that in Fig. 12.1. That is, with mazes made of wood or composition board, as is common in such experiments, the appearance and texture of each arm are bound to be slightly different. If G1 always points east and G2 always points west, then we cannot tell whether the rats are alternating stimuli coming from within the maze, *intramaze stimuli,* or stimuli coming from outside the maze, *extramaze stimuli.*

Walker et al. (1955) painted the arm leading to one of the goal boxes black and the arm leading to the other goal box white to increase

PI   PII

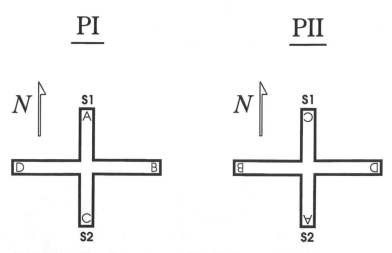

FIG. 12.2.   Two floor plans used by Walker et al. (1955) to separate intramaze stimuli from extramaze stimuli. Copyright © 1997 by R. Allen Gardner.

the stimulus difference between the two arms. The maze had wooden walls and a wire mesh roof through which the rats could see the major landmarks of the experimental room. In their first experimental condition, PI in Fig. 12.2, they used the same floor plan (Fig. 12.1) that Tolman et al. (1946), Montgomery (1952), and Glanzer (1953) had used, and started each rat from S1 on Trial 1 and then from S2 on Trial 2. A rat in Condition 1 that ran to B on Trial 1 and D on Trial 2 was repeating left turns but alternating both intramaze stimuli and extramaze stimuli. Similarly, a rat in Condition 1 that ran to D on Trial 1 and B on Trial 2 was repeating right turns but alternating both intramaze stimuli and extramaze stimuli.

In their second experimental condition, Walker et al. used the same floor plan as before for Trial 1, PI in Fig. 12.2, and started each rat from S1, but then they rotated the whole cross-maze by 180°, as shown in PII of Fig. 12.2, before starting each rat from S2 on Trial 2. Thus, B pointed east and D pointed west on Trial 1, but after the rotation B pointed west and D pointed east on Trial 2. Consequently, an animal in the second condition that ran from S1 to B on Trial 1 and then from S2 to D on Trial 2 was alternating intramaze stimuli but repeating left turns and westerly extramaze stimuli. Similarly, an animal in the second condition that ran from S1 to D on Trial 1 and then from S2 to B on Trial 2 was also alternating intramaze stimuli while repeating right turns and easterly extramaze stimuli. In the third and fourth conditions, Walker et al. started each rat from the same point, either S1 or S2, on both Trial 1 and Trial 2. They used floor plan PI for both trials of the third condition and rotated from PI to PII for the second trial of the fourth condition.

In this way, Walker et al. pitted all three alleged sources of alternation against each other in different combinations in the four different conditions so that they could measure the contribution of each to spontaneous alternation. They found 80% alternation of intramaze stimuli and virtually no alternation of extramaze stimuli or responses. Note that Walker et al. deprived their rats of food during the experiment, but they never gave the rats any food in the cross-maze.

Odor Trails

Many mammals, including laboratory rats, have scent glands on the underside of their bodies and mark their trails with a variety of odors. A rat can tell a lot from an odor trail. It can tell whether the trail was laid down by itself, another familiar rat, or a stranger. It can tell the sex of the rat that laid down the trail. It can tell how old the trail is. It can tell whether the rat that laid down the trail was running away frightened or foraging for food. It can even tell whether the rat that laid down the trail had just detected food or stimuli predicting food (Ludvigson & Sytsma, 1967). Scientists have known for a very long time that odor trails have significant effects on behavior, and careful experimenters have always cleaned out the floors of mazes after every trial to eliminate this source of stimulation. Sad to say, more experimenters failed to observe this precaution as if rats cared as little about odor trails as human beings. Fortunately, the effect of odor trails is irrelevant to the objectives of many experiments.

It is scandalous that there were so many experiments on spontaneous alternation before anyone considered the question of the odor trail left behind on Trial 1. Douglas (1966) pointed out that in all previous experiments on spontaneous alternation—like those of Montgomery (1952), Glanzer (1953), and Walker et al. (1955)—odor trails left behind on Trial 1 were completely confounded with intramaze stimuli. That is, when rats alternated goal arms in these experiments they could have responded to the odor trail that they, themselves, had left behind on Trial 1 and ignored all other differences between G1 and G2, such as the fact that the goal arms were painted different colors. On Trial 2, rats can tell which alley they tried on Trial 1 by sniffing. They do not have to remember anything.

Douglas eliminated odor trails by spreading fresh paper on the floor of the maze between Trial 1 and Trial 2. With the additional control for odor trails, Douglas repeated all of the alternation tests of previous experiments and added a few new ones. He tested for response alternation in isolation by using one T-maze on Trial 1 and then using a different T-maze in a different experimental room with fresh paper on Trial 2. He tested for the effects of extramaze stimuli in isolation by using one T-maze on Trial 1 and a different T-maze with fresh floor paper on Trial 2 while placing the second T-maze in the same location in the same experimental room as Trial 1. He tested for intramaze stimuli in isolation by keeping the T-maze used on Trial 1 the same, including the paper floor and moving the whole business to a different experimental room. As in Walker et al. (1955), Douglas never gave his animals any food in the T-mazes. This is an easier procedure for the experimenter and may also increase the amount of alternation.

In his first series of tests, Douglas found that the effect of extramaze stimuli alone was 75% alternation, the effect of intramaze stimuli alone was 61.5% alternation, and the effect of response alone was exactly 50% or chance-level alternation. Douglas next performed a series of tests to isolate the stimuli responsible for intramaze alternation. He varied the composition of the walls of the goal arms as well as the color, but the only stimulus that led to alternation was an odor trail on the floor paper. No matter how Douglas varied other intramaze stimuli, whenever he put down fresh paper on Trial 2, alternation dropped to chance level. Yet, even when Douglas used a different T-maze in a different room on Trial 2, he got 65.5% alternation when he used the same floor paper on Trial 1 and Trial 2.

An animal can save itself the trouble of storing a cognitive map and studying it later if it can leave behind a trail of markers as Hansel and Gretel did when they were kidnapped in the forest. It is embarrassing that experimental psychologists required so many decades to discover that nocturnal animals, like rats, are much more interested in patterns of odor and much less interested in patterns of light than human beings. With a little more interest in the ethology and ecology of their experimental subjects, experimental psychologists could have discovered long ago the well-known fact that rats, like many mammals, have scent glands that they use to mark places.

Compass Bearing

Douglas then made an unexpected discovery. His next series of experiments aimed at isolating the extramaze stimuli responsible for alternation. He tried moving all sorts of visual, auditory, and olfactory sources of stimuli from the Trial 1 room to the Trial 2 room, but alternation always dropped back to the 50% chance level in the second room. Douglas only got extramaze alternation when he retested the animals in the same room in the same maze location on Trial 1 and Trial 2.

In one of these futile searches for the source of extramaze alternation, he made a slight change in procedure. Up to that point, Douglas had rotated the T-maze 90° (see Fig. 12.3) whenever he changed rooms, so that the goal arms were running from east to west in one room and from north to south in the other room. As he became more and more discouraged, he neglected to rotate the maze when he changed rooms in one set of tests. The effect was an immediate recovery of the roughly 75% alternation level found when the maze was kept in the same location in the same room.

Douglas next showed that when he changed everything—T-maze, room, and floor paper—but kept the goal arms in the same east–west or north–south orientation, he always got roughly 75% alternation. If he rotated the maze 90°, however, alternation dropped to chance in every condition except the one in which he reused the same paper from Trial 1 to Trial 2. He also found the usual 75% alternation when he moved the T-maze around in the same room, but kept the east–west or north–south orientation of the goal arms constant. Soon, Sherrick and Dember (1966a, 1966b) confirmed Douglas' findings in their laboratory.

How can rats tell the difference between an east–west orientation and a north–south orientation? Douglas guessed that they did this with the *semicircular canals* in their inner ears. Mammals have an interesting set of organs in their inner ears consisting of three semicircular canals at right angles to each other so that they respond to

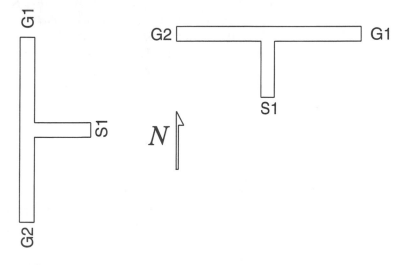

FIG. 12.3.   T-maze with 90° rotation. Copyright © 1997 by R. Allen Gardner.

rotation in all three major planes of the body. Rotation in any direction stimulates the sensors in the semicircular canals. This is the rotation that makes children dizzy when they spin themselves around. Douglas guessed that the rats could tell which way they had turned last and which way they were pointed next if they could sense horizontal rotation.

Douglas found that he could reduce the effect of compass bearing on alternation by holding a rat at chest level, horizontally, head pointing outward, and then pirouetting rapidly around for a full 360°. He could eliminate alternation by compass bearing, entirely, by making eight rapid turns in succession. He worried that the pirouetting of the big man might disturb the little rats so he controlled for the disturbance. When he held a rat at chest level, horizontally pointing outward, but now rotated the rat vertically head over heels, the animals continued to alternate compass direction.

Recently, Etienne and her associates (see Etienne, 1992, for a summary) studied the stimuli that hamsters use to find their way back to a home nest after foraging. The experimental apparatus consisted of a circular arena, two meters in diameter, with a nest box attached to the outside of the boundary wall. The hamsters entered the arena from the nest box through an opening in the wall of the arena. When hamsters find a source of food (Etienne et al. provided little piles of filbert nuts), they seldom eat on the spot. Instead, they stuff as much as they can into their cheek pouches and bring the lot back to hoard in their home nests. Next time a hamster is away on a foraging trip, the experimenter can empty the nest and reuse the nuts. In this way, hamsters never get satiated for nuts and go on foraging, indefinitely.

In the course of foraging, a hamster may travel various distances and make many turns. Nevertheless, a hamster returns directly to its home nest by a fairly accurate linear path, as shown in Fig. 12.4. They can use various kinds of visual landmarks to find their way home, but they can also find their way in total darkness. In total darkness, the experimenters monitored the movements of the hamsters with infrared light. Human beings need special optical aids to see in infrared light and without such special aids hamsters are in the equivalent of total darkness. Etienne et al. used a variety of devices to eliminate other kinds of differential stimuli that might arise from the experimental room and the experimental apparatus.

Etienne et al. could lead a hamster around the arena by baiting a spoon with food and holding it close to the hamster's nose but just beyond its reach. In this way they could lead a hamster by an experimentally controlled path to a pile of nuts. The hamster then promptly filled its cheek pouches and returned home on a direct line. If the

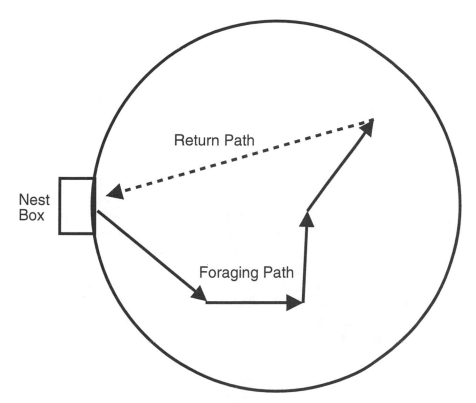

FIG. 12.4.   A hamster forages in an arena and returns to its nest box. (After Etienne, 1992) Copyright © 1997 by R. Allen Gardner.

devious experimental path included as many as five 360° turns in the same clockwise or counterclockwise direction, the hamsters started to make errors. If the experimental path out had six complete turns in the same direction, the hamsters made serious errors in their return path. After eight 360° turns in the same direction, they acted quite lost. If the turns in the foraging path were alternately clockwise and counterclockwise, the hamsters acted as if turns in opposite directions cancel each other out.

Another way that Etienne et al. confused a hamster was by letting it find the pile of nuts on a circular dish-shaped platform after foraging on its own. The platform had a hook on its edge and the experimenter rotated the platform with a long pole while the hamster was busy stuffing its cheek pouches with nuts. One or two passive 360° clockwise or counterclockwise turns on the platform and hamsters began to make significant errors on the return path. Three or more complete passive turns and hamsters acted as though they were completely lost. Like rats, hamsters must use information about rotation from the semicircular canals in their inner ears to guide them back to their home nests.

Rats and hamsters seem to navigate in the dark by first noting the direction that they take when leaving the home nest. With each turn and each excursion in a particular direction, they can judge the angle between themselves and the home nest. It is as if they have a horizontal dial in their heads with a pointer that always points toward home. As long as they stay on the first heading, the pointer indicates that a return path 180° from the present heading is the best path home. If the animal makes a 90° turn to the right and proceeds on this new heading, the pointer keeps pointing home (at first 90° to the right of the new heading) and indicates a larger and larger angle for the correct path home. If the animal next turns 120° to the left, then the pointer begins to indicate a smaller and smaller angle for the correct path home. Equipped with an internal device such as this, an animal never has to form a cognitive map of the territory and never has to store more than one bit of information in memory. A forager only has to follow the angle that currently indicates the way home. If there is still food left at the last foraging sight, the hamster can find its way back by reversing the last return direction when it starts out the next time.

Navigation

Hamsters and rats must rely on odor trails and semicircular canals when they are in total darkness. Etienne and her associates and other modern experimenters (see Poucet, 1993) have also shown that animals can use visual landmarks to guide themselves home and also to guide themselves outward to return to a good foraging site. Etienne and her associates have placed landmarks such as a small light or a silhouette at the edge of the arena or at some distance beyond the arena. Hamsters usually orient to relatively distant landmarks corresponding to the relatively stable landmarks that they would see on the horizon in a natural habitat (Etienne, Lambert, Reverdin, & Teroni, 1993). Under natural conditions they can use visual landmarks together with their semicircular canals. That way they avoid confusion when important visual landmarks are obscured by obstacles or after they have made many turns while foraging. Navigation is for getting home and getting back to a good foraging site when there is a distance to travel. Once an animal gets near home base or back to the foraging neighborhood, it can use distinctive local cues such as particular plants or rocks (Poucet, 1993).

Navigation is based on compass bearing and distance traveled rather than map location. That way a hamster in a natural habitat can get home even though it has to travel a zigzag path to get around bushes and rocks. All it has to do is to keep returning along the same compass bearing. It is unnecessary to hold the actual zigzag path in memory, because following the compass bearing and actual distance traveled will get them back to the neighborhood of the forage site. When they get close, odor and other local cues can take over. It is also quite unnecessary to store in memory an elaborate map of the foraging territory and the obstacles that define the many alternative routes between home base and all possible foraging sites. Nor is it necessary for the little hamster inside the big hamster to pour over such a map in order to tell the big hamster how to get from place to place.

Honeybees forage over even larger territories than hamsters. When bees find a good foraging site they use the sun to guide themselves back to the hive on a beeline. Exploring for food in the usual haphazard path can take them to some places where they cannot return to the hive on a beeline. If there is an obstacle, for example a hill, the scouts interrupt their beeline to the hive in order to fly around the obstacle, leaving the obstacle at the beeline angle (see Fig. 12.5). Back at the hive, their dances communicate the total amount of flight as well as the compass bearing. Followers can retrace this path by reckoning the detour into their flight path. It is so easy that they can do it with their tiny bee brains. Robotics engineers should take note.

In an ingenious experiment, Kirchner and Braun (1994) showed how bees navigate by means of compass bearing and flight distance. The experimenters managed to attach tiny magnets to the backs of foraging bees. They placed the bees in a bee-sized wind tunnel that was about 10 meters from the hive. When the bees flew against the artificial wind, the magnets tethered them so that they flew in place for varying amounts of time. The top half of the wind tunnel was open to the sky so the bees could maintain their bearing with respect to the sun. The bottom half of the wind tunnel had a pattern of lines on it that appeared to move beneath the bees much as the ground moves in normal flight. The direction of flight in the wind tunnel was perpendicular to the angle between the hive and the tunnel. When released, the bees found a rich source of food just outside the exit.

When Kirchner and Braun allowed some of the bees to return to the hive without further intervention, the bees flew at right angles to the correct bearing of the hive as if returning along the path they had flown in the wind tunnel. Some of these bees flew more than 200

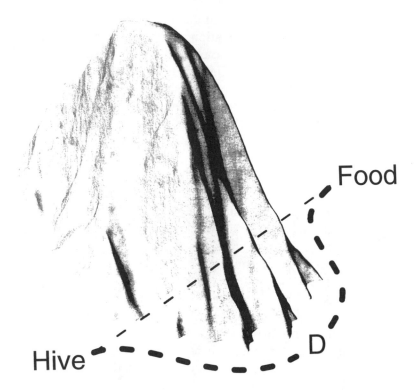

FIG. 12.5.   A steep hill between hive and food requires a detour. The bearing is the line from Hive to Food and the distance is the detour line, Hive to D plus D to Food (after von Frisch, 1953, pp. 124–125). Copyright © 1997 by R. Allen Gardner.

meters in the wrong direction before giving up and circling back to find the hive. That these lost bees found their way home agrees with experimental evidence (Dyer, 1993; Dyer, Berry, & Richard, 1993) that bees, like hamsters, can also use distant landmarks on the horizon for navigation. Since the wind tunnel and the food source were only 10 meters from the hive, the bees could have used local landmarks to return to the hive. That they relied on flight distance, instead, indicates the flexibility of a navigational strategy. They navigate until they are near the hive and then they use local landmarks to find the hive, precisely. Dead reckoning only has to get them to an area near the hive. While they are navigating they can ignore local landmarks along the flight path, which they might otherwise confuse with similar landmarks near the hive (see also Chittka, Geiger, & Kunze, 1995).

When most of the bees finished feeding outside the tunnel, Kirchner and Braun replaced them in the wind tunnel and retethered them for a return flight of the same length as the outward-bound flight, but in the opposite direction. When these bees left the tunnel at the original entrance, they found their way directly back to the hive. Only

10% of them danced in the hive after this experience, but those dances signaled a food site in the direction of the wind tunnel flight and at a distance proportional to the amount of time that they had flown in the tunnel. Once again, dead reckoning only has to get a bee to the general area of a good feeding site. Pinpointing a precise place such as a single flower is quite unnecessary.

Notice another advantage of remembering only the direction and distance of each flight and then only one flight at a time. A foraging animal must exploit adventitious discoveries. The forager should return to a site only if it continues to find food there. The first time that a forager fails to find food at a site should be the last time that it returns. The forager should immediately start exploring for a new site. When a good forager finds a new site, the new distance and direction should immediately govern navigation. A Hullian forager that had to build up reinforcement, or a Tolmanian map reader that had to build up cognitive expectancy after repeatedly finding food at a site would have to return many times to the empty food site before the reinforcement or expectancy could extinguish and a fresh search could begin. Both Hullian reinforcement and Tolmanian expectancy would have negative survival value in the natural world of foraging animals.

Radial Arm Maze

In the 1970s experiments with an apparatus called a radial arm maze revived interest in the traditional concept of a cognitive map. In Fig. 12.6, the eight arms leading away from a central platform are open without walls or with very low walls to expose rat subjects to a rich array of extramaze stimuli. Typically, experimenters bait the end of each arm with a small amount of food, allowing each rat to explore the arms in any sequence. Experimenters only refill the food wells at the ends of the arms after a complete trial which lasts until a rat has made eight excursions out to the ends of the arms or when a fixed amount of time has passed, whichever happens first.

A rat forages most efficiently by exploring each arm exactly once. This is much more like natural foraging than the usual maze-learning task. Typically, rats get five trials per day in this apparatus and they soon learn to explore on average about 7.5 out of the possible 8 arms per trial. Cognitive psychologists claim that rats accomplish this by forming a cognitive map of the apparatus and the room around it.

In a critical experiment, Olton and Collison (1979) separated in-tramaze stimuli from extramaze stimuli by an ingenious device. They modified the apparatus so that the arms could be rotated inde-

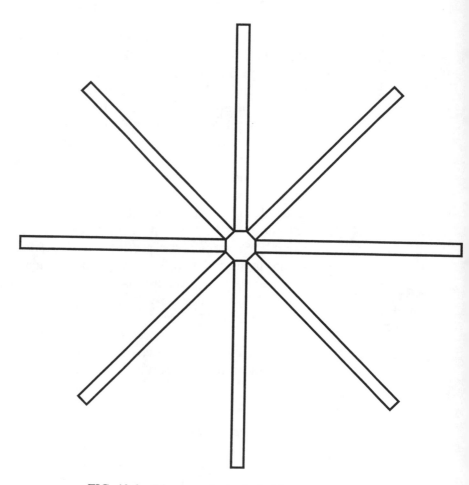

FIG. 12.6. Diagram of a typical eight-arm radial maze.

pendently of the central platform. For half of the rats Olton and Collison put the food in small wells at the end of the arms, which is the usual procedure. For the other half of the subjects Olton and Collison put the food in identical wells placed on small platforms just beyond the ends of the arms, but in easy reach of the rats. When the arms rotated, the outer platforms and the food wells on the outer platforms remained in place.

In Phase I of the experiment, which lasted for 15 daily sessions of 1 trial each, Olson and Collison allowed each rat to explore the arms and consume the food while the arms remained in place as in the usual procedure. Soon, all of the rats reached criterion performance, visiting on average about 7.5 out of the possible 8 arms on each trial. In Phase II, each time that a rat returned from an excursion to the end of an arm, the experimenters trapped it on the central platform with a system of gates and rotated the arms haphazardly one, two, three, or four times 45°, half clockwise and half counterclockwise. After each rotation the experimenter opened all gates and the rat was free to make its next excursion.

The animals that found food at the end of the arms could use intramaze stimuli to avoid repeating excursions to previously visited arms. The animals that found food on the outer platforms could use extramaze stimuli to avoid repeating excursions to previously visited places in the room. The results were decisive. The rats that found food on the outer platforms were only slightly disturbed by the rotations and quickly recovered their Phase I scores of about 7.5 out of the possible 8 radial directions. The rats that found food at the end of the arms dropped to chance performance as soon as the rotations started and remained at chance for 30 days at one trial per day after which the experiment ended. Clearly, the rats in this experiment avoided repeating radial directions and ignored intramaze stimuli such as odor cues.

Animals avoid repeating excursions to the same place in the room rather than the same arm of a radial arm maze. The most popular view of this finding attributes efficient foraging in the radial arm maze to a cognitive map of the room that forms in the brains of the animals and which they have to consult when they make choices (M. F. Brown, Rish, VonCulin, & Edberg, 1993; Poucet, 1993). In Brown et al. Experiment 5, however, rats foraged efficiently in a radial arm maze when their only extramaze cue was a small gap in a curtain hanging well beyond the arms of the maze and blocking all other extramaze cues. They could navigate with this single directional cue, just as the hamsters in Etienne et al. (1993) could navigate with a single directional light on the horizon of their experimental room. Later, M. F. Brown and Moore (1997) showed that rats could also use cues from their semicircular canals to forage in a radial arm maze completing the pattern of agreement with the results of Douglas (1966) and Etienne (1992).

Morris Water Maze

In 1981, Morris introduced a simple apparatus that virtually eliminates intramaze cues. A Morris water maze consists of a large tank filled with a milky opaque fluid. Rats must swim in the tank until they find safety on a small submerged platform. They cannot see the platform or any other cues in the tank. The milky fluid also prevents them from leaving odor trails. They must use extramaze stimuli to find the safe platform. The measures are crude, but a Morris water maze is inexpensive to build and to use and rats master the task very quickly. Consequently, it is a popular apparatus with experimenters who are interested in the effects of physiological factors such as brain lesions, drugs, and age (Poucet, 1993). It should be easy to see that rats could use both internal cues from their middle ears and distant cues on the horizon to guide themselves to the hidden platform as many animals do in the other spatial tasks discussed in this chapter. In an outdoor version of a Morris maze Kavaliers and Galea (1994) showed that meadow voles performed poorly under an overcast sky, indicating that they used celestial cues to guide them to the hidden platform.

Caching

Honeybees and hamsters store their food in large home nests. This is called *larder hoarding*. Many other animals store their food in small scattered *caches*, and this is called *scatter hoarding* (Vander Wall, 1990). While larder hoarders find their way between their home nests and new foraging sites, scatter hoarders have to find their way back to many small caches. Vander Wall (1991) allowed individual chipmunks to cache food at different times in the same laboratory enclosure. Later, individual chipmunks found significantly more of their own caches than the caches made by other chipmunks. Similar results were found, for example, by Vander Wall (1982) with a species of bird called Clark's nutcrackers and by Jacobs and Liman (1991) with squirrels. These findings rule out the possibility that scatter hoarders cache food at random and then find it by searching at random and they also rule out the possibility that scatter hoarders cache food in species-specific places and then find it by searching at random in similar species-specific places.

Both in laboratory (Herz, Zanette, & Sherry, 1994; Vander Wall, 1982, 1991) and in field conditions (Barnea & Nottebohm, 1995) scatter hoarders use landmarks on the horizon to orient to their caches. Under laboratory conditions Clark's nutcrackers also used local landmarks such as stones and pieces of wood to find particular caches (Vander Wall, 1982). Scatter hoarders, like larder hoarders, can use a combination of distant and local landmarks to find specific places without having to construct, carry with them, and then consult detailed cognitive maps.

SUMMARY

Modern ethologically based research has taken us a long way from S-R-S* reinforcement theories such as Hull's and cognitive map theories such as Tolman's. Both of the great schools that were so influential in the early 20th century seem backward now. Clearly, the error of both schools was their disregard for the ethology of the animals in their experiments.

Foraging animals evolved in a very different world from the world of mazes. They may have evolved to explore in a haphazard, zigzag path until they find food, but they certainly did not evolve to wait at the food site for a kindly human to take them back to home base. In nature, their problem is to get directly home from an arbitrary site. If the site is worth a return trip, they need to get directly back when they return. They certainly did not evolve to wait for a kindly human to take them back to the beginning of the exploratory path so they could try again. Under natural foraging conditions, a map of an arbitrary exploratory route is hardly worth memorizing. That animals have learned to repeat an arbitrary route after many trials is a tribute to the adaptability of these amazing creatures, but it is hardly a tribute to the biological insight of the experimenters and theorists.

The practical navigational systems that foraging animals actually use to get from place to place in the natural world are elegant in their simplicity. They are also much more economical than the cognitive maps imagined by cognitive psychologists early in the 20th century. When engineers design robots for exploring sites in space, such as the moon, they have practical tasks in mind. For example, a likely task for a robot would be to prospect for valuable minerals. A robot prospector would have to explore in a haphazard way until it found "pay dirt." Then it would have to get back to the space ship with a load, and remember how to return to the source, perhaps recruiting other prospectors, if it found a rich source. A bottom-up design that took advantage of cheap navigational devices and local landmarks would be a practical solution, significantly more practical than a design that depended on detailed cognitive maps built up trial by trial by extensive exploration packaged together with a sophisticated cognitive map reader (see discussion of one-trial, bottom-up learning in chap. 8).

CHAPTER 13

Transfer

No animal, human or nonhuman, steps twice into the same perceptual stream. A young monkey that picks a ripe mango in a tree must learn something general about ripe mangoes, because it will certainly never see that particular mango again. A young lion that stalks and kills an impala must learn something general about hunting impalas, because it will certainly never meet that particular impala again. A college course in ethology or learning, or any other subject, is valuable only to the extent that it teaches general principles that students can apply in new situations to events that are still in the future. The same is true of job experience, whether it be teaching school, building circuits, or selling shoes; the value of the experience depends on the general usefulness of the learning. Whatever may be learned about a particular object or event, the most valuable things that are learned have to do with variable aspects of general stimulus classes. Theories of learning must explain how past experience *transfers* to new situations.

STIMULUS GENERALIZATION

After conditioning with a particular stimulus, S^a, similar stimuli, S^b, S^c, . . . S^n, can also evoke the same conditioned response, even though these other stimuli never appeared during training. This phenomenon, which has direct implications for transfer, is called *stimulus generali-*

zation. Interest in this phenomenon has generated an enormous volume of research showing that any experimental procedure that produces conditioning also produces stimulus generalization.

Basic Phenomenon

Hovland's (1937) study of the generalization of the conditioned galvanic skin response along a pitch dimension is a good reference experiment. Hovland used psychophysical judgments to select four tones that were separated in pitch by 25 just noticeable differences (JNDs). These frequencies were 153, 468, 1,000, and 1,967 cycles. For one group of subjects, the S^a during conditioning was the lowest tone and the test stimuli during extinction were the three higher tones. For a second group, the S^a during conditioning was the highest tone and the test stimuli during conditioning were the three lower tones. Hovland presented the test stimuli in different counterbalanced orders to different subjects to distribute the effects of extinction evenly among the test stimuli. Figure 13.1 shows the response to tones separated in pitch from

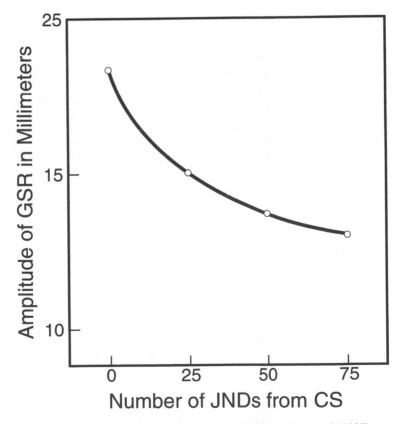

FIG. 13.1.   Stimulus generalization gradient. From Hovland (1937).

the original S^a by 25, 50, and 75 JNDs. The amount of response decreased progressively with the stimulus distance in JNDs from the S^a, which is the typical result of generalization experiments.

Another way to test for generalization is to mix conditioning trials with *probe trials* in which test stimuli replace the S^a, but this introduces other difficulties. If S* appears on the probe trials, then it is paired with the test stimuli and they can become conditioned stimuli in their own right. If S* is omitted on probe trials, then the procedure becomes a partial reward procedure, which can introduce even more complications. These problems of measurement only matter when experimenters are attempting to find the precise shape of the generalization curve, usually to test a particular theory of generalization. The basic phenomenon of stimulus generalization that decreases with stimulus distance from the original conditioned stimulus is so well documented that it is beyond dispute.

Stimulus generalization raises a fundamental theoretical problem for a reinforcement theory. If response to the S^a is a measure of reinforcement strength, then how can other stimuli that the subject never experienced before gain reinforcement strength from S^a?

Implications

The reason for intense interest in gradients of stimulus generalization is that they describe transfer from original learning to new situations in terms of stimulus similarity. A rule for predicting, or better still enhancing, transfer from one learned task to another would be a valuable tool in practical teaching and training situations. In principle, it should be possible to measure the stimulus similarity between any two situations by analyzing each into basic dimensions, such as color, brightness, temperature, loudness, and so on, and then calculating the amount of transfer that should take place from any original object to any transfer object.

Peak Shift

Pigeons have very good vision so they are a favorite subject for the study of stimulus generalization in the Skinner box. The wavelength, or hue, of the light on the key is a favorite dimension because these birds also have very good color vision. In original training, pigeons see light of only one particular wavelength on the key and receive reward for pecking when that light is on the key. The wavelength in original training particular wavelength that corresponds to the CS in classical conditioning. During tests for generalization carried out under extinction, lights of different wavelengths appear on the key in a counterbalanced order to sample response to the spectrum of colors like the CS.

Hanson (1957, 1959) was the first to investigate the effect of *discrimination training* on generalization gradients in the Skinner box. He projected lights of a single wavelength on the key in a Skinner box. He first rewarded pigeons for pecking the key when the wavelength of the light on the key was 550 nm. Human beings describe 550 nm as a yellowish green. Next he administered discrimination training, which consisted of lighting the key for brief periods with 550 nm during half of the periods and with a different wavelength during the other half. Hanson rewarded the pigeons with grain for pecking during the 550 nm on a VI 60 schedule, but never rewarded them for pecking during the other stimulus. Thus, 550 nm was S+ and the other wavelength was S−. For different groups of pigeons, 555, 560, 570, or 590 nm served as S−. Human beings usually describe 580 nm as yellow and 600 as the beginning of reddish yellow (with 620 as true orange). After this discrimination training, Hanson (1959) tested the pigeons with different wavelengths ranging from 480 nm (greenish blue) to 620 nm (orange). Thus, the generalization test measured the response to a series of lights of different colors that included the former S+ and S− as well as a variety of colors that the pigeons had never seen before in this experiment.

In the usual generalization test, the former S+ evokes the maximum response and the other stimuli evoke less response the farther they are from the former S+. That is, responding usually peaks at the former S+ and falls off more or less symmetrically with distance from the former S+. Figure 13.2 illustrates the *peak shift* effect that Hanson found instead.

In Fig. 13.2, the curve traced with a solid line is the control condition in which birds only saw the S+ of 550 nm during original training and saw the range of test wavelengths during extinction. The maximum response or highest point of this curve is at 550 nm as we would expect, and the amount of response to the test wavelengths falls off for lower wavelengths, or bluer lights, and for higher wavelengths, or yellower lights. The solid curve shows that generalization is roughly symmetrical, falling off in roughly equal amounts for lower and higher wavelengths. If anything the control group generalized more to the higher, yellower, wavelengths.

The other curves in Fig. 13.2 show the generalization to the test stimuli and labels with arrows, S− = 555, S− = 560, S− = 570, and S− = 590, identify each curve. After discrimination training, the curves are all displaced away from the S−. The pigeons in these groups responded more to test stimuli that they had never seen before in

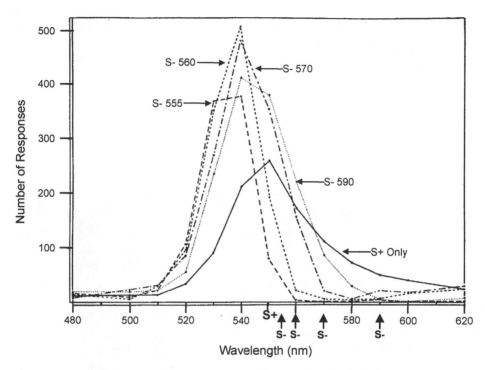

FIG. 13.2.   Mean generalization gradients for a control group and four discrimination groups in Hanson (1959). Arrows indicate the values of the negative stimuli.

their lives than they did to the former S+. Many other studies using a variety of different stimulus dimensions, tones, or angles of lines as well as colors, have replicated the peak shift effect (Cheng, Spetch, & Johnston, 1997; Rilling, 1977; Thomas, 1993). From the point of view of reinforcement theory, this is a puzzling finding. If amount of response measures reinforcement strength, how can a new stimulus have even more strength than the original S+?

Spence (1936, 1937) based his reinforcement model (Fig. 13.3) on the notion that discrimination training produces two gradients, one positive gradient of reinforcement and one negative gradient of extinction. Spence's model would yield a pattern like the peak shift with the peak response to a new stimulus that is displaced away from the former S–. While Spence's model predicts the general pattern of results, the results of peak shift experiments fail to confirm specific predictions of the theory.

Suppose that the traditional view is wrong to say that pigeons in the Hanson experiments learn that 550 nm is positive and 590 nm is negative. Suppose they learn instead that greener is positive and yellower is negative. Then during the generalization test, they respond more to a light that is greener (or, perhaps, bluer) than the original CS. Helson (1964) proposed a theory of perception based on relative values of stimulus dimensions, which he called *adaptation-level theory.* Thomas (1993) shows in detail how Helson's theory describes the results of many experiments in discrimination that followed Hanson's discovery of the peak shift.

TRANSPOSITION

Hanson's results depend on the relation between S+ and S– along the dimension of color. This agrees well with experiments on transposition that present one pair of stimuli S+ and S– in a simultaneous discrimination and measure the transfer to a second pair of stimuli.

Suppose that in a two-choice apparatus, like the one illustrated in Fig. 3.4, the two visual stimuli are a 4-cm circle that serves as S+ and a 2-cm circle that serves as S–. Suppose further that, after a sufficient number of training trials, the animals are choosing the 4-cm circle on nearly every trial. What should happen if the experimenter alters the problem so that now the animals must choose between a new 8-cm circle and the old 4-cm circle?

If all they learned in the original problem was to choose the 4-cm circle, then they should continue to choose the 4-cm circle because they never received either reward or nonreward for choosing the 8-cm circle. Indeed, they never saw the 8-cm circle before in their lives. On the other hand, if they learned to choose the larger of the two circles, then they should pick the new 8-cm circle at once rather than choosing the formerly correct 4-cm circle. The better they learned to choose the 4-cm circle in the original 4-cm versus 2-cm problem, the more certain the transfer to choosing the 8-cm circle in the new 8-cm versus 4-cm problem.

Transfer experiments of this type have appeared throughout this century using a wide variety of stimulus values and the results are decisive. Animals respond to the relation between the original and the transfer stimuli (larger/smaller, brighter/darker, and so on) rather than to the absolute values. In experiments like the one just described, the animals mostly choose the new 8-cm circle, which is larger than the formerly correct 4-cm circle. This result is called *transposition* because the subjects transpose the dimensional values of the stimuli in the training problem to the stimuli in the test problem. Cognitive psychologists claimed that reinforcement theory must predict that animals should choose the 4-cm circle in the transposition test between 4-cm and 8-cm. The cognitivists called their theory the *relational*

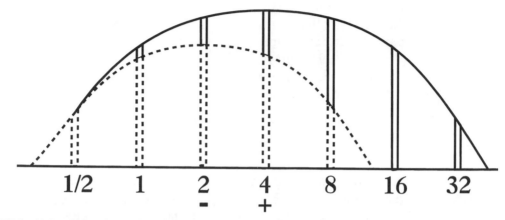

FIG. 13.3. Spence's model of discrimination learning, which predicts transposition at near test values, breakdown of transposition at more distant test values, and reversal of transposition at extreme test values. Copyright © 1997 by R. Allen Gardner.

theory and claimed that habit theories can only predict transfer on the basis of the *absolute* values of stimuli.

Spence's Model

Spence (1936, 1937), a close associate of Hull, developed a model based on reinforcement theory plus generalization gradients, which is illustrated in Fig. 13.3. Spence, quite reasonably, pointed out that reinforcement theory entails two gradients of generalization that arise from training on the first problem, a *positive gradient* of reinforcement originating from the 4-cm circle (solid curve) and a *negative gradient* of inhibition originating from the 2-cm circle (dotted curve). In Hull's theory, the negative gradient subtracts from the positive gradient. Figure 13.3 represents the amount of inhibition as dotted bars rising from each stimulus value and represents the difference between excitation and inhibition as white bars between the positive and negative gradients.

Spence assumed that the positive effect of reward is greater than the negative effect of nonreward, which is immanently reasonable. Otherwise, a mixture of reward for going to S+ and nonreward for going to S– would make rats stop running altogether. This assumption is also confirmed by the fact that partial reward is sufficient to maintain most responses. If reward excites and nonreward inhibits, then the excitation of a few rewards must be worth more than the inhibition of many nonrewards.

Notice that the stimulus values in Fig. 13.3 appear in logarithmic units. That is, each stimulus value on the horizontal axis of the graph

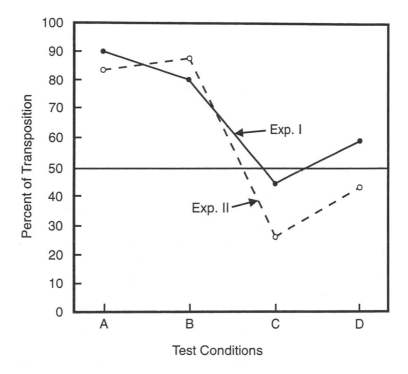

FIG. 13.4. Transposition depends on the difference between training and test stimuli. Test values A, B, C, and D are a series of approximately equal steps from the training stimuli. From Ehrenfreund (1952).

is double the one before, even though each linear distance along the axis is equal to the one before. This agrees well with the known facts of psychophysics. Psychologically equal stimulus intervals are usually separated by logarithmic stimulus values of units such as length, area, or intensity. In making this move, Spence based his model on the dimensionality of stimuli. The model assumes dimensionality rather than deriving it from a theory of learning or cognition.

In this graph of Spence's model, the white bar that shows the positive strength at 4 cm is longer than the positive bar at 2 cm, but it is still not the longest positive bar. This is because the negative gradient arising from 2 cm subtracts from the positive value at 4 cm. The positive differential value at 8 cm is greater than the positive differential value at 4 cm, and so Spence's model also predicts transposition even though it is based on S-R reinforcement principles. The second thing we see is that the white bar at 16 cm is still greater than the white bar at 8 cm, although the difference is less than the difference between 4 cm and 8 cm. This means that there should be some transposition when the test problem is 8 cm versus 16 cm. The rats should choose 16 cm over 8 cm, but transposition should be weaker than transposition to 4 cm versus 8 cm.

The third thing that we see from Fig. 13.3 is that the white bar at 32 cm is actually smaller than the white bar at 16 cm. This means that in a 16-cm versus 32-cm transfer problem, transposition should fail and the rats should choose the smaller 16-cm circle over the larger 32-cm circle. This is the most important prediction in Spence's model because it predicts that transposition will fail or even reverse at extreme values. Cognitive theory, on the other hand, must predict that transposition will go on forever, because all the animals learn is relations between stimuli, such as larger or brighter. Thus, Spence's dimensional model predicts a new result that contradicts cognitive theories.

Experimental tests of Spence's predictions (see Hebert & Krantz, 1965; Schwartz & Reisberg, 1991, for reviews) have generally confirmed his prediction that transposition eventually breaks down, but tests have only partly confirmed the more daring prediction of reversed transposition. Ehrenfreund's (1952) experiment shown in Fig. 13.4 is typical. He tested rats in a T-maze with cards that varied in brightness serving as the stimuli. In Experiment I, S– was white and S+ was a light grey in the original training. In Experiment II, S– was black and S+ was a dark gray. In the transposition tests, the stimuli were intermediate grays presented in pairs chosen to appear at roughly equal steps apart in brightness. The results of the transfer tests appear in Fig. 13.4, which shows that transposition broke down when the transfer pairs were farthest from the original pairs and there was some evidence for transposition reversal in Experiment II. The eventual breakdown of transposition in all experiments confirms Spence's model. The lack of evidence for eventual reversal of transposition indicates that the model is only partly successful. All of these results plainly contradict the cognitive relational model.

Psychophysics

Riley (1958) conducted the definitive transposition experiment. Riley used a Lashley jumping stand, which is a two-choice apparatus for simultaneous discrimination (see Fig. 3.4). He presented his animals with an original brightness discrimination problem and different transfer problems as in the usual transposition experiment. The difference was that Riley also varied the brightness of the front of the apparatus that surrounded the stimulus cards. As most readers should know, the apparent brightness of a gray patch depends on the brightness of the surround. If the surround is white, a gray patch looks dark, and if the surround is black, a gray patch looks light.

TABLE 13.1
Design of the Transposition Tests Conducted by Riley (1958)

	Surround	S−	S+
Training	1	3	10
Near Absolute	1	30	100
Far Absolute	1	300	1000
Near Relative	10	30	100
Far Relative	100	300	1000

Note. These are simplified numbers for illustration purposes. The exact values that Riley used are slightly different.

The design of Riley's experiment appears in Table 13.1. All of the rats first mastered a discrimination between brightness value 3 and brightness value 10, in which 10 was S+ and 1 was the brightness value of the surround. Then they were tested on four different transfer problems.

In what Riley called the *near absolute* test, the surround remained at 1, while the brightnesses of the test stimuli increased to 30 and 100. In Riley's *far absolute* test, the surround remained at 1, and the test pairs increased to 300 and 1,000. In what Riley called the *near relative* test, he raised the brightness of the surround to 10 and the brightness of the test pairs to 30 and 100. In Riley's *far relative* test, he raised the surround to 100 and the test pairs to 300 and 1,000. Thus, in one set of tests, called the absolute tests, the relative brightness of the test stimuli increased while the brightness of the surround stayed constant, as in all other experiments on transposition up to that time. In the other set of tests, that Riley called relative, all three brightnesses including the surround increased in the same proportion.

Riley's absolute tests replicated the earlier transposition experiments. The animals transposed when given the near absolute test in which the surround was constant from training to transfer. That is, they continued to choose the brighter of the new test stimuli even though the new S+ was 10 times brighter than the original S+. Transposition broke down on the far absolute test. The animals failed to choose the brighter of the two new test stimuli when Riley kept the brightness of the surround the same as in original training, but raised the brightnesses of the test stimuli by a factor of 100.

As in earlier experimental tests, which had kept the surround constant, transposition failed at the far absolute test just as Spence predicted. Spence's most dramatic prediction failed, however. Even at the extreme when the new S+ was 100 times brighter than the original S+, transposition only failed; there was no reversal. That is, the rats failed to chose brightness 300 (which is closer to brightness 3) over brightness 1,000. Instead they chose 300 and 1,000 about equally.

The animals transposed completely on both the near and the far relative tests in which Riley raised the brightness of the surround along with the brightnesses of the test stimuli. When the ratio of the test stimuli to the surround stimulus was the same as in original training, transfer was perfect. The animals responded as if nothing had changed. Indeed, the graduate research assistant complained that he, a human, had difficulty telling the relative transfer stimuli apart and had to check the labels on the back of stimulus panels to be sure which set was which.

So, animals can transpose indefinitely as cognitive theories should predict, but they transpose for bottom-up perceptual rather than top-down cognitive reasons. Real animals see only relative brightness. Without an artificial meter, human beings also see only relative brightness. Psychological theories that treat living organisms as though they can respond to particular levels of brightness, size, color, and so on, treat the animals and the tasks as abstractions. Real animals are very different from meters. Animals respond to relative values rather than absolute values because they see only relative values in the first place.

SIGN STIMULI

Ethologists soon recognized the dimensionality of the *sign stimuli* that evoke *species-specific action patterns* (discussed in chap. 4). Herring gulls only sit on nests that contain eggs. What is the sign stimulus that makes a herring gull brood egglike objects? Tinbergen (1953a, pp. 144–159) removed eggs from temporarily unattended nests of herring gulls and placed them in a nearby empty and unattended nest. At the same time, he placed artificial eggs in a third nest, equally nearby. Sometimes he placed artificial eggs in both test nests. The gulls chose by brooding on the objects in one of the nests. Tinbergen varied such things as shape and color and found that the gulls usually chose gull eggs over artificial eggs, but they chose some artificial eggs over others. He found that size was a dimension that mattered very much to brooding gulls. When he offered them a choice between a Herring gull egg and an artificial egg that had the same shape and color but was only half the normal size, all of the gulls chose the normal gull's egg. When he offered them a choice between a normal egg and an artificial egg that was double the normal linear size—that is, eight times the volume of a normal egg—all gulls chose the giant egg. "All birds which were given the large egg became very excited and made frantic attempts to cover it. In doing so, they invariably lost their balance, and their evolutions were, I must confess, most amusing to watch" (p. 158).

Magnus (1963) found the same phenomenon in the mating behavior of the fritillary butterfly, *Argynnis paphia.* Butterflies live to mate, but how do they recognize females fluttering about in the fields? How do they discriminate female *Argynnis paphia* from other butterflies or even flowers in a meadow? Magnus moved artificial lures in pairs in an experimental room to see what sort of lure would attract males of this species. His lures were many times larger than normal fritillaries, but this seemed to be acceptable to the butterflies. The lures were cylinders with black stripes alternating with yellow stripes made by pasting the wings of female butterflies on to the cylinders. When Magnus rotated the cylinders, they presented a flickering pattern to the male butterflies like the flickering pattern of the wings of a flying female butterfly. The males chose lures with a flicker speed like the flicker of normal wings over slower flicker speeds, but they also chose faster speeds over the normal speed. In fact, like the Herring gulls who chose the giant eggs, the fritillaries overwhelmingly chose a flicker speed far faster than any that a live butterfly could ever produce.

Magnus also varied the color of the stripes. He offered a cylinder with yellow stripes made of fritillary wings and cylinders with painted yellow stripes. The artificial yellows varied in saturation, which in the present context is similar to intensity of colors. The butterflies chose the normal fritillary yellow over less saturated yellows, but they also chose more saturated yellows over the normal yellow. Just as with flicker speed, their favorite yellow was much more saturated than anything that they could ever see on a female's wings.

Human beings are also sensitive to species-specific sign stimuli. The profiles of newborn mammals are very different from the profiles of adults. Their jaws and snouts are severely reduced relative to their eyes and brain cases. It is a nursing face. Jaws and snouts develop adult proportions when the animals have to eat for themselves. Human babies also have a nursing face that attracts human beings. Artists take advantage of this and draw *superbabies* on greeting cards and illustrations, babies with impossibly large eyes and brain cases relative to their tiny mouths and noses. The nursing faces of other baby mammals also attract both juvenile and adult humans. Artists use this dimension very effectively to create super-adorable animals in animated films.

B. T. Gardner and Wallach (1965) showed that university students are sensitive to the dimension of shape that defines the relationship between human adults and human babies. They measured silhouettes

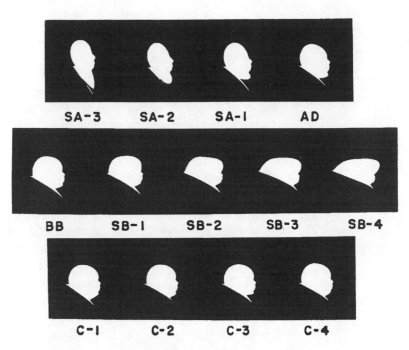

FIG. 13.5. Silhouettes used by B. T. Gardner and Wallach (1965). AD = normal adult silhouette; BB = normal baby silhouette. SB-x = increases in shape dimension beyond BB. SA-x = increases in shape dimension beyond AD. C-x = other variations from the normal baby head. Copyright © 1997 by R. Allen Gardner.

of babies and adults to define the dimension of shape and used this dimension to create the superbabies illustrated in Fig. 13.5. In paired comparisons, undergraduates chose all of the superbabies as more babyish than the silhoutte of an actual baby. This shape dimension is fairly complex, but it has the dimensional properties of sign stimuli.

Ethologists call sign stimuli that are impossible in nature, but more effective than naturally occuring stimuli, *supernormal stimuli*. They show that sign stimuli are dimensional. Eggs that are too small repel brooding gulls, but eggs that are too large attract them. Flickering wings that are not yellow enough repel male butterflies, but superyellow wings attract them. Why are living animals sensitive to impossible stimuli? The reason is that relative sensation is cheaper and more efficient than absolute sensation.

Dimensional Stimuli

Gradients of generalization and transposition only puzzle those who imagine separate receptors for each stimulus, in the case of Fig. 13.2, separate retinal receptors for each wavelength in the visible spectrum.

Sensory research plainly contradicts this view. Research on human color vision (Kaiser & Boynton, 1996; Webster, 1996) points to a system of three color receptors with overlapping ranges of sensitivity that work like the overlapping categories of Kipersztok and Patterson's (1995) fuzzy controller described in chapter 9. As in the case of fuzzy controllers, a relatively small set of overlapping sensors does the job more economically and efficiently than a large array of separate receptors for each value on a dimension (Erickson, Di Lorenzo, & Woodbury, 1994).

Chapter 4 introduced the principle of parsimony in scientific theories. In comparisons between theories, the best theory is the one that accounts for the most evidence with the least amount of assumptions. Biologists place a high value on parsimony for an additional reason. Competition for survival favors economical and efficient biology. Kipersztok and Patterson's (1995) fuzzy controller appeals to biologists for the same reason that it appeals to the Boeing Aircraft Company; it does the job economically and efficiently.

Throughout science and industry, from antique beam balances to electronic strain gauges, the most economical and efficient measuring devices sense relative values of overlapping categories. It is cheaper and more efficient for fritillary butterflies to respond to relative yellow rather than to the absolute yellow of actual female wings.

Neural Networks

Animals extract dimensional and patterned information—color, brightness, curvature, angularity, and so on—from the blooming buzzing confusion of the natural world around them. This baffled early psychologists who often attributed dimensional and patterned perception to mysterious cognitive abilities. Early simple-minded mechanistic models, such as Spence's outlined here, had more power than systems that only considered specific stimulus-response conditioning. They were also more parsimonious than cognitive systems and they made precise and even counterintuitive predictions, but they were clearly too crude to cope with the whole problem.

In modern times, fairly simple-minded electronic computers have taken some of the mystery out of complex psychological phenomena. The idea that a mechanical device could solve complex problems has a long history. In 1936 the mathematician and logician, Turing, showed how a mechanical device that could only write either a 1 or a 0 on squares of paper could write any logical proposition, given enough paper and time. Turing's proof described a machine that would work in principle but was far beyond the technology of the 1930s, not to mention all that paper and time.

There were dramatic advances in computer technology during World War II, however, and Turing, himself, was a leader in these advances. By 1943, McCulloch and Pitts showed how a network of logical units that operated as switches with two positions, on or off corresponding to Turing's 1s and 0s, could compute sophisticated logical propositions limited only by the number of units in the network. They proposed a model of a brain based on existing computer technology and introduced the term *neural networks*. Next, Hebb (1949) showed how a neural network could extract patterned information from sensory input by a self-organizing system that he called *cell assembly*. Hebb conjectured that, if units that fired together had an increased likelihood of firing together again, then groups of cells could organize themselves into cell assemblies that recognized repeating patterned and dimensional information.

The limited speed and capacity of early computers plagued the first attempts to build an electronic computer based on Hebb's cell assemblies and McCulloch and Pitts' neural networks. Computer scientists persisted, however, and more powerful computers appeared that use artificial neural networks to extract useful amounts of dimensional and patterned information from the natural world (J. A. Anderson, 1995). Webster (1996) shows how previously intractable problems of dimensional adaptation and contrast in human color vision can be solved if the visual system uses mechanisms like those found in artificial neural networks. Bateson and Horn (1994) proposed a model based on artificial neural networks that simulates major perceptual phenomena of imprinting (chap. 2), such as recognition of fine detail, while generalizing to classes of stimuli. The mysteries of patterned and dimensional perception are fading away.

HABITS, HYPOTHESES, AND STRATEGIES

The first part of this chapter discussed transfer based on stimulus similarity. This next part considers transfer based on problem-solving strategy.

Habits Versus Hypotheses

In a two-choice, simultaneous discrimination, the experimenter makes the left–right arrangement of S+ and S– random, or at least unpredictable. The subjects, however, respond in predictable ways because they are natural biological systems. Truly *random behavior* must be rare in nature. Gambling casinos try very hard to produce truly random sequences of events, but they always fail to some extent. Casinos must constantly change equipment such as dice and roulette wheels to prevent their customers from winning by memorizing slight deviations from randomness that appear in all such devices.

Usually, animals in a two-choice apparatus respond exclusively left or right for dozens, even scores, of trials. Sometimes, particularly early in training, they make alternate runs of trials to one side or the other, and even switch from side to side trial by trial for several trials. Experimenters take pains to see that the left–right arrangement of S+ and S– varies unpredictably so that the nonrandom choices of the animals earn rewards 50% of the time on average. In terms of correct and incorrect choices, the typical learning curve of an individual animal stays flat around 50% for many trials.

Once response to S+ starts to rise above 50%, it rises steeply until it reaches 100%. Group learning curves look much more gradual because experimenters pool and average the data for many subjects. Because different subjects start rising at different points, the average rise looks smooth. In reinforcement theories, correct choices of S+ and avoidance of S– grow out of reward and nonreward. In feed forward theory, a rhythm of responding within trials builds up because, by definition, rhythms require repetition. Both theories assume that animals are learning even when their choices yield only 50% reward in what is called the *presolution period.*

Cognitive theorists have taken a different view of the function of the presolution period. According to Lashley (1929), the form of the learning curve "suggests that the actual association is formed very quickly and that both the practice preceding and the errors following are irrelevant to the actual formation of the association." According to Krechevsky (1932), "Learning consists of changing from one systematic, generalized, purposive way of behaving to another and another until the problem is solved" (p. 532). In Krechevsky's (1938) analysis of discrimination learning, the subject tries out *hypotheses* during the presolution period:

> Once the animal is immersed in a given problem-situation, the animal selects out of the welter of possible stimuli certain sets of discriminanda to which he reacts. Each time (while "paying attention to" this particular set of discriminanda) he makes what proves to be "correct response," he learns (wrongly perhaps) something about the significance of this particular stimulus; each time he makes a "wrong" response he learns something else, but he does not learn anything about the "correctness" or "wrongness" of the to-be-final-learned set

of discriminanda. Eventually he gives up responding to his first set
of discriminanda and responds to another set, and another set, etc.
(p. 111)

In this view, subjects actually learn nothing about S+ and S– during the
presolution period because they are trying out hypotheses about other
solutions to the discrimination problem. It is only after they have tried
and rejected the other hypotheses that they begin to try hypotheses
about which is correct, S+ or S–, and only then do they form a
preference for S+ over S–. This suggested an experimental test.

Suppose that the experimenter reverses the correctness of the two
stimuli during the presolution period. If black was serving as S+ and
white as S–, then the experimenter would switch to reward for white
choices and nonreward for black choices. If the animals had, indeed,
learned nothing about the correctness of black and white before the
reversal, as Krechevsky claimed, then they should do as well as animals
that had the original problem, black+ versus white– throughout.
According to reinforcement theory, of course, there should be negative
transfer with S+ and S– reversed because the differential strength of
black over white had already begun to form even though the subjects
were still responding according to position or alternation biases.

Krechevsky's own experiments and several others conducted by
cognitive theorists agreed with his prediction. Groups of rats that had
S+ and S– reversed during the presolution period performed roughly
as well as groups of rats that stayed on the same problem from start to
finish. Krechevsky tested this, however, by counting the first trial of
reversal as Trial 1 for the reversed groups and counting the first trial of
original training as Trial 1 for the group that had the same problem
throughout.

The error here is an error in operational definition. It is very similar
to the error that cognitive theorists made in the latent learning
experiments discussed in chapter 5. Karn and Porter (1946) showed
how familiarity with general aspects of the experimental procedure,
such as handling, deprivation schedules, the type of apparatus, and
so on, are critical factors for a rat that must solve an experimental
learning task. During the presolution period, both the reversed and
the constant groups are learning all of these nonspecific aspects of
their task as well as learning to choose S+ over S–. For the groups
that stayed on the same problem from start to finish, Krechevsky and
his cognitive colleagues counted all of the trials from start to finish.
For the groups that had S+ and S– reversed, however, they counted
only the trials after the reversal. Obviously, they failed to count some
important trials. When trials to the solution criterion are counted
from the start to finish for both groups, then the groups that reversed

during the presolution period always required more total trials than the groups that continued with the same problem throughout. That is, the reversed groups showed the negative transfer that habit theories predict (see Hall, 1976, pp. 360–363; Kimble, 1961, pp. 128–134, for more extensive discussions of this problem).

Overtraining and Reversal

In another claim for the superiority of cognitive theory over reinforcement theory, rats were overtrained, that is, run for many trials after reaching criterion, before reversal. Reid (1953) was the first to demonstrate the overtraining reversal effect. He trained three groups of rats to make a black–white discrimination in a Y-maze. All groups first reached a criterion of 9 out of 10 correct responses. Following this, one group was reversed immediately, a second group continued on the original problem for 50 trials of overtraining before reversal, and a third group received 150 overtraining trials before they were reversed. Counting trials from the point of reversal, the immediate reversal group required a mean of 138.3 trials to reach criterion on the reversal problem, while the 50-trial overtrained group required a mean of 129 trials, and the 150-trial reversal group required a mean of only 70 trials.

The overtraining reversal effect attracted a great deal of experimental and theoretical interest for many years (see Gardner, 1966; Hall, 1976, pp. 370–373; Mackintosh, 1974, pp. 602–607, for detailed reviews). A popular cognitive view was that overtrained subjects learn to attend better to critical aspects of the stimuli (Flaherty, 1985; Sutherland & Mackintosh, 1971). But, why should overtraining have an attentional effect? In other situations, repetitious drill lowers attention and impairs problem solving as illustrated in the section on learning sets and problem solving later in this chapter.

A positive effect of overtraining on reversal only contradicts reinforcement theory if reinforcement theory must always predict that repetition only strengthens a discrimination. This grossly underestimates the depth and generality of reinforcment theories such as those of Hull and Spence. As explained in chapter 10, those theories predict the opposite: that overtraining eventually produces a reduction in response strength as confirmed by runway experiments. In addition, Wolford and Bower (1969) applied Hull–Spence theory directly to overtraining and reversal in a two-choice discrimination and showed how it predicted faster reversal after overtraining.

In either case, however, there is an experimental error in the usual interpretation of the overtraining reversal effect. This is the same error as in the latent learning experiments and presolution hypothesis experiments. A fair test must add the overtraining trials to the reversal trials because the overtrained animals did receive these trials. In the case of Reid's (1953) typical finding, the immediate reversal group only took 138.3 trials to master the reversal after reaching the 9 out of 10 criterion on the original problem, the 50-trial overtraining group took 129 + 50 or 179 trials to reach criterion on the reversed problem, and the 150-trial overtraining group required 70 + 150 or 220 trials for reversal. That is, the sooner they got the reversed problem, the sooner they solved it—if we count total trials. The following example illustrates this point.

Suppose that a colleague at a university medical school needs to study the effect of diet on vision and consults a comparative psychologist about the best way to solve the following practical problem. To study vision our medical colleague trained rats on a black versus white discrimination in a T-maze and rewarded them all for choosing black. Now, our colleague realizes that to test the physiological hypothesis all of the rats should approach white rather than black. Furthermore, the research project is running behind schedule, so the time it takes to reverse the animals is important. What should we advise? Should we tell our colleague in the medical school to give the rats the reversal problem immediately, or should we advise 100 or 200 trials of overtraining before the reversal?

Coate and R. A. Gardner (1965) tested this directly when they trained two groups of rats to criterion on the same discrimination problem in the apparatus of Fig. 3.4. They varied the amount of experience with the experimental procedure by mixing in different numbers of trials on a second problem. The group that had more experience with the experimental procedure reversed faster even though both groups should have performed equally well according to the cognitive theory of reversal.

In the case of latent learning without reward, presolution hypotheses, and overtraining reversal, cognitive theorists insisted that reinforcement theories can only explain strengthening by reward and weakening by nonreward. In the traditional cognitive view, anything else that animals learn from experience must be cognitive. Both human and nonhuman animals learn a great deal from their experience in the experimental procedure, and experimental operations must control for the amount of experience before attributing results either to cognition or to reinforcement.

Learning Sets

The phenomenon that Harlow called learning sets is one of the great discoveries of 20th-century psychology. It was the work of an ingenious experimenter trying to find out how intelligent his monkeys were, rather than the work of a clever theorist out to prove how intelligent he was.

To test his monkeys Harlow designed an apparatus that he called the *Wisconsin General Testing Apparatus* (WGTA) shown in Fig. 13.6. In the WGTA, the experimenter places various pairs of objects over two food wells. One well is baited with food; the other is empty. The left–right arrangement of baited and unbaited wells varies in a counterbalanced and unpredictable sequence. If a monkey displaces S+, the object over the baited food well, it gets the food. If the monkey displaces S–, the object over the empty well, it gets nothing. In either case, the experimenter immediately removes the tray bearing the objects and food wells to set up the next trial. Harlow took advantage of the fact that monkeys can respond to a very large range of stimuli and used what he called "junk" objects as S+ and S–. That is, he and his assistants shopped at large stores and bought a variety of cheap objects, such as buttons, spools of thread, control knobs, and so forth. With these "junk" objects, Harlow and his associates could present hundreds of problems to a monkey over a long period of time without repeating any given pair of objects.

The monkeys could try to solve these problems by always choosing, say, the larger object of each pair because the larger object was correct on a previous problem. Or, they could always choose the rounder, or

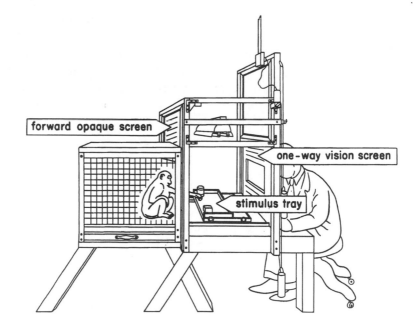

FIG. 13.6. H. F. Harlow's apparatus for studying learning sets in monkeys. From H. F. Harlow (1949).

the darker, or the redder object for the same reason. Such strategies would have to fail because the positive and negative objects varied randomly in size, shape, color, and so on, from problem to problem.

Harlow found that, while naive monkeys could take as many as 100 trials to reach criterion with the early pairs of objects, they steadily improved and solved later problems in fewer and fewer trials. If we call a particular pair of objects A and B, and A serves as S+, then on the first trial with A and B the monkey cannot know which object is S+. On average, the best it can do is 50% correct. If the monkey correctly chooses A on Trial 1, then it can be correct 100% of the time from then on, if it chooses A on Trial 2 and on every trial after that. If the monkey chooses B on Trial 1, then it is incorrect on that trial, but it has enough information to choose A on Trial 2 and every trial after that and can also choose correctly 100% of the time starting with Trial 2. Each problem consists of a fresh pair of objects. After the first trial with a new pair of objects, the monkeys can win every time if they always repeat their correct choices and never repeat their incorrect choices—that is, if they use a *win-stay/lose-shift* strategy.

Harlow found that, as the monkeys proceeded from the first problem, A versus B, to the next problem, C versus D, and the next, E versus F, and so on, they improved steadily. Eventually, they were solving new problems within the minimum possible two trials. Figure 13.7 shows the improvement on Trials 2 through 6. Each line shows the averages at successive stages of improvement. During the latest stage, Problems 201 to 312, the monkeys were nearly always correct from Trial 2 onward. They had learned a *strategy* for solving this kind of problem. Harlow and others replicated this finding many times. Later experiments with the WGTA showed that monkeys can also adopt other strategies such as *win-shift/lose-stay*. Monkeys can even shift from strategy to strategy as the task demands (McDowell & Brown, 1963a, 1963b).

These animals can learn general strategies that are independent of the particular objects that serve as S+ and S−, even more general than broad stimulus qualities such as color and shape. This ability to develop an overall *strategy* to solve a series of problems, regardless of the particular stimuli, is really much more intelligent than the *hypotheses* or the *cognitive maps* proposed by theorists such as Krechevsky and Tolman.

In the original 1949 study, Harlow gave his monkeys 50 trials per problem at first, and then gradually reduced the number of trials to 6 per problem since he was only interested in performance on the second trial and the first few after that. In later experiments, Levine, Harlow, and Pontrelli (1961) and Levine, Levinson, and Harlow

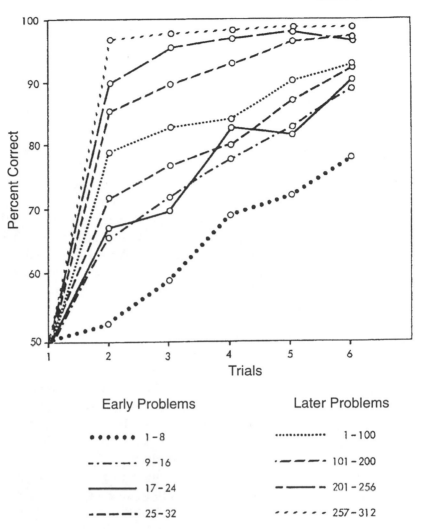

FIG. 13.7. Performance of monkeys on the first six trials of a long series of two-choice problems in the WGTA. From H. F. Harlow (1949).

(1959) gave different groups of monkeys 3, 6, or 12 trials per problem from the start and found that they required fewer problems to achieve learning sets—100% correct choices starting on Trial 2—if they had fewer trials per problem. That is, the fewer the trials per problem up to what must be a minimum of three, the faster the monkeys learned the winning strategy.

In the early problems, as Fig. 13.7 shows, it took much more than 12 trials for a monkey to master a problem. At only three trials per problem, Harlow and his associates were certainly switching to new pairs of objects before the monkeys mastered the early problems. Other experiments have shown that monkeys can form learning set strategies with only two trials per problem. They can do this even if the first trial on each of 16 different problems appears on one day and the second trial appears on the next day with the sequence of the 16 problems randomly shuffled from Day 1 to Day 2 (Bessemer & Stollnitz, 1971).

Monkeys, at least, perform more intelligently with less drill and more varied experience. It is rather the reverse of the traditional doctrine that human learners progress faster if they are drilled on each succeeding problem until they have overlearned it—the "one-step-at-a-time" strategy of the Skinnerian behaviorists. The problem may be that conventional reinforcement theory applies to habit and skill rather than to intelligent strategies. Habits and skills depend on rhythmic repetition, actually getting into a rut. Intelligent problem solving is quite different. A problem usually begins when a well-practiced habit fails. The more practice, the more difficult it is to abandon the old solution and try new solutions.

PROBLEM SOLVING VERSUS HABIT

Here is a little test that you can try on trusting friends. Try asking them to pronounce the words you spell out loud. Try M - A - C - D - U - F - F. Then a few like M - A - C - T - A - V - I - S - H, or M - A - C - H - E - N - R - Y, and then, perhaps, M - A - C - H - I - N - E - R - Y. Presented orally, this little test in negative transfer trips up many English-speaking people.

R. A. Gardner and Runquist (1958) used a variant of this pronunciation test to study an everyday type of problem-solving skill in college students. Each student subject had the following type of problem. They were to imagine that they had three empty jars, and each jar was a different size. The problem was to measure out a fourth volume of water using just those three jars and an unlimited supply of tap water. Each problem consisted of a 3×5 inch index card with four numbers on it as in the following example:

A	B	C	X
50	81	7	17

It could take the average undergraduate a few minutes to solve this problem by filling Jar B with 81 units and then measuring out 50 units into Jar A and 7 units out into Jar C twice. They had to indicate this by writing $81 - 50 - 7 - 7 = 17$ on the card for that trial. Each student solved 6, 11, or 21 problems of the same kind one after the other in rapid succession as a training series. Each problem had different numbers but could only be solved by the same formula as the first, B - A - C - C. At the end of the training series they got the following problem:

A	B	C	X
21	52	9	12

This problem is much easier than the problems in the training series. It can be solved by writing $21 - 9 = 12$. After training with the difficult problems, the easy problem became very difficult. After solving 21 examples of B - A - C - C problems, some subjects worked for more than 10 minutes before they could solve the first A - C problem. The students acted as if conditioned to solve all the problems with B - A - C - C. They failed, of course. But, they repeated the same thing again and again as if blaming their failure on some error in their arithmetic. Next, they tried variations of B - A - C - C, such as B - C - C - A or B - C - A - C. They acted as if they had to extinguish the solution that had worked so many times in the past by repeating it and failing over and over again. Next, they tried other difficult solutions with many steps. But, these also failed. They acted as if they had to extinguish the strategy of looking for a complicated solution before they could try something simple like A - C.

With practice, the subjects took less and less time to solve the hard problems as shown in the line labeled "Pre-Test" in Fig. 13.8. If speed of response measures strength of conditioning, then the stronger the conditioning the less time it should take to solve the training problems, and that is what happened. The more practice they had with hard problems, the longer it took them to solve the first easy problem as shown in the line labeled "Extinction" in Fig. 14.3. That is just what should happen if they had to extinguish the hard solution before they could solve the easy problem.

Now, if the students had to extinguish the hard solution before they could solve the easy problem, then that one trial of extinction should bring all of the subjects down to the same level of extinction of the hard solutions. To test this, Gardner and Runquist followed the easy A - C trial with one more problem of the hard type, B - A - 2C. All of the subjects took about the same time to solve the post-extinction problem, even though some had practiced that solution for only 6 trials during the training series and others had practiced it for 21 trials. This appears in the line labeled "Post-Test" in Fig. 13.8. The Post-Test averages are not precisely level, but they come very

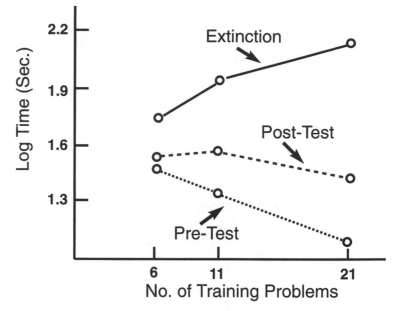

FIG. 13.8. Mean log time to solve the three test problems in R. A. Gardner and Runquist (1958). Copyright © 1997 by R. Allen Gardner.

close and the differences were statistically insignificant. The substantially equal performance of all three groups on the Post-Test agrees with the notion that they had to extinguish the hard solution to a similar level before they could try the easy solution.

The response times in the graph of Fig. 13.8 are in logarithmic units. This is a common practice with time scores because the actual results of response time measures are often badly skewed. That is, there was a floor on the scores because the subjects had to take a few seconds at least to write their answers. But there was no ceiling; they could take a few minutes, or in the case of extinction trials, many minutes to solve the problem, and many did. The very high scores tend to distort the averages, but using logarithm of time scores often corrects the problem.

The highly intelligent college students in this experiment discovered a relatively difficult solution to a problem and got better and better at solving fresh problems with the same solution. The more they practiced the difficult solution, however, the harder it got for them to solve a much easier problem. The Post-Test results show that the habit of trying the difficult solution first made it harder for them to find the easy solution (see A. S. Luchins & E. H. Luchins, 1994, for a history of the use of water jar problems to study the negative effect of drill on human problem solving).

There is a lesson here. Most of the research discussed in the early part of this book deals with habits and skills, with well-practiced rhythmical patterns of response to predictable rhythmical patterns of stimuli. Habit and skill are essential modes of response. What happens when a well-practiced habit fails? Many people start out for work or school by getting their things together and going out to the car. They start the car and drive off. Often, they cannot remember the well-practiced steps that got them to their destination. But, suppose that the car fails to start when you turn the key in the ignition. Then you have a problem. Most people turn the key a few more times to make sure. Those who persistently turn the key in the ignition over and over again are failing to face the problem. The most likely result for them is a dead battery and more problems. You can also start swearing or go out and kick the tires. Responses of that sort can be well-practiced habits also.

Clearly, there is a conflict between habit and problem solving. Both are necessary for survival, but they interfere with each other. Even simple problem-solving strategies like the learning sets formed by Harlow's monkeys suffer from overtraining, but thrive in conditions that foster variability. A truly powerful theory must account both for well-practiced habit and for variable problem solving. The lesson for the student is to profit from skills, and even to be persistent in the face of failure, but at the same time to recognize when failure reveals a problem that requires a fresh and variable attack.

COMPARATIVE INTELLIGENCE AND INTELLIGENT COMPARISONS

At the beginning of the 20th century, Köhler (1925/1959) studied a group of captive chimpanzees on the island of Tenerife off the coast of Africa. Köhler invented ingenious problems that the chimpanzees had to solve with objects that they could find in a large testing arena. To get a banana suspended from the ceiling, they had to drag a large box from a distance to a point under the lure. When Köhler raised the banana higher, the chimpanzees had to drag two, three, and even four boxes and then stack them before they could reach the lure.

Köhler's chimpanzees also solved problems by pulling in lures attached to strings and by reaching through barriers with sticks. In a particularly difficult, and therefore interesting, problem the chimpanzee had two bamboo sticks to work with, but neither stick was long enough to reach the lure. At least one young chimpanzee, named Sultan, spontaneously inserted the thin end of one stick into the hollow end of the second, thus making a longer stick. Sultan then ran with this new object to draw in food that was out of reach with either of the short sticks. Sultan extended this skill to a situation in which the food was so far away that he had to join three sticks together. The three-stick tool was awkward to handle, so Sultan would shorten the tool by disconnecting sections of bamboo as he drew the food closer (pp. 113–119).

Köhler revealed intelligence by giving chimpanzees interesting problems to solve and keeping them in relatively free and stimulating conditions, as opposed to the usual mind-numbing confinement of caged life. As Köhler (1925/1959) put it:

> ... there has arisen among animal psychologists a distinct negativistic tendency, according to which it is considered particularly exact to establish *non*-performance, *non*-human behavior, mechanically-limited actions and stupidity in [nonhuman] animals. ... For my part, I have tried to be impartial, and I believe that my description is not influenced by any emotional factor, beyond a deep interest in these remarkable products of nature. (p. 241)

Köhler's chimpanzees were captured in the jungle and sold to the laboratory by traders, so he could not know their past experience or even their ages at the beginning of his experiments. Later, working with laboratory-born and -reared chimpanzees, Birch (1945) discovered how skill with sticks depended on past experience with sticks. Birch studied six juvenile chimpanzees who were between 4 and 5 years old, which is quite young for chimpanzees (see chap. 14). He gave them a series of problems that they had to solve by using strings and sticks to reach food on a special table just outside of their testing cage.

After a series of string problems, Birch gave each chimpanzee the problem shown in Fig. 13.9. One end of a stick was within reach of the chimpanzee. The other end had a cross-bar. Near the cross-bar was the usual banana. All the chimpanzees had to do was to pull on the stick and rake in the food. Of the six subjects, only Jojo solved the problem by raking in the lure. A second subject, Bard, solved the problem without using the stick as a rake. While agitated by frustration, Bard happened to hit the cage end of the rake in such a way that the other end hit the food and moved it closer to the bars of the testing cage. After observing this, Bard hit the stick repeatedly until he could reach the food with his hand. The remaining four chimpanzees failed to solve the rake problem within one hour.

One striking difference between Jojo and the other five chimpanzees was that Jojo had previous experience using a stick as a tool.

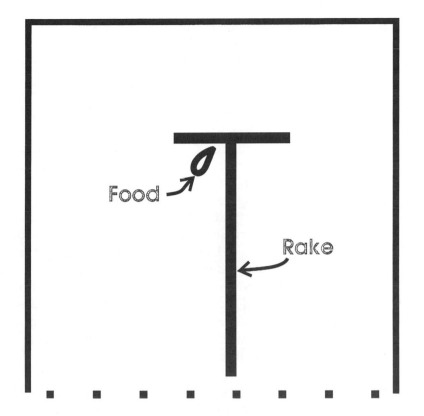

FIG. 13.9.   H. G. Birch's (1945) rake problem. Copyright © 1997 by R. Allen Gardner.

She had already taught herself to use a stick to operate a light switch that was outside of her living cage, and had also taught herself to use a stick to unscrew light bulbs from a socket that was also outside of her living cage.

Birch next released the chimpanzees as a group into a large outdoor area and left them there to run and climb and play freely for 3 days. Birch had left many 1 × 1 inch sticks—some 16 inches long, some 23 inches long—for the chimpanzees to find in the play area. Providing that their previous confinement has not been too severe or has not lasted too long, all chimpanzees play with any objects they can find. All six chimpanzees of Birch's study group were soon playing with the sticks, running with them, hitting with them, and poking with them. The sticks evoked manipulation. After only 3 days of free play with sticks, Birch returned the chimpanzees to the rake problem and the slowest of them took only 20 seconds to rake in the food.

Birch then gave the chimpanzees eight more problems in which they had to use straight sticks without cross-bars to bring in food that was out of reach. In the first problem the stick was beside the food, just as in the rake problem. In another problem it was entirely inside the cage, but near the bars separating the chimpanzees from the lure. In another problem the stick was at the opposite side of the cage from the bars, so the chimpanzees had to turn away from the lure to find the stick. In another problem the chimpanzees had to use a short stick to bring in a longer stick and then use the longer stick to bring in the food.

After eight problems of that sort, Birch gave them a ninth problem that was quite different. In the ninth problem, Birch let the chimpanzees watch him place food inside a length of pipe. The only way that the chimpanzees could get the food out of the pipe was by poking it out with the stick that Birch left lying near the pipe. This problem baffled these otherwise clever and stick-wise chimpanzees. The first thing that they all did, of course, was to pick up the stick and run to the bars to find the food on the table outside of the cage because they had practiced that so many times before. Within the allotted hour, only three of them stopped trying the old problem solution and took the stick back to poke through the pipe. Jojo solved the new problem faster than the others, as we might expect. The remaining three became frustrated and agitated when they failed to find any food outside of the cage, and eventually lost all interest in the problem. The young chimpanzees behaved very much like the college students in Gardner and Runquist (1958) and in many other studies of humans reviewed by Luchins and Luchins (1994).

Chapter 9 described an experiment in which Harlow et al. (1950) left special latching hardware mounted on the walls of cages for monkeys to solve without any extrinsic reward. Figure 13.10 is a diagram of the latching devices. To unlatch these devices, a monkey had to remove the pin attached to the chain, then lift the hook holding the hasp in place, then open the hasp by swinging it on its hinge. A monkey had to perform all three steps in that fixed order to open the hasp.

There were two groups of four monkeys in this experiment. In Phase I, the experimenters set one latch in each cage for 12 days. For Group A the latches were assembled as shown in Fig. 13.10. For Group B the latches were disassembled with the hasps in their open position. The experimenters checked several times a day and reassembled any of the Group A latches that they found opened. They also checked the latches of Group B in order to reset them to their disassembled positions, but none of the monkeys in Group B ever reassembled a latch.

Phase II tested for learning during Phase I and consisted of 10 1-hour tests for each monkey in both groups with the latches assem-

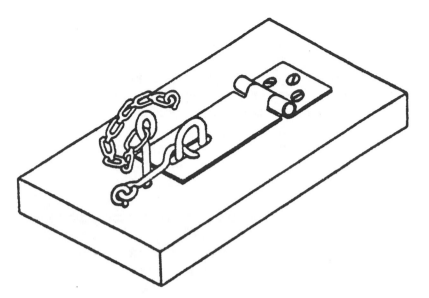

FIG. 13.10.   Latch problem in H. F. Harlow et al. (1950) set for monkeys with and without extrinsic reward. From H. F. Harlow et al. (1950).

bled. The monkeys in Group A disassembled their latches within the hour on 31 out of these 40 opportunities and they usually succeeded within a minute. The monkeys in Group B succeeded in disassembling the latches on only 4 of these 40 opportunities and none of them succeeded within 1 minute. Clearly, experience in Phase I developed a skill in Group A, even though the monkeys never received any extrinsic rewards in either Phase I or Phase II.

In Phase III the monkeys in Group A had to open the hasps to get food reward. During Phases I and II, the experimenters also adapted each monkey in Group A to the WGTA shown in Fig. 13.6 for 1 hour each day. As in the usual preliminary procedure for the WGTA, both food wells contained food, in this case raisins. At first the wells were open, then they were covered with identical junk objects and the monkeys had to displace the objects to get the raisins. After this experience and immediately after Phase II, the monkeys found a single food well in the WGTA closed by an assembled latch. After the test with food reward in the WGTA, the experimenters brought each monkey back to its home cage and reassembled a latch attached to the wall as before (Fig. 9.2) after sticking a raisin under the hasp so that the monkey had to disassemble the latch to get the raisin. Immediately after the test with food under the hasp, an experimenter reassembled the latch in the home cage without food and again in full view of the monkey.

Food incentives significantly disrupted performance. Only one of the monkeys succeeded in opening the hasp to get the food in the WGTA. Three out of the four monkeys succeeded in opening the hasps in their home cages to get food rewards, but all four succeeded after the experimenters removed all food. Even when they succeeded, the monkeys made many more errors in Phase III than they had in Phase II. The main type of error was anticipatory; they tried to open the hasp without disassembling the rest of the latch. Food incentive disrupted performance by inducing anticipatory errors as in the experiments reviewed in chapter 10. The monkeys improved markedly when food incentive was withdrawn at the end of Phase III, but they continued to make more errors than they had before the experimenters introduced extrinsic reward.

Near the end of the 20th century, Visalberghi and Limongelli (1994) carried on the tradition of testing intelligence by practicing clever, nonhuman animals on repetitive tasks. Their subjects were four capuchin monkeys who had learned to get a piece of candy out of a transparent tube by poking with a stick. Three of the monkeys were young adult females between 5 and 8 years old and had years of various kinds of unspecified laboratory experience including "more than 80" repetitive trials of overtraining with the transparent tube. The fourth subject was a 3-year-old juvenile female who had much less experience with laboratory *drill* and who had only "about 20" successful trials with the transparent tube.

Visalberghi and Limongelli next gave the monkeys the following challenge. They modified the transparent tube so that it had a trap in the center as shown in Fig. 13.11 and they placed the food randomly either to the right or to the left of the trap. When the food was on the right in the diagram of Fig. 13.11, a monkey could only poke it out by inserting the stick through the left end of the tube. If a monkey poked from the right end, then the food fell into the trap where it was impossible to reach by any means available to monkeys.

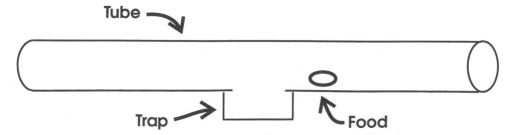

FIG. 13.11. A tube with a trap (after Visalberghi & Limongelli, 1994). Copyright © 1997 by R. Allen Gardner.

The three well-practiced adults adopted a strategy of always poking from the same end of the tube although sometimes they switched ends across days. In this way they earned food 50% of the time, with stereotyped, repetitive habits (chap. 11). The three adults stuck to this strategy for the entire course of 140 trials. Visalberghi and Limongelli concluded that the overtrained adults, that they described as "expert tool users," failed to understand the problem in spite of their training.

A relatively inexperienced juvenile female, Rb, did solve the problem about halfway through the course, but the experimenters kept her repeating this for another 40 or 50 trials. Doubting that Rb understood tools better than the well-trained adults, Visalberghi and Limongelli tested Rb further. In the first test, for example, they rotated the tube so that the trap was above rather than below the path of the food. Starting from either end of the tube in this arrangement, Rb could poke the food safely past the trap, but she stuck to the strategy she had practiced so well before. She always started the stick from the end of the tube that was farthest from the lure, and poked the food out through the near end. She persisted in this habitual strategy even with straight tubes that lacked any traps at all.

Visalberghi and Limongelli concluded that the now well-practiced Rb also failed to understand the problem. All she had learned, according to them, was to poke the food out by starting the stick from the far end. On their part, the experimenters failed to consider the uniformly negative effect of mind-numbing drill on both human and nonhuman animals throughout the history of research on problem solving.

SUMMARY

Extending the findings of earlier chapters to problem-solving strategy reveals a basic conflict between skill at repetitive sequences and flexible attack on new problems. Chapter 11 showed how partial reward increases resistance to extinction because it separates sequential skill from reward. Repetitive practice with minimum reward perfects skill at repetitive tasks, but tolerance for failure delays, even prevents, problem solving.

Early cognitive approaches like Krechevsky's transposed the effect of contingency to the reinforcement and extinction of abstract hypotheses without taking into account the practical benefit that a learner gets from general experience with experimental procedures. Later cognitive approaches like MacKintosh's transposed Skinner's notions of stamping in responses to the idea that overtraining stamps in attention to stimulus dimensions. In both cases, support for the cognitive position depended on confusion about noncognitve alternatives and the operational definition of efficient problem solving.

Harlow's research on problem solving by monkeys revealed the development of problem-solving strategies and showed how repetitive drill and extrinsic reward retard problem solving in monkeys as well as human beings. The notion that rigorous application of Skinnerian reinforcement is the best way to train other animals has made them fail at laboratory tasks. The next chapters of this book extend these findings to research on teaching sign language to chimpanzees.

CHAPTER 14

Teaching Sign Language
to Chimpanzees

How do the principles of ethology and experimental design in this book apply to learning outside of the conditioning chamber? From the point of view of the teacher or the trainer, does it really matter whether a teaching and training technique depends on feed forward or feed backward, on operant conditioning or Pavlovian conditioning, or even on errors in experimental design? The result is the same—or is it? Everything depends on what the teacher aims to teach. If the target behavior resembles obligatory responses evoked by food, then rewarding a hungry learner with food will work as it does in the Skinner box. Otherwise, food will favor the obligatory responses over the target behavior regardless of positive or negative consequences. In that case, the evidence reviewed throughout this book shows that the more rigorous the contingency the poorer the performance. Learners will often appear to be avoiding reward and seeking pain.

Suppose that the learner is a well-fed, free-living being, such as a human child or an infant chimpanzee that is living in a human home like a human child. Suppose that the target behavior is quite unlike lever-pressing or object discrimination, something complex like a human language. What then? We, Allen and Beatrix Gardner, found ourselves in just this situation when we began our sign language studies of chimpanzees.

Our objective was to compare infant chimpanzees with human children. This required a special sort of laboratory. Early in the 20th century, psychologists and biologists taught that all animals develop according to an inexorable species-specific plan. Provided with sufficient food, water, and shelter, each child should develop into a typical child, each chimpanzee into a typical chimpanzee, and so on. It was in those days that B. F. Skinner recommended a small, sterile, climatically controlled chamber as the best place to raise a human infant. Everyone hated Skinner for this proposal, but few questioned its scientific and practical merit.

To this day comparisons betweeen human children and other animals often overlook the contribution of behavioral environments. Experiments compare chimpanzees that live in cages—lucky if they have a rubber tire to play with or a rope to swing from—with children that live in the rich environment of suburban homes. In many so-called "developmental studies" of captive animals, the developmental variable is the number of years that the animal lived under deprived conditions. Most modern psychologists would expect human children to lose rather than develop intelligent behavior under comparable conditions. Indeed, older captives often score lower than younger captives at intelligent tasks (e.g., Tomasello, Davis-Dasilva, Camak, & Bard, 1987).

Experimental comparison requires comparable conditions. In our sign language studies, the chimpanzees had to live like human children. This rich environment provided a stringent test of traditional teaching methods. At about the same time, fresh ethological observations in the operant conditioning chamber revealed more and more flaws in the traditional view of the learning process. The new ethological studies combined with the patterns that we saw in our sign language studies led directly to this book. The next two chapters illustrate the patterns of success and failure and the novel adventures in teaching that tested the feed forward, ethological principles outlined in this book. We begin with a description of our cross-fostering laboratory.

CROSS-FOSTERING

On June 21, 1966, an infant chimpanzee arrived in our laboratory. We named her Washoe, for Washoe County, the home of the University of Nevada. To a casual observer Washoe's new home may not have looked very much like a laboratory. In fact, it was the Gardner residence in the suburbs of Reno, originally purchased as a home for junior faculty, a small, one-story, brick and wood house with an attached garage and a largish garden in the back. To that same casual observer, Washoe's daily life may not have looked much like laboratory routine, either. It was more like the daily life of human children of her age in the same suburban neighborhood.

Washoe was about 10 months old when she arrived in Reno, and almost as helpless as a human child of the same age. In the next few years she learned to drink from a cup and to eat at a table with forks and spoons. She also learned to set and clear the table and even to wash the dishes, in a childish way. She learned to dress and undress herself and she learned to use the toilet to the point where she seemed embarrassed when she could not find a toilet on an outing in the woods, eventually using a discarded coffee can that she found on a hike. She had the usual children's toys and was particularly fond of dolls, kissing them, feeding them, and even bathing them. She was attracted to picture books and magazines almost from the first day and she would look through them by herself or with a friend who would name and explain the pictures and tell stories about them. The objects and activities that most attracted her were those that most engaged the grownups. She was fascinated by household tools, eventually acquiring a creditable level of skill with hammers and screwdrivers.

Washoe lived in a used house trailer, parked in a garden behind the house. With a few minor alterations, it was the same trailer that its previous owners had used as a traveling home. It had the same living-room and bedroom furniture and the same kitchen and toilet facilities. Someone came in to the trailer to check her each night and all through the night, every night, someone listened to her by means of an intercom connected to the Gardner home.

Ethologists use the procedure called *cross-fostering* to study the interaction between environmental and genetic factors by having parents of one genetic stock rear the young of a different genetic stock. It seems as if no form of behavior is so fundamental or so distinctively species-specific that it is not deeply sensitive to the effects of early experience. Ducklings, goslings, lambs, and many other young animals learn to follow the first moving object that they see, whether it is their own mother, a female of another species, or a shoebox. The mating calls of many birds are so species-specific that an ornithologist can identify them by their calls alone without seeing a single feather. Distinctive and species-specific as these calls may be, they, too, depend upon early experience (Slater & Williams, 1994; West, King, & Freeberg, 1997).

How about our own species? How much does our common humanity depend on our common human genetic heritage and how much on the equally species-specific character of a human childhood? The question is as traditional as the story of Romulus and Remus and so tantalizing that even alleged but unverified cases of human cross-fostering, such as the wolf children of India (Singh & Zingg, 1942) and the monkey boy of Burundi (Lane & Pillard, 1978), attract serious scholarly attention. An experimental case of a human infant cross-fostered by nonhuman parents would require an unlikely level of cooperation from both sets of parents. In a few cases, however, chimpanzees have been cross-fostered by human parents (Kellogg, 1968).

Cross-fostering a chimpanzee is very different from keeping one in a home as a pet. Many people keep pets in their homes. They may treat their pets very well, and they may love them dearly, but they do not treat them like children. True cross-fostering—treating the chimpanzee infant like a human child in all respects, in all living arrangements, 24 hours a day every day of the year—requires a rigorous experimental regime that has rarely been attempted.

SIBLING SPECIES

Chimpanzees are an obvious first choice for cross-fostering. They look and act remarkably like human beings and recent research reveals closer and deeper biological similarities of all kinds (Goodall, 1986). In blood chemistry, for example, the chimpanzee is not only the closest species to the human, but the chimpanzee is closer to the human than the chimpanzee is to the gorilla or to the orangutan (Ruvolo, 1994; Stanyon, Chiarelli, Gottlieb, & Patton, 1986).

For cross-fostering, the most important resemblance is that chimpanzees and humans mature very slowly. Infant chimpanzees are quite helpless: Adults must provide warmth, bodily care, and food (Plooij, 1984). The infants in our cross-fostering laboratory, Moja, Pili, Tatu, and Dar, only began to roll over by themselves when they were 4 to 7 weeks old, to sit at 10 to 15 weeks, and to creep at 12 to 15 weeks. The change from milk teeth to adult dentition begins at about 5 years. Under natural conditions in Africa, infant chimpanzees depend on their mothers' care almost completely until they are 2 or 3. They cannot survive if their mother dies before they are 3, even when older siblings attempt to care for them. Weaning only begins when they are between 4 and 5. In Africa, young chimpanzees usually live with their mothers until they are 7; and females often stay with their mothers until they are 10 or 11. Menarche occurs when wild females are 10 or 11, and their first infant is born when they are between 12 and 15 (Goodall, 1986, pp. 84–85, 443). Captive chimpanzees have remained vigorously alive, taking tests and solving experimental problems when they were more than 50 verified years old (Maple & Cone, 1981).

Under favorable conditions, their behavioral repertoire continues to expand and develop throughout their long childhood (Goodall,

1967; Hayes & Nissen, 1971; Plooij, 1984). This gives us a detailed scale of comparative development for measuring the progress of cross-fostered chimpanzees.

SIGN LANGUAGE

Perhaps the most prominent feature of a human childhood is the development of two-way communication in a natural human language. Without conversational give and take in a common language, cross-fostering conditions could hardly simulate the environment of a human infant. Before Project Washoe, the human foster parents spoke to their adopted chimpanzees as human parents speak to human children. In contrast to the close parallels in all other aspects of development, the chimpanzees acquired hardly any speech. For decades, the failure of a few cross-fostered chimpanzees to learn to speak supported the traditional doctrine of an absolute, unbridgeable discontinuity between human and nonhuman intelligence. There is another possibility: that speech is an inappropriate medium of communication for chimpanzees. In that case we must find a naturally occurring human language that does not require human speech. This was the innovation of Project Washoe. For the first time, the human foster family used a gestural rather than a vocal language.

American Sign Language (ASL) is the naturally occurring gestural language of the deaf in North America. Word-for-sign translation between English and ASL is about as difficult as word-for-word translation between English and any other spoken language. English has many common words and idiomatic expressions that can only be paraphrased in ASL, and ASL has its own complement of signs and idioms that can only be paraphrased in English. There are also radical differences in grammar. Where English relies heavily on word order, ASL is like the many other human languages that convey most of the same distinctions through inflection. Where English makes heavy use of auxiliary verbs such as the copula, *to be*, ASL is like the many other human languages that manage without the copula.

The signs of ASL, like the words of English, represent whole concepts. Finger spelling is based on a manual alphabet in which each letter of a written language is represented by a particular configuration of the fingers. It is a code in which messages of a written language can be spelled out in the air. Literate signers mix finger spelling with sign language as a way of referring to seldom-used proper names and technical terms, and we used finger spelling for this purpose in our laboratory. We also used finger spelling from time to time as a code to prevent understanding, the way human parents commonly spell out messages that they want to keep secret from their children. In general, we avoided finger spelling because our still-illiterate subjects could not understand or copy it, and also because too much finger spelling could easily lapse into manual English and defeat the objective of a good adult model of ASL.

Contrary to popular belief, ASL is not an artificial system recently invented by the hearing for use by the deaf. ASL existed in the United States more than 100 years before Project Washoe, and its roots in European sign languages can be traced back for hundreds of years (Stokoe, 1960, pp. 8–19). Outsiders have sometimes invented artificial gestural systems and taught them to their deaf clients. Within the deaf community, however, artificial sign languages have never competed successfully with the indigenous sign languages developed by the deaf, themselves, over the centuries.

Contrary to another popular belief, ASL does not consist of about 50 iconic gestures, understandable to all normal human beings. Instead, ASL is one of many, mutually unintelligible sign languages that have developed among the separate deaf communities around the world. International meetings of the deaf require simultaneous translators (R. A. Gardner & B. T. Gardner, 1989, pp. 56–57).

In ASL, new signs appear and old signs drop out, just as in spoken languages. Historically, the shapes of the signs of ASL have changed continuously, moving toward simplicity and smoothness of articulation in ways that parallel historical trends in the sounds of spoken languages. New signs appear as technical and social needs arise. Fluent signers tend to create the same new coinages for the same concepts, independently, and they tend to agree also on the relative appropriateness of suggested candidates for the same concepts (Kannapell, Hamilton, & Bornstein, 1969). This is what we would expect if there are structural rules for coining new signs.

Sign Language Only

Attempting to speak correct English while simultaneously signing correct ASL is about as difficult as attempting to speak correct English while simultaneously writing correct Russian. Often, teachers and other helping professionals who only learn to sign in order to communicate with deaf clients, attempt to speak and sign simultaneously. They soon find that they are speaking English sentences while adding the signs for a few of the key words in each sentence (Bonvillian, Nelson, & Charrow, 1976). When a native speaker of English practices ASL in this way, the effect is roughly the same as practicing Russian by speaking English sentences and saying some of the key words both in English and in Russian. It is obviously not a good way to master a foreign language.

It was clear from the start of Project Washoe, that the human foster family would provide a poor model of sign language if they spoke and signed at the same time. Signing to the infant chimpanzee and speaking English among ourselves would also be inappropriate. That would lower the status of signs to something suitable for nursery talk, only. In addition, Washoe would lose the opportunity to observe adult models of conversation, and the human newcomers to sign language would lose significant opportunities to practice and to learn from each other.

When the cross-fosterlings were present, all business, all casual conversation was in ASL. Everyone in the foster family had to be fluent enough to make themselves understood under the sometimes hectic conditions of life with these lively youngsters. There were occasional lapses in the rule of sign language only, as when outside workmen or the pediatrician entered the laboratory, but such lapses were brief and rare. Visits from nonsigners were strictly limited. Visitors from the deaf community who were fluent in ASL were always welcome.

The rule of sign language only required some of the isolation of a field expedition. We lived and worked with Washoe on that corner of suburban Reno as if at a lonely outpost in a hostile country. We were always avoiding people who might speak to Washoe. On outings in the woods, we were as stealthy and cautious as Indian scouts. On drives in town, we wove through traffic like undercover agents. We could stop at a Dairy Queen or a McDonald's fast-food restaurant, but only if they had a secluded parking lot in the back. Then one of Washoe's companions could buy the treats while another waited with her in the car. If Washoe was spotted, the car drove off to return later for the missing passenger and the treats, when the coast was clear.

Ethological Considerations

The exquisite development of the human vocal apparatus is matched by the evolution of peculiarly human vocal habits. Human beings are unusually noisy animals. There is a hubbub of voices at almost every social gathering, a great din at the most peaceful cocktail party or restaurant dining room. It is a mark of discipline and respect when an audience settles down in silence to listen to a single speaker. In the rest of the animal kingdom there are very few creatures—perhaps only whales and dolphins, and some birds—that make nearly so much vocal racket when they are otherwise undisturbed.

Chimpanzees are silent most of the time. A group of ten wild chimpanzees of assorted ages and sexes feeding peacefully in a fig tree at the Gombe stream in Africa may make so little sound that an inexperienced observer passing below can altogether fail to detect them. Since the time of the Tarzan films, chimpanzee movie stars have appeared to chatter incessantly on the screen. The effect is created by harassing the chimpanzees when they are off camera, and then dubbing their cries of distress onto the soundtrack. To those who are familiar with the natural vocal repertoire of chimpanzees the result is irritating and distracting. The distressed voice on the sound track clashes with the facial expressions and the postures on the screen, while it is easy to imagine the unpleasant scenes that evoked those high-pitched, nattering cries. When chimpanzees use their voices, they are usually too excited to engage in casual conversation. Their vocal habits, much more than the design of their vocal apparatus, keep them from learning to speak.

We confirmed these ethological considerations by comparing vocal and gestural behavior under controlled experimental conditions. In one experiment we used ASL to announce emotionally charged events to the cross-fostered chimpanzees, Tatu and Dar. Examples of positively charged events would be going outdoors to play or getting an ice-cream cone from the refrigerator. Examples of negatively charged events would be the departure of a favorite friend or the removal of a favorite toy. The key to this investigation was systematic presentation of planned announcements and events in a balanced experimental design during the course of normal daily activities in the cross-fostering laboratory. Tatu and Dar were more likely to sign than to vocalize under all conditions. But, there was more signing in response to the announcements than to the events that followed, while there was more vocalization in response to the events than to the signed announcements. The further from the exciting event the easier it was to evoke arbitrary gestural responses, and the closer to the source of excitement, the easier it was to evoke obligatory emotional cries (R. A. Gardner et al., 1989).

Because their vocalization is so closely tied to emotional excitement, attempts to teach chimpanzees to speak were probably doomed to failure, even under the most favorable conditions, as in the cross-fostering experiments before Project Washoe. As obvious as this may seem now, in those early days influential followers of B. F. Skinner still claimed that almost anything could be taught to almost any animal by the force of operant conditioning. The earlier research, particularly the 7-year, thoroughgoing, and highly professional, cross-fostering experiment of the Hayeses with Viki, was a necessary preliminary to Project Washoe. Before the definitive work of the Hayeses with Viki (see Hayes & Nissen, 1971), it would have been much more difficult to abandon spoken language in favor of sign language.

CHIMPANZEE SUBJECTS

Washoe was captured wild in Africa. She arrived in Reno on June 21, 1966, when she was about 10 months old and lived as a cross-fosterling until October 1, 1970. In the next project, we started new-born chimpanzees at intervals to capitalize on the relationships between older and younger foster siblings. Moja, Pili, Tatu, and Dar, were born in American laboratories and each arrived within a few days of birth. Moja, a female, was born at the Laboratory for Experimental Medicine and Surgery in Primates, New York, on November 18, 1972, and arrived in our laboratory in Reno on the following day. Cross-fostering continued for Moja until late spring 1979. Pili, a male, was born at the Yerkes Regional Primate Research Center, Georgia, on October 30, 1973, and arrived in our laboratory on November 1, 1973. (Pili died of leukemia on October 20, 1975, so that his records cover only the first 2 years.) Tatu, a female, was born at the Institute for Primate Studies, Oklahoma, on December 30, 1975, and arrived in our laboratory on January 2, 1976. Dar, a male, was born at Albany Medical College, Holloman AFB, New Mexico, on August 2, 1976, and arrived in our laboratory on August 6, 1976. Cross-fostering continued for Tatu and Dar until May 1981.

TEACHING METHODS

In teaching sign language to Washoe, Moja, Pili, Tatu, and Dar we imitated human parents teaching young children in a human home. We called attention to everyday events and objects that might interest the young chimpanzees, for example, THAT CHAIR, SEE PRETTY BIRD, MY HAT. We asked probing questions to check on communication, and we always tried to answer questions and to comply with requests. We expanded on fragmentary utterances using the fragments to teach and to probe. We also followed the parents of deaf children by using an especially simple and repetitious register of ASL and by making signs on the youngsters' bodies to capture their attention (Maestas y Moores, 1980; Marschark, 1993; Schlesinger & Meadow, 1972).

Washoe, Moja, Pili, Tatu, and Dar signed to friends and to strangers. They signed to themselves and to each other, to dogs, cats, toys, tools, even to trees. We did not have to tempt them with treats or ply them with questions to get them to sign to us. Most of the signing was initiated by the young chimpanzees rather than by the human adults. They commonly named objects and pictures of objects in situations in which we were unlikely to reward them.

When Washoe signed to herself in play, she was usually in a private place—high in a tree or alone in her bedroom before going to sleep. All of the cross-fosterlings signed to themselves when leafing through magazines and picture books, but only Washoe resisted our attempts to join in this activity. If we persisted in joining her or if we watched her too closely, she often abandoned the magazine or picked it up and moved away. Washoe not only named pictures to herself in this situation, she also corrected herself. In a typical example, she indicated a certain advertisement, signed THAT FOOD, then looked at her hand closely and changed the phrase to THAT DRINK, which was correct.

The cross-fosterlings also signed to themselves about their own ongoing or impending actions. We sometimes saw Washoe moving stealthily to a forbidden part of the garden signing QUIET to herself, or running pell-mell for the potty chair while signing HURRY.

Contrast With Operant Conditioning

The procedures of operant conditioning were plainly inappropriate. Withholding food or water or any other necessity, administering formal trial by trial training, paying the youngsters with treats for each sign or each sentence, all would have defeated the primary purpose of the cross-fostering laboratory. In fact, we found that most attempts at drill or bribery only interfered with the task at hand (see for example, B. T. Gardner & R. A. Gardner, 1971, pp. 123–140). Skinnerian methods failed whenever attempted with Washoe, Moja, Pili, Tatu, and Dar, just as they failed in other laboratories. The pattern of failure confirms the feed forward principles presented throughout this book.

It is, nevertheless, a tribute to the success of the cross-fostering studies that so many followers of B. F. Skinner have insisted that the results were "established in chimps through rigorous application of conditioning principles" (Schwartz, 1978, p. 374). We began early and explicitly to describe our departures from the prescriptions of operant behaviorism (B. T. Gardner & R. A. Gardner, 1971, pp. 123–140), but the extent of the departure seems to come out more clearly in films and tapes (e.g., R. A. Gardner & B. T. Gardner, 1973). A letter that we received from B. F. Skinner following a public television show, for example, attributes our positive results to operant conditioning and scolds us for our feed forward departures from his operant prescriptions:

> I recently saw your Nova program and want to congratulate you. I have done enough of that sort of thing myself to know how difficult it is. . . .
>
> [However] I was quite unhappy about your new recruits—the young people working with the new chimps. They were not arranging effective contingencies of reinforcement. Indeed, they were treating the subjects very much like spoiled children. A first course in behavior modification might save a good deal of time and lead more directly to results. (B. F. Skinner, personal communication, May 24, 1974)

Eventually, a prominent student of B. F. Skinner fielded a rigorously operant version of Project Washoe, with the chimpanzee Nim (Terrace, 1979). This was carried to the point where research assistants were forbidden to treat Nim like a child (p. 118). They were even forbidden to comfort him if he cried out in the night (p. 71). Training sessions took place in a small room designed to simulate an operant conditioning chamber (p. 49). Mostly, training sessions consisted of demonstrating signs for Nim to imitate and showing him things to name, then rewarding correct responses promptly with the requested object or with some other treat (see Terrace, Petitto, Sanders, & Bever, 1980, pp. 377 378 for detailed descriptions). It is hardly surprising that videotape records of these training sessions showed Nim mostly imitating the trainer's signs and begging for treats (Sanders, 1985; Terrace, 1979).

Terrace concluded that Nim lacked

> the motivation needed to sign about things other than requests. . . . Can one instill a greater motivation to sign than we managed to instill in Nim? . . .
>
> The ease with which a child learns language may be less a consequence of superior intellectual machinery than of a child's willingness to inhibit its impulses to grab and to use words instead. In contrast to a child, a chimpanzee seems less disposed to inhibit its impulses, preferring to operate upon the world in a physical, as opposed to a verbal, manner. To get a chimpanzee into the habit of signing, it would help to begin instruction in sign language at an age at which its physical coordination is limited. During the chimpanzee's first year, it is essentially as helpless as a human infant: its locomotion is rather limited, and it is quite uncoordinated in its attempts to grasp things. . . . While Nim was quite helpless, I should have required him to sign, or at least attempt to sign, for anything he wanted. (Terrace, 1979, p. 223)

From an ethological, feed forward point of view, however, it is easy to see that Nim grabbed so much because his trainers provided conditions that evoked grabbing rather than communication. Nim's signs were usually requests because his trainers taught him to use signs for requests rather than for communication. The relentless application of extrinsic incentives evoked extrinsic responses that stifled communication. If Terrace had the opportunity to try the more extreme operant procedure that he describes in the quoted passage, he would only find, as the Brelands found, more "misbehavior" (chap. 8) and less communication. Human children are not born with some mysterious "willingness to inhibit impulses to grab"; they are, instead, reared in an environment that evokes communication rather than grabbing.

Approaching the problem in much the same way as Terrace, Rumbaugh and his associates taught the chimpanzee, Lana, to use a multiple-choice response panel to obtain a variety of goods and services (mostly foods and drinks) with strict Skinnerian schedules of reinforcement. "With regard to the intensity of training, it was decided that Lana would live in the language environment 24 hours a day. There, her linguistic expressions would provide repeated, reinforcing engagement with the system, since she would have to obtain all of her necessities and social interactions by making appropriate requests of it" (Gill & Rumbaugh, 1977, p. 158).

After this intensive overtraining, it was very difficult for Lana to transfer from one problem to the next. She often required extensive retraining to master simple variants of sequences of responses even though she had used the same responses correctly for tens of thousands of trials in other sequences (Gill & Rumbaugh, 1974). Overtraining, the hallmark of the Rumbaugh laboratory, had the negative effects on intelligent behavior we would expect from the evidence reviewed in chapter 13.

Later, Savage-Rumbaugh and her associates used a similar multiple-choice response panel with the chimpanzees Sherman and Austin. The second project concentrated on naming rather than pressing keys in specific sequences, and trainers handed rewards to the chimpanzees directly rather than relying on automatic dispensers. The greater social interaction between experimenters and chimpanzees and the relaxation of some of the operant rigor of reward delivery seemed to help Sherman and Austin. But the Rumbaughs taught Sherman and Austin to use the panel step by step according to the same Skinnerian model of language learning as before. Each step in the conditioning program consisted of a still more elaborate way to get food rewards (Savage-Rumbaugh, 1984, pp. 230–247).

Failure of Extrinsic Incentives

Lepper, Greene, and Nisbett (1973) studied the effect of extrinsic incentives on toddlers in a nursery school. Ordinarily, freehand drawing is a very popular activity in nursery school. Lepper et al. measured the amount of freehand drawing when they left toddlers by themselves with drawing materials. Next, the experimenters told half the children that they would reward them for drawing more and the more the drawing the more the reward. The other half were treated the same and received the same amount of reward, but the amount of reward was independent of the amount of drawing, and the experimenters never told the control children that rewards would depend on amount of drawing. The result was a dramatic decline in the amount of drawing by the contingent group. Extrinsic incentives actually suppressed the otherwise attractive activity of freehand drawing.

Freehand drawing is also a popular activity for young chimpanzees and extrinsic incentives have the same depressing effect on their art. In his study of a young captive named Congo, Morris (1962) made food contingent on freehand drawing and described his results as follows:

> The outcome of this experiment was most revealing. The ape quickly learnt to associate drawing with getting the reward but as soon as this condition had been established the animal took less and less interest in the lines it was drawing. Any old scribble would do and then it would immediately hold out its hand for the reward. The careful attention the animal had paid previously to design, rhythm, balance and composition was gone and the worst kind of commercial art was born! (pp. 158–159)

To take an example that is directly relevant to communication, consider Hayes and Nissen's (1971) report of the cross-fostered chimpanzee Viki:

> . . . one hot summer day [Viki] brought a magazine illustration of a glass of iced tea to a human friend. Tapping it, she said "Cup! Cup!" and ran to the refrigerator, pulling him along with her. It occurred to us that pictures might be used to signify needs more explicitly than words. . . .
> A set of cards was prepared showing magazine illustrations in natural color of those things she solicited most frequently. [For 4 days Viki consistently used the picture-cards for requests, but on the 5th day] . . . suddenly she acted as if imposed upon. She had to be coaxed to cooperate and then used the pictures in a completely random way.

> [After 7 months of erratic performance] . . . the technique which had seemed so promising was dropped, pending revision. Spring weather, plus a new car, gave Viki a wanderlust so that no matter what situation sent her to the picture-communication pack, when she came upon a car picture she made happy noises and prepared to go for a ride. We eliminated all car pictures from the pack, but it was too late. Long afterwards Viki was tearing pictures of automobiles from magazines and offering them as tickets for rides. (pp. 107–108)

Viewed from this perspective, the positive results of the cross-fostering studies with Washoe, Moja, Pili, Tatu, and Dar and the disappointing results of the operant conditioning studies that followed in other laboratories should be easier to understand. Terrace (1979) in his studies of Nim, Rumbaugh and his associates (see Gill & Rumbaugh, 1977) in their studies of Lana, and Savage-Rumbaugh (1984) in her studies of Sherman and Austin, all insisted on operant rigor in their laboratories and all obtained relatively negative results.

Modern psychobiologists recognize many primary motives rather than a few basic ones, such as hunger and thirst. Other motives, such as contact comfort (chap. 9), can be more powerful determinants of behavior than hunger and thirst. Human children learn to speak as if they were born with a powerful motive to communicate; extrinsic incentives are unnecessary. Many other animals behave as if they, too, were born with a powerful motive to communicate. Contact comfort and communication have obvious selective advantages, and the existence of many such basic motives is clearly more compatible with Darwinism than the elaborate process of conditioning based on hunger and thirst so often proposed in traditional theories.

There are important lessons to be learned here for those who teach children with special speech and language problems. There is much to be gained by assuming a motive to communicate and much to be lost by imposing ethologically irrelevant, extrinsic incentives (see also F. Levine & Fasnacht, 1974).

USES OF THE SIGNS

When teaching a new sign, we usually began with a particular exemplar—a particular toy for BALL, a particular shoe for SHOE. At first, especially with very young subjects, there would be very few balls and very few shoes. Early in Project Washoe we worried that the signs might become too closely associated with their initial referents. It turned out that this was no more a problem for Washoe or for any of the other cross-fosterlings than it is for human children.

The chimpanzees easily transferred the signs they had learned for a few balls, shoes, flowers, or cats to the full range of the concepts wherever found and however represented, as if they divided the world into the same conceptual categories that human beings use.

The human members of the foster families observed the cross-fostered chimpanzees constantly throughout the day and attempted to record all of the significant activities of the day, but particularly the sign language and its verbal and nonverbal contexts. We grouped the signs of Washoe, Moja, Tatu, and Dar at 5 years of age into *functional categories* according the contexts in which they were used, such as names (DAR, ROGER), pronouns (ME, YOU), animates (BABY, DOG), inanimate objects (BALL, TREE), noun/verbs (BRUSH, DRINK), verbs (GO, OPEN), locatives (DOWN, OUT), colors (BLACK, RED), possessives (MINE, YOURS), material (GLASS, WOOD), numbers (ONE, TWO), comparatives (BIG, DIFFERENT), qualities (HOT, SWEET), markers (AGAIN, CAN'T), and traits (SORRY, GOOD).

Table 14.1 shows examples of context descriptions from the daily field records of Washoe, Moja, Tatu, and Dar grouped according to functional categories. For one representative sign from each category, Table 14.1 shows a summary description of contexts together with typical questions that evoked that sign and examples of verbal exchanges and phrases in which it appeared. Table 14.1 lists separately each of the signs in the category that we have called *markers* and *traits*, because these cases are both more complex and more significant. The examples and the summaries were all taken from the formal field records described in B. T. Gardner, R. A. Gardner, and Nichols (1989).

Functional categories such as those in Table 14.1 are called *sentence constituents* because they seem to serve constituent functions in the early fragmentary utterances of human children. One way to demonstrate the functional roles of these categories is to ask a series of questions about the same object. When Greg asked Washoe a series of questions about her red boot, her reply to WHAT THAT? was SHOE, to WHAT COLOR THAT? was RED, and to WHOSE THAT? was MINE. Replies to questions can establish the functional character of lexical categories. At the time of this example (filmed in R. A. Gardner & B. T. Gardner, 1973), Washoe had four color signs in her vocabulary: RED, GREEN, WHITE, and BLACK. If her only color sign had been RED, then all she would have had to do was to reply RED whenever anyone asked WHAT COLOR? With a group of color signs in the vocabulary, she could reply at different levels of correctness. If she had replied GREEN when asked WHAT COLOR THAT? of the red boot, it would have been an error, but a different

TABLE 14.1

Contexts and Uses of the Signs in the Vocabularies of Washoe, Moja, Tatu, and Dar at 5 Years of Age

		In response to:	Used in phrases such as:
Names, Chimpanzees DAR, MOJA, TATU, WASHOE	e.g., DAR - Chimpanzee Dar, and pictures of Dar	WHO THAT?/ WHO YOU?/ WHAT YOUR NAME?/ WHO CHASE?/ (During breakfast) JOHN: WHO DRINK MILK? DAR: MILK DAR/ (Indoors before playtime with Dar) R.A.G.: WHO MEET?/ TATU: OUT GO DAR/	CHASE DAR/ DRINK DAR/ MILK DAR/ GOOD DAR/
Names, Human Companions ARLENE K., GREG G., LINN A., NAOMI R., R.A.G., SUSAN N., TOM V., and other names	e.g., NAOMI R. - Naomi Rhoades, a human companion, and pictures of Naomi	WHO THAT?/ WHO ME?/ WHO TICKLE NOW?/ (Looking at photos) TATU: THAT WHO?/ BETTY: THAT TOM, WHO THAT?/ TATU: NAOMI/	YOU NAOMI/ NAOMI TICKLE/ NAOMI COME/ NAOMI GOOD/
Names, Generic BOY, FRIEND, GIRL	e.g., BOY - Males, especially male strangers or familiar males who do not have name signs; pictures of men in magazines	WHO THAT?/ WHICH-SEX THAT?/ WHICH-SEX ME?/ WHAT THAT?/ (During lesson in ASL) SUSAN: WHICH-SEX YOU?/ DAR: BOY DAR/ (Of magazine picture of man) SUSAN: WHAT THAT?/ DAR: BOY/	THAT BOY/ GOOD DAR BOY/ R.A.G. BOY/ BIRD BOY/ (eagle and man on coin)
Pronouns ME, WE, YOU	e.g., YOU - The addressee, during food sharing, games with turns such as tickle and hide, and other activities	WHO TICKLE?/ WHO EAT?/ WHO OUT?/ (Sharing sodapop) DAR: SODAPOP DAR/ SUSAN: AND WHO OTHER?/ DAR: YOU/	YOU JIM/ YOU PEEKABOO/ YOU TICKLE ME WASHOE/
Nouns, Animates BABY, BEAR, BIRD, BUG, BUTTERFLY, CAT, COW, DOG, HORSE	e.g., BIRD - Sparrows, ducks, pigeons, and other species of birds; toy birds; pictures, draw-ings, and cartoons of birds; birdcalls and human renditions of birdcalls	WHAT THAT?/ WHO SAY "quack, quack"?/ NAME THAT?/ (Of hidden bird, calling) PAT: WHAT THERE YOU HEAR?/ DAR: HEAR/ PAT: NAME/ DAR: BIRD/	THAT BIRD/ RED BIRD/ LISTEN BIRD/

Words	e.g.	In response to:	Used in phrases such as:
Nouns, Edibles APPLE, BANANA, BERRY, BREAD, CANDY, CARROT, CEREAL, CHEESE, COFFEE, COOKIE, CORN, CRACKER, CUCUMBER, GRAPES, GUM, ICE, ICE CREAM, MEAT, MEDICINE, MILK, NUT, ONION, ORANGE, PEA-BEAN, PEACH, SANDWICH, SODAPOP, TOMATO, WATER	e.g., COFFEE - Coffee and tea in mugs, cups, thermos bottles; jars of instant coffee; pictures of cups of coffee	WHAT THAT?/ WHAT NAME THAT?/ WHAT WANT?/ (Of a cup of coffee) TATU: DRINK/ BETTY: WHAT THAT DRINK?/ TATU: COFFEE/	COFFEE DRINK/ THAT COFFEE/ BABY DRINK MORE COFFEE/ (when Susan pretended to give coffee to doll)
Nouns, Inanimate Objects AIRPLANE, BALL, BELT, BIB, BLANKET, BOOK, CLOTHES, COAT, CUP, DIAPER, EARRING, FLOOR, FLOWER, FORK, GARBAGE, GLASSES, GLOVE, GRASS, HAMMER, HANDS, HAT, HOLE, HOSE, HOUSE, HURT, KEY, KNIFE, LEAF, LIPSTICK, LOCK, MIRROR, PANTS, PIN, PURSE, RING, ROCK, SHIRT, SHOE, SPOON, STAMP, STRING, SWAB, TABLE, TELEPHONE, TOOTHPASTE, TREE, WINDOW, WIPER, WRISTWATCH	e.g., WRISTWATCH - Wristwatches, whether being worn or not; pictures of wristwatches	WHAT THAT?/ WHAT NAME THAT?/ NAME THAT/ (Of Naomi's watch) TATU: THAT BLACK/ NAOMI BLACK WHAT? TATU: WRISTWATCH/	THAT WRISTWATCH/ WRISTWATCH GIMME/ WRISTWATCH BLACK/
Noun-Verbs BATH, BED, BLINDFOLD, BLOW, BRUSH, CAR, CHAIR, CLEAN, CLIMB, COMB, COVER-BLANKET, DRINK, FOOD-EAT, HANKY, HEAR-LISTEN, LIGHT, OIL, PEEKABOO, PEN-WRITE, PIPE, POTTY, RIDE, SCHOOL, SEE, SMELL, SMOKE, SWING, TOOTHBRUSH, VACUUM	e.g., TOOTHBRUSH - Toothbrushes; brushing teeth	WHAT THAT?/ WHAT NOW?/ WHAT DO?/ (Susan toothbrushes a doll) DAR: BABY/ SUSAN: WHAT DO?/ DAR: TOOTHBRUSH BABY/ (At end of meal) BETTY: WANT THAT?/ TATU: TOOTHBRUSH TOOTHBRUSH/	TOOTHBRUSH THAT/ TIME TOOTHBRUSH/ TOOTHBRUSH DAR/
Verbs BITE, BREAK, CATCH, CHASE, CRY, GO, GROOM, HUG, KISS, LAUGH, OPEN, QUIET, RUN, SLEEP, SPIN, SWALLOW, TICKLE, WRESTLE	e.g., CHASE - Chasing and being chased in play	WHAT WANT?/ WHAT DO?/ WHAT PLAY?/ (During chase game) MOJA: CHASE/ TIM: WHO CHASE?/ MOJA: CHASE ME/	CHASE DAR/ TATU CHASE/ YOU CHASE/

305

TABLE 14.1
(Continued)

	In response to:	Used in phrases such as:
Locatives DOWN, HOME, IN-ENTER, OUT, THAT-THERE, UP e.g., OUT - Requesting change in location, as going outdoors or re-moving an object from a container; designating current location of a person or an object	WHERE GO?/ WHERE DAR?/ WHAT WE DO?/ WHAT NOW?/ (Near closed door) MOJA: OUT OUT/ TIM: SORRY CAN'T NOW/	YOU ME OUT/ CAN'T OUT OUT/ PLEASE BLANKET OUT/ (at blanket cupboard) OUT HOME MILK DRINK/ (when in playroom)
Modifiers, Colors BLACK, GREEN, ORANGE, RED, WHITE e.g., BLACK - Purse, dog, shoe, and other items that are black; indicating the part of a multicolored item that is black	WHAT COLOR THAT?/ NAME COLOR THAT/ WHAT COLOR HAT?/ (During lesson in ASL) KEN: WHAT COLOR YOU?/ MOJA: BLACK/	THAT BLACK/ SHOE BLACK/ BLACK BERRY/ (raisin)
Modifiers, Possessives MINE, YOURS e.g., YOURS - Watches, shoes, coffee, and other belongings of the companion	WHOSE THAT?/ WHOSE SHOE?/ WHOSE LISTEN?/ (Of Betty's can of soda) BETTY: WHOSE DRINK?/ TATU: MINE/ BETTY: NO, NO/ TATU: YOURS/	HAT YOURS/ CANDY YOURS/ SUSAN YOURS/
Modifiers, Materials GLASS, METAL, WOOD e.g., METAL - Pans, pliers, spoons, and other items made of metal	WHAT THAT MAKE FROM?/ (Of a key that Dar found) PAT: WHAT THAT?/ DAR: KEY/ PAT: WHAT THAT MAKE FROM?/ DAR: METAL/	THAT METAL/ METAL HOT/ (cigarette lighter) METAL CUP DRINK COFFEE/ (thermos flask)
Modifiers, Numbers ONE, TWO e.g., ONE - When single items such as a nut, a match, a glove are displayed	HOW MANY?/ HOW MANY NUT?/ HOW MANY CANDY?/ (Of grapes in icebox) CHRIS: HOW MANY GRAPE WANT EAT?/ TATU: ONE ONE/	ONE BLACK/ ONE NUT/ ONE GUM/
Modifiers, Comparatives BIG, DIFFERENT, SAME, SMALL e.g., BIG - When pairs of items that differ in size are displayed, such as balls, spoons, or toy animals	WHAT SIZE THAT?/ THAT SMALL, WHAT THAT?/ (Of two toy horses) JIM: THIS SMALL HORSE, WHAT THAT?/ MOJA: BIG/	BIG BALL/ BIG HORSE/ BIG SPOON/

		In response to:	Used in phrases such as:
Modifiers, Qualities HOT, SOUR, SWEET	e.g., HOT - Substances that are hot, such as water or soup or meat; sources of heat, such as stove or furnace, whether lit or not	WHAT TEMPERATURE THAT?/ (Of cigarette lighter) KEN: TEMPERATURE THAT?/ MOJA: HOT/	THAT HOT/ HOT WATER/ SANDWICH HOT/
Markers and Traits AGAIN	Requesting continuation and repetition of grooming, swinging, tossing, and other activities	WHAT WANT?/ (After Moja breaks a balloon) MOJA: BLOW AGAIN/ KATHY: NO, FINISH PLAY BLOW, YOU BREAK THAT/ MOJA: BLOW/	AGAIN TICKLE/ AGAIN UP/ AGAIN AGAIN PEEKABOO/
CAN'T	Unable to do a task, as after many attempts to unlock a door, open a jar, break a stick; unable to answer a question; often used in toilet situations; could also be understood as a refusal	CAN YOU POTTY MORE?/ YOU TRY POTTY/ CAN YOU BREAK THAT?/ (After putting on outdoor clothes) DAR: CAN'T/ PAT: CAN'T WHAT?/ DAR: OUT/	DIRTY CAN'T/ POTTY CAN'T/ OUT OPEN CAN'T/
COME-GIMME	Requesting someone to approach; requesting an out-of-reach object or an object someone is holding	WHAT WANT?/ WHAT NOW?/ WHAT ME DO?/ (Betty working in kitchen) TATU: COME/ BETTY: WANT WHAT?/ TATU: CHASE/	COME HUG/ GIMME MILK/ GIMME BLANKET/
DIRTY	Feces; stains on clothes, furniture, shoes, and soiled items; defecating and urinating	WHAT THAT?/ NAME THAT/ WHO POTTY THERE?/ (Of toilet in playroom) CHRIS: THAT WHAT?/ TATU: POTTY/ CHRIS: WHAT NAME SMELL?/ TATU: POTTY ... DIRTY/	THAT DIRTY/ THAT THAT SHOE DIRTY/ DIRTY DIRTY SORRY/ DIRTY GOOD/(potty chair)
ENOUGH	Ending routine activities such as a meal, a bath, a lesson	YOU FINISH?/ (At end of lunch) WASHOE: ENOUGH/ ROGER: ENOUGH WHAT?/ WASHOE: ENOUGH EAT TIME/	ENOUGH FOOD/ ENOUGH SWALLOW ENOUGH/ OUT ENOUGH ENOUGH TOOTHBRUSH/ (end of supper)

(Continued)

TABLE 14.1
(Continued)

FINISH	Ending routine activities, such as a meal, a toilet session, a bath	In response to: WHAT NOW?/ MORE EAT?/ MORE CLEAN/ (Toothbrushing after breakfast) VAUGHN: MORE TOOTHBRUSH/ TATU: FINISH/ Used in phrases such as: SCHOOL FINISH/ FINISH POTTY/ FINISH HURRY/
FUNNY	An epithet, usually for oneself; during tickling, chasing, and other playful interactions; occasionally, when being pursued after mischief	In response to: WHO FUNNY?/ (During lesson in ASL) SUSAN: WHO FUNNY?/ WASHOE: FUNNY FUNNY YOU/ Used in phrases such as: FUNNY ME/ FUNNY FUNNY WASHOE/ TICKLE FUNNY/ FUNNY SUSAN FUNNY/
GOOD	An epithet, usually for oneself; part of requests, especially for eyeglasses, watch, or other breakable belongings of companion; part of apologies and appeasement after mischief; could also be understood as a promise to "be good"	In response to: YOU BAD GIRL/ YOU GOOD GIRL?/ NO CAN'T GO THERE/ (Before going outdoors) TATU: GOOD GOOD OUT/ NAOMI: YOU SURE?/ TATU: GOOD OUT/ Used in phrases such as: GOOD GOOD GOOD ME/ GOOD MOJA/ SORRY GOOD/ TATU GOOD OUT GO/
GOODBYE	At departures, when persons announce they will leave or as they actually depart	In response to: WHAT SAY NOW?/ TIME ME LEAVE/ HE LEAVE/ (Greg preparing to leave) GREG: ME LEAVE NOW/ MOJA: GOODBYE/ Used in phrases such as: GOODBYE DAR/ OUT GOODBYE/
HELP	Requesting someone to assist with difficult tasks, such as operating locks and keys, cracking nuts, opening bottles, also with signs that are difficult to produce	In response to: WHAT WANT?/ (Of garage door) WASHOE: IN HELP KEY/ ROGER: WHERE IN?/ WASHOE: IN OPEN THERE/ (Of a book) SUSAN: WHAT THAT?/ MOJA: HELP/ SUSAN: THAT BOOK/ MOJA: BOOK/ Used in phrases such as: OPEN HELP/ IN HELP/ HELP UP/

HURRY	Requesting someone to approach, bring an object, unlock a door, or do other things quickly	In response to: WHAT WANT?/ WHAT NOW?/ YOU WANT OUT?/ (During supper preparations) DAR: HURRY GIMME/ TONY: WANT?/ DAR: CARROT/	Used in phrases such as: HOME HURRY/ HURRY COME/ OPEN HURRY/ EAT TATU HURRY/
MORE	Requesting continuation and repetition of tickling, chasing, brushing, and other activities; requesting additional helpings of milk, juice, cookies, and other edibles	In response to: WHAT WANT?/ WHAT DO?/ FINISH?/ (Washoe hands weeding tool to Susan) WASHOE: MORE/ SUSAN: MORE WHAT?/ WASHOE: MORE OPEN/ (on ground) (Susan holding grape) WASHOE: MORE/ SUSAN: MORE WHAT?/ WASHOE: MORE ME BERRY/	Used in phrases such as: MORE GO/ MORE TICKLE/ MORE MILK/ MORE SODAPOP DAR/
NO	Negation; used in reply to commands, questions, and statements; also, in response to actions such as a stranger's offer to pick up subject, threats to throw snowballs or splash water at the subject, and occasionally, offers of food	In response to: YOU WANT SHOE THERE?/ WANT GO HOME?/ ME EAT THAT?/ COME, TIME SLEEP/ FINISH OUT/ (Of Washoe's doll) B.T.G.: THAT MY BABY?/ WASHOE: NO NO MINE/ (simultaneous signs) (Of toy cow) TIM: WHAT THAT?/ MOJA: HORSE/ TIM: "uh uh" (vocalizes) MOJA: NO COW/	Used in phrases such as: BATH NO/ BED NO NO/ HOT NO/ (after unplugging heater)
PLEASE	Requesting a drink, a berry, a hat, going outside, and other objects and activities	In response to: ASK POLITE/ ASK NICE/ (Pat holding a cookie) DAR: GIMME COOKIE/ PAT: ASK NICE/ DAR: PLEASE GIMME/	Used in phrases such as: PLEASE FLOWER/ PLEASE OUT/ PLEASE TICKLE THERE/
SORRY	An epithet for oneself; part of apology and appeasement after an escape, a toilet accident, breaking something, and other offenses	In response to: YOU GOOD NOW?/ ASK PARDON/ YOU SIGN!/ (After a potty accident) BETTY: YOU POTTY THERE, BAD/ TATU: SORRY/	Used in phrases such as: SORRY GOOD/ ME SORRY/ WASHOE SORRY/ COME HUG SORRY SORRY/

(Continued)

309

TABLE 14.1
(*Continued*)

TIME	Announcing or requesting the next event of the daily routine and other imminent events	Used in phrases such as:
		TIME VACUUM/
		TIME EAT?/
		TIME TOOTHBRUSH/
		TIME DAR OUT/
		
		In response to:
		WHAT NOW?/ WHAT TIME NOW?/
		(In barn, at lunch time)
		  MOJA: TIME/
		  KEN: WHAT TIME?/
		  MOJA: HOME/

WANT	Requesting objects and activities	Used in phrases such as:
		WANT IN/
		WANT MORE DRINK/
		WASHOE WANT
		  CEREAL/
		WANT ROGER
		PEEKABOO/
		
		In response to:
		WHAT YOU WANT?/ YOU WANT TICKLE?/
		  WANT GROOM?/
		(Before going outdoors)
		  LINN: WHAT TIME?/
		  WASHOE: OUT OUT/
		  LINN: WHO OUT?/
		  WASHOE: WASHOE WANT OUT/

WHAT	Interesting out-of-view objects, such as contents of backpack, pocket, clasped hands; pictures or objects for which the sign is unknown to subject; could be understood as inquiry	Used in phrases such as:
		WHAT THAT?/
		PLEASE WHAT/
		WHAT SEE EAT/ (closed
		  refrigerator)
		
		In response to:
		ASK/, but usually self-initiated
		(Of picture of gorilla)
		  MOJA: THAT WHAT/
		  TOM: THAT GORILLA/
		  MOJA: THAT ME/
		(During tickle play with teddy bear)
		  SUSAN WANT TICKLE MORE?/
		  MOJA: TICKLE/
		  SUSAN WHO TICKLE YOU?/
		  MOJA: THAT WHAT/ (of teddy bear)
		  SUSAN BABY/
		  MOJA: BABY/

WHO	Persons or their pictures, and subject's mirror image; could be understood as inquiry	Used in phrases such as:
		WHO THAT?/
		THAT WHO?/
		WHO YOU?/
		
		In response to:
		I KNOW WHO COME SOON/ ASK ME MY
		  NAME/, but usually self-initiated
		(Of Naomi's photo on driver's license)
		  TATU: THAT WHO?/
		  NAOMI: THAT ME NAOMI/
		  TATU: THAT NAOMI/

YES	Agreement; used in reply to questions offering objects or activities	Used in phrases such as:
		MILK YES/
		WRISTWATCH YES/
		OUT YES/
		
		In response to:
		YOU WANT THAT?/ YOU WANT TICKLE?/
		  WANT MORE?/
		(Sharing crackers)
		  TIM: WANT MORE?/
		  MOJA: YES/

sort of error from a reply such as SHOE or HAT or MINE. A reply can be functionally appropriate without being factually correct.

R. Brown (1968) and others reviewed by Van Cantfort, B. T. Gardner, and R. A. Gardner (1989) used the replies of human children to *WH questions* of this sort to show that children use different functional categories of words as sentence constituents, even when the children are still so immature that they cannot frame WH questions on their own. Washoe, Moja, Tatu, and Dar also used appropriate sentence constituents in their replies to WH questions. As an additional parallel, longitudinal samples of the replies of the chimpanzees show the same developmental pattern that has been found in human children. Children and cross-fostered chimpanzees reply to WHAT questions with nominals and to WHERE questions with locatives before they reply to WHAT DO questions with verbs and to WHO questions with proper names and pronouns, while reliably appropriate replies to HOW questions appear even later (Van Cantfort et al., 1989).

PHRASES

As soon as Washoe had 8 or 10 signs in her vocabulary, she began to construct phrases of 2 or more signs. Before long, multiple-sign constructions were common. The last column of Table 14.1 shows typical examples of phrases. The individual terms within these phrases and sentences formed basic meaningful patterns such as agent-action (SUSAN BRUSH, YOU BLOW), action-object (CHASE DAR, OPEN BLANKET), action-location (GO UP, TICKLE THERE), possession (BIB MINE, HAT YOURS), nomination (THAT CAT, THAT SHOE), and recurrence (MORE COOKIE, MORE GO). Longer constructions could specify more than one agent of an action (YOU ME IN, YOU ME GREG GO), or specify agents, actions, and locations (YOU ME DRINK GO, YOU ME OUT SEE), or specify agents, actions, and objects of action (YOU GIVE GUM MOJA, YOU TICKLE ME WASHOE).

Table 14.1 may seem a little formidable at first, but we heartily recommend it as a realistic sample of the way sign language appeared in the casual conversations of the cross-fosterlings.

Word-for-Sign Translation

In our reports, the English glosses of ASL signs appear in captial letters and transcribe signed utterances into word-for-sign English. More liberal translations must add words and word endings that are without signed equivalents either in the vocabularies of the chimpanzees or in ASL. Literal word-for-sign transcription makes the utterances appear to be in a crude or pidgin dialect, but the reader should understand that equally literal word-for-word transcriptions between Russian or Japanese and English appear equally crude.

Creativity

Without deliberately teaching the chimpanzees to construct multiple-sign utterances, the human signers normally modeled simple phrases and sentences in their daily conversation. Washoe, Moja, Pili, Tatu, and Dar could all invent novel combinations for themselves. Washoe called her refrigerator the OPEN FOOD DRINK and her toilet the DIRTY GOOD even though her human companions referred to these as the COLD BOX and the POTTY CHAIR. When asked WHAT THAT? of assorted unnamed objects, Moja described a cigarette lighter as a METAL HOT, a Thermos flask as a METAL CUP DRINK COFFEE, and a glass of Alkaseltzer as a LISTEN DRINK (B. T. Gardner et al., 1989; R. A. Gardner & B. T. Gardner, 1991).

FIG. 14.1.   Moja (30 months) at brunch with Allen and Beatrix Gardner. Moja is signing *APPLE*. Copyright © 1997 by R. Allen Gardner.

FIG. 14.2.   Moja (33 months) signed TICKLE on (21-month-old) Pili's hand, equivalent in a sign language to inflection for agent as in *you*/TICKLE/*me* (see Rimpau, Gardner, & Gardner, 1989). Pili affirms (see Gardner, Gardner, & Drumm, 1989) by signing TICKLE on his own hand. Copyright © 1997 by R. Allen Gardner.

In Oklahoma, Washoe frequently called the swans in the moat around her island WATER BIRD even though Roger Fouts called the swans DUCK. Fouts (1975) reported a systematic study of the chimpanzee Lucy in Oklahoma in which he asked Lucy to name a series of fruits and vegetables that no one had ever named for her in ASL. Among the objects that Lucy had to name for herself were radishes, which she called CRY HURT FOOD, and watermelon, which she called CANDY DRINK. Perhaps the clearest evidence that the chimpanzees learned signs as meaningful parts of meaningful phrases is the frequency and variety of new, chimpanzee-invented terms.

Development

Exciting as they are, first steps are only the beginning of walking and first words are only the beginning of talking. If the earliest utterances of human infants represent language, then they are best described as primitive, childish language. Gradually and piecemeal, but in an orderly sequence, the language of toddlers develops into the language of their parents. The well-documented record of human development provides a scale for measuring the progress of cross-fostered chimpanzees.

In a cross-fostering laboratory, the sign language of chimpanzees grows and develops. B. T. Gardner and R. A. Gardner (1994) studied the growth and development of phrases in the sign language of Moja, Tatu, and Dar, who were cross-fostered from birth for about 5 years. Size of vocabulary, appropriate use of sentence constituents, number of utterances, proportion of phrases, inflection, all grew robustly throughout 5 years of cross-fostering. The growth was patterned growth and the patterns were consistent across chimpanzees. Wherever there are comparable measurements, the patterns of growth for cross-fostered chimpanzees paralleled the characteristic patterns reported for human infants.

More advanced developments appeared with each succeeding year of cross-fostering. The proof that Moja, Tatu, and Dar had not yet reached any limit at 3 years is their growth during the 4th year, and the proof that they had not yet reached a limit at 4 years is the growth during the 5th year. Nevertheless, after 3 years of cross-fostering, they had clearly fallen behind human 3-year-olds, and they fell further behind after 4 years, and still further behind after 5 years. Chimpanzees should be even further behind human children after 6 years of cross-fostering, but by the same token, they should continue to advance and at 6 years they should be ahead of themselves at 5 years.

Sign language studies of cross-fostered chimpanzees reveal robust growth and development. Further intellectual development should continue until sexual maturity, which takes more than 12 years. Much more can be accomplished in future studies with long-term support.

MODULAR APPROACHES

Traditionally, comparative psychologists have analyzed language into theoretically defined components, such as concept formation or rules of order, and then studied each component separately. In this modular tradition scientists train, or attempt to train, nonhuman animals to perform arbitrary tasks that theory relates to hypothetical cognitive functions. Success at an experimentally isolated, concrete task is evidence that this or that nonhuman being possesses this or that abstract, cognitive function. The conclusions depend entirely on the theoretical reasoning that ties the task to the cognitive target.

In this modular spirit, Harlow used his learning set procedure (chap. 13) to train rhesus monkeys to solve oddity problems. In oddity problems the monkeys had to choose the correct object from among three alternatives. Presented with two circles and a triangle, the monkey had to choose the triangle. Presented with two green squares and one red square, the monkey had to choose the red square. Harlow (1958) argued that, "We would be very much surprised if there is any fundamental difference in the learning of the oddity problem and the learning of differential equations—other than that of complexity" (p. 288).

The success of Project Washoe stimulated modular studies of a variety of nonhuman animals (e.g., Herman, Richards, & Wolz, 1984; Matsuzawa, 1985; Pepperberg, 1990; Premack, 1971; Rumbaugh, 1977; Savage-Rumbaugh, 1984; Schusterman & Gisiner, 1988; Terrace et al., 1980), each study with its own theoretically defined components, highly specific tasks, and relentless application of operant conditioning. In modular studies, of course, it would be pointless to avoid operant conditioning or any other training techniques, regardless of how foreign these techniques would be in a human nursery. The entire performance usually consists of requests for goods and services or answers to questions with goods or services as reward.

Appropriately, the "symbol systems" of modular studies are usually synthetic and deliberately designed to be different from any naturally occurring human language. The more arbitrary the task, the stronger the argument that mastery depends on some abstract, cognitive function. In the typical "language-training" experiment, animals only have access to their apparatus-based symbols during formal testing sessions and formal tests usually represent the entire population of relevant responses. Conversation and communication are irrelevant. Comparisons with what human beings actually do or say are equally irrelevant. Growth and development is also irrelevant because investigators test only one module, or only one module at a time in an arbitrary sequence. The modular approach is very different from the developmental approach of cross-fostering.

Modular studies often make grand theoretical claims like Harlow's claim about oddity problems and differential equations, but they are always claims about aptitudes and capacities. Both investigators and commentators find it easy to label them as studies of "ape language" or "animal language," hence set apart from language proper.

Modular Semantics

In a typical modular study, Premack invented an artificial system of plastic tokens to test his chimpanzee Sarah. Figure 14.3 illustrates Premack's "features analysis of apple" (Premack, 1971, pp. 224–226). At the top of Fig. 14.3, the object on the left represents an actual example of an apple and the object on the right represents the flat plastic token, colored blue and shaped like a triangle, that represented "apple" in Premack's token language. The first pair of columns in the figure

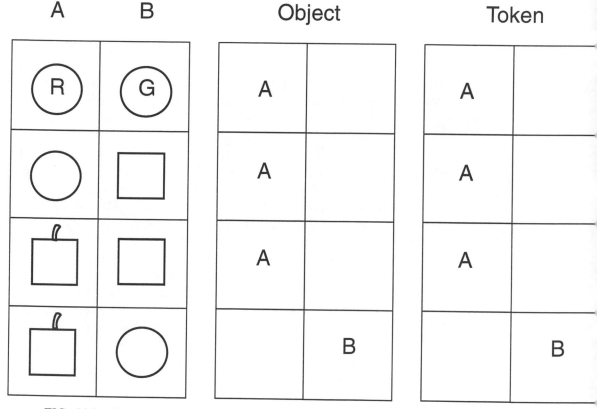

FIG. 14.3. Features analysis of "apple" (after Premack, 1971). Copyright © 1997 by R. Allen Gardner.

represent a series of tests in which Sarah had to choose between the following alternatives: (a) a red-colored patch versus a green-colored patch, (b) a round shape versus a square shape, (c) a square shape with a stemlike protuberance at the top versus a plain square shape, and finally, (d) a square shape with a stemlike protuberance at the top versus a round shape. The second pair of columns represents the choices that Sarah made when an actual apple was present, and the third pair of columns represents the choices that Sarah made when the apple object was removed and replaced by the apple token. She made the same choices for both, proving to Premack that the object and the token were equivalent for her.

What would happen if someone presented a 3-year-old human child with the same series of choices? In the experience of most toddlers only some apples are red. Apples also come in green, yellow, and many shades in between. Some apples are more than one color at the same time. Peeled or sliced apples are white until they sit for a while and become brownish. Apples also come in many shapes, particularly when cut up for eating. Only some apples have stems, and so on. Premack's feature analysis of apple may appeal to traditional Aristotelian philosophers, but it has little to do with the experience of a human child or a cross-fostered chimpanzee growing up in a human world.

Outside of certain special laboratory conditions, the natural world resists Aristotelian attempts to divide it into true and false, red and nonred, apple and nonapple, fruit and nonfruit, and so on. For certain natural philosophers, this only means that the modular approach is more faithful to the underlying truths of philosophy. Yet the terms of natural languages mostly represent fuzzy categories that are faithful to the variegated, overlapping categories of the natural world (Zadeh & Kacprzyk, 1992). Moreover, human speakers and signers of natural languages use these fuzzy terms with great ease, beginning in infancy. This prominent characteristic of the human use of natural language is, perhaps, the clearest evidence that traditional Aristotelian logic is irrelevant to human language.

As early as 1923, Bertrand Russell said:

> Let us consider the various ways in which common words are vague. . . . [Aristotle's] law of the excluded middle is true when precise symbols are employed, but it is not true when symbols are vague, as, in fact, all symbols are. All words describing sensible qualities have the same kind of vagueness which belongs to the word 'red'. This vagueness exists also, though in a lesser degree, in the quantitative words which science has tried hardest to make precise, such as metre or second. . . . (pp. 84–92)

Modular Conversation

Savage-Rumbaugh and her associates (Greenfield & Savage-Rumbaugh, 1990; Savage-Rumbaugh, McDonald, Sevcik, Hopkins, & Rubert, 1986) have made particularly strong claims for their modular studies of the *bonobo*, Kanzi. Bonobo is the common name of an animal that seemed at one time to be a pygmy variety of chimpanzee. Modern taxonomists distinguish two separate species, the bonobo (*Pan paniscus*) and the true chimpanzee (*Pan troglodytes*). Genetically and physiologically, bonobos are more specialized and further removed than chimpanzees from the main hominid line, though not so far removed as gorillas and orangutans (Stanyon et al., 1986).

Kanzi communicated with human beings by pointing at abstract forms displayed on a large response panel. Savage-Rumbaugh and her associates called these forms "lexigrams," "words," "elements," and "symbols," interchangeably. When Kanzi pointed at someone or touched someone present, this was transcribed as if he had pointed at a lexigram for "person." Nearly all Kanzi's lexigrams stand for different kinds of foods, drinks, destinations, or services (Savage-Rumbaugh et al., 1986, Table 1) in contrast to the varied vocabularies of Washoe, Moja, Tatu, and Dar (B. T. Gardner et al., 1989, Table 3.2).

Earlier work in the Rumbaugh laboratory with chimpanzees used a computer-assisted device that recorded all responses, automatically (Rumbaugh, Gill, & von Glasersfeld, 1973). Because the computer-assisted device became too cumbersome for use outside of a cage, it was mostly replaced by a folding panel with painted patches representing the array of lexigrams. When Kanzi moved from place to place, his trainers folded the response panel for portability and opened it up and spread it out again when they were ready to receive Kanzi's next utterance.

Without automatic recording, records of Kanzi's lexigram utterances depended on observer reports like the records of the signed utterances of Washoe, Moja, Pili, Tatu, and Dar. Like other serious investigators, Savage-Rumbaugh et al. (1986) saw that this procedure requires some evaluation of observer reliability. Accordingly, they videotaped a sample of Kanzi's sessions with the response panel when he was in his 4th year. Independent transcriptions of the videotape agreed with the written reports of observers on the scene for 80% of individual lexigrams (Savage-Rumbaugh et al., 1986, p. 217).

When they were also 4 years old, very similar videotaped samples of Dar and Tatu yielded interobserver agreement of 84% and 81% for individual signs (R. A. Gardner & B. T. Gardner, 1994, pp. 217–218). This makes three comparable videotape records, two for cross-fostered chimpanzees using sign language, and one for a laboratory bonobo touching lexigrams on a panel. All three were made under comparable conditions with comparable interobserver reliability when the subjects were at comparable ages. In their taped records, Tatu averaged 441 signed utterances per hour and Dar averaged 479 signed utterances per hour. In his tapes Kanzi averaged 10.2 lexigram utterances per hour.

In Tatu's tapes 35% of her utterances consisted of combinations of two or more signs, and in Dar's tapes 49% of his utterances consisted of combinations of two or more signs. Savage-Rumbaugh has not yet published the proportion of phrases in Kanzi's videotaped sample, but Greenfield and Savage-Rumbaugh (1990) described a sample of Kanzi's utterances written down by observers on the scene when he was 60–69 months old. In this larger and later sample, Kanzi averaged 10.1 utterances per hour and 10.4% of these contained two or more elements.

There are several differences that could explain why Dar and Tatu were so much more fluent than Kanzi. First, bonobos are further removed from the hominid line than chimpanzees (Stanyon et al., 1986). Perhaps they have less aptitude for conversation. Second, the lexigram panel impedes the communication of any species. Greenfield and Savage-Rumbaugh (1990) report that Kanzi's human trainers, themselves, "most frequently inserted only one or two lexigrams per sentence, reflecting the mechanical difficulty of the lexigram mode" (p. 568). Third, the laboratory regimen of modular training and testing, itself, probably depresses spontaneous communication.

A ROBUST PHENOMENON

In October 1970, after 51 months in Reno, when Washoe was about 5 years old, she went to the University of Oklahoma with Roger Fouts (R. S. Fouts & D. H. Fouts, 1989). In November 1972, we began a second venture in cross-fostering. The objectives were essentially the same, but there were several improvements in method. For example, Washoe was nearly 1 year old when she arrived in Reno. A newborn subject would have been more appropriate, but newborn chimpanzees are very scarce and none were offered to us at the time. After Project Washoe, it was easier for us to obtain newborn chimpanzees from laboratories.

Replication

For the scientific objectives of cross-fostering, the replication with Moja, Pili, Tatu, and Dar was essential to verify the original discoveries with Washoe. The second project also included many improvements over Project Washoe.

The chimpanzees of the second project interacted with each other and this, in itself, added a new dimension to the cross-fostering. In a human household, children help in the care of their younger siblings who, in their turn, learn a great deal from older siblings. Sibling relationships are also a common feature of the family life of wild chimpanzees. In the wild, older offspring stay with their mothers while their younger siblings are growing up and they share in the care of their little brothers and sisters. Close bonds are established among the older and younger members of the same family who remain allies for life. Equally significant for cross-fostering, the younger siblings follow and imitate their big sisters and big brothers (Goodall, 1986).

Seven-year-old Flint for example, followed and imitated his young adult brother, Faben, in a way that would certainly be described as hero worship if they had been human brothers. Faben was partially paralyzed as an aftereffect of polio and had a peculiar and striking way of supporting his lame arm with one foot while he scratched the lame arm with the good arm. During our 1971 visit to Gombe, we Gardners observed how Flint copied even this peculiar scratching posture of his brother Faben.

In order to capitalize on the relationships between older and younger foster siblings, we started them newborn, but at intervals, so that there would be age differences. Starting the subjects at intervals in this way also had the practical advantage of allowing us to add human participants to the project more gradually. In each family group, there was always a core of experienced human participants for the new recruits to consult as well as a stock of records and films to study. This helped us achieve the necessary stability and continuity in the foster families. Fifteen years after the start of Project Washoe there were still five human participants who had been long-term members of Washoe's original foster family.

The second project became a fairly extensive enterprise by the time that there were three chimpanzee subjects. At that point, the laboratory moved from the original suburban home to a secluded site that used to be a guest ranch. The chimpanzees lived in the cabins that formerly housed ranch hands. Some members of the human families lived in the guest apartments and the rancher's quarters. The human bedrooms were wired to intercoms in the chimpanzee cabins so that at least one human adult monitored each cross-fosterling throughout each night. There were great old trees and pastures, corrals and barns, to play in. There were also special rooms for observation and testing as well as office and shop facilities. The place was designed to keep the subjects under cross-fostering conditions until they were nearly grown up, perhaps long enough for them to begin to care for their own offspring.

Throughout the second project, several human members of the family were deaf themselves, or were the offspring of deaf parents. Others had already learned ASL and had used it extensively with members of the deaf community. With the deaf participants it was always sign language only, whether or not there were chimpanzees present. The native signers were the best models of ASL, for the human participants who were learning ASL as a second language as well as for the chimpanzees who were learning it as a first language. The native signers were also better observers because it was easier for them to recognize babyish forms of ASL. Along with their own fluency they had a background of experience with human infants who were learning their first signs of ASL.

Loulis

After she left Reno, Washoe continued to sign, not only to humans but to other chimpanzees whether or not there were any human beings in sight (R. S. Fouts & D. H. Fouts, 1989). This is more remarkable when we consider the procedure of Project Loulis. When Loulis was 10 months old he was adopted by 14-year-old Washoe, shortly after she lost her own newborn infant. To show that Washoe could teach signs to an infant without human intervention, Roger Fouts introduced a drastic procedure. All human signing was forbidden when Loulis was present. Because Loulis and Washoe were almost inseparable for the first few years, this meant that Washoe lost almost all her input from human signers. It was a deprivation procedure for Washoe. Later, Moja joined the group in Oklahoma, and still later Tatu and Dar joined the group in Ellensburg, Washington. The cross-fostered chimpanzees were allowed to sign to each other; indeed there was no way to stop them. They became part of Project Loulis.

Washoe taught signs to Loulis the way we taught her when she was an infant. During the first few days after Loulis arrived, Washoe often turned toward him signing COME, approaching him, and finally grasping his arm and drawing him close. During the next 5 days she signed COME and only approached without touching him. After about a week, Washoe only signed COME as she turned toward Loulis and faced him until he came to her. Washoe also molded Loulis' hands to form signs. In one observation, as a human friend was bringing candy, Washoe repeated the FOOD sign, jiggling about and grunting with excitement. Loulis was watching her. Abruptly, Washoe stopped signing, molded Loulis' hand into a FOOD sign and moved his molded hand to his lips. Washoe formed the GUM sign with her hands, but placed it on Loulis' cheek. She also formed DRINK with her own hand and brought it to Loulis' lips, and formed HAT with her own hands and brought it to Loulis' head. In still another observation, Washoe placed a small chair in front of Loulis and repeated the CHAIR sign while watching him intently. Notice that Washoe always used feed forward rather than feed backward methods. Loulis learned more than

50 signs from the cross-fostered chimpanzees during the 5 years in which they were his only models and tutors. Meanwhile, Washoe, herself, learned some new signs from Moja, Tatu, and Dar (R. S. Fouts, D. H. Fouts, & Van Cantfort, 1989).

As Loulis grew older and moved freely by himself from room to room in the laboratory, there were more opportunities for the human beings to sign to the other chimpanzees when Loulis was not in sight. As expected, however, the rule against signing to Loulis had a generally negative effect on all human signing. There was little incentive for the research assistants to become fluent in ASL, and only a few of the most senior personnel acquired any signing facility. Thus, whether or not Loulis was in sight, there was little human signing to be seen in the laboratory. Human signing was almost completely withdrawn for 5 years.

Washoe, Moja, Tatu, and Dar continued to sign to each other and also attempted to engage human beings in conversation throughout the period of deprivation. The cross-fostered chimpanzees signed among themselves, even when there was no human being present and the conversations were recorded with remotely controlled cameras. Mainly the cross-fosterlings signed to each other about activities such as play, grooming, and moving together from room to room (R. S. Fouts & D. H. Fouts, 1989).

Once introduced and integrated into daily life, sign language was robust and self-supporting. The regimen that the Foutses enforced to demonstrate that the infant Loulis could learn signs from Washoe, Moja, Tatu, and Dar, was a drastic procedure for the cross-fosterlings. It slowed the growth of their sign language, but it proved that sign language, once acquired by cross-fostered chimpanzees, becomes a permanent and robust aspect of their behavior.

CHAPTER 15

Concepts and Communication

W hen Washoe was 27 months old, she made a hole in the then flimsy inner wall of her house trailer. The hole was located high up in the wall at the foot of her bed. Before we repaired the hole, she managed to lose a toy in the hollow space between the inner and outer walls. When Allen Gardner arrived that evening, she attracted his attention to an area of the wall down below the hole at the level of her bed, signing OPEN OPEN many times over that area. He easily understood her problem and fished out the toy. It was exciting to realize that a chimpanzee had used a human language to communicate new and unexpected information. Soon situations of this sort became commonplace. For example, Washoe's playground was in the garden behind a single-story house. High in her favorite tree, Washoe was often the first to know who had arrived at the front of the house and her companions on the ground learned to rely on her to tell them who was arriving and departing.

COMMUNICATION AND INFORMATION

Washoe could tell her human companions things that they did not already know. This is what *Clever Hans* could not do. Clever Hans was a German horse that seemed to do arithmetic by tapping out numbers with his hoof. Hardly anyone besides his owner believed that Clever Hans could really do arithmetic, but for a long time no one could figure out how he got the right answers. Not the circus trainers or the cavalry officers, not the veterinarians or the zoo directors, not even the philosophers and the linguists who studied the case could explain how Clever Hans did it. Eventually, an experimental psychologist, Oskar Pfungst (1911), unraveled the problem with the following test. Pfungst whispered one number into Clever Hans's left ear and Herr von Ost, the trainer, whispered a second number into the horse's right ear. When Clever Hans was the only one who knew the answer, he could not tap out the correct sums. He could not tell his human companions anything that they did not already know.

Now that he knew the source of information, Pfungst observed Herr von Ost more carefully. He soon noticed that the trainer always wore a hat with a large brim which he pointed down toward Clever Hans' hoof when it was time to start tapping and raised up again when it was time to stop tapping. Pfungst soon demonstrated that he could get whatever number he wanted from Clever Hans by lowering and raising the brim of his hat.

The truly interesting thing that Clever Hans was doing has become more clear in recent times with studies of *pragmatic devices* in everyday human conversation. The speech of normal conversation is embedded in other sorts of behavior—tone of voice, gestures, facial expressions—called pragmatic devices. Most structural theories of language (e.g., Chomsky, 1972) ignore pragmatic devices even though they are obviously criticial aspects of everyday communication. The meaning of a sentence can be completely altered by a lifted eyebrow or a shrugging shoulder, for example.

The glances of a human speaker and listener play a vital role in conversational turn taking. The listener looks at the face of the speaker, usually the lower face, presumably focusing on the mouth of the speaker. At the beginning of a turn, the speaker looks away from the listener and only looks back at the listener's face (a) when checking for approval or understanding, after which the speaker looks away again and continues to talk, and (b) when turning the initiative over to the listener, after which the new speaker looks away and the new listener gazes at the face of the speaker (Argyle & Cook, 1976, pp. 98–124; Kendon, 1967).

Apparently, Clever Hans had learned how to take turns in a European conversation. At the end of a question, German speakers looked down at Clever Hans' organ of communication, his hoof. At the end of an answer they looked up, often exclaiming their approval of the answer. All Clever Hans had to know was when to start his turn by tapping his hoof and when to end a turn by ending his tapping.

This explains why perfect strangers, even hatless strangers, could get correct answers from Clever Hans.

Since Pfungst (1911), controls for *Clever Hans errors* have been standard procedure in comparative psychology. As late as 1997, forced choice tests of comprehension by human infants continue to omit such controls (for example, Girouard, Ricard, & Décarie, 1997; Hill, Collis, & Lewis, 1997; Shwe & Markman, 1997). Students of child development seem to believe that, whereas horses and chimpanzees may be sensitive to subtle nonverbal communication, human children are totally insensitive to pragmatics.

A classic study by Fraser, Bellugi, and Brown (1963) is typical of many studies of human children. Fraser et al. showed pairs of pictures to individual 3-year-old children. Each pair of pictures was untitled, of course, and illustrated a grammatical contrast, such as "the dog is biting the cat" versus "the cat is biting the dog." As the experimenters showed each pair of pictures, they asked the child to point at the picture that illustrated one of the contrasts. Fraser et al. comment that "S sometimes pointed quickly, then reflected and corrected himself; the last definite pointing is the one we always scored" (p. 129). As they were in full view of the children, the experimenters could indicate the correct picture by gaze direction alone, or by approving and disapproving facial expressions. They could do this without uttering a word, without being any more aware of their hints than the baffled experts who tested Clever Hans.

What is wrong with the procedure of Fraser et al. is that the observers knew the correct answer before the children replied. The tests described in this chapter kept the observers from knowing the correct answer until after the chimpanzee responded. As in the case of Washoe telling us where she lost her toy and who was coming, in these tests the chimpanzees knew something that the observer did not know. They had information to communicate.

VOCABULARY TESTS

Early in Project Washoe, we devised vocabulary tests to demonstrate that chimpanzees could use the signs of ASL to communicate information. For Washoe's first test, we mounted color photographs (mostly cut from magazine illustrations) on 8.5 × 5.5 inch cards. An experimenter selected a random sample of 6 to 10 cards and placed them facedown in a cupboard of Washoe's trailer the night before a test session. Early in the morning an observer held up the cards one by one and asked Washoe to name them. For each card, the observer wrote down the first sign that Washoe made and then looked at the card and scored the response as correct or incorrect.

In order to extend the test to three-dimensional exemplars, we put objects into specially designed $12 \times 13 \times 9.5$ inch plywood boxes. One side of each box was clear Plexiglas; the other sides were opaque. An experimenter selected exemplars randomly from a pool of photographs and objects and placed them one by one in a box. Again, the observer exposed the window side of the box to Washoe without looking inside and wrote down the first sign that Washoe made. We soon abandoned the box test because it was too cumbersome, but it gave us a valuable piece of information about the difference between photographs and three-dimensional exemplars.

Three-dimensional exemplars of objects like bibs and brushes fit easily into a small box, but exemplars of CAT, DOG, COW, BIRD, and CAR are another matter. In order to present both photographs and three-dimensional exemplars for all categories, we used high-quality figurines and models as well as photographs for the larger objects. We soon noticed that the expensive replicas produced significantly more errors than the photographs. Washoe's favorite error for replicas of cats, dogs, cows, birds, and cars was BABY, but she rarely called any of the photographs of these items BABY. In a sense, she treated the three-dimensional replicas as less real than the photographic replicas (B. T. Gardner & R. A. Gardner, 1971, pp. 160–161).

On the basis of these results, we developed a procedure that used photographs exclusively. For a more detailed description of the testing procedures and results, see R. A. Gardner and B. T. Gardner (1984) and Campbell-Jones (1974).

Objectives

The first objective of these tests was to demonstrate that the chimpanzee subjects could communicate information under conditions in which the only source of information available to a human observer was the signing of the chimpanzees. To accomplish this, nameable objects were photographed on 35-mm slides. During testing, the slides were back-projected on a screen that could be seen by the chimpanzee subject, but not by the observer. The slides were projected in a random sequence that changed from test to test so that neither the observer nor the subject could memorize the sequence.

The second objective of these tests was to demonstrate that *independent observers* agreed with each other. To accomplish this, there were two observers. The first observer (O1) served as interlocutor in the testing room with the chimpanzee subject. The second observer

(O2) was stationed in a second room and observed the subject from behind one-way glass, but could not see the projection screen. The two observers gave independent readings; they could not see each other and they could not compare observations until after the test.

The third objective of these tests was to demonstrate that the chimpanzees used the signs to refer to *natural language categories*—that the sign DOG could refer to any dog, FLOWER to any flower, SHOE to any shoe, and so on. This was accomplished by preparing a large library of slides to serve as exemplars. Some of the slides appeared in pretests that served to adapt subjects, observers, and experimenters to the testing procedure. The slides that were reserved for the tests never appeared in pretests so that the first time that a particular chimpanzee subject saw any one of the test slides was on a test trial and each test slide appeared on one and only one test trial. Consequently, it was impossible for a chimpanzee to memorize particular pairs of exemplars and signs. Scores on these tests depended on the ability to name new exemplars of natural language categories.

Teaching and Testing

In most laboratory studies of nonhuman beings, the same procedures serve both for teaching and for testing. A monkey or a rat, for example, learns trial-by-trial to associate one stimulus with reward and the other with an empty food dish, and the very same trials are scored for correct and incorrect choices and plotted to show learning curves. Washoe, Moja, Tatu, and Dar spent virtually all of their waking hours in the company of some human member of their foster families. During that time, their exposure to objects and the ASL names for objects was very large compared with the brief samples of the vocabulary tests. These tests were as different from the routines of the rest of their daily lives as similar testing would be for young children. For caged subjects, a session of testing is probably the most interesting thing that happens in the course of a laboratory day. For Washoe, Moja, Tatu, and Dar, most of the activities of daily life were more attractive than their formal tests. The cross-fostering regime precluded any attempt to starve them like rats or pigeons to make them earn their daily rations by taking tests.

Getting free-living, cross-fostered chimpanzees to do their best under these stringent conditions required ingenuity and patience. A basic strategy was to establish the testing routine by a regular program of pretests that were short, usually less then 30 minutes, and infrequent, rarely more than two sessions per week. We used the pretests to pilot variations in procedure and to ensure that experimenters, observers, and subjects were all highly practiced at the procedure before the tests.

Rewards

Early in Project Washoe, we learned that when she was too anxious to earn her reward—when she was too hungry or the reward too desirable—then we could expect no more from Washoe than the absolute minimum amount or quality of response necessary to get the reward. If used, food rewards had to be very small—half of a raisin or a quarter of a peanut—more symbolic than nourishing. Attempting to reward Washoe for correct replies in the testing situation created procedural difficulties, which we avoided with Moja, Tatu, and Dar by rewarding them for prompt, clear replies, regardless of correctness. Unlike Washoe, the other subjects were distracted by the treats and would often ask for the rewards by name at critical points in the procedure, so that O1 and O2 could not tell whether the chimpanzees were asking for a treat or naming a picture. Consequently, we abandoned this procedure entirely for Tatu and Dar, and they rarely received any rewards after we discovered this problem during the initial stages of pretesting.

Additional personnel frequently monitored both the procedure in the observation room and the procedure in the testing room (Fig. 15.1). Whether those serving as O1 were aware of it or not, they often revealed their approval or disapproval of a cross-fosterling's performance by smiling or frowning and by nodding or shaking their heads as well as by signing such things as GOOD GIRL and SMART CHIMP. Gestures and signing evoked more communication from the cross-fosterlings, just as edible treats evoked begging (chap. 8).

ITEMS AND EXEMPLARS

Here the term *vocabulary item* refers to a category of objects—such as shoes, flowers, dogs—named by a particular sign; and the term *exemplar* refers to a unique member of such a category in these tests—the 16 × 11 inch back-projected image of a 35-mm color slide.

Photography

Outside of the testing situation, we could use the pictures in ordinary books and magazines—even when the pictures contained objects of many different kinds—because we could point to particular objects

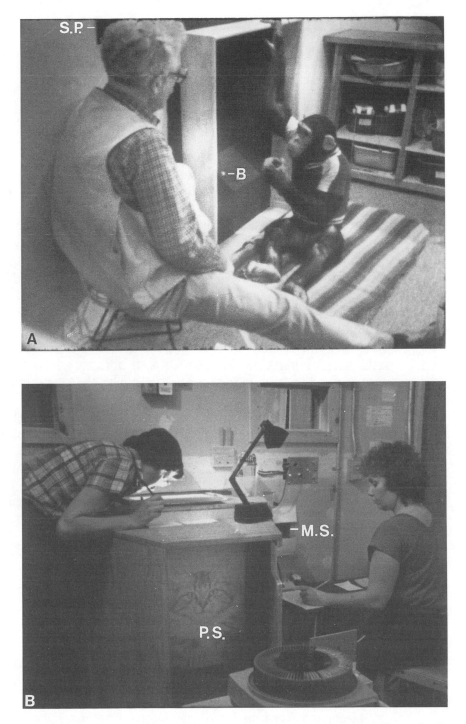

FIG. 15.1. Testing Apparatus. Top: O1 can see Dar's signs but cannot see the projection screen. Dar pushes button (B) to show himself the pictures. Bottom: O2 can see the chimp through one-way glass, but cannot see the projection screen (P.S.). Experimenter checks procedure and receives messages directly from O2 and—via the message slot (M.S.)—from O1. Copyright © 1997 by R. Allen Gardner.

or ask questions such as, WHAT BIRD EAT? Under the blind conditions of the tests, however, the objects had to dominate the field of view. The backgrounds had to be very plain, since vividly colored backgrounds were often so distracting that the chimpanzees named the background colors instead of the objects. Note in the examples of Fig. 15.2 that the objects filled the screen regardless of their normal relative size, whether they were bugs, shoes, or cars.

Some of the things the chimpanzees often named, such as grass or water, seemed impossible to present in test slides because they lack any characteristic shape and appear as meaningless forms against a blank background. Some otherwise shapeless objects, such as coffee or facial tissues, made acceptable test slides because they appear in distinctive containers. Still other objects, such as houses and windows, seemed impossible to photograph without backgrounds or fore-grounds that contain distracting extraneous detail. An important function of the pretests was to try out different photographic tech-niques. It was in this way that we learned to avoid vividly colored backgrounds because the chimpanzees sometimes named the color of the background instead of the featured object.

We had to learn to look at the slides with the eyes of our subjects. For example, dramatic slides of leafy trees yielded mixed results, but shortly after Christmas one year, Tatu suggested something better. As she played with her discarded Christmas tree she named it to herself many times. It turned out that Christmas trees, photographed close up against the sky, made highly acceptable exemplars both for Tatu and for Dar. The tops of live evergreens photographed with a telephoto lens were also highly acceptable. Even though evergreens come in some variety, we wanted to demonstrate that chimpanzees can also name deciduous trees under test conditions. Once more, Tatu showed us the way. That winter, on outings in the woods, Tatu frequently called our attention to trees by signing THAT TREE at their bare trunks. With this hint, we discovered that photographs of bare trees in winter made excellent exemplars.

Novelty

Each slide was unique and each slide appeared only once on each test or pretest. An exemplar could be unique because the chimpanzee subject had never seen that object before or because it was the first time that the subject had ever seen a photograph of that particular object or because it was the first time that the subject had ever seen that particular photograph of that particular object. When different exemplars con-sisted of different photographs of the same object, each was unique in

FIG. 15.2.   Some of the photos used in the vocabulary tests. Copyright © 1997 by R. Allen Gardner.

that the object appeared (a) at a different distance, (b) at a different angle, (c) against a different background, (d) under different light, or (e) in a different arrangement of a group, such as fruits, nuts, or shoes. At least three, but usually four, of the five dimensions varied from slide to slide. All except four of the slides used in all of Tatu's and Dar's tests were photographs of objects that neither chimpanzee had ever seen before, either directly or in photographs.

Target Signs

The correct sign for each vocabulary item was designated in advance of the tests. That sign and that sign only was scored as correct for that item. Although there were aspects of the pictures for which superordinate terms, such as FOOD, or descriptive terms, such as BLACK, might be correct or incorrect, neither the presence or absence nor the correct or incorrect use of such terms was considered in the scoring of these tests.

Most of the replies consisted of a single sign which was the name of an object. Sometimes, the single noun in the reply appeared in a descriptive phrase, as when Tatu signed RED BERRY for a picture of cherries, or when Dar signed THAT BIRD for a picture of a duck. These replies contained only one object name and that was the sign that was scored as correct or incorrect. Occasionally, a test reply contained more than one object name, as when Washoe signed FLOWER TREE LEAF FLOWER for a picture of a bunch of daisies. In such cases, the observers designated a single sign for scoring (usually the first) without looking at the picture themselves. For each trial and each observer, then, one sign and one sign only in each report was used to score agreement between O1 and O2 and agreement between the reports of the observers and the name of the exemplar.

Table 15.1 lists the vocabulary items that appeared in the tests of Washoe, Moja, Tatu, and Dar. Differences among the subjects in this table reflect differences in their vocabularies as well as a strategy of overlapping tests that sampled the range of picturable objects in the vocabularies without making the tests excessively long. For each test, we chose four exemplars of each vocabulary item to illustrate the range of objects that a subject could name with the same sign. Different breeds represented CAT and DOG, different species represented BIRD and BUG, different makes and models represented CAR, and so on (see Fig. 15.2). The number of vocabulary items and the resulting number of trials (items × exemplars) appear in Table 15.2.

TABLE 15.1
Vocabulary Items in the Tests of Four Chimpanzees

Items	Chimpanzees				Items	Chimpanzees			
Animates	W	M	T	D	*Foods*	W	M	T	D
BABY	+		+	+	APPLE		+	+	+
BIRD	+	+	+	+	BANANA		+	+	+
BUG	+	+	+	+	BERRY		+	+	+
CAT	+	+	+	+	CARROT			+	+
COW	+	+	+	+	CEREAL		+		
DOG	+	+	+	+	CHEESE	+		+	+
HORSE		+			CORN		+	+	+
					FRUIT	+			
					GRAPES		+		
Plants					GUM		+		
FLOWER	+	+	+	+	ICECREAM		+	+	+
LEAF	+	+			MEAT	+		+	+
TREE	+	+	+	+	NUT	+	+	+	+
					ONION		+		
Clothing					ORANGE		+		
CLOTHES	+				PEA/BEAN		+		
HAT	+	+	+	+	PEACH		+	+	+
PANTS	+				SANDWICH			+	+
SHOE	+	+	+	+	TOMATO	+			
Grooming					*Drinks*				
BRUSH	+	+	+		COFFEE			+	+
COMB		+	+		DRINK	+			
HANKIE			+		MILK		+		
LIPSTICK			+		SODAPOP		+	+	+
OIL	+		+	+					
TOOTHBRUSH	+	+	+	+	*Other*				
WIPER	+				BALL			+	+
					BOOK	+	+		
Sensory					CAR	+		+	+
LISTENS	+	+			HAMMER	+			
LOOKS	+	+	+		KEY	+	+	+	
SMELLS	+				KNIFE		+		
					PEEKABOO			+	
					PIPE	+			
					SMOKE	·+	+		

Note.   W = Washoe, M = Moja, T = Tatu, D = Dar.

TEST RESULTS

Table 15.2 shows how the tests accomplished their major objectives. The agreement between O1 and O2 was high for all seven tests; except for Moja, the agreement ranged between 86% and 95% and all agree-

TABLE 15.2
Scores on the Vocabulary Tests of Four Chimpanzees

Chimpanzee Subject		Washoe		Moja	Tatu		Dar	
Test		1	2	1	1	2	1	2
Vocabulary Items (#)		16	32	35	25	34	21	27
Trials (#)		64	128	140	100	136	84	108
Inter-Observer Agreement (%)		95	86	70[a]	89	91	90	94
Scored Correct by <	Observer 1 (%)	86	72	54[b]	84	80	79	83
	Observer 2 (%)	88	71	54[b]	85	79	80	81
Expected* (%)		15	4	4	6	4	7	5

*assuming that the observer was guessing on the basis of perfect memory for all previous trials that that observer had seen (see text).
[a]based on 135 trials; O2 missed 5 trials. [b]based on 132 trials; 8 unscorable trials.

ment was far beyond *chance expectancy*. Note that this is the agreement for both correct and incorrect signs. Clearly, the signs made by the chimpanzees were distinct and intelligible. The agreement between the signs reported by O1 and O2 and the correct names of the categories is also high; except for Moja, correct scores ranged between 71% and 88% and all scores were far beyond chance expectancy.

Chance Expectancy

The line labeled *expected* in Table 15.2 needs some explanation. From the point of view of Washoe, Moja, Tatu, and Dar, the chance of being correct by guessing alone would be $1/N$ where N is the number of vocabulary items on a test and all items have the same number of exemplars. For example, Tatu's first test had 25 items. With the usual four exemplars of each item, the total number of trials was 100. If Tatu was only guessing on each trial, but selected each guess from 1 of the 25 items on the test, then her average performance would be $1/25$ or 4 correct by chance alone. The $1/N$ estimate may be too low, because it only considers the guesses of the chimpanzees and fails to consider the possibility that the human observers could also be guessing. This is important because we can never know what the chimpanzees were signing; we only know what the observers reported. Indeed, a major objective of the tests was to verify the independent agreement between observers.

After each and every trial, we could have randomly reshuffled the 100 items on Tatu's first test. That procedure is called *random sampling with replacement* and the odds of guessing correctly would remain the same $1/25$ on each and every trial. The trouble with this version of random sampling is that some exemplars could reappear on more than one trial and some might never appear. To make sure that each exemplar appeared only once and also that each vocabulary item appeared exactly four times, we assigned all 100 exemplars to trials in a random but fixed sequence. This is called *random sampling without replacement.* The trouble with this procedure is that it makes probabilities shift during the course of the test. Because O1 and O2 knew that there were only four exemplars of each item on each test, they could have used this information to improve their guesses in later trials. The last trial is completely predictable, because there is only one exemplar of only one item left in the series. The next to the last trial may be completely predictable, but there are at most two vocabulary items still to appear, and so on.

In random sampling without replacement, the probabilities of later events in a fixed sequence depend on earlier events. Thus, gamblers who can remember the cards in the deck that have already appeared can win significant amounts at games such as blackjack. Dealers in casinos routinely reshuffle the cards at the 50% to 75% point in a deck to defeat "card counters."

As small as the effect of sampling without replacement might be in these vocabulary tests, good scientific practice demands an exact estimate of chance. Accordingly, Patterson, B. T. Gardner, and R. A. Gardner (1986) developed a general mathematical expression to calculate the effect of random selection without replacement on chance expectancy under the conditions of these tests. As applied to the vocabulary tests, this expression assumes that both observers (a) saw each slide after each trial, (b) had perfect memory for the number of exemplars of each vocabulary item that had appeared before the beginning of each trial, and (c) guessed the correct sign on the basis of the number of exemplars of each vocabulary item that remained on the test. The expected chance scores for each test appear in Table 15.2. In all cases, this estimate is negligibly small compared to the number of correct responses. Since O1 and O2 reported extralist intrusions (signs that were not on the target lists), they were using a less efficient strategy. Small as they are, the values in the expected line of Table 15.2 overestimate chance expectancy.

The expected score for Washoe's first test is small but appreciably larger than the expected scores for the other tests in Table 15.2 for two reasons. First, this test was shorter than the other tests and predictability depends on the number of vocabulary items—the fewer the items the greater the predictability. Second, and more significantly for this discussion, predictability increases as we approach the end of the test. In all of the tests in Table 15.2, except for Washoe's first test, each individual observer served for only half of the trials. We did this to demonstrate that at least four different human observers could read the signs of the chimpanzees. The effect on chance expectancy is the same as a dealer in a casino reshuffling the cards halfway through the deck. The smaller number of items and the assignment of the same two observers to all trials of Washoe's first test account for the higher, but still quite small, expected score on that test.

PRODUCTIVE TESTS VERSUS FORCED CHOICES

Because these were productive tests, Washoe, Moja, Tatu, and Dar could respond with any item in their vocabularies on any trial. This reduces the chance probability of correct responses to a negligibly small number. Tests in other laboratories have often used forced choice tests of understanding with very few response alternatives, usually only two, rarely more than four. With a small number of alternatives, subjects can succeed at these tests with strategies that are irrelevant to the cognitive objectives of the experiment. Once again, the scientist must think like a detective eliminating prime suspects.

For example, a classic test for extrasensory perception (ESP) uses a standard deck of 25 ESP cards consisting of five exemplars of each of five symbols. An experimenter shuffles the deck and then makes a list of the sequence of symbols. A percipient in another room attempts to perceive the sequence without looking at the cards. By chance the percipient should average $1/N$ or five hits on each run through the deck. Anything significantly greater than that means that the percipient has ESP. Careful experimenters average the number of hits over many runs through the deck to reduce the possibility of chance runs of success.

Tart (1976), arguing for ESP as well as for postive reinforcement, reasoned that percipients would improve their powers if the experimenter gave them positive feedback for every hit. Sure enough, under these conditions percipients got more hits as they progressed through the deck and their average score was greater than chance indicating that postive reinforcement heightens ESP. There is another prime suspect for the results in this case, however. Running through the deck in a fixed order is random sampling without replacement so a percipient can use information about past hits to improve later scores (Read, 1962).

A standard ESP deck of 25 cards samples without replacement every 25 trials. Suppose that Tart (1976) had used a rigorous Skinnerian procedure that ended each trial with a hit and a reward.

Suppose that he had allowed percipients to correct for misses. That is, when they missed a card Tart could have allowed a percipient to guess again until each trial ended with a hit. This is called a *correction procedure*. Suppose further that Tart had sampled without replacement every 5 trials instead of every 25 trials. It is easy to calculate the effect of the correction procedure together with random sampling every five trials. On the first trial of any set of five, chance would be 1/5 or 20%. On the second trial there would be only four possibilities left so chance would be 1/4 or 25%. On the third trial chance would be 1/3 or 33.3%, on the fourth trial 1/2 or 50%, and on the last trial there would be only one possibility so a percipient with ordinary human memory could always get a hit on the last trial. Average chance expectancy under these rigorous reinforcment conditions is 20% + 25% + 33.3% + 50% + 100% divided by five or 45.7%. Under these conditions, a percipient would have to average significantly more than 45.7% hits before a scientist could attribute the results to ESP.

It may seem more conventional to argue that pigeons can learn concepts from pictures by Skinnerian reinforcement than to argue that human clairvoyants can learn ESP by Skinnerian reinforcement, but the rules of evidence are the same. For example, Wasserman and his associates (Bhatt, Wasserman, Reynolds, & Knauss, 1988; Wasserman, 1993; Wasserman, Kiedinger, & Bhatt, 1988) presented four different conceptual categories of pictures—such as human beings, cats, flowers, or cars—and trained pigeons to peck at four different locations depending on which category appeared on a projection screen. They used trial-by-trial correction and sampling without replacement every four trials. They estimated chance as $1/N$ or 25% hits. The correct value, however, should be 25% + 33.3% + 50% + 100% divided by four, or 52%. Consequently, many of their demonstrations fail as evidence for conceptual transfer because correct performance was less than or indistinguishable from 52%. Some of their claims for transfer based on hierarchical categories actually show negative transfer when the pigeons were correct less than 52% of the time.

Chapter 3 described the original procedure that Skinner recommended to measure discrimination between stimuli. With pigeons, Skinner recommended presenting stimuli one at a time on a single response key. When S+ appears on the screen, the apparatus dispenses rewards for key-pecking during S+ periods and never dispenses rewards for key-pecking during S− periods. If the pigeon pecks at a higher rate during S+ periods than during S− periods, then, according to Skinnerian tradition, the pigeon is discriminating between S+ and S−. Jenkins (1965) showed that under these conditions pigeons can discriminate between S+ and S− periods without looking at the stimuli.

All they have to do is peck after reward and stop pecking after nonreward. In the feed forward view of this book, food in S+ evokes pecking and the lack of food in S− evokes other behavior even if the pigeon is blind.

In spite of Jenkins' (1965) analysis, respected experimenters frequently offer such measures as evidence of discrimination and even of categorical concepts as if Skinner's approval guarantees scientific validity. In a series of experiments, Herrnstein and his associates (Herrnstein, 1979, 1985) projected photographs of natural scenes on the key in a Skinner box. Exemplars of the target category appeared in half of the scenes but were absent from the other half of the scenes. The pigeons received food reward for pecking at exemplars of the target category but never received food when the target category was absent. With training, the pigeons pecked more often at exemplars of the target category than at other pictures. The pigeons could have done quite well without looking at the photographs; all they had to do was peck when rewarded and stop pecking when not rewarded. Jenkins described how proper control groups and transfer tests could provide valid evidence of discrimination in the Skinner box.

Forced-choice tests with very few alternatives create serious problems of measurement that productive tests avoid by allowing a large number of alternatives. The smaller the number of response alternatives, the cruder the measurement and the worse the effect of trial-by-trial reinforcement and sampling without replacement. R. Gardner and Gardner (1978, pp. 61–65, 68) discusses the problems of interpretation raised by forced-choice tests of understanding in chimpanzees.

SIGNS OF ASL

The field records summarized in B. T. Gardner et al. (1989, Table 3.2) show how closely the signs in the vocabularies of Washoe, Moja, Tatu, and Dar approximated the target signs of ASL that human companions modeled for them, allowing of course for childish diction. Fluent signers frequently visited the cross-fostering laboratory and observed the cross-fosterlings signing under naturalistic conditions. The double-blind testing procedures permitted more rigorous confirmation. Two fluent deaf signers, both then recent graduates of Gallaudet College, each served as O2 in Washoe's pretests in the summer of 1970. Each of these young men participated in two pretests at a time when each had observed Washoe for less than one hour. Their agreement with O1 (who had in each case years of experience with

Washoe) rose from 67% and 71% on their first session to 89% for both on their second session.

The task that these fluent signers faced was the same as the task of fluent English speakers identifying words in the speech of equally immature human children after equally brief preexposure to the immature speakers and under equally stringent conditions. These two outside observers who were expert at ASL, but unfamiliar with Washoe, read her signs fairly well at first and then improved markedly in their second test session. The first and second sessions contained different items so the improvement did not depend on the deaf observers learning specific vocabulary items. The initially good agreement with O1 together with the improvement indicates that Washoe's signs were intelligible to fluent signers with, perhaps, a childish or chimpanzee accent that they could learn fairly quickly.

CONCEPTS

To make sure that the signs referred to conceptual categories, all of the test trials were first trials; that is, the one and only test trial in which a slide appeared was the first time that that chimpanzee ever saw that slide. All of the specific stimulus values varied, as they do in natural language categories; that is to say, most human beings would agree that the exemplars in each set belong together. Apparently, Washoe, Moja, Tatu, and Dar agreed with this assignment of exemplars to conceptual categories.

Significant variation among exemplars and testing with true first trials are essential to the definition of natural language categories. More concerned with theoretical definitions of language than with conceptual behavior, the Rumbaughs and their associates (Rumbaugh, 1977; Savage-Rumbaugh, Pate, Lawson, Smith, & Rosenbaum, 1983) administered hundreds of trials of training and testing with identical exemplars or with minimally varied exemplars. To be sure, in their tests of chimpanzees the Rumbaughs concentrated on the arbitrariness of what they called "lexigrams" as used in arbitrarily fixed sequences. It seems likely that the Rumbaugh chimpanzees could have used natural language categories, given the opportunity to do so.

In 4 years of work with the chimpanzee Nim, Terrace (1979) never attempted any systematic tests at all. His work is unique in this field in that it was entirely restricted to adventitious naturalistic observation without any controls for Clever Hans errors, whatsoever. Terrace's claims that all of Nim's sign language could have been cued by his human companions only reflects Terrace's failure to conduct properly controlled tests.

COMMUNICATION AND LANGUAGE

If the development of human verbal behavior requires any significant expenditure of biological resources, then it must return some biological advantages to its possessors. Before it can return any profit, however, a biological trait must operate on the world in some way; it must be instrumental in obtaining benefit or avoiding harm. If clarifying one's ideas is biologically profitable, it must be because in some way clarified ideas provide superior means for operating in the biological world. As for establishing social relations, a system of displays and cries is sufficient to maintain group cohesiveness in most animals. The advantage of a wider variety of signals would seem to be the communication of more information. But, unless verbal behavior refers to objects and events in the external world, it cannot communicate information and it cannot have any such advantage. From this point of view, reference is the biological function of verbal behavior, and the function of grammar or structure in verbal behavior must be to enlarge the scope and to increase the precision of reference.

In the naturally occurring languages of the world, the pairing of words and signs with conceptual categories is arbitrary. This is amply demonstrated by the mutual unintelligibility of languages and the well-documented history of shifts in forms and usage. Washoe, Moja, Tatu, and Dar, if they had been human children—if they had been angels for that matter—could succeed in these vocabulary tests only by associating the signs of ASL with their referents. Angels may have other ways of associating responses with stimuli, but children and chimpanzees must learn arbitrary associations. Thus, to the extent that the communication of information depends on the arbitrary connection of terms to conceptual categories, then that biological function of a natural language depends on rote learning.

DUALITY OF PATTERNING

Hockett (1978) describes *duality of patterning* as one of the design features of human languages. The meaningful units or morphemes are composed of smaller units such as vowel and consonant sounds that are meaningless in themselves. There are structural rules for combining sounds or phonemes into meaningful units and there are different structural rules for combining the morphemes into messages. Duality of patterning was a significant source of errors in these vocabulary tests.

Errors often tell a great deal about basic processes. Sometimes more can be learned from errors than from correct responses. In their vocabulary tests, the cross-fostered chimpanzees were free to use any sign in their vocabularies. They chose their errors for themselves rather than from a set of forced choices chosen by the experimenters. The probability of any particular error, like the probability of any particular correct response, was very low, permitting us to detect patterns of errors. Most errors fell into one of two patterns: *conceptual errors* and *form errors.* Thus, DOG was a common error for a picture of a cat, SODAPOP for a picture of ice cream, and so on, showing that conceptual groups such as animals and foods were a major source of confusion. Similarly, signs made on the nose such as BUG and FLOWER were confused with each other, as were signs made on the hand such as SHOE and SODAPOP, showing that the *cheremic structure* of ASL was a source of errors the way the *phonemic structure* of English is the source of errors in the verbal behavior of human beings (R. A. Gardner & B. T. Gardner, 1984, pp. 393–398).

The daily laboratory procedure discouraged the cross-fosterlings from answering a question with a string of guesses, particularly during testing. When a reply contained more than one sign for an object, we scored the first object sign as the only reply. Inspecting the 14% of the replies that contained two or more names for objects, we found that Washoe, Moja, Tatu, and Dar made more errors on these trials than on the trials in which they only offered a single object name as a reply. They seemed to be groping about for the correct sign in these cases as if unsure of themselves.

Pairs of signs within these indecisive replies formed patterns. Conceptual pairs, such as CAT and DOG, or SODAPOP and ICECREAM, and form pairs, such as CAT and APPLE, or BUG and FLOWER, were the most common. Sometimes, pairs were repeated as in, CAT DOG CAT DOG, or BUG FLOWER BUG FLOWER. Sometimes, replies contained a string of related signs as when Washoe signed CAT BIRD DOG MAN for a picture of a kitten, or FLOWER TREE LEAF FLOWER for a picture of daisies.

There are several signs that are made by grasping points along the edge of one hand with the thumb and index finger of the active hand; the end of the thumb is grasped in BERRY, the upper edge of the palm in MEAT, the lower edge of the palm in OIL. In a typical case, Washoe signed OIL BERRY MEAT for a picture of frankfurters, as if the correct sign was on the tip of her fingers. Thus, not only the

correct replies, but the errors and the very dithering between alternatives depended on conceptual relations among the referents and cheremic relations among the signs of ASL.

Hockett (1978, pp. 275–276) points out that, when errors depend
on phonology as well as on semantics, we have evidence for duality
of patterning. Perhaps an example can make this point more clear.
Warden and Warner (1928) demonstrated that the German shepherd
dog Fellow, a star of movies and vaudeville, could understand instructions in spoken English. In the most critical tests, Fellow's master
spoke from behind a screen and instructed him to fetch objects from
the next room. Fellow was good at this task, but he also made
interesting errors—such as fetching a collar instead of a dollar—that
depend on the sounds of English. We would argue that only a chimpanzee that had learned the shapes of the ASL signs would confuse
CAT with APPLE or BUG with FLOWER. In their test errors as
well as in their use of cheremic *inflections* (Rimpau, R. A. Gardner,
& B. T. Gardner, 1989), the cross-fostered chimpanzees exhibited
Hockett's duality of patterning.

ETHOLOGY AND OPERATIONAL DEFINITION

Chapter 14 described the ethological considerations that dictated the
procedure of cross-fostering and the use of ASL as a naturally occurring human language. In this rich environment and with this rich
repertoire of ASL signs, the cross-fosterlings could name quite new
examples of a wide variety of objects. In spite of the sharp break with
traditional laboratory procedures, the ethologically sound laboratory
was entirely compatible with rigorous testing.

Members of the human foster family served as testers who could
get the chimpanzees to communicate information in signs. They could
do this without forcing the animals to beg for food. They responded
with social approval, which fed forward to more communication. By
separating communication from extrinsic reward, they widened the
range of communication. The chimpanzees could tell them about
many things that had nothing to do with eating or drinking. Given
the social relationship between the human adults and the cross-fostered chimpanzees, it was a relatively easy matter to construct a testing
situation in which the only source of information available to the
human testers was the signing of the chimpanzees.

Ethological consisiderations dictated the use of a naturally occurring human language that left Washoe, Moja, Tatu, and Dar free to use
any of the signs in their ASL vocabularies at any time, including testing

time, so their errors were their own errors rather than arbitrary alternatives forced upon them by the test. These open tests showed more than numbers of correct and incorrect choices. They showed how errors as well as correct replies depended on the conceptual structure of the vocabularies and the cheremic structure of ASL. The program of research that combined cross-fostering, naturalistic observation, and systematic experiments yielded operational definitions of communication, concepts, and structure. The ethological validity of the laboratory conditions contributed to the experimental operations.

Like all of the methods described in this book, sign language studies of cross-fostered chimpanzees are a tool for studying intelligent behavior. It seems unlikely that a phenomenon as rich as language could be based on an isolated, unitary biological trait, unrelated to the rest of human nature. It is more reasonable to suppose that language is embedded in a complex pattern that relates all aspects of human intelligence. This book argues further that, like other significant biological phenomena, the general laws that govern human intelligence are instances of the general laws that govern the intelligent behavior of all animals. The search for underlying patterns and general biological laws of intelligence led to sign language studies of cross-fostered chimpanzees.

Like the other tools described in this book, sign language studies aim to open up new fields of discovery from the bottom-up rather than to answer traditional philosophical questions from the top-down. The following comment of Bruner (1978) applies directly to the last two chapters. Hopefully, readers can see how it applies in spirit to the bottom-up, feed forward approach of the whole book.

> A third trend is also discernible: the bridging of gaps that before were not so much empty as they were filled with corrosive dogmatism. The gaps between prelinguistic communication and language proper as the child develops, the gap between gesture and word, between holophrases and sentences, between chimps signing and man talking, between sign languages and spoken ones, between the structure of action and the structure of language. I think that the renewal of interest in language as an interactive, communicative system has made these 'gaps' less like battlegrounds where one fights and dies for the uniqueness of man and more like unknown seas to be mapped. (p. viii)

References

Adelman, H. M., & Maatsch, J. L. (1955). Resistance to extinction as a function of the type of response elicited by frustration. *Journal of Experimental Psychology, 50*, 61–65.

Ainsworth, M. D. S., & Bell, S. M. (1977). Infant crying and maternal responsiveness: A rejoinder to Gewirtz and Boyd. *Child Development, 48*, 1208–1216.

Akins, C. K., Domjan, M., & Guitiérrez, G. (1994). Topography of sexually conditioned behavior in male Japanese quail depends on the CS-US interval. *Journal of Experimental Psychology: Animal Behavior Processes, 20*, 199–209.

Albert, M., & Ayres, J. J. B. (1989). With number of preexposures constant latent inhibition increases with preexposure CS duration or total CS exposure. *Learning and Motivation, 20*, 278–294.

Albert, M., Ricker, S., Bevins, R. A., & Ayers, J. J. B. (1993). Extending continuous versus discontinuous conditioned stimuli before versus after unconditioned stimuli. *Journal of Experimental Psychology: Animal Behavior Processes, 19*, 255–264.

Amsel, A. (1958). The role of frustrative nonreward in noncontinuous reward situations. *Psychological Bulletin, 55*, 102–119.

Amsel, A. (1962). Frustrative nonreward in partial reinforcement and discrimination learning: Some recent history and a theoretical extension. *Psychological Review, 69*, 306–328.

Amsel, A. (1992). *Frustration theory: An analysis of dispositional learning and memory.* Cambridge, England: Cambridge University Press.

Amsel, A. (1994). Précis of *Frustration theory: An analysis of dispositional learning and memory. Psychonomic Bulletin & Review, 1*, 280–296.

Anderson, J. A. (1995). *An introduction to neural networks.* Cambridge, MA: MIT Press.

Anderson, M. C., & Shettleworth, S. J. (1977). Behavioral adaptation to fixed-interval and fixed-time food delivery in golden hamsters. *Journal of the Experimental Analysis of Behavior, 27*, 33–49.

Argyle, M., & Cook, M. (1976). *Gaze and mutual gaze.* Cambridge, England: Cambridge University Press.

Ayres, J. J. B., Axelrod, H., Mercker, E., Muchnik, F., & Vigorito, M. (1985). Concurrent observations of barpress suppression and freezing: Effects of CS modality and on-line vs off-line training upon posttrial behavior. *Animal Learning and Behavior, 13*, 44–50.

Ayres, J. J. B., Haddad, C., & Albert, M. (1987). One-trial excitatory backward conditioning as assessed by conditioned suppression of licking in rats: Concurrent observations of lick suppression and defensive behaviors. *Animal Learning and Behavior, 15*, 212–217.

344

Azrin, N. H., Hutchinson, R. R., & Hake, D. F. (1966). Extinction-induced aggression. *Journal of the Experimental Analysis of Behavior, 9*, 191–204.

Bachrach, J. A., & Karen, R. L. (1969). *Complex behavior chaining* [Film]. Available from Psychological Cinema Register, University Park, PA.

Badia, P., Coker, C., & Harsh, J. (1973). Choice of higher density signalled shock over lower density unsignalled shock. *Journal of the Experimental Analysis of Behavior, 20*, 47–55.

Badia, P., Culbertson, S., & Harsh, J. (1973). Choice of longer or stronger signalled shock over shorter or weaker unsignalled shock. *Journal of the Experimental Analysis of Behavior, 19*, 25–32.

Bahrick, H. P. (1952). Latent learning as a function of the strength of unrewarded need states. *Journal of Comparative and Physiological Psychology, 45*, 192–197.

Barlow, G. W. (1977). Modal action patterns. In T. A. Sebeok (Ed.), *How animals communicate* (pp. 98–134). Bloomington: Indiana University Press.

Barnea, A., & Nottebohm, F. (1995). Patterns of food storing by black-capped chickadees suggest a mnemonic hypothesis. *Animal Behaviour, 49*, 1161–1176.

Bateson, P., & Horn, G. (1994). Imprinting and recognition memory: A neural net model. *Animal Behaviour, 48*, 695–715.

Berger, D. F., & Brush, F. R. (1975). Rapid acquisition of discrete-trial lever-press avoidance: Effects of signal-shock interval. *Journal of the Experimental Analysis of Behavior, 24*, 227–239.

Bersh, P. J. (1951). The influence of two variables on the establishment of a secondary reinforcer for operant responses. *Journal of Experimental Psychology, 41*, 62–73.

Bessemer, D. W., & Stollnitz, F. (1971). Retention of discriminations and an analysis of learning set. In A. M. Schrier & F. Stollnitz (Eds.), *Behavior of nonhuman primates* (Vol. 4, pp. 1–58). New York: Academic Press.

Bhatt, R. S., Wasserman, E. A., Reynolds, W. F., & Knauss, K. S. (1988). Conceptual behavior in pigeons: Categorization of both familiar and novel examples from four classes of natural and artificial stimuli. *Journal of Experimental Psychology: Animal Behavior Processes, 14*, 219–234.

Birch, D., Ison, J. R., & Sperling, S. E. (1960). Reversal learning under single stimulus presentation. *Journal of Experimental Psychology, 60*, 36–40.

Birch, H. G. (1945). The relation of previous experience to insightful problem solving. *Journal of Comparative Psychology, 38*, 367–383.

Bitterman, M. E., Reed, P. C., & Kubala, A. L. (1953). The strength of sensory preconditioning. *Journal of Experimental Psychology, 46*, 178–182.

Bogoslovski, A. I. (1937). An attempt at creating sensory conditioned reflexes in humans. *Journal of Experimental Psychology, 21*, 403–422.

Bolles, R. C. (1970). Species-specific defense reactions and avoidance learning. *Psychological Review, 77*, 32–48.

Bolles, R. C. (1988). The bathwater and everything. *Behavioral and Brain Sciences, 11*, 449–450.

Bonvillian, J. D., Nelson, K. E., & Charrow, V. R. (1976). Language and language-related skills in deaf and hearing children. *Sign Language Studies, 12*, 211–250.

Bornstein, M. H., & Benasich, A. A. (1986). Infant habituation: Assessments of individual differences and short-term reliability at five months. *Child Development, 57*, 87–99.

Bornstein, M. H., & Sigman, M. D. (1986). Continuity in mental development from infancy. *Child Development, 57*, 251–274.

Bouton, M. E. (1993). Context, time, and memory retrieval in the interference paradigms of Pavlovian learning. *Psychological Bulletin, 114*, 80–99.

Breland, K., & Breland, M. (1951). A field of applied animal psychology. *American Psychologist, 6*, 202–204.

Breland, K., & Breland, M. (1961). The misbehavior of organisms. *American Psychologist, 16*, 681–684.

Brogden, W. J. (1939a). Higher order conditioning. *American Journal of Psychology, 52*, 579–591.

Brogden, W. J. (1939b). Sensory preconditioning. *Journal of Experimental Psychology, 25*, 323–332.

Brogden, W. J. (1939c). Unconditioned stimulus-substitution in the conditioning process. *American Journal of Psychology, 52*, 46–55.

Brogden, W. J. (1947). Sensory preconditioning of human subjects. *Journal of Experimental Psychology, 37*, 527–539.

Brooks, R. A. (1990). Elephants don't play chess. *Robotics and Autonomous Systems, 6*, 3–15.

Brower, L. P. (1984). Chemical defence in butterflies. In R. I. Vane-Wright & P. R. Ackery (Eds.), *The biology of butterflies* (pp. 109–134). Orlando, FL: Academic Press.

Brower, L. P. (1988). Avian predation on the monarch butterfly and its implications for mimicry theory. *American Naturalist, 131*, Supplement, 4–6.

Brown, M. F., & Moore, J. A. (1997). In the dark II: Spatial choice when access to extrinsic spatial cues is eliminated. *Animal Learning and Behavior, 25*, 335–336.

Brown, M. F., Rish, P. A., VonCulin, J. E., & Edberg, J. A. (1993). Spatial guidance of choice behavior in the radial-arm maze. *Journal of Experimental Psychology: Animal Behavior Processes, 19*, 195–214.

Brown, P., & Jenkins, H. M. (1968). Auto-shaping of the pigeon's key-peck. *Journal of the Experimental Analysis of Behavior, 11*, 1–8.

Brown, R. (1968). The development of wh questions in child speech. *Journal of Verbal Learning and Verbal Behavior, 7*, 277–290.

Bruner, J. (1978). Foreword to A. Lock. In A. Lock (Ed.), *Action gesture and symbol: The emergence of language* (pp. vii–viii). New York: Academic Press.

Bugelski, B. R. (1938). Extinction with and without sub-goal reinforcement. *Journal of Comparative and Physiological Psychology, 26*, 121–134.

Campbell, B. A., & Sheffield, F. D. (1953). Relation of random activity to food deprivation. *Journal of Comparative and Physiological Psychology, 46*, 320–322.

Campbell-Jones, S. (Producer & Director). (1974). *The first signs of Washoe* [Film]. Available from WGBH, Nova series, Boston.

Candland, D., Faulds, B., Thomas, D., & Candland, M. (1960). The reinforcing value of gentling. *Journal of Comparative and Physiological Psychology, 53*, 55–58.

Candland, D. K., Horowitz, S. H., & Culbertson, J. L. (1962). Acquisition and retention of acquired avoidance with gentling as reinforcement. *Journal of Comparative and Physiological Psychology, 55*, 1062–1064.

Cannon, W. B. (1932). *The wisdom of the body*. New York: Norton.

Capaldi, E. J., Ziff, D. R., & Godbout, R. C. (1970). Extinction and the necessity or non-necessity of anticipating reward on nonrewarded trials. *Psychonomic Science, 18*, 61–63.

Carney, R. E., & Mitchell, G. L. (1978). Reactions of planarians after cannibalization of planarians exposed to four stimulus combinations. *Journal of Biological Psychology, 20*, 44–49.

Cason, H. (1936). Sensory conditioning. *Journal of Experimental Psychology, 19*, 572–591.

Catania, A. C. (1984). *Learning* (2nd ed.). New York: Prentice-Hall.

Chen, J.-S., & Amsel, A. (1980). Recall (versus recognition) of taste and immunization against aversive taste anticipations based on illness. *Science, 209*, 831–833.

Cheng, K., Spetch, M. L., & Johnston, M. (1997). Spatial peak shift and generalization in pigeons. *Journal of Experimental Psychology: Animal Behavior Processes, 23*, 469–481.

Chernikoff, R., & Brogden, W. J. (1949). The effect of instructions upon sensory preconditioning of human subjects. *Journal of Experimental Psychology, 39*, 200–207.

Chittka, L., Geiger, K., & Kunze, J. (1995). Influence of landmarks on distance estimation of honey bees. *Animal Behaviour, 50*, 23–31.

Chomsky, N. (1972). *Language and mind* (Extended ed.). New York: Harcourt Brace.

Chomsky, N. (1972). *Language and mind*. New York: Harcourt Brace.

Coate, W. B. (1956). Weakening of conditioned bar-pressing by prior extinction of its subsequent discriminated operant. *Journal of Comparative and Physiological Psychology, 49*, 135–138.

Coate, W. B., & Gardner, R. A. (1964). Reward vs. nonreward in a successive discrimination. *Journal of Experimental Psychology, 68*, 119–124.

Coate, W. B., & Gardner, R. A. (1965). Sources of transfer from original training to discrimination reversal. *Journal of Experimental Psychology, 70*, 94–97.

Cohen, P. S., & Looney, T. A. (1984). Induction by reinforcer schedules. *Journal of the Experimental Analysis of Behavior, 41*, 345–353.

Collias, N. (1990). Statistical evidence for aggressive responses to red by male three-spined sticklebacks. *Animal Behaviour, 39*, 401–403.

Colwill, R. M., & Rescorla, R. A. (1985a). Instrumental responding remains sensitive to reinforcer devaluation after extensive training. *Journal of Experimental Psychology: Animal Behavior Processes, 11*, 520–536.

Colwill, R. M., & Rescorla, R. A. (1985b). Postconditioning devaluation of a reinforcer affects instrumental responding. *Journal of Experimental Psychology: Animal Behavior Processes, 11*, 120–132.

Colwill, R. M., & Rescorla, R. A. (1986). Associative structures in instrumental learning. In G. H. Bower (Ed.), *The psychology of learning and motivation* (Vol. 20, pp. 55–104). New York: Academic Press.

Coppock, W. J. (1958). Pre-extinction in sensory preconditioning. *Journal of Experimental Psychology, 55*, 213–219.

Cotzin, M., & Dallenbach, K. M. (1950). "Facial vision": The role of pitch and loudness in the perception of obstacles by the blind. *American Journal of Psychology, 63*, 485–515.

Cowles, J. T. (1937). Food-tokens as incentives for learning by chimpanzees. *Comparative Psychology Monographs, 14*(No. 5), 1–96.

Crum, J., Brown, W. L., & Bitterman, M. E. (1951). The effect of partial and delayed reinforcement on resistance to extinction. *American Journal of Psychology, 64*, 228–237.

Culler, E., Finch, G., Girden, E., & Brogden, W. J. (1935). Measurements of acuity by the conditioned-response technique. *Journal of General Psychology, 12*, 223–227.

Curio, E., Ernst, U., & Vieth, W. (1978). The adaptive significance of avian mobbing: II. Cultural transmission of enemy recognition in blackbirds: Effectiveness and some constraints. *Zeitschrift für Tierspychologie, 48*, 184–202.

Dallenbach, K. M. (1959). Twitmeyer and the conditioned response. *American Journal of Psychology, 72*, 633–638.

D'Amato, M. R., & Schiff, D. (1964). Long-term discriminated avoidance performance in the rat. *Journal of Comparative and Physiological Psychology, 57*, 123–126.

Deaux, E. B., & Patten, R. L. (1964). Measurement of the anticipatory goal response in instrumental runway conditioning. *Psychonomic Science, 1*, 357–358.

Deese, J. (1951). The extinction of a discrimination without performance of the choice response. *Journal of Comparative and Physiological Psychology, 44*, 362–366.

Dember, W. N., & Richman, C. L. (1989). *Spontaneous alternation behavior.* New York: Springer-Verlag.

Denny, M. R. (1971). Relaxation theory and experiments. In F. R. Brush (Ed.), *Aversive conditioning and learning* (pp. 235–296). New York: Academic Press.

Domjan, M. (1980). Ingestional aversion learning: Unique and general processes. In J. S. Rosenblatt, R. A. Hinde, C. Beer, & M. Busnel (Eds.), *Advances in the study of behavior* (Vol. 11, pp. 275–336). New York: Academic Press.

Douglas, R. J. (1966). Cues for spontaneous alternation. *Journal of Comparative and Physiological Psychology, 62*, 171–183.

Drew, G. C. (1939). The speed of locomotion gradient and its relation to the goal gradient. *Journal of Comparative and Physiological Psychology, 27*, 333–372.

Dunham, P. J. (1972). Some effects of punishment upon unpunished responding. *Journal of the Experimental Analysis of Behavior, 17*, 443–450.

Dyer, F. C. (1993). How honey bees find familiar feeding sites after changing nesting sites with a swarm. *Animal Behaviour, 46*, 813–816.

Dyer, F. C., Berry, N. A., & Richard, A. S. (1993). Honey bee spatial memory: Use of route-based memories after displacement. *Animal Behaviour, 45*, 1028–1030.

Ehrenfreund, D. (1952). A study of the transposition gradient. *Journal of Experimental Psychology, 43*, 81–87.

Ekman, P. (1973). Cross-cultural studies of facial expression. In P. Ekman (Ed.), *Darwin and facial expression* (pp. 169–222). New York: Academic Press.

Ellen, P., & Wilson, A. S. (1964). Two patterns of avoidance responding. *Journal of the Experimental Analysis of Behavior, 7*, 97–98.

Epstein, R., Kirshnit, C. E., Lanza, R. P., & Rubin, L. C. (1984). "Insight" in the pigeon: Antecedents and determinants of an intelligent performance. *Nature, 308*, 61–62.

Erickson, R. P., Di Lorenzo, P. M., & Woodbury, M. A. (1994). Classification of taste responses in the brain stem: Membership in fuzzy sets. *Journal of Neurophysiology, 71*, 2139–2150.

Etienne, A. S. (1992). Look homeward hamster. *Current Directions in Psychological Science, 1*, 48–52.

Etienne, A. S., Lambert, S. J., Reverdin, B., & Teroni, E. (1993). Learning to recalibrate the role of dead reckoning and visual cues in spatial navigation. *Animal Learning and Behavior, 21*, 266–280.

Falk, J. L. (1971). The nature and determinants of adjunctive behavior. *Physiology and Behavior, 6*, 577–588.

Fenner, D. (1980). The role of contingencies and "principles of behavioral variation": in pigeons pecking. *Journal of the Experimental Analysis of Behavior, 34*, 1–12.

Flaherty, C. F. (1985). *Animal learning and cognition.* New York: Knopf.

Fleure, H. J., & Walton, C. L. (1907). Notes on the habits of some sea anemones. *Zoologischer Anzeiger, 31*, 212–220.

Forgione, A. G. (1970). The elimination of interfering response patterns in lever-press avoidance situations. *Journal of the Experimental Analysis of Behavior, 13*, 51–56.

Fouts, R. S. (1975). Communication with chimpanzees. In G. Kurth & I. Eibl-Eibesfeld (Eds.), *Hominisation und Verhalten* (pp. 137–158). Stuttgart, Germany: Gustav Fischer Verlag.

Fouts, R. S., & Fouts, D. H. (1989). Loulis in conversation with the cross-fostered chimpanzees. In R. A. Gardner, B. T. Gardner, & T. E. Van Cantfort (Eds.), *Teaching sign language to chimpanzees* (pp. 293–307). Albany: State University of New York Press.

Fouts, R. S., Fouts, D. H., & Van Cantfort, T. E. (1989). The infant Loulis learns signs from cross-fostered chimpanzees. In R. A. Gardner, B. T. Gardner, & T. E. Van Cantfort (Eds.), *Teaching sign language to chimpanzees* (pp. 280–292). Albany: State University of New York Press.

Fraser, C., Bellugi, U., & Brown, R. (1963). Control of grammar in imitation, comprehension and production. *Journal of Verbal Learning and Verbal Behavior, 2*, 121–135.

French, J. W. (1940). Trial-and-error learning in the paramecium. *Journal of Experimental Psychology, 26*, 609–617.

Friedman, S., Carpenter, G. C., & Nagy, A. N. (1973). Decrement and recovery of response to visual stimuli in the newborn human. In L. J. Stone, H. T. Smith, & L. B. Murphy (Eds.), *The competent infant: Research and commentary* (pp. 361–365). New York: Basic Books.

Gamboni, W. R. (1973). Anticipatory errors in rats as a function of delayed reward. *Journal of Experimental Psychology, 97*, 98–104.

Garcia, J., & Koelling, R. A. (1966). Relation of cue to consequence in avoidance learning. *Psychonomic Science, 4*, 123–4.

Gardner, B. T., & Gardner, R. A. (1971). Two-way communication with an infant chimpanzee. In A. Schrier & F. Stollnitz (Eds.), *Behavior of nonhuman primates* (Vol. 4, pp. 117–184). New York: Academic Press.

Gardner, B. T., & Gardner, R. A. (1994). Development of phrases in the utterances of children and cross-fostered chimpanzees. In R. A. Gardner, B. T. Gardner, A. B. Chiarelli, & F. X. Plooij (Eds.), *The ethological roots of culture* (pp. 223–255). Dordrecht, Netherlands: Kluwer Academic.

Gardner, B. T., Gardner, R. A., & Nichols, S. G. (1989). The shapes and uses of signs in a cross-fostering laboratory. In R. A. Gardner, B. T. Gardner, & T. E. Van Cantfort (Eds.), *Teaching sign language to chimpanzees* (pp. 55–180). Albany: State University of New York Press.

Gardner, B. T., & Wallach, L. (1965). Shapes of figures identified as a baby's head. *Perceptual and Motor Skills, 20*, 135–142.

Gardner, E. T., & Lewis, P. (1977). Parameters affecting the maintenance of negatively reinforced key pecking. *Journal of the Experimental Analysis of Behavior, 28*, 117–131.

Gardner, R. A. (1957). Probability learning with two and three choices. *American Journal of Psychology, 70*, 174–185.

Gardner, R. A. (1961). Multiple-choice decision-behavior with dummy choices. *American Journal of Psychology, 74*, 205–214.

Gardner, R. A. (1966). On box score methodology as illustrated by three reviews of overtraining reversal effects. *Psychological Bulletin, 66*, 416–418.

Gardner, R. A., & Coate, W. B. (1965). Reward vs. nonreward in a simultaneous discrimination. *Journal of Experimental Psychology, 69*, 579–582.

Gardner, R. A., & Gamboni, W. R. (1971). Anticipatory responses in a linear maze. *Psychonomic Science, 25*, 277–278.

Gardner, R. A., & Gardner, B. T. (1973). *Teaching sign language to the chimpanzee, Washoe* [Film]. Available from Psychological Cinema Register, State College, PA.

Gardner, R. A., & Gardner, B. T. (1978). Comparative psychology and language acquisition. In K. Salzinger & F. Denmark (Eds.), *Psychology: The state of the art*. Annals of the New York Academy of Sciences, *309*, 37–76.

Gardner, R. A., & Gardner, B. T. (1984). A vocabulary test for chimpanzees. *Journal of Comparative Psychology, 98*, 381–404.

Gardner, R. A., & Gardner, B. T. (1988a). Feedforward versus feedbackward: An ethological alternative to the law of effect. *Behavioral and Brain Sciences, 11*, 429–447.

Gardner, R. A., & Gardner, B. T. (1988b). Truth or consequences. *Behavioral and Brain Sciences, 11*, 479–487.

Gardner, R. A., & Gardner, B. T. (1989). A cross-fostering laboratory. In R. A. Gardner, B. T. Gardner, & T. E. Van Cantfort (Eds.), *Teaching sign language to chimpanzees* (pp. 1–28). Albany: State University of New York Press.

Gardner, R. A., & Gardner, B. T. (1991). Absence of evidence and evidence of absence. *Behavioral and Brain Sciences, 14*, 558–560.

Gardner, R. A., & Gardner, B. T. (1992). Feedforward: The ethological basis of animal learning. In F. J. Variela & P. Bourgine (Eds.), *Toward a practice of autonomous systems* (pp. 399–410). Cambridge, MA: MIT Press.

Gardner, R. A., & Gardner, B. T. (1994). Ethological roots of language. In R. A. Gardner, B. T. Gardner, A. B. Chiarelli, & F. X. Plooij (Eds.), *The ethological roots of culture* (pp. 199–222). Dordrecht, Netherlands: Kluwer Academic.

Gardner, R. A., Gardner, B. T., & Drumm, P. (1989). Voiced and signed responses of cross-fostered chimpanzees. In R. A. Gardner, B. T. Gardner, & T. E. Van Cantfort (Eds.), *Teaching sign language to chimpanzees* (pp. 29–54). Albany: State University of New York Press.

Gardner, R. A., & Runquist, W. N. (1958). Acquistion and extinction of problem-solving set. *Journal of Experimental Psychology, 55*, 274–277.

Gelber, B. (1952). Investigations of the behavior of paramecium aurelia: I. Modification of behavior after training with reinforcement. *Journal of Comparative and Physiological Psychology, 45*, 58–65.

Gelber, B. (1956). Investigations of the behavior of paramecium aurelia: III. The effect of the presence and absence of light on the occurence of a response. *Journal of Genetic Psychology, 68*, 31–36.

Gelber, B. (1957). Food or training in paramecium? *Science, 125*, 1340–1341.

Gelber, B. (1958). Retention in paramecium aurelia. *Journal of Comparative and Physiological Psychology, 51*, 110–115.

Gelber, B. (1965). Studies of the behavior of paramecium aurelia. *Animal Behavior, 13*(Suppl. 1), 21–29.

Gill, T. V., & Rumbaugh, D. M. (1974). Mastery of naming skills by a chimpanzee. *Journal of Human Evolution, 3*, 483–492.

Gill, T. V., & Rumbaugh, D. M. (1977). Training strategy and tactics. In D. M. Rumbaugh (Ed.), *Language learning by a chimpanzee* (pp. 157–162). New York: Academic Press.

Girouard, P. C., Ricard, M., & Décarie, T. G. (1997). The acquisition of personal pronouns in French-speaking and English-speaking children. *Journal of Child Language, 24*, 311–326.

Glanzer, M. (1953). The role of stimulus satiation in spontaneous alternation. *Journal of Experimental Psychology, 45*, 387–393.

Goodall, J. (1967). Mother–offspring relationships in free-ranging chimpanzees. In D. Morris (Ed.), *Primate ethology* (pp. 287–346). London: Weidenfeld & Nicolson.

Goodall, J. (1986). *The chimpanzees of Gombe*. Cambridge, MA: Harvard University Press.

Goodrich, K. P. (1959). Performance in different segments of an instrumental response chain as a function of reinforcement schedule. *Journal of Experimental Psychology, 57*, 57–63.

Gormezano, I. (1965). Yoked comparisons of classical and instrumental conditioning of the eyelid response; and an addendum on "voluntary responders." In W. F. Prokasy (Ed.), *Classical conditioning: A symposium* (pp. 48–70). New York: Appleton–Century–Crofts.

Gormezano, I., & Hiller, G. W. (1972). Omission training of the jaw-movement response of the rabbit to a water US. *Psychonomic Science, 29*, 276–278.

Gould, J. L. (1975). Honeybee recruitment: The dance-language controversy. *Science, 189*, 685–692.

Gould, J. L. (1985). How bees remember flower shapes. *Science, 227*, 1492–1494.

Gould, J. L., Henerey, M., & MacLeod, M. C. (1970). Communication of direction by the honey bee. *Science, 169*, 544–554.

Grant, D. A. (1973). Cognitive factors in eyelid conditioning. *Psychophysiology, 10*, 75–81.

Greenfield, P. M., & Savage-Rumbaugh, E. S. (1990). Grammatical combination in Pan paniscus: Processes of learning and invention. In S. T. Parker & K. R. Gibson (Eds.), *"Language" and intelligence in monkeys and apes: Comparative developmental perspectives* (pp. 540–578). New York: Cambridge University Press.

Grether, W. F. (1938). Pseudo-conditioning without paired stimulation encountered in attempted backward conditioning. *Journal of Comparative Psychology, 25*, 91–96.

Hall, D., & Suboski, M. D. (1995). Sensory preconditioning and second-order conditioning of alarm reactions in zebra danio fish (*Brachydanio rerio*). *Journal of Comparative Psychology, 109*, 76–84.

Hall, J. F. (1976). *Classical conditioning and instrumental learning*. Philadelphia: Lippincott.

Hanson, H. M. (1957). Discrimination training effect on stimulus generalization gradient for spectrum stimuli. *Science, 125*, 888–889.

Hanson, H. M. (1959). Effects of discrimination training on stimulus generalization. *Journal of Experimental Psychology, 58*, 321–334.

Harlow, H. F. (1949). The formation of learning sets. *Psychological Review, 56*, 51–65.

Harlow, H. F. (1958). The nature of love. *American Psychologist, 13*, 673–685.

Harlow, H. F., Harlow, M. K., & Meyer, D. R. (1950). Learning motivated by a manipulation drive. *Journal of Experimental Psychology, 40*, 228–234.

Harlow, H. F., & Toltzien, F. (1940). Formation of pseudo-conditioned responses in the cat. *Journal of General Psychology, 23*, 367–375.

Harris, J. D. (1941). Forward conditioning, backward conditioning, and pseudo-conditioning, and adaptation to the conditioned stimulus. *Journal of Experimental Psychology, 28*, 491–502.

Harrison, R. G., & Schaeffer, R. W. (1975). Temporal contiguity: Is it a sufficient condition for reinforcement? *Bulletin of the Psychonomic Society, 5*, 230–232.

Hayes, K. J., & Nissen, C. H. (1971). Higher mental functions of a home-raised chimpanzee. In A. M. Schrier & F. Stollnitz (Eds.), *Behavior of nonhuman primates* (Vol. 4, pp. 59–115). New York: Academic Press.

Hebb, D. O. (1949). *The organization of behavior*. New York: Wiley.

Hebert, J. A., & Krantz, D. L. (1965). Transposition: A reevaluation. *Psychological Bulletin, 63*, 244–257.

Hediger, H. (1955). *Studies of the psychology and behavior of captive animals in zoos and circuses*. London: Butterworth.

Helson, H. (1964). *Adaptation-level theory*. New York: Harper & Row.

Herman, L. M., Richards, D. G., & Wolz, J. P. (1984). Comprehension of sentences by bottle-nosed dolphins. *Cognition, 16*, 129–219.

Herrnstein, R. J. (1979). Acquisition, generalization, and discrimination reversal of a natural concept. *Journal of Experimental Psychology: Animal Behavior Processes, 5*, 116–129.

Herrnstein, R. J. (1985). Riddles of natural categorization. *Philosophical Transactions of the Royal Society, London, B308*, 129–144.

Herrnstein, R. J., & Hineline, P. N. (1966). Negative reinforcement as shock frequency reduction. *Journal of the Experimental Analysis of Behavior, 9*, 421–430.

Herz, R. S., Zanette, L., & Sherry, D. F. (1994). Spatial cues for cache retrieval by black-capped chickadees. *Animal Behaviour, 48*, 343–351.

Heth, C. D. (1976). Simultaneous and backward fear conditioning as a function of number of CS-UCS pairings. *Journal of Experimental Psychology: Animal Behavior Processes, 2*, 117–129.

Heynen, A. J., Sainsbury, R. S., & Montoya, C. P. (1989). Cross-species responses in the defensive burying paradigm: A comparison between Long-Evans rats, Richardson's ground squirrels, and thirteen-lined ground squirrels. *Journal of Comparative Psychology, 103*, 184–190.

Hill, R., Collis, G. M., & Lewis, V. A. (1997). Young children's understanding of the cognitive verb *forget*. *Journal of Child Language, 24*, 57–79.

Hinde, R. A. (1973). Constraints on learning: An introduction to the problems. In R. A. Hinde & E. Stevenson-Hinde (Eds.), *Constraints on learning* (pp. 1–19). New York: Academic Press.

Hineline, P. N. (1977). Negative reinforcement and avoidance. In W. K. Honig & J. E. R. Staddon (Eds.), *Handbook of operant conditioning* (pp. 364–414). Englewood Cliffs, NJ: Prentice-Hall.

Hineline, P. N. (1981). The several roles of stimuli in negative reinforcement. In P. Harzem & M. D. Zeiler (Eds.), *Advances in analysis of behavior: Predictability, correlation, and contiguity* (pp. 203–246). New York: Wiley.

Hittesdorf, M., & Richards, R. W. (1982). Aversive second-order conditioning in the pigeon: Elimination of conditioning to CS1 and effects on established second-order conditioning. *Canadian Journal of Psychology, 36*, 462–477.

Hockett, C. F. (1978). In search of Jove's brow. *American Speech, 53*(4), 243–313.

Hoffeld, D. R., Thompson, R. F., & Brogden, W. J. (1958). Effect of stimuli time relations during preconditioning training upon the magnitude of sensory preconditioning. *Journal of Experimental Psychology, 56*, 437–442.

Holland, P. C., & Rescorla, R. A. (1975). The effect of two ways of devaluing the unconditioned stimulus after first- and second-order appetitive conditioning. *Journal of Experimental Psychology: Animal Behavior Processes, 1*, 355–363.

Horswill, I. D., & Brooks, R. A. (1988). Situated vision in a dynamic world: Chasing objects. In *Seventh National Conference on Artificial Intelligence* (Vol. 2, pp. 796–800). Palo Alto, CA: Morgan Kaufmann.

Hovland, C. I. (1937). The generalization of conditioned responses: I. The sensory generalization of conditioned responses with varying frequencies of tone. *Journal of General Psychology, 17*, 125–148.

Huber, J. C., Rucker, W. B., & McDiarmid, C. G. (1974). Retention of escape training and activity changes in single paramecia. *Journal of Comparative and Physiological Psychology, 86*, 258–266.

Hull, C. L. (1932). The goal-gradient hypothesis and maze learning. *Psychological Review, 39*, 25–43.

Hull, C. L. (1934). The rat's speed-of-locomotion gradient in the approach to food. *Journal of Comparative Psychology, 17*, 393–422.

Hull, C. L. (1939). The problem of stimulus equivalence in behavior theory. *Psychological Review, 46*, 9–30.

Hull, C. L. (1947). Reactively heterogeneous compound trial-and-error learning with distributed trials and terminal reinforcement. *Journal of Experimental Psychology, 37*, 118–135.

Hull, C. L. (1952). *A behavior system*. New Haven, CT: Yale University Press.

Hull, J. H. (1977). Instrumental response topographies of rats. *Animal Learning and Behavior, 5*, 207–212.

Hull, J. H., Bartlett, T. J., & Hill, R. C. (1981). Operant response topographies of rats receiving food or water reinforcers on FR or FI reinforcement schedules. *Animal Learning and Behavior, 9*, 406–410.

Hulse, S. H., Egeth, H., & Deese, J. (1980). *The psychology of learning*. New York: McGraw-Hill.

Hunt, E. L. (1949). Establishment of conditioned responses in chick embryos. *Journal of Comparative and Physiological Psychology, 42*, 107–117.

Huston, J., & Agee, J. (1951). *The African Queen* [Film]. London: Horizon Enterprises.

Inglis, I. R., Forkman, B., & Lazarus, J. (1997). Free food or earned food? A review and fuzzy model of contrafreeloading. *Animal Behaviour, 53*, 1171–1191.

Irion, A. L. (1969). A brief history of research on the acquisition of skill. In E. A. Bilodeau (Ed.), *Principles of skill acquisition* (pp. 1–31). New York: Academic Press.

Jacob, T. C., & Fantino, E. (1988). Effects of reinforcement context on choice. *Journal of the Experimental Analysis of Behavior, 49*, 367–381.

Jacobs, L. F., & Liman, E. R. (1991). Grey squirrels remember the locations of buried nuts. *Animal Behaviour, 41*, 103–110.

Janssen, M., Farley, J., & Hearst, E. (1995). Temporal location of unsignaled food deliveries: Effects on conditioned withdrawal (inhibition) in pigeon signtracking. *Journal of Experimental Psychology: Animal Behavior Processes, 21*, 116–128.

Jenkins, H. M. (1965). Measurement of stimulus control during discriminative operant conditioning. *Psychological Bulletin, 64*, 365–376.

Jenkins, H. M., & Moore, B. R. (1973). The form of the autoshaped response with food or water reinforcers. *Journal of the Experimental Analysis of Behavior, 20*, 163–181.

Jensen, D. D. (1957). Experiments of "learning" in paramecium. *Science, 125*, 191–192.

Jensen, G. D. (1963). Preference for bar pressing over "freeloading" as a function of number of rewarded presses. *Journal of Experimental Psychology, 65*, 451–454.

Kaiser, P. K., & Boynton, R. M. (1996). *Human color vision.* Washington, DC: Optical Society of America.

Kannapell, B. M., Hamilton, L. B., & Bornstein, H. (1969). *Signs for instructional purposes.* Washington, DC: Gallaudet College Press.

Karn, H. W. (1947). Sensory preconditioning and incidental learning in human subjects. *Journal of Experimental Psychology, 37*, 540–544.

Karn, H. W., & Porter, J. M., Jr. (1946). The effect of certain pretraining procedures upon maze performance and their significance for the concept of latent learning. *Journal of Experimental Psychology, 36*, 461–469.

Katz, M. S., & Deterline, W. A. (1958). Apparent learning in the paramecium. *Journal of Comparative and Physiological Psychology, 51*, 243–247.

Kavaliers, M., & Galea, L. A. M. (1994). Spatial water maze learning using celestial cues by the meadow vole, *Microtus pennsylvanicus. Behavioural Brain Research, 61*, 97–100.

Kehoe, E. J., Horne, P. S., & Horne, A. J. (1993). Discrimination learning using different CS-US intervals in classical conditioning of the rabbit's nictitating membrane response. *Psychobiology, 21*, 277–285.

Kehoe, E. J., Horne, P. S., Macrae, M., & Horne, A. J. (1993). Real-time processing of serial stimuli in classical conditioning of the rabbit's nictitating membrane response. *Journal of Experimental Psychology: Animal Behavior Processes, 19*, 265–283.

Kehoe, E. J., & Napier, R. M. (1991). Real-time factors in the rabbit's nictitating membrane response to pulsed and serial conditioned stimuli. *Animal Learning and Behavior, 19*, 195–206.

Keith-Lucas, T., & Guttman, N. (1975). Robust-single-trial delayed backward conditioning. *Journal of Comparative and Physiological Psychology, 88*, 468–476.

Kelleher, R. T. (1956). Intermittent conditioned reinforcement in chimpanzees. *Science, 124*, 679–680.

Kelleher, R. T. (1957a). Conditioned reinforcement in chimpanzees. *Journal of Comparative and Physiological Psychology, 50*, 571–575.

Kelleher, R. T. (1957b). A multiple schedule of conditioned reinforcement with chimpanzees. *Psychological Reports, 3*, 485–491.

Kelleher, R. T. (1958a). Fixed-ratio schedules of conditioned reinforcement with chimpanzees. *Journal of the Experimental Analysis of Behavior, 1*, 281–289.

Kelleher, R. T. (1958b). Stimulus producing responses in chimpanzees. *Journal of the Experimental Analysis of Behavior, 1*, 87–102.

Kellogg, W. N. (1938). Evidence for both stimulus-substitution and original anticipatory responses in the conditioning of dogs. *Journal of Experimental Psychology, 22*, 186–192.

Kellogg, W. N. (1968). Communication and language in the home-raised chimpanzee. *Science, 162*, 423–427.

Kelly, E. L. (1934). An experimental attempt to produce artificial chromaesthesia by the technique of the conditioned response. *Journal of Experimental Psychology, 17*, 315–341.

Kendler, H. H. (1946). The influence of simultaneous hunger and thirst drives upon the learning of two opposed spatial responses of the white rat. *Journal of Experimental Psychology, 36*, 212–220.

Kendon, A. (1967). Some functions of gaze direction in social interaction. *Acta Psychologica, 26*, 1–47.

Kimble, G. A. (1961). *Hilgard and Marquis' conditioning and learning.* New York: Appleton–Century–Crofts.

King, A. P., & West, M. J. (1989). Presence of female cowbirds affects vocal imitation and improvisation in males. *Journal of Comparative Psychology, 103*, 39–44.

Kipersztok, O., & Patterson, J. C. (1995). Intelligent fuzzy control to augment the scheduling capabilities of network queuing systems. In *Computer Science Lecture Notes* (Vol. 949, pp. 3–23). Santa Barbara, CA: Springer-Verlag.

Kirchner, W. H., & Braun, U. (1994). Dancing honey bees indicate the location of food sources using path integration rather than cognitive maps. *Animal Behaviour, 48*, 1437–1441.

Kirchner, W. H., Dreller, C., & Towne, W. F. (1991). Hearing in honeybees: Operant conditioning and spontaneous reactions to airborne sound. *Journal of Comparative Physiology, 168*(1), 85–89.

Kish, G. B. (1955). Learning when the onset of illumination is used as reinforcing stimulus. *Journal of Comparative and Physiological Psychology, 48*, 261–264.

Kish, G. B. (1966). Studies of sensory reinforcement. In W. K. Honig (Ed.), *Operant behavior: Areas of research and application* (pp. 109–134). New York: Appleton–Century–Crofts.

Köhler, W. (1959). The mentality of apes (2nd ed., E. Winter, Trans.). New York: Vintage Books. (Original work published 1925)

Konorski, J. (1948). *Conditioned reflexes and neuron organization.* New York: Cambridge University Press.

Kosko, B. (1993). *Fuzzy thinking: The new science of fuzzy logic.* New York: Hyperion.

Krasne, F. B., & Glanzman, D. L. (1995). What we can learn from invertebrate learning. *Annual Review of Psychology, 46*, 585–624.

Krechevsky, I. (1932). "Hypotheses" in rats. *Psychological Review, 39*, 516–532.

Krechevsky, I. (1938). A study of the continuity of the problem-solving process. *Psychological Review, 45*, 107–133.

Lane, H., & Pillard, R. (1978). *The wild boy of Burundi.* New York: Random House.

Lashley, K. S. (1929). *Brain mechanisms and intelligence.* Chicago: University of Chicago Press.

Lawhon, D. K., & Hafner, M. S. (1981). Tactile discriminatory ability and foraging strategies in kangaroo rats and pocket mice. *Oecologia, 50*, 303–309.

Lehrman, D. S. (1955). The physiological basis of parental feeding behaviour in the ring dove. *Behaviour, 7*, 241–286.

Lepper, M. R., Greene, D., & Nisbett, R. E. (1973). Undermining children's intrinsic interest with extrinsic reward: A case of the "overjustification" hypothesis. *Journal of Personality and Social Psychology, 28*, 129–137.

Levine, F., & Fasnacht, G. (1974). Token rewards may lead to token learning. *American Psychologist, 29*, 816–820.

Levine, M., Harlow, H. F., & Pontrelli, T. (1961). The effects of problem length on transfer during learning-set performance. *Journal of Experimental Psychology, 61*, 192.

Levine, M., Levinson, B., & Harlow, H. F. (1959). Trials per problem as a variable in the acquisition of discrimination learning set. *Journal of Comparative and Physiological Psychology, 52*, 396–398.

Levison, M. J., & Gavurin, E. I. (1979). Truly random control group in Pavlovian conditioning of planaria. *Psychological Reports, 45*, 987–992.

Leyland, C. M. (1977). Higher order autoshaping. *Quarterly Journal of Experimental Psychology, 29*, 607–619.

Liddell, H. S. (1942). The conditioned reflex. In F. A. Moss (Ed.), *Comparative psychology* (pp. 178–216). New York: Prentice-Hall.

Liddell, H. S. (1956). *Emotional hazards in animals and man.* Springfield, IL: Thomas.

Lindauer, M. (1961). *Communication among social bees.* Cambridge, MA: Harvard University Press.

Lubow, R. E. (1989). *Latent inhibition and conditioned attention theory.* Cambridge, England: Cambridge University Press.

Luchins, A. S., & Luchins, E. H. (1994). The water jar experiments and Einstellung effects: Part II. Gestalt psychology and past experience. *Gestalt Theory, 16*, 205–270.

Ludvigson, H. W., & Sytsma, D. (1967). The sweet smell of success: Apparent double alternation in the rat. *Psychonomic Science, 9*, 283–284.

MacCorquodale, K., & Meehl, P. E. (1951). On the elimination of cul entries without obvious reinforcement. *Journal of Comparative and Physiological Psychology, 44*, 367–371.

MacCorquodale, K., & Meehl, P. E. (1954). Edward C. Tolman. In W. K. Estes, S. Koch, K. MacCorquodale, P. Meehl, C. G. Mueller, W. N. Schoenfeld, & W. S. Verplanck (Eds.), *Modern learning theory* (pp. 177–266). New York: Appleton–Century–Crofts.

Mackintosh, N. J. (1974). *The psychology of animal learning.* New York: Academic Press.

Mackintosh, N. J. (1983). *Conditioning and associative learning.* New York: Oxford University Press.

Maestas y Moores, J. (1980). Early linguistic environment: Interactions of deaf parents with their infants. *Sign Language Studies, 26,* 1–13.

Magnus, D. B. E. (1963). Sex limited mimicry: II. Visual selection in the mate choice of butterflies. *Proceedings of the XVI International Congress of Zoology, 4,* 179–183.

Maple, T. L., & Cone, S. G. (1981). Aged apes at the Yerkes Regional Primate Research Center. *Laboratory Primate Newsletter, 20,* 10–12.

Marquis, D. P. (1931). Can conditioned responses be established in the newborn infant? *Journal of Genetic Psychology, 39,* 479–492.

Marschark, M. (1993). *Psychological development of deaf children.* New York: Oxford University Press.

Matsuzawa, T. (1985). Color naming and classification in a chimpanzee. *Journal of Human Evolution, 14,* 283–291.

McCulloch, T. L. (1939). The role of clasping activity in adaptive behavior of the infant chimpanzee: III. The mechanism of reinforcement. *Journal of Psychology, 7,* 305–316.

McCulloch, W. S., & Pitts, W. (1943). A logical calculus of the ideas immanent in nervous activity. *Bulletin of Mathematical Biophysics, 5,* 115–133.

McDowell, A. A., & Brown, W. L. (1963a). The learning mechanism in response shift learning set. *Journal of Comparative and Physiological Psychology, 56,* 572–574.

McDowell, A. A., & Brown, W. L. (1963b). Learning mechanism in response perseveration sets. *Journal of Comparative and Physiological Psychology, 56,* 1032–1034.

McNeil, D., & Freiberger, P. (1993). *Fuzzy logic.* New York: Touchstone Press.

Meachum, C. L., & Bernstein, I. L. (1990). Conditioned responses to a taste conditioned stimulus paired with lithium chloride administration. *Behavioral Neuroscience, 104,* 711–715.

Meehl, P. E., & MacCorquodale, K. (1951). A failure to find the Blodgett effect, and some secondary observations on drive conditioning. *Journal of Comparative and Physiological Psychology, 44,* 178–183.

Mendelsohn, E. (1964). *Heat and life: The development of the theory of animal heat.* Cambridge, MA: Harvard University Press.

Meyer, D. R., Cho, C., & Wesemann, A. F. (1960). On problems of conditioning discriminated lever-press avoidance responses. *Psychological Review, 67,* 224–228.

Mogenson, G., & Cioé, J. (1977). Central reinforcement: A bridge between brain function and behavior. In W. K. Honig & J. E. R. Staddon (Eds.), *Handbook of operant behavior* (pp. 570–595). Englewood Cliffs, NJ: Prentice-Hall.

Moltz, H. (1955). Latent extinction and reduction of secondary reward value. *Journal of Experimental Psychology, 49,* 395–400.

Moltz, H., & Maddi, S. R. (1956). Reduction of secondary reward value as a function of drive strength during latent extinction. *Journal of Experimental Psychology, 52,* 71–76.

Montgomery, K. C. (1952). A test of two explanations of spontaneous alternation. *Journal of Comparative and Physiological Psychology, 45,* 287–293.

Morato, S., & Brandão, M. L. (1996). Transporting rats to the test situation on a cart can modify rat exploratory behavior in the elevated plus-maze. *Psychobiology, 24,* 247–252.

Morgan, C. T., & Stellar, E. (1950). *Physiological psychology.* New York: McGraw-Hill.

Morris, D. (1962). *The biology of art.* New York: Knopf.

Morris, R. G. M. (1981). Spatial localization does not require the presence of local cues. *Learning and Motivation, 12,* 239–260.

Morse, W. H., & Kelleher, R. T. (1977). Determinants of reinforcement and punishment. In W. K. Honig & J. E. R. Staddon (Eds.), *Handbook of operant conditioning* (pp. 174–200). Englewood Cliffs, NJ: Prentice-Hall.

Mowrer, O. H. (1960). *Learning theory and behavior.* New York: Wiley.

Mowrer, O. H., & Aiken, E. G. (1954). Contiguity vs. drive-reduction in conditioned fear: Temporal variations in conditioned and unconditioned stimulus. *American Journal of Psychology, 67,* 26–38.

Murphy, J. V., & Miller, R. E. (1957). Higher-order conditioning in the monkey. *Journal of General Psychology, 56,* 67–72.

Nairne, J. S., & Rescorla, R. A. (1981). Second-order conditioning with diffuse auditory reinforcers in the pigeon. *Learning and Motivation, 12,* 65–91.

Newton, I. (1730/1952). *Opticks.* New York: Dover.

Olton, D. S., & Collison, C. (1979). Intramaze cues and "odor trails" fail to direct choice behavior on an elevated maze. *Animal Learning and Behavior, 7,* 221–223.

Osborne, S. R. (1977). The free food (contrafreeloading) phenomenon: A review and analysis. *Animal Learning and Behavior, 5,* 221–235.

Osborne, S. R. (1978). A note on the acquisition of responding for food in the presence of free food. *Animal Learning and Behavior, 6,* 368–369.

Osborne, S. R., & Shelby, M. (1975). Stimulus change as a factor in response maintenance with free food available. *Journal of the Experimental Analysis of Behavior, 24,* 17–21.

Parker, L. A. (1988). Positively reinforcing drugs may produce a different kind of CTA than drugs which are not postively reinforcing. *Learning and Motivation, 19,* 207–220.

Parker, L. A. (1993). Taste reactivity responses elicited by cocaine-, phencyclidine-, and methamphetamine-paired sucrose solutions. *Behavioral Neuroscience, 107,* 118–129.

Parker, L. A. (1996). LSD produces place preference and flavor avoidance but does not produce flavor aversion in rats. *Behavioral Neuroscience, 110,* 503–508.

Parker, L. A., Hills, K., & Jensen, K. (1984). Behavioral CRs elicited by a lithium- or an amphetamine-paired contextual test chamber. *Animal Learning and Behavior, 12,* 307–315.

Patten, R. L., & Rudy, J. W. (1967). The Sheffield omission of training procedure applied to the conditioning of the licking response in rats. *Psychonomic Science, 8,* 463–464.

Patterson, J. C., Gardner, B. T., & Gardner, R. A. (1986). Chance expectancy with trial-by-trial feedback and random sampling without replacement. *American Mathematical Monthly, 93,* 520–530.

Pavlov, I. P. (1960). *Conditioned reflexes* (G. V. Anrep, Trans.). New York: Dover. (Original work published 1927)

Pepperberg, I. M. (1990). Cognition in the African grey parrot: Further evidence for comprehension of categories and labels. *Journal of Comparative Psychology, 104,* 41–52.

Pfungst, O. (1911). *Clever Hans* (C. L. Rahn, Trans.). New York: Holt.

Pinel, J. P., Mana, M. J., & Ward, J. A. (1989). Stretched-approach sequences directed at a localized shock source by *Rattus norvegicus. Journal of Comparative Psychology, 103,* 140–148.

Pinel, J. P. J., Symons, L. A., Christensen, B. K., & Tees, R. C. (1989). Development of defensive burying in *Rattus norvegicus*: Experience and defensive responses. *Journal of Comparative Psychology, 103,* 359–365.

Plonsky, M., Driscoll, C. D., Warren, D. A., & Rosellini, R. A. (1984). Do random time schedules induce polydipsia in the rat? *Animal Learning and Behavior, 12,* 355–362.

Plooij, F. X. (1984). *The behavioural development of free-living chimpanzee babies and infants.* Norwood, NJ: Ablex.

Plooij, F. X., & Rijt-Plooij, H. C. (1994). Learning by instinct, developmental transitions, and the roots of culture in infancy. In R. A. Gardner, B. T. Gardner, A. B. Chiarelli, & F. X. Plooij (Eds.), *The ethological roots of culture* (pp. 357–373). Dordrecht, Netherlands: Kluwer Academic.

Plowright, C. M. S. (1997). Function and mechanism of mirror-image ambiguity in bumblebees. *Animal Behaviour, 53,* 1295–1303.

Poucet, B. (1993). Spatial cognitive maps in animals: New hypotheses on their structure and neural mechanisms. *Psychological Review, 100,* 163–182.

Powell, D. A., Gibbs, C. M., Maxwell, B., & Levine-Bryce, D. (1993). On the generality of conditioned bradycardia in rabbits: Assessment of CS and US modality. *Animal Learning and Behavior, 21,* 303–313.

Powell, R. W. (1972). Some effects of response-independent shocks after unsignaled avoidance conditioning in rats. *Learning and Motivation, 3,* 420–441.

Powell, R. W., & Peck, S. (1969). Persistent shock-elicited responding engendered by a negative-reinforcement procedure. *Journal of the Experimental Analysis of Behavior, 12,* 1049–1062.

Prechtl, H. R. F. (1974). The behavioral states of the newborn infant. *Brain Research, 76,* 185–189.

Premack, D. (1959). Toward empirical behavior laws: I. Positive reinforcement. *Psychological Review, 66,* 219–233.

Premack, D. (1962). Reversibility of the reinforcement relation. *Science, 136*, 255–257.

Premack, D. (1965). Reinforcement theory. In D. Levine (Ed.), *Nebraska symposium on motivation* (pp. 123–180). Lincoln: University of Nebraska Press.

Premack, D. (1971). Language in chimpanzee? *Science, 172*, 808–822.

Prokasy, W. F. (1960). Postasymptotic performance decrements during massed reinforcements. *Psychological Bulletin, 57*, 237–247.

Prokofiev, G., & Zeliony, G. P. (1926). Des modes d'associations cerebrales chez l'homme et chez les animaux. *Journal de Psychologie, 23*, 1020–1028.

Pryor, K. W., Haag, R., & O'Reilly, J. (1969). The creative porpoise: Training for novel behavior. *Journal of the Experimental Analysis of Behavior, 12*, 653–661.

Pullen, M. R., & Turney, T. H. (1977). Response modes in simultaneous and successive visual discriminations. *Animal Learning and Behavior, 5*, 73–77.

Rashotte, M. E., Griffin, R. W., & Sisk, C. L. (1977). Second-order conditioning of the pigeon's keypeck. *Animal Learning and Behavior, 5*, 25–38.

Razran, G. H. S. (1955). A note on second-order conditioning—and secondary reinforcement. *Psychological Review, 62*, 327–332.

Read, R. C. (1962). Card-guessing with information—a problem in probability. *American Mathematical Monthly, 69*, 506–511.

Reberg, D., Innis, N. K., Mann, B., & Eizenga, C. (1978). Superstitious behavior resulting from periodic response-independent presentations of food or water. *Animal Behaviour, 26*, 507–519.

Reed, J. D. (1947). Spontaneous activity of animals: A review of the literature since 1929. *Psychological Bulletin, 44*, 393–412.

Reid, L. S. (1953). The development of non-continuity behavior through continuity learning. *Journal of Experimental Psychology, 46*, 107–112.

Rescorla, R. A. (1979). Aspects of the reinforcer learned in second-order Pavlovian conditioning. *Journal of Experimental Psychology: Animal Behavior Processes, 5*, 79–95.

Rescorla, R. A. (1980). Simultaneous and successive associations in sensory preconditioning. *Journal of Experimental Psychology: Animal Behavior Processes, 6*, 207–216.

Rescorla, R. A. (1987). A Pavlovian analysis of goal-directed behavior. *American Psychologist, 42*, 119–129.

Rescorla, R. A., & Cunningham, C. L. (1979). Spatial contiguity facilitates Pavlovian second-order conditioning. *Journal of Experimental Psychology: Animal Behavior Processes, 5*, 152–161.

Restle, F. (1957). Discrimination of cues in mazes: A resolution of the "place vs response" question. *Psychological Review, 64*, 217–228.

Riley, D. A. (1958). The nature of the effective stimulus in animal discrimination learning: Transposition reconsidered. *Psychological Review, 65*, 1–7.

Rilling, M. (1977). Stimulus control and inhibitory processes. In W. K. Honig & J. E. R. Staddon (Eds.), *Handbook of operant behavior* (pp. 432–480). Englewood Cliffs, NJ: Prentice-Hall.

Rimpau, J. B., Gardner, R. A., & Gardner, B. T. (1989). Expression of person, place, and instrument in ASL utterances of children and chimpanzees. In R. A. Gardner, B. T. Gardner, & T. E. Van Cantfort (Eds.), *Teaching sign language to chimpanzees* (pp. 240–268). Albany: State University of New York Press.

Rizley, R. C., & Rescorla, R. A. (1972). Associations in second-order conditioning and sensory preconditioning. *Journal of Comparative and Physiological Psychology, 81*, 1–11.

Rumbaugh, D. M. (Ed.). (1977). *Language learning by a chimpanzee.* New York: Academic Press.

Rumbaugh, D. M., Gill, T. V., & von Glasersfeld, E. (1973). Reading and sentence completion by a chimpanzee. *Science, 182*, 731–733.

Russell, B. (1923). Vagueness. *Australasian Journal of Psychology and Philosophy, 1*, 84–92.

Ruvolo, M. (1994). Molecular evolutionary processes and conflicting gene trees: The hominoid case. *American Journal of Physical Anthropology, 94*, 89–113.

Saltzman, I. J. (1949). Maze learning in the absence of primary reinforcement: A study of secondary reinforcement. *Journal of Comparative and Physiological Psychology, 42*, 161–173.

Sameroff, A. J., & Cavanaugh, P. J. (1979). Learning in infancy: A developmental perspective. In J. D. Osofsky (Ed.), *Handbook of infant development* (pp. 344–392). New York: Wiley.

Sanders, R. J. (1985). Teaching apes to ape language: Explaining the imitative and nonimitative signing of a chimpanzee. *Journal of Comparative and Physiological Psychology, 99,* 197–210.

Savage-Rumbaugh, E. S. (1984). Verbal behavior at a procedural level in the chimpanzee. *Journal of the Experimental Analysis of Behavior, 41,* 223–250.

Savage-Rumbaugh, E. S., McDonald, K., Sevcik, R. A., Hopkins, W. D., & Rubert, E. (1986). Spontaneous symbol acquisition and communicative use by pigmy chimpanzees. *Journal of Experimental Psychology: General, 115,* 211–235.

Savage-Rumbaugh, E. S., Pate, J. L., Lawson, J., Smith, S. T., & Rosenbaum, S. (1983). Can a chimpanzee make a statement? *Journal of Experimental Psychology: General, 112,* 457–492.

Savoy, C. (1993). A yearly mental training program for a college basketball player. *The Sport Psychologist, 7,* 173–190.

Schaal, D. W., McDonald, M. P., Miller, M. A., & Reilly, M. P. (1996). Discrimination of methadone and cocaine by pigeons without explicit discrimination training. *Journal of the Experimental Analysis of Behavior, 66,* 193–203.

Schlesinger, H. S., & Meadow, K. P. (1972). *Deafness and mental health: A developmental approach.* Berkeley: University of California Press.

Schoenfeld, W. N., Antonitis, J. J., & Bersh, P. J. (1950). A preliminary study of training conditions necessary for secondary reinforcement. *Journal of Experimental Psychology, 40,* 40–45.

Schusterman, R. J., & Gisiner, R. C. (1988). Artificial language comprehension in dolphins and sea lions: The essential cognitive skills. *The Psychological Record, 38,* 311–348.

Schwartz, B. (1978). *Psychology of learning and behavior.* New York: Norton.

Schwartz, B., & Gamzu, E. (1977). Pavlovian control of operant behavior. In W. K. Honig & J. E. R. Staddon (Eds.), *Handbook of operant behavior* (pp. 53–97). Englewood Cliffs, NJ: Prentice-Hall.

Schwartz, B., & Reisberg, D. (1991). *Learning and memory.* New York: Norton.

Seidel, R. J. (1958). An investigation of mediation in preconditioning. *Journal of Experimental Psychology, 56,* 220–225.

Servatius, R. J., & Shors, T. J. (1994). Exposure to inescapable stress persistently facilitates associative and nonassociative learning in rats. *Behavioral Neuroscience, 108,* 1101–1106.

Seward, J. P., & Levy, N. (1949). Sign learning as a factor in extinction. *Journal of Comparative and Physiological Psychology, 39,* 660–668.

Sheffield, F. D. (1949). Hilgard's critique of Guthrie. *Psychological Review, 56,* 284–291.

Sheffield, F. D. (1965). Relation between classical conditioning and instrumental learning. In W. F. Prokasy (Ed.), *Classical conditioning: A symposium* (pp. 302–322). New York: Appleton–Century–Crofts.

Sheffield, V. F. (1949). Extinction as a function of partial reinforcement and distribution of practice. *Journal of Experimental Psychology, 39,* 511–526.

Sherrick, M. F., & Dember, W. N. (1966a). The tendency to alternate direction of movement as reflected in starting stem running speed. *Psychonomic Science, 6,* 29–30.

Sherrick, M. F., & Dember, W. N. (1966b). Trial-two goal arm alternation to direction of movement in trial-one straight alley. *Psychonomic Science, 6,* 317–318.

Shettleworth, S. J. (1972). Constraints on learning. In D. S. Leherman, R. A. Hinde, & E. Shaw (Eds.), *Advances in the study of behavior* (Vol. 4, pp. 1–68). New York: Academic Press.

Shettleworth, S. J., & Juergensen, M. R. (1980). Reinforcement and the organization of behavior in golden hamsters: Brain stimulation reinforcement for seven action patterns. *Journal of Experimental Psychology: Animal Behavior Processes, 6,* 352–375.

Shwe, H. I., & Markman, E. M. (1997). Young children's appreciation of the mental impact of their communicative signals. *Developmental Psychology, 33,* 630–636.

Sidman, M. (1953). Two temporal parameters of the maintenance of avoidance behavior in the white rat. *Journal of Comparative and Physiological Psychology, 46,* 253–261.

Sidman, M. (1958). Some notes on "bursts" in free-operant avoidance experiments. *Journal of the Experimental Analysis of Behavior, 1*, 167–172.

Siegel, S. (1967). Overtraining and transfer processes. *Journal of Comparative and Physiological Psychology, 64*, 471–477.

Silver, C. A., & Meyer, D. R. (1954). Temporal factors in sensory preconditioning. *Journal of Comparative and Physiological Psychology, 47*, 57–59.

Singh, J. A. L., & Zingg, R. M. (1942). *Wolf children and feral man.* Hamden, CT: Shoe String Press. (Reprinted in 1966 by Harper & Row)

Skinner, B. F. (1938). *The behavior of organisms: An experimental analysis.* New York: Appleton–Century.

Skinner, B. F. (1948). "Superstition" in the pigeon. *Journal of Experimental Psychology, 38*, 168–172.

Skinner, B. F. (1953). *Science and human behavior.* New York: Macmillan.

Skinner, B. F. (1977). The evolution of behaviorism. *American Psychologist, 32*, 1006–1012.

Skinner, B. F. (1988). Signs and countersigns. *Behavioral and Brain Sciences, 11*, 466–467.

Slater, P. J. B., & Williams, J. M. (1994). Bird song learning: A model of cultural transmission? In R. A. Gardner, B. T. Gardner, A. B. Chiarelli, & F. X. Plooij (Eds.), *The ethological roots of culture* (pp. 95–106). Dordrecht, Netherlands: Kluwer Academic.

Small, W. S. (1900). An experimental study of the mental processes of the rat. *American Journal of Psychology, 11*, 133–165.

Solomon, R. L., & Wynne, L. C. (1953). Traumatic avoidance learning: Acquisition in normal dogs. *Psychological Monographs, 67*, 19.

Spelt, D. K. (1938). Conditioned responses in the human fetus in utero. *Psychological Bulletin, 35*, 712–713.

Spelt, D. K. (1948). The conditioning of the human fetus *in utero. Journal of Experimental Psychology, 38*, 338–346.

Spence, K. W. (1936). The nature of discrimination learning in animals. *Psychological Review, 43*, 427–449.

Spence, K. W. (1937). The differential response in animals to stimuli varying within a single dimension. *Psychological Review, 44*, 430–444.

Sperling, S. E., & Valle, F. P. (1964). Handling-gentling as a positive secondary reinforcer. *Journal of Experimental Psychology, 67*, 573–576.

Spetch, M. L., Wilkie, D. M., & Pinel, J. P. J. (1981). Backward conditioning: A reevaluation of the empirical evidence. *Psychological Bulletin, 89*, 163–175.

Spooner, A., & Kellogg, W. N. (1947). The backward-conditioning curve. *American Journal of Psychology, 60*, 321–324.

Sprow, A. J. (1947). Reactively homogeneous compound trial-and-error learning with distributed trial and terminal reinforcement. *Journal of Experimental Psychology, 37*, 197–213.

Staddon, J. E. R. (1983). *Adaptive behavior and learning.* Cambridge, England: Cambridge University Press.

Staddon, J. E. R., & Simmelhag, V. L. (1971). The "superstition" experiment: A reexamination of its implications for the principles of adaptive behavior. *Psychological Review, 78*, 3–43.

Stanyon, R., Chiarelli, B., Gottlieb, K., & Patton, W. H. (1986). The phylogenetic and taxonomic status of *Pan paniscus*: A chromosomal perspective. *American Journal of Physical Anthropology, 69*, 489–498.

Stewart, J., De Wit, H., & Eikelboom, R. (1984). Role of unconditioned and conditioned drug effects in the self-administration of opiates and stimulants. *Psychological Review, 91*, 251–268.

Stokoe, W. C. (1960). Sign language structure: An outline of the visual communications systems of the American deaf. *Studies in Linguistics*, Occasional Papers 8. New York: University of Buffalo Press.

Suboski, M. D. (1990). Releaser-induced recognition learning. *Psychological Review, 97*, 271–284.

Suboski, M. D. (1994). Social transmission of stimulus recognition by birds, fish and molluscs. In R. A. Gardner, B. T. Gardner, A. B. Chiarelli, & F. X. Plooij (Eds.), *The ethological roots of culture* (pp. 173–198). Dordrecht, Netherlands: Kluwer Academic.

Suboski, M. D., Bain, S., Carty, A. E., McQuoid, L. M., Seelen, M. I., & Seifert, M. (1990). Alarm reaction in acquisition and social transmission of simulated-predator recognition in zebra danio fish. *Journal of Comparative Psychology, 104*, 101–112.

Supa, M., Cotzin, M., & Dallenbach, K. M. (1944). "Facial vision": The perception of obstacles by the blind. *American Journal of Psychology, 57*, 133–183.

Sutherland, N. S., & Mackintosh, N. J. (1971). *Mechanisms of animal discrimination learning.* New York: Academic Press.

Tait, R. W., & Suboski, M. D. (1972). Stimulus intensity in sensory preconditioning of rats. *Canadian Journal of Psychology, 26*, 374–381.

Tart, C. T. (1976). *Learning to use ESP.* Chicago: University of Chicago Press.

Terrace, H. S. (1979). *Nim.* New York: Knopf.

Terrace, H. S., Petitto, L., Sanders, R. J., & Bever, T. G. (1980). On the grammatical capacity of apes. In K. E. Nelson (Ed.), *Children's language* (Vol. 2, pp. 371–495). New York: Gardner.

Thomas, D. R. (1993). A model for adaptation-level effects on stimulus generalization. *Psychological Review, 100*, 658–673.

Thomas, D. R., & Morrison, S. K. (1994). Novelty versus retrieval cue value of visual contextual stimuli in pigeons. *Animal Learning and Behavior, 22*, 90–95.

Thompson, R., & McConnell, J. (1955). Classical conditioning in the planarian, dugesia dorotocephala. *Journal of Comparative and Physiological Psychology, 48*, 65–68.

Thorndike, E. L. (1898). Animal intelligence: An experimental study of the associative process in animals. *Psychological Review Monographs, 2*, No. 8, 1–109.

Thorndike, E. L. (1911). *Animal intelligence.* New York: Macmillan.

Thorpe, W. (1961). *Bird-song.* Cambridge, England: Cambridge University Press.

Timberlake, W. (1983). Rats' responses to a moving object related to food or water: A behavior-systems analysis. *Animal Learning and Behavior, 11*, 309–320.

Timberlake, W. (1986). Unpredicted food produces a mode of behavior that affects rats' subsequent reactions to a conditioned stimulus: A behavior-system approach to "context blocking." *Animal Learning and Behavior, 14*, 276–286.

Timberlake, W., & Lucas, G. A. (1985). The basis of superstitious behavior: Chance contingency, stimulus substitution, or appetitive behavior. *Journal of the Experimental Analysis of Behavior, 44*, 279–299.

Timberlake, W., & Silva, F. J. (1994). Observation of behavior, inference of function and the study of learning. *Psychonomic Bulletin & Review, 1*, 73–89.

Timberlake, W., Wahl, G., & King, D. (1982). Stimulus and response contingencies in the misbehavior of rats. *Journal of Experimental Psychology: Animal Behavior Processes, 8*, 62–85.

Tinbergen, N. (1953a). *The herring gull's world.* London: Collins.

Tinbergen, N. (1953b). *Social behaviour in animals.* New York: Wiley.

Tolman, E. C., & Honzik, C. H. (1930). Introduction and removal of reward, and maze performance in rats. *University of California Publications in Psychology, 4*, 257–275.

Tolman, E. C., Ritchie, B. F., & Kalish, D. (1946). Studies in spatial learning: II. Place learning versus response learning. *Journal of Experimental Psychology, 36*, 221–229.

Tomasello, M., Davis-Dasilva, M., Camak, L., & Bard, K. (1987). Observational learning of tool use by young chimpanzees. *Human Evolution, 2*, 175–183.

Tugendhat, B. (1960). The disturbed feeding behavior of the three-spined stickle-back. Electric shock is administered in the feeding area. *Behaviour, 16*, 159–187.

Turing, A. M. (1936). On computable numbers, with an application to the *Entscheidungsproblem. Proceedings of the London Mathematical Society, Ser. 2-42*, 230–265.

Turkkan, J. S. (1989). Classical conditioning: The new hegemony. *Behavioral and Brain Sciences, 12*, 121–137.

Twitmeyer, E. B. (1974). A study of the knee jerk. *Journal of Experimental Psychology, 103*, 1047–1066.

Underwood, B. J. (1957). *Psychological research.* New York: Appleton–Century–Crofts.

Van Cantfort, T. E., Gardner, B. T., & Gardner, R. A. (1989). Developmental trends in replies to Wh-questions by children and chimpanzees. In R. A. Gardner, B. T. Gardner, & T. E. Van Cantfort (Eds.), *Teaching sign language to chimpanzees* (pp. 198–239). Albany: State University of New York Press.

Van Willigen, F., Emmett, J., Cote, D., & Ayres, J. J. B. (1987). CS modality effects in one-trial backward and forward excitatory conditioning as assessed by conditioned suppression of licking in rats. *Animal Learning and Behavior, 15*, 201–211.

Vander Wall, S. B. (1982). An experimental analysis of cache recovery in Clark's nutcracker. *Animal Behaviour, 30*, 84–94.

Vander Wall, S. B. (1990). *Food hoarding in animals.* Chicago: University of Chicago Press.

Vander Wall, S. B. (1991). Mechanisms of cache recovery by yellow pine chipmunks. *Animal Behaviour, 41*, 851–863.

Visalberghi, E., & Limongelli, L. (1994). Lack of comprehension of cause–effect relations in tool-using capuchin monkeys. *Journal of Comparative Psychology, 108*, 15–22.

Vogel, G. W. (1975). Review of REM sleep deprivation. *Archives of General Psychiatry, 32*, 749–761.

von Frisch, K. (1950). Bees: *Their vision, chemical senses, and language.* Ithaca, NY: Cornell University Press.

von Frisch, K. (1953). *The dancing bees.* New York: Harcourt Brace.

Walker, E. L. (1948). Drive specificity and learning. *Journal of Experimental Psychology, 38*, 39–49.

Walker, E. L., Dember, W. N., Earl, R. W., & Karoly, A. J. (1955). Choice alternation: I. Stimulus vs. place vs. response. *Journal of Comparative and Physiological Psychology, 48*, 19–23.

Warden, C. J., & Warner, L. H. (1928). The sensory capacities and intelligence of dogs with a report on the ability of the noted dog "Fellow" to respond to verbal stimuli. *Quarterly Review of Biology, 3*, 1–28.

Wasserman, E. A. (1993). Comparative cognition: Beginning the second century of the study of animal intelligence. *Psychological Bulletin, 113*, 211–228.

Wasserman, E. A., Kiedinger, R. E., & Bhatt, R. S. (1988). Conceptual behavior in pigeons: Categories, subcategories, and pseudocategories. *Journal of Experimental Psychology: Animal Behavior Processes, 14*, 235–246.

Webster, M. A. (1996). Human color perception and its adaptation. *Network: Computation in Neural Systems, 7*, 587–634.

Weigl, P. D., & Hanson, E. V. (1980). Observational learning and the feeding behavior of the red squirrel: The ontogeny of optimization. *Ecology, 61*, 213–218.

Weinstock, S. (1954). Resistance to extinction of a running response following partial reinforcement under widely spaced trials. *Journal of Comparative and Physiological Psychology, 47*, 318–322.

Weinstock, S. (1958). Acquistion and extinction of a partially reinforced running response at a 24-hour intertrial interval. *Journal of Experimental Psychology, 56*, 151–158.

West, M. J., King, A. P., & Freeberg, T. M. (1997). Building a social agenda for the study of bird song. In C. T. Snowdon & M. Hausberger (Eds.), *Social influences on vocal development* (pp. 41–56). Cambridge, England: Cambridge University Press.

Westergaard, G. C. (1988). Lion-tailed macaques (*Macaca silenus*) manufacture and use tools. *Journal of Comparative Psychology, 102*, 152–159.

Westergaard, G. C., Greene, J. A., Babitz, M. A., & Suomi, S. J. (1995). Pestle use and modification by tufted capuchins. *International Journal of Primatology, 16*, 643–651.

Whitlow, J. W., Jr., & Wagner, A. R. (1984). Memory and habituation. In H. V. S. Peeke & L. Petrinovich (Eds.), *Habituation, sensitization and behavior* (pp. –). Orlando, FL: Academic Press.

Wickens, C. D. (1984). *Engineering psychology and human performance.* Columbus OH: Merrill.

Williams, D. R., & Williams, H. (1969). Automaintenance in the pigeon: Sustained pecking despite contingent non-reinforcement. *Journal of the Experimental Analysis of Behavior, 12*, 511–520.

Wohleber, C. (1996). The rocket man. *Invention & Technology, 12*(1), 36–45.

Wolfe, J. B. (1936). Effectiveness of token-rewards for chimpanzees. *Comparative Psychology Monographs, 12*(60), 1–72.

Wolford, G., & Bower, G. H. (1969). Continuity theory revisited: Rejected for the wrong reasons? *Psychological Review, 76*, 515–518.

Wright, A. A., Cook, R. G., Rivera, J. J., Sands, S. F., & Delius, J. D. (1988). Concept learning by pigeons: Matching-to-sample with trial-unique video picture stimuli. *Animal Learning and Behavior, 16*, 436–444.

Wright, A. A., & Sands, S. F. (1981). A model of detection and decision processes during matching to sample by pigeons: Performance with 88 different wavelengths in delayed and simultaneous matching tasks. *Journal of Experimental Psychology: Animal Behavior Processes, 7*, 191–216.

Zadeh, L. A., & Kacprzyk, J. (Eds.). (1992). *Fuzzy logic for the management of uncertainty.* New York: Wiley.

Zalaquette, C. P., & Parker, L. A. (1989). Further evidence that CTAs produced by lithium and amphetamine are qualitatively different. *Learning and Motivation, 20*, 413–427.

Zeiler, M. D. (1968). Fixed and variable schedules of response-independent reinforcement. *Journal of the Experimental Analysis of Behavior, 11*, 405–414.

Zener, K. (1937). The significance of behavior accompanying conditioned salivary secretion for theories of the conditioned response. *American Journal of Psychology, 50*, 384–403.

Zimmerman, D. W. (1957). Durable secondary reinforcement: Method and theory. *Psychological Review, 64*, 373–383.

Zimmerman, D. W. (1959). Sustained performance in rats based on secondary reinforcement. *Journal of Comparative and Physiological Psychology, 52*, 353–358.

Author Index

Subject Index